# *The*
# Literary Universe
## *of*
# Jorge Luis Borges

# *The*
# Literary Universe
# *of*
# Jorge Luis Borges

An Index to References and Allusions
to Persons, Titles, and Places in His Writings

*Compiled by*
Daniel Balderston

Bibliographies and Indexes in World Literature, Number 9

GREENWOOD PRESS
New York • Westport, Connecticut • London

LIBRARY OF CONGRESS CATALOGING-IN-PUBLICATION DATA

Balderston, Daniel, 1952-
  The literary universe of Jorge Luis Borges.

  (Bibliographies and indexes in world literature,
ISSN 0742-6801 ; no. 9)
  Bibliography: p.
  1. Borges, Jorge Luis, 1899-      —Dictionaries,
indexes, etc.   2. Borges, Jorge Luis, 1899-      —
Knowledge—Literature—Indexes.   I. Title.   II. Series.
PQ7797.B635Z459   1986        868        86-14947
ISBN 0-313-25083-9 (lib. bdg. : alk. paper)

Library of Congress Catalog Card Number: 86-14947
ISBN: 0-313-25083-9
ISSN: 0742-6801

First published in 1986

Greenwood Press, Inc.
88 Post Road West, Westport, Connecticut 06881

Printed in the United States of America

The paper used in this book complies with the
Permanent Paper Standard issued by the National
Information Standards Organization (Z39.48-1984).

10 9 8 7 6 5 4 3 2 1

to the memory of Borges

"esa esfera intelectual, cuyo
centro está en todas partes
y la circunferencia en ninguna"

# Contents

# Acknowledgments

I am particularly grateful to Les Perelman, for the extended loan of an Eleventh Edition of the *Encyclopaedia Britannica;* to Daniel Heiple, for help with preparing the copy; and to Marco Plumari, for help with the cross-checking of some of the references to the *Obras completas.* Thanks are also due to Susan Jordan, Mario Ullivarri, and Richard Matzinger for assistance in getting started with the data processing; to Sylvia Molloy, Marina Kaplan, and Magdalena García Pinto for their help with some of the Argentine references; and to Gwen Kirkpatrick and my parents for encouragement along the way. Special thanks also to those who initiated me in the study of Borges: L. A. Murillo, James Irby, and Sylvia Molloy.

# Abbreviations

| | |
|---|---|
| OC | *Obras completas*. Buenos Aires: Emecé, 1974 |
| OCC | *Obras completas en colaboración*. Buenos Aires: Emecé, 1979 |
| A | *Atlas*. Buenos Aires: Sudamericana, 1984 |
| BC | *Borges y el cine*. Edgardo Cozarinsky, ed. Buenos Aires: Sudamericana, 1974 |
| BO | *Borges, oral*. Buenos Aires: Emecé/Universidad de Belgrano, 1979 |
| C | *La Cifra*. Buenos Aires: Emecé, 1981 |
| CONJ | *Los conjurados*. Madrid: Alianza, 1985 |
| HE | *La hermana de Eloísa*. Buenos Aires: Ene Editorial, 1955 |
| I | *Inquisiciones*. Buenos Aires: Editorial Proa, 1925 |
| IA | *El idioma de los argentinos*. Buenos Aires: M. Gleizer, 1928 |
| ILN | *Introducción a la literatura norteamericana*. Buenos Aires: Editorial Columba, 1967 |
| LA | *El libro de arena*. Buenos Aires: Emecé, 1975 |
| NED | *Nueve ensayos dantescos*. Madrid: Espasa-Calpe, 1982 |
| OP | *Obra poética, 1923-1977*. Madrid: Alianza, 1981 |
| P | *Prólogos*. Buenos Aires: Torres Aguero, 1975 |
| PB | *Páginas de Jorge Luis Borges*. Buenos Aires: Celtia, 1982 |

PJ      *Poesía juvenil de Jorge Luis Borges.* Carlos Meneses,
        ed. Barcelona: Olañeta, 1923

SN      *Siete noches.* México: Fondo de Cultura Económica, 1982

TE      *El tamaño de mi esperanza.* Buenos Aires: Editorial
        Proa, 1926

VA      *Veinticinco Agosto 1983 y otros cuentos.* Madrid:
        Ediciones Siruela, 1983

# Introduction

> And in such indexes, although small pricks
> To their subsequent volumes, there is seen
> The baby figure of the giant mass.
> *Troilus and Cressida* I.3

Borges opens his famous story "La biblioteca de Babel" with the words: "El Universo (que otros llaman la Biblioteca) . . . " (OC, 465). The Universe as Library: the equivalence is central to Borges's work. He reminds us on numerous occasions that for the Kabbalists and other medieval thinkers the Creation was dual: the invention *ex nihilo* of our universe, the "Book of the World," and of the Bible, the "Book of the Book" (OC, 715-716, 775). And he quotes with evident approval Mallarmé's dictum that everything exists so that it can become a book (OC, 716).

Borges, perhaps the most bookish of modern writers, fashioned what Robert Burton would have called centos or anatomies. Quotations, allusions, and references of every kind are everpresent in his writing. In a 1977 lecture he asserted that his reliance on quotation was due to an incapacity to think abstractly (SN, 108), that is, on a need to base his thought on some authority. His use of these authorities is, however, deeply subversive, as Sylvia Molloy has observed in *Las letras de Borges* (183, 187). Borges's lists tend to jumble together famous names, the authors of the so-called Great Books, with others who seem to have purely local importance, or are utterly imaginary, and these juxtapositions serve to turn the "Great Tradition" upside down.

Borges insistently presented himself to his readers as a librarian, though he spent relatively few years of his long life in that profession. As a librarian, he was of course concerned with taxonomies and classification systems--not only that of the apocryphal Chinese encyclopedia which so fascinated Foucault, but also the Brussels system in which God is number 162. He also had a reference librarian's knack for consulting manuals and encyclopedias as a way to avoid getting lost in the stacks.

The profession of librarian is one that he assumed in his slightly disguised portrayals of himself--notably in the blind librarian in "El milagro secreto"--and one in which other writers have cast him, as for instance the librarian Burgos in Umberto Eco's *The Name of the Rose*. Borges even claimed that there is a likeness of sorts between the task of the critic and that of the librarian:

> Ordenar bibliotecas es ejercer,
> de un modo silencioso y modesto,
> el arte de la crítica. (OC, 998)

The density of references in Borges's central works--those from *Discusión* to *Otras inquisiciones*--is overwhelming, with many thousands of allusions recorded from each book of essays and stories. The earlier and later works are less dense, and references in them are frequently to the same authors and titles mentioned in the central works. (The notable exceptions, however, are the manuals of Buddhism and North American literature, which are full of names Borges does not mention elsewhere.) Even in his second book of essays, Borges aspired to a book wholly made of quotations (TE, 154), and extensive and recondite quotation is one of the marks of his writings. Already in his early essays Borges proposed that reality is verbal, and that all is allusion.


ENCYCLOPEDIC LEARNING


In the preparation of this index I have been able to confirm that many of the seemingly fanciful references are nothing of the kind, and that most of the fictional characters have names that also belong to the philosophers and theologians and scholars who figure in Borges's wide and eccentric readings. One well-known example of this is Ireneo Funes, whose first name is that of an early Christian theologian, and whose last name is that of an Argentine religious and political figure from the period of the wars of independence. Others include Nils Runeberg in "Tres versiones de Judas," who has the last name of the major patriotic poet of nineteenth-century Finland, and Erik Lonnrot in "La muerte y la brújula," who must be kin to the nineteenth-century Finnish scholar Elias Lonnrot, modern editor of the *Kalevala*. Jaromir Hladík takes his surname (including what is an anomalous accent in the Spanish text) from the Czech writer Václav Hladík. Borges refers just once to Conrad's *Victory*, to the hotelkeeper Schomberg, but other names that figure in that novel include Zangiacomo and Ricardo, used by Borges and Bioy in one of the outrageous detective stories that they published under the name of Honorio Bustos Domecq. Yu Tsun, the Chinese spy-narrator of "Jardín de los senderos que se bifurcan," is, as Murillo observes in his study *The Cyclical Night* (160), a character in the *Hung Lu*

*Meng*, the Chinese novel known in English as *Dream of the Red Chamber*. One of the most alarming and curious of these intrusions of extratextual realities into the world of Borges's fiction is that although Pierre Menard may not have rewritten *Don Quixote*, he (or some namesake) did write a number of books on French history in the middle of this century. An earlier Pierre Menard, a seventeenth-century polymath, has been discovered by Dante Medina ("Diez años de *Terra Nostra*," 65).

Indeed, it could be argued that Borges did not invent anything. He worked with the detritus of a culture, shuffling and picking through the shards. The ruined culture is that of Europe: the fragments of the cultures of Islam, India and the Orient are those brought back by the plundering imperial missionaries, governors and merchants. Borges was, as he would say himself, unsurpassingly ignorant of Arabic, Hebrew, Farsi, Sanskrit, and Chinese, and only slightly conversant in his later years in Japanese; his knowledge of these cultures is to a large extent drawn from the infinite pages of the *Encyclopaedia Britannica* and the manuals of Buddhism, Persian and Chinese literatures and the like that he cited so often. His learning was indeed encyclopedic, but often at several removes from its subject.

This kind of encyclopedic learning was, in fact, one of his main subjects. When the universe is conceived of as a library, knowledge deals with ideas, not things. Thus, Persian literature exists as it manifests itself in Edward G. Browne's *Literary History of Persia*, and a knowledge of Stuart Gilbert's summary of Joyce's *Ulysses* is better than so-called direct knowledge of the Joyce novel. The perversity of this idea is immeasurable, yet it is recognizable throughout Borges's work: in the chaos of the library of Babel, in the infinite rubbish-heap of the memory of Ireneo Funes, in the reviews of non-existent works, even in the insistence that, had Argentina consecrated Sarmiento's *Facundo* as its canonical work instead of Hernández's *Martín Fierro*, the country would be better (P, 139). Borges's universe, like the universe of the thinkers of Tlön, was radically idealist. Curiously, though, Borges undermined the idealist conception with a contrary insistence on the reality of the physical world. One of the characteristic gestures of his paradoxical idealist realism was his bibliophilia. In his later years, he lovingly acquired Brockhaus's encyclopedia and numerous other works, which he mentioned in his recent poetry, and reflected (as he had previously in "Poema de los dones" on his appointment as director of the National Library at the very time he was going blind) on the paradox that only now did he "have" these books, now when they could only exist for him as ideas.

Similarly, he dwelled in loving memory on quotations from his favorite poets and philosophers, and even on the sounds of words. Thus, books as physical objects and words in their concreteness became icons of a reality that to Borges as thinker seemed an entirely dubious proposition. The evidence of this "unreal reality," presented in such abundance in Borges's writings, was names. By naming--and Borges frequently recalled the example of

Adam here--human beings give a shape or form to a nebulous reality, above all a mental shape or form. Cratylus, in one of Plato's dialogues, dreamed of a world where the name would be the thing itself, and Borges is persuaded of the importance of that desire, as well as of the impossibility of realizing it in human language.

As a result, names are invested with a magical power in Borges's writing. At one extreme, words can give a power over reality to certain characters. For example, Tzinacán in "La escritura del dios" searches for the magical word that will release him from his Spanish prison and restore the Mayan way of life, and the rabbi in the poem "El Golem" would conjure up a malignant and powerful being, the Golem, by his combinations of the secret letters of the Holy Name. Conversely, though, the idolatrous love of names and ideas reduces the obsessed idolator to the mere status of a name or an idea. Erik Lonnrot is the key example of this revenge of an intractable reality that cannot be reduced to one's idea of it: the detective in "La muerte y la brújula" is destroyed when he loses sight of the fact that, in the world in which we live, ideas correspond only inexactly to the things that they represent.

## ATLAS

Most of the references to places recorded here are to real places, as Borges insisted on the importance of particular places in all their concreteness since his earliest writing. The double movement discussed earlier--the notion that the world exists only as idea or representation, and the paradoxical acknowledgment that it exists despite our ideas of it--is apparent here too.

Buenos Aires, for example, existed for Borges at least in part as an idea--the city of his famous poem "Fundación mítica de Buenos Aires" exists entire and solid from the moment of its foundation, that is, from the moment when it was named. But Buenos Aires exists also in the fact that it is a collective fiction, an idea which millions of people have conspired to make up together, over and over again. Ideal objects have a weight and a density all their own, as the startled character named Borges discovers near the end of "Tlon, Uqbar, Orbis Tertius," when oddly heavy coins, a compass and a cone, figments of somebody's imagination, weigh on his hand.

One quirk displayed by Borges is his practice of the classical usage of associating people with their places of origin (Zeno of Elea, Augustine of Hippo). So he often referred not to David Hume but to Hume of Edinburgh. Similarly, he frequently noted the nationality of the people he mentioned (references that I have indexed under the countries in question).

It would be interesting to plot the places that Borges mentions on a globe. Argentina and Uruguay, most of Europe, the United States, the Mediterranean and the Middle East, Persia, India and a few places in China and Japan would be highlighted, but the Antilles, Brazil, Central America and the northern part of South America, sub-Saharan Africa, the Soviet Union, and the populous mainland and islands of southeast Asia would hardly appear.

Curiously, one of Borges's last books is called *Atlas*. These travel writings of a blind man are frequently reflections on the tension caused by the discrepancy between the experience of a place and the cultural idea one has of it. In one of the brief sections of this book, for instance, Borges asserted that at a bakery called Aux Brioches de la Lune he encountered the perfect brioche: the brioche which is all brioches, or rather the Platonic idea of a brioche. He conceived of travel to a place as a pilgrimage in search of the idea of that place, as much as (indeed, more than) for the experience itself. It was fitting that he chose to return to Geneva to die, the place where he went to school, learned several languages and began to write.

## NAMING NAMES

Those mentioned most frequently in Borges's pages are: Borges himself, God, Jesus Christ, and then, in descending order, Shakespeare, Schopenhauer, Cervantes, Plato, Virgil, Quevedo, Whitman, Homer, Milton, Poe, Lugones, Dante, Stevenson, and then a multitude of others, including Goethe, Rosas, Chesterton, De Quincey, Hernández and Góngora.

I have counted as a reference to Borges not only the explicit references, that is, the various characters named Borges who appear in several of the stories, the signed prefaces, and so on, but also references to his blindness, his works, his unsurpassable ignorance of Hebrew, and so on. Borges held that all literature is autobiographical (TE, 146), and his own example seems to support that idea.

The frequent references to God and Jesus Christ would seem odd for an unbeliever, were it not for Borges's assertion that religion and philosophy can be taken as a kind of fantastic literature. Among the writers, the one mentioned most often is Shakespeare, who is for Borges paradoxically the most impersonal and most un-English of English writers. Borges refers to several of the tragedies, most notably *Hamlet*, *Macbeth*, and *Julius Caesar*, and to *The Tempest* and the sonnets. Of the great late plays, he refers rarely to *Lear* and not at all to *The Winter's Tale*. Among the philosophers, Plato is mentioned most frequently, followed by

Schopenhauer, Aristotle, Berkeley and Nietzsche. Some Victorian
and Edwardian writers are alluded to often--Stevenson, Kipling
and Chesterton most notably--but of course references to others
(Morris, Wells, Shaw, Wilde, Rossetti and so forth) are very
common, making this the period of English literature to which
Borges refers the most. The Argentine writers mentioned most
frequently are Lugones, Carriego, and Hernández, with Sarmiento,
Almafuerte and Macedonio Fernández not far behind. One also notes
the preponderance of references to epic poets--Homer, Virgil,
Dante, Camoes, Tasso, Milton--as this genre has obviously engaged
Borges's sensibility very deeply, although it could not be more
different from his own work. Indeed, the only time he set himself the task of writing a few lines of epic verse, the intention
was to mock the poem and the entire enterprise, as he did in his
description of Carlos Argentino Daneri's poem *La tierra* in the
story "El Aleph."

Though this affirmation may seem odd, Borges's encyclopedic
allusions are not all-encompassing. A simple example of this
occurs in the essay "La esfera de Pascal," in which he refers to
a wide variety of philosophers and writers who, over the centuries, have used the metaphor of an infinite sphere, the center of
which was everywhere. At least one illustrious name is not in
this list: the great poet of colonial Mexico, Sor Juana Inés de
la Cruz, who uses this image in her autobiographical letter
(4:450).

QUOTATION MARKS

Many of Borges's references are not explicit but implicit. Some
of them were easy to identify and have been included (a white
whale, an immortal poem about a gaucho outlaw, a time traveler),
while some of them of course escape me. In addition to quotations, various kinds of textual reference are embedded in
Borges's writing. He calls attention to this process in the final
note to the story "El inmortal," where the narrator takes stock
of the "intrusiones, o hurtos" from Pliny, Shaw, Descartes, and
others that are present in the tale. Several critics have called
attention to the ironically incomplete nature of this information: Ronald Christ and James Irby have discussed other borrowings in that story.

The story ends with the words: "Palabras, palabras desplazadas
y mutiladas, palabras de otros, fue la pobre limosna que le
dejaron las horas y los siglos," words that, as I have shown
elsewhere (*El precursor velado: R. L. Stevenson en la obra de
Borges*, 171), have been borrowed from Conrad's preface to the
*Nigger of the "Narcissus"*:

it is only through an unremitting, never-discouraged
care for the shape and ring of sentences that an
approach can be made to plasticity, to colour; and the
light of magic suggestiveness may be brought to play
for an evanescent instant over the commonplace surface
of words; of the old, old words, worn thin, defaced by
ages of careless usage. (146)

Thus, Borges plagiarized the justification for plagiarism; the
"old words" can be made to live again in a changed context, if
only for a moment.

This index, then, bears witness to one of the fundamental
features of Borges's art: fiction as patchwork, or as what Nahum
Cordovero in "El inmortal" termed the "coat of many colors." At
best, an index of this kind can only point to the more obvious of
these borrowings; the others must wait for a critical edition
with full critical apparatus.

AN INDEX OF FORBIDDING BOOKS

Le fantastique est un monde sans indices.
Compagnon, 376

This book is the fruit of an individual effort, and has evident
strengths and weaknesses for that reason. Because of previous
research I am well-acquainted with most of Borges's British
sources, but must confess to a less than adequate grasp of the
cultural ephemera recorded so profusely in the Bustos Domecq
stories. The annotations are complete for those items that can be
researched through normal sources--encyclopedias, atlases, etc.--
but weak in the area of personal reference ("nuestro amigo
Cuttini," for instance, is not of my acquaintance) and sometimes
in the realm of local Argentine allusions. I have made every
effort to include in this index not only explicit references but
also implicit ones, but it was impossible to catch them all. Some
references necessarily escape me or are obvious to all; these
have been left without annotation.

I have indexed all of Borges's books, and a number of collections by other people of his uncollected articles (on cinema, on
Dante, etc.). There are significant omissions: of the uncollected
articles, the interviews, and most of the anthologies Borges
compiled. The uncollected articles number in the hundreds, and
the sheer task of devising a code that would differentiate between them in an index such as this was sufficient reason for
their omission. No doubt Emecé will come out fairly soon with a
volume of Borges's suppressed writings, the first three books of

essays most notably, and with a volume of the dispersed articles. (One hopes these volumes will be more carefully edited and proof-read than the two existing volumes of collected works.) Some of the most important of the dispersed articles have been collected recently by Alicia Jurado in *Páginas de Jorge Luis Borges*, but many others are still waiting to be compiled in a careful schol-arly edition. (Another very extensive body of articles, Borges's contributions to the magazine *El Hogar* from 1936 to 1939, has been the subject of a dissertation by Enrique Sacerio Gari; he has published an index of sorts to those articles in the *Revista Interamericana de Bibliografía.*)

I have included two volumes of Borges's talks--*Borges, oral* and *Siete noches*--but have excluded the several dozen volumes of interviews. The interviews are very uneven in quality, and Borges has not been involved in the editing of them (with perhaps a few exceptions), with the inevitable result that the items that are of interest here--names, titles, places--have often been hope-lessly mangled. For a thorough study of any of the points of contact between Borges and the literary universe, the interviews are, however, indispensable: approximately one quarter of the references to Stevenson, for example, are found in them. I leave the thankless task of indexing the interviews--the several dozen books of interviews and numerous others published as parts of books and in periodicals--to some other harmless drudge. Finally, I have omitted the anthologies (with the exception of those included in the *Obras completas en colaboración*): anthologies of writings about the *gaucho matrero* and the *compadrito*, the two volumes of detective stories, the book of dreams, anthologies of Argentine and Latin American poetry, a book of writings about heaven and hell, and last but not least the famous anthology of fantastic literature. For the most part these anthologies have few notes by the editors that would be worth indexing, and the most important of the Borges prefaces to these anthologies are included in *Prólogos* and in *Páginas de Jorge Luis Borges*. Again, however, I would urge readers, scholarly and otherwise, not to ignore the anthologies. They give vital information about the particular writings by Léon Bloy and Max Beerbohm and so many others that were of most interest to Borges.

We urgently need a critical edition of Borges showing the variants between different editions of his works. Borges was obsessive in his revisions, with scarcely a sentence left un-touched. Even such reeditions of earlier essays as those included in *Prólogos* and *Nueve ensayos dantescos* show extensive revision, some in matters that affect this index. Were it not for our writer's prodigious memory, it would be difficult to imagine that a man who was blind for the last thirty years of his life would bother to rewrite essays published forty or even sixty years ago, sometimes inserting new references to secondary material that he had read years ago, and yet still remembered.

Borges often referred to very obscure scholars and writers as if it were obvious to whom he was referring. Indeed, his readers (myself included) have often imagined that his frame of reference is fairly manageable or predictable. However, in the course of

trying to trace several thousand of these references, I can
assure others that this is anything but the case. The references
could only be truly obvious to someone whose reading overlapped
precisely with that of Borges himself. In trying to identify many
of the figures mentioned here, I often had very little to work
with. Many times the only indications would be a fairly common
last name and the assertion that the person in question had said
something about Buddhism, the fourth dimension, or the Icelandic
sagas. Similarly, many of the titles were translated into Spanish
or were incomplete, with little or erroneous information about
publication dates or authors' names. I have spent six months on
the annotations, brief as they are, and fear I could easily have
spent another ten years without ever achieving a sense of finality.

In *Through the Looking Glass*, Lewis Carroll writes of running
as fast as one can only to stay in the same place. The compiler
of this index must confess to feeling that same way, considering
that Borges published several books during the time in which I
have been working on this index. I have paused--like the runners
over the golden apples dropped by Atalanta--to include them also.

This work complements David William Foster's recent annotated
bibliography on Borges, and completes the task, initiated years
ago by Emile Berveiller in *Le Cosmopolitisme de Jorge Luis
Borges*, of cataloguing his allusions in a fairly thorough manner.


A MODEST PROPOSAL


> Durante muchos años, yo creí que la casi infinita
> literatura estaba en un hombre. Ese hombre fue
> Carlyle, fue Johannes Becher, fue Whitman, fue
> Rafael Cansinos-Assens, fue De Quincey. (OC, 641)


It is devoutly to be wished that this index will be but the first
of such efforts: within a few years, when a more adequate edition
of Borges's works should be available, it is to be hoped that
there will be an annotated index that takes stock more completely
of Borges's references. One may envision some decades hence a
Borges encyclopedia, with brief articles resuming the critical
books and articles--which by then will fill the libraries--on
Shakespeare, Heine and Pliny in Borges, on Borges and Balvanera
Street, on Borges and *The Mind of Man*, works provoked, alas, at
least in part by the existence of the present index. This encyclopedia will of necessity be a collective project: the work of a
group of people devoted to the annihilation of the external
universe and its replacement with a universe made by a human
being, with its own inevitable logic and order. That human being
will in time recede as a physical being and achieve the status of
an idea. Then those future generations of scholars will forget
the existence of English or Argentine or Latin literatures. The
world will be Borges.

# A Guide to This Index

The index is divided into three parts: indexes to persons, to titles and to places. The index to persons includes gods and monsters, real people and fictional characters. The index to titles similarly includes a mixture of real works and of apocrypha of every variety. The index to places consists to a large extent of actual places. Initially I sought to distinguish between reality and fiction, but that enterprise contradicted Borges's endeavor as a writer, and consequently had to be abandoned. I have characterized many of the fictitious references as such, but *caveat lector*--may the reader beware: many of the apparently fictitious references are based on some element of fact, as witness the examples given in the introduction to Pierre Menard, Yu Tsun, and Erik Lonnrot among others.

The index to persons includes information about the principal works of many of the writers. Many of these works are found listed in the title index.

The title index lists titles, when possible, in the original language for the major Western European languages: Spanish, Portuguese, French, English, German, Latin and Italian. When Borges has translated the title into Spanish a cross-reference is provided to the original title. Titles in Russian, Chinese, Arabic, Greek, and other languages (which Borges, by the way, could not read) have been translated into Spanish, following his usage, except in cases where a transliteration of the original title has become more familiar, as for example with the *Rig-Veda* or the *Zohar*. I have generally followed Borges's transliterations in the main entry, providing a corrected version in some cases where necessary to confirm the identification. Information concerning the author and the date of publication is provided for the purposes of identification, and has been cross-checked with other sources as much as possible.

The index to places includes a large number of references to streets and landmarks of Buenos Aires, the identification of which is doubtless unnecessary for Argentine readers but may prove useful to others.

References to the *Obras completas* and *Obras completas en colaboración* are listed first, followed by references to the other books in alphabetical order. A chronological ordering of the references, though highly desirable, was impossible because the collected works are not themselves organized by any rigorous chronology.

The *Obras completas* and *Obras completas en colaboración* contain a large number of works that were first published separately. It was not practical to include these works under their separate titles, but some users of this index may find it useful to have the two collected volumes broken down here by title and date of first publication. The *Obras completas* consists of the following works:

| | |
|---|---|
| *Fervor de Buenos Aires* (1923) | 13-52 |
| *Luna de enfrente* (1925) | 55-73 |
| *Cuaderno San Martín* (1929) | 79-96 |
| *Evaristo Carriego* (1930) | 101-172 |
| *Discusión* (1932) | 177-286 |
| *Historia universal de la infamia* (1935) | 289-345 |
| *Historia de la eternidad* (1936) | 351-423 |
| *Ficciones* (1944) | 429-530 |
| *El Aleph* (1949) | 533-630 |
| *Otras inquisiciones* (1952) | 633-775 |
| *El hacedor* (1960) | 779-854 |
| *El otro, el mismo* (1964) | 857-954 |
| *Para las seis cuerdas* (1965) | 953-972 |
| *Elogio de la sombra* (1969) | 975-1018 |
| *El informe de Brodie* (1970) | 1021-1078 |
| *El oro de los tigres* (1972) | 1081-1140 |

The *Obras completas en colaboración* consists of the following works:

| | |
|---|---|
| *Seis problemas para don Isidro Parodi* (1942) | 3-121 |
| *Dos fantasías memorables* (1946) | 125-142 |
| *Un modelo para la muerte* (1946) | 145-195 |
| *Los orilleros--El paraíso de los creyentes* (1955) | 199-296 |
| *Crónicas de Bustos Domecq* (1967) | 299-371 |
| *Nuevos cuentos de Bustos Domecq* (1977) | 375-451 |
| *Leopoldo Lugones* (1965) | 457-508 |
| *El "Martín Fierro"* (1953) | 513-565 |
| *El libro de los seres imaginarios* (1967) | 569-714 |
| *Qué es el budismo* (1976) | 719-781 |
| *Breve antología anglosajona* (1978) | 787-801 |
| *Introducción a la literatura inglesa* (1965) | 807-857 |
| *Literaturas germánicas medievales* (1966) | 861-975 |

Dates cited above are for the book publication only. The first publication of the individual texts can be ascertained in most cases by consulting the bibliographies to Ana María Barrenechea's *La expresión de la irrealidad*, and the bibliography included in the volume of *L'Herne* devoted to Borges.

This is not an index to translations of Borges, though that would be a worthwhile project in itself. Information on translations in English and numerous other languages is available in David William Foster's bibliography on Borges. The English translations are widely scattered, uneven in quality, and by no means complete. Users of this index who do not read Spanish should be able to locate some of the references by consulting the Spanish works indexed here and comparing them with the myriad translations.

Information in the annotations has been derived from a large variety of sources. Most frequent use was made of: the Eleventh Edition of the *Encyclopaedia Britannica*, the *Columbia Encyclopedia*, the *Encyclopedia of Philosophy*, the French and Spanish *Larousse*, the *Oxford Classical Dictionary*, the *Oxford Companions* to English, American, French, Spanish and German literatures, the

five volume *Historia de la literatura argentina*, published by the
Centro Editor de América Latina in 1982, the *Enciclopedia de la
literatura argentina*, edited by Roberto Yahni and Pedro Orgambide, and OCLC, the computerized data base system for library
holdings in the United States. Information on film was drawn from
Leslie Halliwell's *Filmgoer's Companion*. References to the world
of the tango were checked against several sources, notably José
Gobello's *Crónica general del tango*, Horacio Ferrer's *El libro
del tango* and the many volumes of *La historia del tango* published
by Corregidor. Many recondite titles were searched in the *Union
Catalog* and the *Cumulative Title Index to the Library of Congress
Shelflist*. Some personal references were checked against Emir
Rodríguez Monegal's biography of Borges. The reference work used
for street names in Buenos Aires was *Guía Bregna de Buenos Aires*
(1983 edition). Extensive use was also made of Scholem's *Major
Trends in Jewish Mysticism*, Donadoni's *History of Italian Litera-
ture*, Rose's *History of German Literature*, Turville-Petre's *Ori-
gins of Icelandic Literature*, Gibb's *Arabic Literature*, Browne's
*Literary History of Persia*, Moses Hadas's histories of Greek and
Roman literatures, MacDonnell's *History of Sanskrit Literature*,
Giles's *History of Chinese Literature*, Diez-Echarri and Roca
Franquesa's *Historia de la literatura española e hispanoamerica-
na*, the historical dictionary of Argentina by Wright and Nekhom
and that of Uruguay by Willis, *Quien es quien en la Argentina* and
numerous other sources, including many of the works to which
Borges alludes.

Because the reference works consulted do not all follow the
same practice, and because Borges's mode of reference is not
always consistent, I have standardized references as much as
possible, with variants listed under the main reference and with
abundant cross-references. Thus, for example, all references to
the *Koran* or *Q'uran* are found in the title index under *Alcorán*,
that being the most frequent form of the name in Borges's work
(and in Spanish), but cross-references have been provided as
necessary. Alphabetization was based on the first word of each
entry, discounting initial articles, and applied the custom of
placing whole words first (as is standard library practice in the
United States); thus, *De fato* and *De sobremesa* precede *Decline
and Fall of the Roman Empire*. Titles, when long, are frequently
alphabetized using the most familiar words: thus, *El ingenioso
hidalgo don Quijote de la Mancha* is found under *Don Quijote*, and
so on. When an author's pseudonym is more familiar than his or
her real name, the main reference is under the pseudonym (Lewis
Carroll, Almafuerte, Mark Twain) with cross-references under the
real name.

Some books were indexed merely in part. Only those portions of
*Borges y el cine Veinticinco de agosto*, *La poesía juvenil de
Jorge Luis Borges* and *Nueve ensayos dantescos* which are by Borges
are treated in this index. In *La hermana de Eloísa*, only the
title story is indexed, as the others are not by Borges or are
included elsewhere. The Alianza edition of the *Obra poética* is
indexed exclusively for books subsequent to publication of the
*Obras completas*. The anthology *Páginas de Jorge Luis Borges* is
indexed for the uncollected articles only (117-248).

Because some works appear more than once in the books listed
below, a few of the references are duplicated. For instance, two
of the essays on Dante included in the *Nueve ensayos dantescos*
also appear in *Páginas de Jorge Luis Borges*; oddly enough, and
consistent with Borges's practice of constant rewriting, the
texts are not exactly the same. Regretfully, some of the texts
are corrupt: Meneses purports to give the original texts of the
Ultraist poems in his *Poesía juvenil*, but an examination of the
texts reveals that in some cases he has included later revisions
rather than the original versions published in Ultraist magazines
in Spain. Also, unfortunately, some of the poems in *Fervor de
Buenos Aires*, *Luna de enfrente* and *Cuaderno San Martín* have been
left out of the *Obras completas* or so radically altered as to
merit inclusion here in both forms. This is, however, neither the
time nor the place to undertake a full study of the variants; the
careful reader is urged to check the texts of the early poems
against their first published versions.

The two large volumes of *Obras completas* and *Obras completas
en colaboración* are full of egregious errors, in many cases
compounded from the earlier editions of the works of Borges also
published by Emecé. An example of this is the acknowledged source
of the story of the Tichborne Claimant, "El impostor inverosímil
Tom Castro": according to earlier editions of *Historia universal
de la infamia*, the source is Thomas Seccombe's article on the
Claimant in the *Encyclopaedia Britannica*. As I have shown in
detail in my book *El precursor velado* (72-90), the Seccombe
article serves Borges as a point of departure, and the many
additions and variations on the Tichborne story derive not from
history but from Borges's reading of the adventure fiction of
Robert Louis Stevenson. In the Emecé single volume edition of the
*Obras completas*, however, the reference to the *Encyclopaedia
Britannica* has vanished, replaced by printer's oversight with
Philip Gosse's *History of Piracy*, a work that has little to do
even with the story of the widow Ching, and nothing at all to do
with Tichborne and Orton.

In the numerous cases where different appellations were used
for the same thing--e. g., Constantinopla, Bizancio, Estambul and
Miklegard--I have consolidated all the entries under the most
frequently used name, in this case *Constantinopla*, even though
the different names are not strictly synonymous. (The same is
done in the case of Jesus Christ, called *Jesús*, *Cristo*, *Jesucristo*, *el Redentor*, *el Hijo* and so on, and found here under *Jesucristo*.)

I would beg my readers' pardon for the lack of written accent
marks with the exception of the accent mark most frequently used
in Spanish. The dieresis or umlaut, grave accent, cedilla, and
circumflex, as well as the tilde marking the nasal sound in
Portuguese, though present in the printer fonts, could not be
printed in the right places in some of the printer modes. The
runic letter *eth* in Icelandic and Old English words has usually
been rendered here as a *d*, though a *th* would have been strictly
speaking more accurate, but the *d*, much closer to it in appearance, is the letter Borges has most frequently used himself in

transliterating old Icelandic names. Similarly, in Icelandic and other languages where *oe* and *ae* occur as single letters, the two letters have been separated here.

Annotations have been kept fairly brief, for the obvious reason that the total number of references is overwhelmingly large. (I have calculated that the total number of allusions catalogued here numbers upwards of 100,000.) The most this index can do in this regard is point the reader toward the reference works that are most appropriate in the given case. The one refer- ence work which clearly is a necessity to the careful reader of Borges--and I speak as a sadder but wiser man, having spent some eighteen months tracking down the many thousands of references in Borges's works--is the eleventh edition of the *Encyclopaedia Britannica.*

In the preface to one of the *Oxford Companions* the editor explains that to his dismay the errors that were corrected during the day crept back during the night. I regret that some more or less fantastic explanation of this kind is necessary in a work of this kind. Like the *hronir* in "Tlon, Uqbar, Orbis Tertius," Error, that demon out of Spenser and Thomas Browne, intrudes into the universe of books to which this index aspires to provide access.

# Works Cited

Balderston, Daniel. *El precursor velado: R. L. Stevenson en la obra de Borges*. Buenos Aires: Editorial Sudamericana, 1985.

Barrenechea, Ana María. *La expresión de la irrealidad en la obra de Borges*. Mexico City: El Colegio de México, 1957.

Berveiller, Emile. *Le Cosmopolitisme de Jorge Luis Borges*. Paris: Publications de la Sorbonne, 1973.

Browne, Edward G. *Literary History of Persia*. 2 vols. New York: Scribner's, 1902.

Christ, Ronald. *The Narrow Act: Borges' Art of Allusion*. New York: New York University Press, 1969.

Compagnon, Antoine. *La Seconde main ou le travail de la citation*. Paris: Editions du Seuil, 1979.

Conrad, Joseph. *The Nigger of the "Narcissus."* New York: Norton, 1979.

Diez-Echarri, Emiliano, and José María Roca Franquesa. *Historia de la literatura española e hispanoamericana*. 2nd ed. Madrid: Aguilar, 1972.

Donadoni, Eugenio. *A History of Italian Literature*. Richard Monges, trans. 2 vols. New York: New York University Press, 1969.

Edwards, Paul, ed. *The Encyclopedia of Philosophy*. New York: Macmillan, 1967.

*Encyclopaedia Britannica*. 11th ed. New York: The Encyclopaedia Britannica Company, 1910–1911.

Ferrer, Horacio. *El libro del tango. Crónica y diccionario 1850–1977*. Buenos Aires: Galerna, 1977.

Ferrer, Manuel. *Borges y la nada*. London: Támesis, 1971.

Foster, David William. *Jorge Luis Borges: An Annotated Primary and Secondary Bibliography*. New York: Garland, 1984.

Foucault, Michel. *Les Mots et les choses*. Paris: Gallimard, 1966.

García-Pelayo y Gross, Ramón. *Pequeño Larousse Ilustrado*. Mexico City: Ediciones Larousse, 1982.

Garland, Henry Burnand. *Oxford Companion to German Literature*. Oxford: Clarendon Press, 1976.

Genette, Gérard. "L'Utopie littéraire." *Figures*. Paris: Editions du Seuil, 1966.

Gibb, H. A. R. *Arabic Literature: An Introduction*. 2nd ed. London: Oxford University Press, 1963.

Giles, Herbert A. *History of Chinese Literature*. New York: Appleton-Century, 1937.

Gobello, José. *Crónica general del tango*. Buenos Aires: Editorial Fraterna, 1980.

*Guía Bregna de Buenos Aires*. Buenos Aires: Editorial Bregna, 1983.

Halliwell, Leslie. *Filmgoer's Companion*. 8th ed. New York: Scribner's, 1985.

Hadas, Moses. *A History of Greek Literature*. New York: Columbia University Press, 1950.

---. *A History of Latin Literature*. New York: Columbia University Press, 1952.

Hammond, N. G. L., and H. H. Scullard. *Oxford Classical Dictionary*. 2nd ed. Oxford: Oxford University Press, 1970.

Harris, William H. and Judith S. Levey, eds. *New Columbia Encyclopedia, The*. New York: Columbia University Press, 1975.

Hart, James D. *The Oxford Companion to American Literature*. New York: Oxford University Press, 1965.

Harvey, Paul and Dorothy Eagle. *The Oxford Companion to English Literature*. 4th ed. Oxford: Oxford University Press, 1967.

Harvey, Paul and Janet E. Haseltine. *The Oxford Companion to French Literature*. Oxford: Oxford University Press, 1984.

*Historia de la literatura argentina*. 5 vols. Buenos Aires: Centro Editor de América Latina, 1980–1982.

Irby, James East. "The Structure of the Stories of Jorge Luis Borges." Ph.D. dissertation. University of Michigan, 1962.

*Jorge Luis Borges.*    Dominique Le Roux, ed.   Paris: Cahiers de L'Herne, 1964.

MacDonnell, Arthur A. *A History of Sanskrit Literature.* 1st pub. 1900. Rpt. ed. New York: Haskell House, 1968.

Martini Real, Juan Carlos and Manuel Pampín, eds. *Historia del tango, La.* 17 vols. Buenos Aires: Corregidor, 1976–1981.

Medina, Dante. "Diez años de *Terra Nostra.*" *Vuelta* 109 (December 1985): 64–66.

Molloy, Sylvia. *Las letras de Borges.* Buenos Aires: Editorial Sudamericana, 1979.

Murillo, L. A. *The Cyclical Night: Irony in James Joyce and Jorge Luis Borges.* Cambridge: Harvard University Press, 1968.

Orgambide, Pedro and Roberto Yahni. *Enciclopedia de la literatura argentina.* Buenos Aires: Editorial Sudamericana, 1970.

*Petit Larousse.* 25th ed. Paris: Librairie Larousse, 1966.

*Quien es quien en la Argentina.* 9th ed. Buenos Aires: Editorial Kraft, 1968.

Rodríguez Monegal, Emir. *Jorge Luis Borges: A Literary Biography.* New York: Dutton, 1978.

Rose, Ernst. *A History of German Literature.* New York: New York University Press, 1960.

Sacerio Garí, Enrique. "La crítica de Borges en *El Hogar.*" *Revista interamericana de bibliografía,* 33.2 (1983): 171–190.

Scholem, Gerschom G. *Major Trends in Jewish Mysticism.* New York: Schocken, 1961.

*Times Atlas of the World.* 7th ed. New York: Times Books, 1985.

Turville-Petre, G. *Origins of Icelandic Literature.* Oxford: Oxford University Press, 1953.

Ward, Philip. *The Oxford Companion to Spanish Literature.* Oxford: Oxford University Press, 1978.

Willis, Jean L. *Historical Dictionary of Uruguay.* Latin American Historical Dictionaries, 11. Metuchen, N. J.: Scarecrow Press, 1974.

Wright, Ione S. and Lisa M. Nekhom. *Historical Dictionary of Argentina.* Latin American Historical Dictionaries, 17. Metuchen, N. J.: Scarecrow Press, 1978.

# Index of Persons

Aarón (in the Bible, high priest of the Hebrews, brother of Moses). OCC, 907. A, 35

Aarón el Ortodoxo. See Harún al-Raschid

Aarón-Ben-Chaim (rabbi). OCC, 682

Abalo. OCC, 127

Abarbanel, Isaac (Portuguese rabbi, philosopher and statesman, 1437–1508). OC, 876

Abaroa, Diego (shopkeeper in Gualeguaychú, in Borges story). OC, 574, 575

Abarrategui. OCC, 127

Abatimarco. OCC, 127

Abbagnato. OCC, 127

Abbasidas (dynasty of caliphs). OC, 324, 412, 417

Abbatantuono. OCC, 127

Abd-el-Melek, Issota (character in Bustos Domecq story). OCC, 28

Abdalmálik or Abdelmélik (caliph, 646–705). OC, 409, 584, 586

Abdul Melek. OCC, 388

Abdulmálik (character in Borges-Bioy filmscript). OCC, 266, 268–70, 289, 292, 296

Abdurrahman. OC, 587

Abeille, Luciano (Argentine author of works on medicine, law, education and language, including the *Idioma nacional de los argentinos*, 1900). TE, 137

Abel (son of Adam and Eve in the Bible, killed by his brother Cain). OC, 154, 701, 853, 934, 948, 956, 1013, 1092, 1113. OCC 533n., 659, 801, 904. BC, 57. CONJ, 95. NED, 93. OP, 387, 436

Abelardo, Pedro (French philosopher and theologian, 1079–1142). OC, 746

Abenabás (Ibn Abbas, Moslem traditionalist theologian, cousin of Mohammed). IA, 52

Abenjacán el Bojarí (character in Borges story). OC, 600–606

Abenjaldún (Abu Zaid ibn Mahommed ibn Khaldun, Arabic historian, born at Tunis, 1332–1406, author of a universal history). OC, 628. P, 134

Abenjaldún (character in Bustos Domecq story). OCC, 23–33

Abensida (Ibn Sidah the Andalusian, Spanish lexicographer, c.1006–1066, author of the *Mohkam*). OC, 583

Abentofail, Abudeker (Ibn Tufail, Spanish-Arabic novelist, 1100–85, author of

the philosophical romance
*Hayy ibn Yaqzan,* "The Living
One, Son of the Waking One").
OC, 356n.

Abercrombie, Lascelles
(English poet, 1881–1938).
OC, 249, 686.   ILN, 46

Ablewhite (character in
Collins).   P, 48

Abnesra (Spanish rabbi,
1098–c.1167).   OC, 509

Abrabanel, Isaac (Jewish
statesman, philosopher,
theologian and commentator,
1437–1508).   OC, 766

Abraham (Biblical patriarch,
sometimes Abram).   OC, 419.
OCC, 904, 925.   NED, 99.
P, 36.   PB, 183

Abraham (prince in Celtic
legend).   PB, 222–23

Abramowicz, Maurice (childhood
friend of Borges in Geneva).
OC, 516n.   OCC, 304.   CONJ,
33–34, 35–36

Abramowicz, Padre.   OCC, 41

Abraxas (emanations of
divine spirit, according to
Basilidian Gnostics).   OC,
214.   A, 35.   LA, 83

Absalom (in the Bible, a son
of David).   P, 79

Abtu (fish in Egyptian
mythology).   OCC, 572

Abu-Bashar Mata.   OC, 583

Abul Hasán (character in
Bustos Domecq story, owner of
taxi cabs).   OCC, 24

Abulbeca de Ronda (Abu'l-Baka
Salih ar-Rundi, Arabic poet
who may have influenced Jorge
Manrique).   OC, 404n.

Abulcásim al-Asharî
(character in Borges story
about Averroes).   OC, 583–87

Abulcásim el Hadramî (12th
century poet).   OC, 850

Abulfeda (Abu-1-Fida Isma'il
ibn 'Ali 'Imad-ud-Dni,
Arabian historian and
geographer, 1273–1331).
OC, 593

Abulgualid Muhammad Ibn-Ahmad
ibn-Muhammad ibn-Rushd.   See
Averroes

Abulhasán (character in the
*Arabian Nights*).   OC, 397

Acebal or Acevedo (character
in Borges).   OC, 1040, 1042

Acevedo (family).   OC, 932,
1003, 1100.   OP, 377, 549.
P, 78

Acevedo, Eudoro (character in
Borges story).   LA, 123–33.
VA, 43–51

Acevedo, Francisco Xavier.   OC,
561

Azevedo, Isidoro (Borges's
maternal grandfather, d. 1905).
OC, 68, 79, 86–87, 994, 1003

Acevedo, Judas Tadeo.   OC,
1100.   OP, 378

Acevedo, Miguel.   OC, 1100.
OP, 378

Acevedo, Pedro Pascual.   OC,
1100.   OP, 378

Acevedo de Borges, Leonor
(Borges's mother, 1876–1975).
OC, 9.   A, 88.   BO, 39.
C, 37.   CONJ, 35.   LA, 13.
OP, 471, 492, 511.   PB, 246.

Acevedo Díaz, Eduardo Inés
(Uruguayan writer, 1851–1919,
author of *Brenda, Ismael* and
*Nativa*).   OC, 627

Acha, Mariano (Argentine
military officer, 1799–1841).
PB, 132, 152

Achamoth.   OC, 215

Achinelli (pharmacist in
Bustos Domecq story).   OCC,
410

Actor (character in
the *Iliad*).   OC, 242n.

Acuario (Aquarius in Greek
mythology and in zodiac).
OCC, 643

Acuña de Figueroa, Francisco
(Uruguayan poet, 1790–1862).
OC, 114, 179

Adam Kadmón (original man
according to the Kabbalah).
P, 67, 161.   SN, 133

Adam von Bremen (German
historian and geographer,
c.1045–1076, author of
*Historia Hammaburgensis
Ecclesiae,* of which the
*Libellus* is the fourth book).
C, 23.   LA, 111.   PB, 200

Adán (Adam, first man in
Bible). OC, 180, 263, 264,
337, 362, 408, 419, 453, 638,
650, 651, 702, 795, 819, 842,
865, 917, 934, 948, 996,
1004, 1085, 1099, 1104, 1131.
OCC, 322, 659, 709, 738-39,
801, 825, 879, 894, 904, 952.
BO, 36. C, 21, 23, 29, 41,
43, 73. CONJ, 49. IA,
182. LA, 83. OP, 376,
382, 408, 431, 487, 504, 507,
513, 552, 554. P, 523. SN,
68, 137-38, 154. VA, 22

Addison, Joseph (English
writer, 1672-1719). OC,
670. OCC 826, 836. ILN, 13.
NED, 120n. SN, 45, 47, 53

Adobrandi, Aldo (character in
Bustos Domecq story, also
known as Arlequín de la
Muerte). OCC, 378

Adonis (youth of great beauty
in classical mythology,
favorite of Aphrodite). PB,
197. TE, 127

Adriano, Publio Elio (Publius
Aelius Hadrianus, Roman
emperor, 76-138). OCC, 809,
824. I, 35. P, 166

Adrogué, Esteban (founder of
town of Adrogué outside of
Buenos Aires). OCC, 417

Aegir (magician mentioned in
the Skaldskaparmal). OC,
369, 376. OCC, 954, 955

Aesón (in Greek mythology,
Jason's father). OC, 226

Aethelstan (West Saxon king,
894-939). OCC, 885, 937

Aetla. See Atila

Africano, el. See Escipión
el Africano

Afrodita (Aphrodite, goddess
of love in Greek mythology).
OC, 782, 863

Agamenón (Agamemnon, Greek
hero, general of Greek forces
in Trojan war). OC, 250.
OCC, 621, 741, 792. BO, 37

Agita, Tony, doctor (probably
a reference to Antonio Aita,
see below). OCC, 145

Agramante (character in
Ariosto). OC, 838

Agripina (Agrippina the
younger, Roman noblewoman,
sister of Caligula and mother
of Nero, 16-59). NED, 93

Agrippa von Nettesheim,
Cornelius (German writer,
soldier, physician and
magician, 1486-1535, author
of De Incertitudine et
Vanitate Scientiarum et
artium atque Excellentia
Verbi Dei Declamatio). OC,
256, 261, 541. C, 41. I, 88

Aguila (eagle in Dante).
NED, 140, 141, 143. PB,
177-80

Aguilera, Rufino (character
in Borges story). OC, 1036,
1037

Agustín, San (St. Augustine,
Aurelius Augustinus, bishop
of Hippo and Church father,
356-430, author of De
Civitate Dei, Confessiones
and other works). OC, 216,
359, 362, 363, 365, 388, 391,
392, 550, 551, 651, 701, 714,
764. OCC, 622, 689, 774,
873, 897. BO, 14, 49, 85,
86, 88, 91, 97. I, 140,
153. NED, 114. OP, 429.
P, 23. PB, 144. SN, 18,
58, 89, 96

Ahab, Captain (character in
Melville's Moby Dick). OC,
591, 1128. NED, 118. OP,
485. P, 116, 117. SN, 30-
31

Ahasverus (Persian king
mentioned several times in
the Bible). OC, 699

Ahmed (prince in the Arabian
Nights). OC, 397

Ahumada, Domingo (character
in Borges-Bioy filmscript).
OCC, 215-216, 217

Aita, Antonio, doctor
(Argentine educator and
writer, b. 1891, past
president of the PEN club in
Argentina and, in the words
of the Enciclopedia de la
literatura argentina,
"entusiasta difusor de la
cultura americana"). OC,
627

Aixa (in some Spanish ballads, Boabdil's mother, who tells him after his loss of Granada that if he had fought like a man he would not have had to flee like a woman). OC, 306

Akbar (Mogul emperor of India, 1542-1605). OC, 613

Akutagawa Ryunosuke (Japanese short story writer and critic, 1892-1927, author of a parody of the story of the forty-seven Ronins, *A Day in the Life of Oishi Kuranosuke*, 1917). P, 48

Al-Mahdi, Mohammed. See Mahdi, Mohammed al-

Al-Moqanna. See Hákim de Merv

Al-Qazwini. See Qazwini, al-

Al-Yahiz. See Yahiz, al-

Alá (Allah, name of God in Islam). OC, 338, 412, 583, 591, 612. OCC, 350, 672, 709. VA, 41

Aladino (character in the *Arabian Nights*). OC, 397. SN, 72, 73

Alain (pseud. of Emile-Auguste Chartier, French philosopher and essayist, 1868-1951, author of *Propos sur l'Esthetique*, *Propos de littérature*, *Histoire de mes pensées* and other works). I, 56

Alain de Lille or Alanus de Insulis (French theologian, poet and Latinist, c.1128-1202). OC, 625, 636

Alba, duquesa de (patroness of Torres Villarroel). I, 8

Albert, Prince (Francis Charles Augustus Albert Emmanuel, prince consort of England, 1819-1861). P, 35

Albert, Stephen (Sinologist, character in Borges story). OC, 474-80

Albertelli, Pilo (author of *Gli Eleati*, 1939). OC, 636

Alberto (character in Herrera's *Hágase hizo*, also known as Ruperto). OCC, 346

Alberto Magno (Albertus Magnus of Cologne, German theologian, philosopher and scientist, c.1200-1280).

OC, 280, 360. OCC, 661. PB, 230

Alberuni (al-Biruni, Arabic writer, d. 1048, author of books on India, on comparative history and on astronomy and astrology). OCC, 729-30

Albino, San. OCC, 897

Albornoz, Alejo (Buenos Aires thug). OC, 128n., 969

Albornoz, Filemón (character in Gutiérrez). PB, 154

Alburak (magical mare in Islamic legend). OC, 361n.

Alceo de Mesena (his epitaph is preserved in the *Greek Anthology*). OC, 700n.

Alcorta, Amancio (Argentine public official and writer, 1842-1902, author of *Espinas de un amor*, *Tratado de derecho internacional*, *Instrucción secundaria* and other works). OCC, 137

Alcorta, Gloria (Argentine writer, b. 1916, author of *En la casa muerta*, *El hotel de la luna* and other works). PB, 166

Alcuino (Alcuin or Albinus Flaccus, English scholar and ecclesiastic, 732-804, author of *Versus de patribus, regibus et sanctis Eboracensis ecclesiae*, *De Fide Trinitatis* and other works). OCC, 880, 903

Aldao, José Félix (Argentine caudillo and priest, 1785-1845, subject of a biography by Sarmiento). OC, 867. P, 64

Aldiger. See Dante Alighieri

Aldrovandi, Ulissi (Italian naturalist, 1522-1605). OCC, 593

Alejandro Bicorne. See Alejandro de Macedonia

Alejandro de Afrodisia (Alexander of Aphrodisias, peripatetic philosopher, fl. 3rd century A. D.). OC, 583

Alejandro de Macedonia (Alexander III of Macedonia, the Great, conqueror of

Persia, 356–323, sometimes
called Alejandro Bicorne,
Alejandro Magno, Iskandar).
OC, 263, 500, 517, 562, 585,
627, 692n.     OCC, 586, 746,
907, 925, 936.     A, 52–53.
BO, 16.     CONJ, 45.     LA,
35.     NED, 110.     OP, 519,
538.     PB, 194, 195.     SN,
58–59, 61, 65, 125–26, 127,
137

Alem, Leandro (Argentine
lawyer and politician, 1842–
1896, head of the Unión
Cívica Radical).     OC, 1036.
OCC, 526.     A, 58.     C, 37

Alemán, Mateo (Spanish
novelist, 1547–1614?, author
of *Guzmán de Alfarache*).
TE, 139, 140

Alessandri, Roberto (Beatriz
Viterbo's husband, character
in Borges story).     OC, 617

Alewih (Danish king mentioned
in the *Widsith*).     OCC, 876

Alexander, Francisco
(Ecuadorian translator of
Whitman).     P, 173

Alfarabi (al-Farabi, Turkish-
Arabian philosopher, d. 950,
author of *The Opinions of
the Citizens of the Virtu-
ous City*).     OC, 688

Alfieri (lawyer, character in
Miller's *View from the
Bridge*).     ILN, 55

Alfredo el Grande (Alfred the
Great, English king, 849–
901).     OCC, 799, 851, 882,
894

Algazel (al-Ghazali, Persian
philosopher, 1058–1111,
author of the *Tahafut-ul-
Tahafut* or *Incoherence of
the Philosophers, The
Revivification of the
Religious Sciences* and other
works).     OC, 582, 705, 715

Alicia (Alice, character in
Carroll's *Alice's Adventures
in Wonderland* and *Through
the Looking Glass*).     OCC, 838.
C, 89.     P, 108–11.     SN, 70

Allaby, rector (character in
Borges story "Abenjacán el
Bojarí").     OC, 601–7

Allan, John (Poe's adopted
father).     ILN, 18

Allen, Myriam (character in
Bustos Domecq stories, also
known as Myriam Allen de
Ford and Myriam Allen Du
Bosc).     OCC, 304, 330

Allende (minor figure in
Borges-Bioy filmscript).
OCC, 236–37

Almada, Juan (knife-fighter
in Borges story).     OC, 1042,
1043

Almafuerte (Argentine poet,
pseud. of Pedro Bonifacio
Palacios, 1854–1917).     OC,
115, 119, 123, 127, 135.     I,
62, 107.     IA, 35–43.     P, 8,
11–16, 40.     PB, 164, 206.
TE, 90, 133, 146

Almansur.     See Yacub Almansur

Almanza, Juan (knife-fighter
in Borges story).     OC, 1043

Almotanabi (Abu-t-Tayyib al-
Mutanabbi, Arabic poet, 916–
965).     OC, 403

Almotásim (in Borges story,
mysterious divine man).     OC,
416, 417, 418

Almotásim el Magrebi (12th
century Arabic poet).     OC,
848

Alonso, Amado (Spanish critic
and philologist, 1896–1952).
OC, 655

Alonso, Dámaso (Spanish poet,
critic and philologist, b.
1898).     IA, 84–85

Alonso y Trelles, José (Uruguayan gauchesque poet, born in
Spain, 1857–1924).     TE, 89

Alp Arslan (Mahommed Ben
Da'ud, second sultan of the
dynasty of Seljuk, in Persia,
1029–1072; the honorific
title Alp Arslan means "a
valiant lion").     OC, 688

Alsina, Adolfo (Argentine
politician, 1829–1877).     OC,
86.     OCC, 526.     P, 28

Alt (character in Borges
story, identified with
Roberto Arlt by Ricardo
Piglia).     OC, 1032

Alto Rey (character in Borges
story).     LA, 101–107

Altsachsen.   OCC, 903

Alvarado, Pedro de   (Spanish conquistador in Mexico and Central America, 1486-1541). OC, 596, 599

Alvarez, José Sixto (Argentine writer, 1858-1903, who used pseudonyms Fray Mocho and Fabio Carrizo; author of *Un viaje al país de los matreros*, *Memorias de un vigilante*, *Vida de los ladrones célebres de Buenos Aires y sus maneras de robar* and other works).   OC, 134. OCC, 21, 92, 393.   IA, 167, 168.   TE, 22, 30

Alvarez de Pineda.   OC, 295

Alvarez de Toledo, Letizia (Argentine writer, author of *Leonardo da Vinci, su vida y su obra*, 1942).   OC, 88, 471n.

Alvear, Carlos de   (Argentine general and politician, 1789-1853).   OC, 1048

Alvear, Dora de   (member of a socially prominent and historically important family).   SN, 44

Alvear, Elvira de   (Argentine poet and patron of the arts, author of *Reposo*, 1934, and publisher of the periodical *Imán*, edited in Paris by Alejo Carpentier).   OC, 816, 1009

Ama   (the housekeeper, minor character in *Don Quijote*). PB, 211

Amadeo, Octavio   (author of prologue to Lugones's posthumous book on Roca). OCC, 487

Amadís de Gaula   (hero of one of the earliest and most influential chivalric novels).   OC, 667.   OP, 527.   PB, 207

Amaro, Eliseo   (character in Borges story).   OC, 1031-33

Amaro, Juan Francisco   (doctor in Paysandú, Uruguay).   OC, 522, 572, 573

Ambapali   (courtesan in Buddhist legend).   OCC, 726

Ambrosio, San   (St. Ambrose, bishop of Milan and Church father, 340-397, author of the *Hexameron*).   OC, 700, 714.   OCC, 588

Ameghino, Florentino (Argentine paleontologist, 1854-1911).   OCC, 431, 486-87

Amenophis IV   (Akhenaton, Egyptian pharaoh and religious reformer, ruled 1370-1350).   OC, 522

Amiel, Henri-Frédéric   (Swiss philosopher and critic, 1821-1881).   A, 38.   CONJ, 97. LA, 12

Amicis, Edmondo de   (writer of travel books, 1846-1908, author of *De los Apeninos a los Andes*).   OCC, 304

Amiothi.   See Hamlet

Amis, Kingsley   (British writer, b. 1922).   ILN, 58, 60

Amitabha   (name for Gautama Buddha meaning "Infinite Light").   OCC, 757

Amleth or Amlodi.   See Hamlet

Ammiano   (Marcellinus Ammianus, Roman historian, c.325-c.391, author of *Rerum Gestarum libri XXXI*).   OC, 152n.

Amódite   (Libyan serpent, according to Lucan).   OCC, 593

Amón   (Egyptian god).   OCC, 627

Amor   (god of love).   OCC, 691.   C, 67

Amorim, Enrique   (Uruguayan novelist and short-story writer, 1900-1960).   OC, 329, 441, 442.   PB, 134

Anacreonte   (Anacreon, Greek lyric poet, 560-478).   OCC, 484

Ananda   (Buddha's cousin). OCC, 725

Anastasio el Pollo   (character in Estanislao del Campo's *Fausto*).   OC, 186-87.   P, 29, 92.   TE, 11, 12

Anastasio el Pollo   (pseud. of Estanislao del Campo).   OC, 186.   OCC, 520

Anaxagoras (Greek philosopher, c.500–c.428). OC, 705, 764, 864

Anderson, Sherwood (American writer, 1876–1941, author of *Winesburg, Ohio* and other works). ILN, 34–35 37, 40, 54

Andrade, Olegario (Argentine Romantic poet and journalist, 1839–1882). OC, 1049

Andrea, Johannes Valentinus (German theologian, founder of Rosicrucianism, 1586–1654, supposed author of *Allgemeine und General-Reformation der ganzen weiten Welt* and *Fama Fraternitatis*). OC, 433, 440

Andrenio (character in Gracián's *Criticón*). TE, 146

Andreoli, Raffaele (Italian literary critic, author of *La Divina Commedia di Dante Aleghieri*, 1891, and various studies of Italian popular poetry, dialects, etc.). OC, 610. NED, 114

Andro-esfinge (Herodotus's name for the Egyptian sphinxes). OCC, 627

Andrómeda (princess of Ethiopia in Greek mythology). OCC, 675

Andrusov, Nikolai V. (Russian engineer who studied the hydrography of the Caspian Sea). OC, 324

Andvari (dwarf in Scandinavian myth, forced by Loki to make a magic ring). OCC, 910, 929, 966

Anet (fish in Egyptian mythology). OCC, 572

Anfisbena (mythical two-headed serpent). OCC, 573, 593. A, 49. CONJ, 51. LA, 77

Angel de la Guarda (guardian angel). C, 67

Angeles (angels of various kinds). OCC, 574. BO, 49, 50, 52, 53, 56, 58, 60. P, 158–59, 162

Angélica (character in Ariosto and Boiardo poems, beloved of Orlando). OC, 837. OP, 456

Angelus Silesius (pseud. of Johannes Scheffler, German mystic poet, 1624–1677, author of *Cherubinischer Wandersmann*, 1657). OC, 641n., 771, 936, 1116. OCC, 734. I, 147. OP, 392, 542, 550. PB, 119. SN, 120–121

Anglada, Carlos (character in Bustos Domecq stories). OCC, 48–61, 62–66, 67, 68, 80, 81, 110n., 352, 353, 411, 414

Anglada, Mariana Ruiz Villalba de. See Ruiz Villalba de Anglada, Mariana

Aníbal (Hannibal, Carthaginian general, 247–183). OC, 633. CONJ, 37

Aniceto el Gallo (pseud. of Hilario Ascasubi). OC, 185. OCC, 520

Aniel (names given in the *Zohar* to the one of the monsters in Ezekiel's vision, the others being Haniel, Kafziel and Azriel). OCC 642–43

Anlaf (Irish king). See Olaf

Anna (beloved of De Quincey). A, 28

Annunzio, Gabriel D' (Italian poet, novelist and playwright, 1863–1938). OC, 445

Anónimo Florentino (early commentator on Dante, sometimes identified as Graziolo de' Bambaglioli). NED, 114

Anónimo Sevillano (author of the important poem "Epístola Moral a Fabio," now held to be Andrés de Fernández). OC, 1129. BO, 33. SN, 118

Anselmi, Dolménico (character in Borges–Bioy filmscript). OCC, 254, 261, 266

Anselmi, Raúl (fictional character in Borges–Bioy filmscript). OCC, 199, 254–78, 281–296. BC, 77

Anselmo, San (St. Anselm, Italian prelate, doctor of

the Church, archbishop of
Canterbury, c.1033–1109,
author of the *Monologion,*
the *Proslogion* and other
writings). OC, 218, 698,
745. BO, 16
Anticristo (in Christian
eschatology, tyrant who will
lead the forces of evil at
the end of time). OCC, 902.
NED, 152n.
Antígona (princess of Thebes
in Greek myth). OCC, 627
Antílopes (six-legged
antilopes in Siberian myth).
OCC, 583
Antonio (black slave belonging
to Camoes). PB, 241
Antonio, Julio (friend of
Gómez de la Serna). I, 126
Antonio, San (St. Anthony of
Egypt, first Christian monk,
c.250–c.350). OCC, 603
Antrobus (family in Wilder's
*The Skin of Our Teeth).*
ILN, 54
Antuñano y Pons, Paco
(character in Bustos Domecq
story). OCC, 405
Aparicio. See Saravia
Apisonador. See Bodendrucker
Aplanador. See Bodendrucker
Apollinaire, Guillaume (pseud.
of Guillaume de Kostrowitsky,
French poet, 1880–1918). I,
96. TE, 70–74
Apolo (god of sun, music and
song in Greek myth). OC,
550, 695, 877. OCC, 604,
818. I, 39. TE, 126
Apolodoro (Apollodorus of
Athens, Greek scholar, b.
c.180 B.C., author of the
*Bibliotheca,* a study of Greek
heroic mythology, and various
other works on time,
geography, theology and
etymology). OC, 228n., 820.
OCC, 645, 696
Apolonio de Rodas (Apollonius
of Rhodes, Alexandrian epic
poet and grammarian, 222–181,
author of the *Argonautica).*
OC, 226, 228n., 249. OCC,
585, 696, 699

Apolonio de Tyana (Apollonius
of Tyana, Greek philosopher
of the neo-Pythagorean
school, c.5 B.C.–95 A.D.).
OCC, 656
Apóstoles (the term refers to
twelve disciples of Jesus
Christ and then more broadly
to others of his early
followers). OCC, 879
Apuleyo, Lucio (Lucius
Apuleius, Latin writer,
rhetorician and philosopher,
b. 125 A.D., author of the
*Metamorphoses* or *Golden Ass,*
*Apologia, Florida, De Deo*
*Socratis* and other works).
OC, 281, 733
Aqueo (character in Homer).
OP, 444
Aqueronte (monster). OCC,
669–70
Aquiles (Achilles, hero in
Greek myth and literature).
OC, 177, 203, 241, 244–48,
254–58, 263, 278n., 393, 445,
543n., 562, 660, 710, 890,
1081, 1112, 1128. OCC 326,
605. BO, 18, 92. I, 91.
ILN, 25. NED, 110, 125. OP,
366, 428. P, 119, 171.
PB, 225, 235, 242. SN, 41
Aquino, Tomás (Thomas Aquinas,
Italian theologian and
scholastic philosopher, 1225–
1274, author of the *Summa*
*Theologiae,* the *Summa*
*Catholicae Fidei contra*
*Gentiles* and other works).
OC, 256, 575, 704. OCC,
851. BO, 33, 38. LA, 125.
PB, 165, 230. VA, 45
Aquino Derisi, señora
(character in Bustos Domecq
story). OCC, 138
Arcángel. BC, 58. PJ, 66,
72
Arcipreste de Hita (Juan Ruiz,
Spanish poet, 1283?–1350?).
IA, 174
Arden, Elizabeth (founder of
cosmetics company). OCC, 54
Arenal, Concepción (Spanish
sociologist, 1820–1893).
OCC, 62

Arnold, Matthew (English poet and critic, 1822–1888). OC, 219, 241, 400, 719, 772. OCC, 833, 837–38, 902n. BC, 60. IA, 22. ILN, 42–43. PB, 217, 222

Arolas, Eduardo (tango composer, 1892–1924, author of "El Marne" and dozens of other works). OC, 139, 889

Arpías (the harpies of Greek mythology). OCC, 585

Arquímedes (Archimedes, Greek mathematician and inventor, c.287–212). LA, 130

Arredondo, Avelino (assassin of the Uruguayan president Idiarte Borda in 1896). OC, 853, 1086. LA, 151–59, 181. OP, 371

Arredondo, Clementina (maid and cousin of Avelino Arredondo). LA, 152, 154

Arrieta, Rafael Alberto (Argentine poet, essayist and literary historian, 1889–1968). I, 155

Arrowsmith (character in Sinclair Lewis novel). ILN, 35

Arruti (minor character in Bustos Domecq story). OCC, 378

Artagnan, D' (character in Dumas's Les trois mousquetaires). OC, 157, 748. OCC, 159. LA, 46. P, 41

Artajerjes (character in Borges-Bioy film synopsis). BC, 83

Artajerjes Mnemon (Artaxerxes, Persian king, reigned c.436–358). OCC, 608, 663, 703

Artemidoro (Artemidorus of Ephesus, fl. 2nd century A.D., author of a treatise on the interpretation of dreams, Oneirocritica). OC, 1132

Artigas, José Gervasio (Uruguayan politician and general, 1764–1850). OC, 655, 968, 999, 1049, 1144. A, 74. LA, 43. P, 64, 130, 132, 138. PB, 132, 152

Artsybashev, Mikhail Petrovich (Russian novelist, 1878–1927, author of Sanine and other works, here Arzibashev). OC, 223. BC, 29

Arturo or Artús (Arthur, legendary British king). OC, 219, 836. OCC, 814, 825, 897. ILN, 46. OP, 431, 466

Arturo (fireman in Bustos Domecq story). OCC, 361

Asbury, Herbert (author of The Gangs of New York, 1927). OC, 311, 345

Ascasubi, Hilario (Argentine gauchesque poet, 1807–1875, author of Paulino Lucero, Aniceto el Gallo, Santos Vega o los mellizos de la Flor and other works). OC, 106, 107, 131, 132n., 139, 154n., 165, 180, 181–86, 188, 193, 267, 268, 656, 684, 734, 735, 965, 976, 1002, 1144. OCC 392, 516, 517–20, 522, 534, 536, 977. I, 51–56, 57. IA, 56. OP, 478. P 17–21, 28, 64–65, 82, 91–93, 95, 97, 112, 113, 136. PB, 133, 134. TE, 8, 15, 19, 60, 88

Asgerd (Egil's daughter in the Egils Saga). OCC, 937–38

Ashe, Herbert (character in Borges story). OC, 433, 434, 440, 441, 483

Asín Palacios, Miguel (Spanish scholar and Arabist, 1871–1944, author of Huellas del Islam and other works). OC, 588, 705. OCC, 599, 711. PB, 230

Asita (Nepalese mystic). OCC, 722

Asno de Tres Patas (monster mentioned in the Bundahish, a Zoroastrian encyclopedic work). OCC, 586

Asoka (Indian emperor, convert to Buddhism, reigned 274–232). OC, 741. OCC, 671, 756. SN, 78

Aspid (Libyan serpent mentioned by Lucan). OCC, 593

Asplanato (the Snake Man).
OCC, 180
Asterión (name given to the
Minotaur in Ovid).  OC, 569–
70, 1091.  OP, 436
Astioque (sister of Priam,
character in the *Iliad*).
OC, 242n.
Astolfo (character in
Ariosto's *Orlando Furioso*).
OCC, 647
Asvaghosha (Indian Buddhist
writer).  OCC, 727
Atahualpa (Inca emperor, c.
1502–1533, treacherously
killed by Pizarro).  OC,
295.  SN, 62
Atalanta (Arcadian Atalanta,
huntress and warrior in Greek
legend).  OCC, 920
Atanarico (Athanaric, Gothic
king, d. 381, ruled 366–80).
OCC, 863
Atanasio (St. Athanasius,
bishop of Alexandria,
theologian, 293–373, author
of important discourses
against the Arians and of
works on the deity and
personality of the Holy
Spirit).  OC, 210
Atheo.  See Theodoro
Athis.  OCC, 621–22
Atila (Hun king, d. 453, ruled
433–53).  OC, 148, 155, 161,
217.  OCC, 787, 827, 872–73,
875, 876, 910, 914, 919, 920,
925, 929, 934, 969–70.  A,
23.  NED, 110.  P, 74
Atlante.  I, 91
Atli (fictional character in
*Grettir Saga*).  PB, 191–92
Atman (the soul according to
Vedanta).  OCC, 733
Atreo (Atreus, mythological
king who killed the children
of his brother Thyestes and
then served their flesh to
Thyestes).  OC, 869
Atropos (the Irresistible,
one of the three Fates of
Greek mythology).  OCC, 311
Attar.  See Farid ud-din Attar
Attis (consort of Cybele in
Phrygian mythology).  OC,
1128

Auden, Wystan Hugh (Anglo-
American poet, playwright and
essayist, 1907–73).  OCC,
842
Augusto César (Caesar Augustus,
Roman emperor, 63 B.C.–14
A.D.).  P, 95.  SN, 14
Aulo Gelio.  See Gelio, Aulo
Aureliano (theologian,
character in Borges story).
OC, 550–56
Aurora (minor character in
Bustos Domecq story).  OCC,
75
Ausonio (Decimus Magnus
Ausonius, Roman poet and
rhetorician, c.310–395,
author of epigrams and other
short poems, as well as works
on history and education).
OCC, 956
Austen, Jane (English novelist,
1775–1817).  P, 47
Avalokitésvara (Buddhist
saint).  OCC, 762, 765, 767
Ave del Alba.  See Gallo
Celestial
Avelino (character in Bustos
Domecq story).  OCC, 381–91
Avellanos, Ricardo (character
in Borges story, grandson of
Dr. Avellanos).  OC, 1062
Avellanos, Doctor (character
in Borges story).  OC, 1062,
1065
Aventura (goddess of
adventure).  OCC, 40
Averroes (Ibn Rushd, Spanish-
Arabic philosopher and
writer, 1126–1198, author of
the *Tahafut-ul-falasifa* or
*Incoherence of the
Incoherence*, a reply to al-
Ghazali's *The Incoherence of
the Philosophers*).  OC, 582–
88.  NED, 99, 117.  PB,
183.  SN, 50
Avicebrón (Salomón ben Gabirol,
Spanish-Jewish philosopher,
c.1020–c.1058).  I, 13
Avicena (Ibn Sina, Persian
philosopher and physician,
980–1037, author of the *Book
of Healing* and *The Canon*).
OC, 688, 715

Axehandle Hound (fabulous animal of North America). OCC, 631

Ayax (Aias or Ajax, king of Salamis and hero in the *Iliad* and later works). OC, 782

Azcárate, Patricio de (Spanish scholar, 1800–1886). OC, 255

Azevedo, Daniel Simón (character in Borges story). OC, 501, 502, 504, 506

Azevedo Bandeira (character in Borges story). OC, 545–49, 629

Azorín (pseud. of José Martínez Ruiz, Spanish writer, 1873–1967). OC, 667. OCC, 13, 49, 77

Azriel (name given in Zohar to one of the monsters in Ezekiel's dream). OCC, 642–43

Baal (ancient Semitic fertility god). CONJ, 37

Baal Shem Tobh, Israel ben Eliezer (founder of Hasidism, 1700–1760). OC, 500, 997

Babaí (monster which helps devour the dead in Egyptian mythology). OCC, 615

Babbitt, George Folansbee (character in Lewis novel). ILN, 35

Babuglia (character in Bustos Domecq story). OCC, 399

Bachelier, Mme. Henri (character in Borges story). OC, 444, 446, 450

Baco (Bacchus or Dionysus, ancient god of wine and ecstasy). OCC, 692. PB, 239, 243

Bacon, Delia (American writer, 1811–1859, leading proponent of the idea that Shakespeare's plays were written by Francis Bacon). P, 143

Bacon, Francis (English philosopher and writer, 1561–1626, author of *The Advancement of Learning, The New Atlantis* and numerous essays). OC, 209, 278n.,

394, 533, 638, 641, 697, 715, 716, 775. OCC, 822. A, 72. BO, 46. C, 9. I, 9. LA, 89. NED, 139. OP, 557. P, 26, 143, 152, 157. PB, 177. SN, 106. TE, 114

Bacon, Roger (English philosopher and scientist, c.1220–1292). OCC, 958

Bacourt, baroness (character in Borges story). OC, 444, 446, 449

Baculard, Germaine (character in Bustos Domecq story). OCC, 363, 364

Baculard, Jean-Christophe (character in Bustos Domecq story). OCC, 364

Badana. OC, 184

Badoglio, Adelma (Argentine educator, author of bio-biographical note on Honorio Bustos Domecq). OCC, 13

Badrbasim (son of Shahriman, character in the *Arabian Nights*). OC, 358n.

Bagnoregio, count (character in Borges story). OC, 444, 445, 449

Bahadur Alí, Mir (Bombay lawyer, author of *The Approach to Al–Mu'tasim*). OC, 414–18

Bahamut (Arabic monster related to the Behemoth). OCC, 590, 651, 654

Bahnsen, Julius Friedrich August (German philosopher, author of *Philosophie und Nationalitat,* 1878, *Zur Philosophie der Geschichte* and other works). I, 74

Bahr, Hermann (Austrian playwright and writer, 1863–1934). OC, 55

Baigent, Francis J. (Tichborne family friend, ally of the Claimant). OC, 304

Baigorri (character in Bustos Domecq story). OCC, 397

Baladhuri (Abu-1-Abbas Ahmad ibn Yahya ibn Jabir al-Baladhuri, Arabian historian born in Persia, d. 892, author of *Ansab ul-Ashraf* or *Genealogies of the Nobles,* and of the *Futuh ul–Buldan* or *Conquests of Lands*, an account of the early conquests of Mohammed and the early caliphs). OC, 324

Balcarce, Florencio (Argentine poet, 1815–1839). OCC, 338

Baldanders (Protean creature in Grimmelshausen's *Simplicissimus*). OCC, 591

Balder or Baldr (Norse god of summer). OCC, 900, 928–29, 953–54, 955, 965. OP, 453, 466, 529

Ballena (whale in various myths and legends). OCC, 712, 892

Balmes Urpiá, Jaime Luciano (Spanish philosopher and political journalist, author of *El criterio, Cartas a un escéptico en materia de religión, Filosofía elemental* and other works). OCC, 185. LA, 57

Balzac, Honoré (French novelist, 1799–1850, author of *Recherche de l'absolu* and numerous other works). OC, 157, 262, 874. OCC, 311, 312, 936. I, 46. ILN, 14, 34. P, 23

Banchs, Enrique (Argentine poet, 1888–1968, author of *La urna*). OC, 119, 137, 163, 269. OCC, 484, 563. CONJ, 65. IA, 78. PB, 164, 166, 167, 215. SN, 112–16. TE, 7, 103, 128

Bancroft, George (American film actor, 1882–1956). BC, 63. CONJ, 75

Bandello, Matteo (Italian bishop and novelist, 1485–1561, author of the *Novelle*). P, 46

Banquo (Scottish general, character in Shakespeare's *Macbeth*). OCC, 825. P, 142, 145, 146

Banshee (supernatural being of Ireland and Scotland, known for howling by the window of a house where someone is about to die). OCC, 592

Banú Abbás (reference to the Abbasid dynasty, opposed to Al-Moqanna). OC, 326

Banville, Theodore (French poet, dramatist and writer, 1823–1891). TE, 117

Barahona de Soto, Luis (Spanish poet, 1548–1595, author of *Las lágrimas de Angélica* and other works). OC, 277

Baralt, Rafael María (Venezuelan critic and poet, 1810–1860, author of a *Diccionario de galicismos, Historia de Venezuela* and an unfinished *Diccionario matriz de la lengua castellana*). OCC, 300, 327, 328, 329

Barbara, Major (major in the Salvation Army, character in Shaw play). OCC, 848

Barbero (character in *Don Quijote*). See Nicolás el barbero

Barbone. OCC, 173

Barbusse, Henri (French writer, 1874–1935, author of *L'Enfer*). OC, 249 PB, 186

Barcia, Roque (Spanish lexicographer, 1823–1885, author of a *Diccionario general etimológico de la lengua española* and a *Diccionario de sinónimos*). OCC, 136

Barcina, la (minor character in Bustos Domecq story). OCC, 71, 80

Bardi (Beatriz Portinari's husband). NED, 159

Barfod. See Magnus Barfod

Barker, Ernest (British historian, 1874–1960, author of *The Crusades*). P, 140

Barlaam (holy man in legend of Barlaam and Josaphat, Christianized version of the Buddha legend). OC, 741. OCC, 936

Barlach, Julius (supposed author of the apocryphal *Urkunden zur Geschichte der Zahirsage*, 1899, perhaps a relative of the writer and

sculptor Ernst Barlach, 1870–
1938). OC, 593, 594
Barnes (translator of
Bergson). OC, 246
Baroja, Pío (Spanish novelist,
1872–1956). P, 59
Baronio, César (Caesar Baronius,
Italian cardinal and church
historian, 1538-1607, author
of *Annales Ecclesiastici* and
the *Martyrologium Romanum*).
OC, 741
Barrabás (Barabbas, Jew of
Malta in Marlowe's play).
OCC, 817
Barrabás (Barabbas, in the
Bible, Jewish prisoner
released in exchange for the
crucifixion of Jesus). LA,
85
Barreiro, Ladislao (character
in Suárez Lynch novella,
nicknamed Potranco,
Pestalozzi, Estatua de
Garibaldi, etc.). OCC, 149,
157, 158, 162, 164–66, 170–
72, 179–83, 192
Barres, Maurice (French novel-
ist, essayist and politician,
1862-1923). OC, 448
Barretero, El (pseud. of
Carriego). OC, 118, 143
Barrett, Elizabeth. See
Browning, Elizabeth Barrett
Barsdorf, Hermann (publisher
of Hladík's translation of
the *Sefer Yetsirah*). OC,
508
Bartholomew, Roy (Argentine
critic, editor of *Cien
poesías rioplatenses*, 1954,
and works of Lugones and
Borges). SN, 118
Bartleby (character in
Melville's *Bartleby the
Scrivener*). P, 117
Barton, Bernard (English poet,
1784-1849, friend of Charles
Lamb and father-in-law of
Edward FitzGerald). OC, 77
Basílides (Gnostic theologian,
fl. c.130 A.D.). OC, 177,
213–16, 468, 514, 750n. SN,
136
Basilio, doctor. OCC, 145

Basil, San (Basil the Great
of Caesarea, Greek church
leader, c.330–379, author of
*De Spiritu Sancto, Moralia*
and *Regulae*). OCC, 956
Basilisco (horrid monster of
the ancients). OCC, 593–94,
603
Bassi, Arturo Vicente de
(Argentine tango composer,
1890–1950). OC, 165
Bastardo. See Guillermo I
Battafuoco, Nana (minor
character in Bustos Domecq
story). OCC, 395n.
Batz, Philipp. See Mainlander
Baudelaire, Charles (French
poet and critic, 1821–1867,
author of *Les Fleurs du mal,
Spleen, Petits poemes en
prose* and other works). OC,
235, 250, 382, 447, 694, 731.
OCC, 304, 464, 468, 471, 472,
736, 833, 834. BO, 68.
CONJ, 33. ILN, 9, 62.
NED, 136n. P, 7, 81, 142,
166. PB, 121, 231
Baudizzone (journalist
mentioned in Bustos Domecq
story). OCC, 30
Baulito. See Pérez, Baulito
Beatriz (Beatrice Portinari,
woman who leads Dante in the
*Purgatorio* and *Paradiso*).
OC, 672, 744. OCC, 933.
NED, 103, 116, 132, 140, 145–
53, 155–61. PB, 177, 185,
191. SN, 10, 18, 26
Beauvais, Vincent de (medieval
French writer, d. 1264,
author of *Speculum*). LA, 47
Becher, Johannes (German poet,
1891–1958). OC, 641. I, 73
Becket, Thomas a (English
politician, bishop and saint,
1118–1170). OCC, 816
Beckford, William (English
writer, 1760–1844, author of
*Vathek*). OC, 250, 729–32.
NED, 95, 96. PB, 181
Beckh, Hermann (German
Orientalist, 1874–1939,
author of *Buddhismus: Buddha
und seine lehre*). OC, 743
Bécquer, Gustavo Adolfo
(pseud. of Gustavo Adolfo

Domínguez Bastida, Spanish poet and painter, 1836–1870, author of *Rimas* and *Leyendas*). OC, 1105. OP, 384. PB, 232

Beda el Venerable (the Venerable Bede, English historian, c.672–735, author of the *Historia ecclesiastica gentis Anglorum*). OC, 468, 643. OCC, 809, 881–85, 888, 897, 903, 907, 972. NED, 125–34. OP, 419, 540. P, 108. PB, 199

Bediver (knight in Arthurian legend). OC, 219

Behemoth or Behemot (monster mentioned in the Bible, often identified with the hippopotamus). OCC, 451, 595–96. SN, 25, 134. VA, 38

Behn, Aphra (English dramatist, novelist and spy, 1640?–1689, author of *Oroonoko, The Forced Marriage, The Amorous Prince* and other works). OCC, 853

Belcebú (Beelzebub, lord of the flies, one of the principal devils). OCC, 813

Belda, Joaquín (Spanish novelist and humorist, 1880–1937?). OCC, 49

Belerofonte (Bellerophon, Greek mythological hero, son of Glaucus, king of Corinth, who killed the chimera and flew on Pegasus). OCC, 685

Belisario (Belisarius, Roman general, c.505–565, in whose honor medals were struck; according to legend, Belisarius later wandered the streets of Constantinople a blind beggar). OC, 591, 895

Belkis (queen in the *Arabian Nights*). OC, 405. OCC, 695

Bella Durmiente (Sleeping Beauty). OCC, 968

Bellay. See Du Bellay

Belleforest, Francois de (French poet, 1530–1585, compiler of the *Histoires tragiques*). OCC, 973

Bellegarde, Mme. de (character in James's *The American*). P, 102

Belleza (personification of beauty). LA, 107

Bello, Andrés (Venezuelan philosopher, grammarian and poet, 1781–1865). OC, 487. IA, 14, 58–59

Belloc, Hilaire (English writer, born in France, 1870–1953). OC, 699, 730. OCC, 300, 847, 851. P, 166

Belluga, Luis de (bishop of Murcia during the War of the Spanish Succession). OCC, 595n.

Beltrán. See Silveira, Beltrán

Benaser, Rafael (character in Cansinos Assens' novel *Las luminarias de Hanukah*). TE, 96, 98

Benavides (knife-fighter in Buenos Aires). OC, 1125. OP, 406

Benda, Julien (French critic and essayist, 1867–1956, author of *La trahison des clercs* and other works). OC, 449, 673

Bengochea (Baulito Pérez's mother's maiden name). OCC, 160

Bengolea, Tigre (member of a socially prominent Buenos Aires family, mentioned in Bustos Domecq story). OCC, 95

Benoit, Hubert (French Orientalist, author of *La doctrine supreme*). OCC, 780

Bentley, Edmund (English poet, 1875–1956, inventor of the clerihew). OCC, 851

Benvenuto da Imola. See Rambaldi da Imola, Benvenuto

Beowulf (hero of Old English epic poem). OC, 904. OCC, 622, 811, 871–74

Beppo (character in Byron's poem *Beppo: A Venetian Story*). A, 23. C, 21, 105

Beppo (cat). CONJ, 69

Beranger, Pierre-Jean (French poet and song-writer, 1780–1857). OC, 181

Berard, Victor (French writer on questions of international law as well as on Homer and other literary subjects). OC, 240. PB, 168

Berazategui. See Frogman

Berceo, Gonzalo de (Spanish poet, c.1180-1264, author of *Milagros de Nuestra Señora* and other works). TE, 119

Bergman, Ingrid (Swedish actress, 1915-1982). OC, 285. BC, 67

Bergson, Henri (French philosopher, 1859-1941, author of *Essai sur les données immédiates de la conscience*, *L'Evolution créatrice* and other works). OC, 245-46, 258, 591, 648, 757. OCC, 749. BO, 38, 85. ILN, 40. P, 86. SN, 92, 118, 146

Bergthora (Njal's wife in the *Njals Saga*). OCC, 939

Berkeley, George (English philosopher, 1685-1753, author of *Dialogues between Hylas and Philonous*, *Principles of Human Knowledge*, *Siris*, *Alciphron* and other works). OC, 38, 39, 217, 253n., 273, 281, 435, 440, 719, 757, 759, 760, 761, 766, 767, 768, 773, 1106. OCC, 756. A, 14. BO, 31. I, 109-19. IA, 11. ILN, 9, 11. LA, 67. OP, 384. P, 32, 49. PB, 144. VA, 47

Berkeley, general (character in Borges story). OC, 493

Bernárdez (shopkeeper, character in Bustos Domecq story). OCC, 393

Bernárdez, Francisco Luis (Argentine poet, b. 1900). OC, 82, 198, 371n. OCC, 393. C, 35. I, 98-99. PB, 166. TE, 86

Bernardo (Prince Bernard of the Netherlands). OCC, 334

Bernardo, San (St. Bernard, French mystic and monk, 1090-1153, here used as a nickname). OCC, 132

Bernardo del Carpio (legendary Spanish medieval knight, subject of well-known ballads). OC, 167n.

Bernasconi, Petite (character in Bustos Domecq story). OCC, 411

Bernheim, Hippolyte (French psychologist, expert on hypnotism). BO, 91

Berón de Astrada, Genaro (Argentine politician, d. 1839, governor of Corrientes and opponent of Rosas). P, 138

Berry, Anita (author of *Art for Children*). A, 48

Bertrand, Aloysius (French poet, 1807-1841, author of *Gaspard de la nuit*). OCC, 468

Bertrand de Born (Provencal warrior and troubadour, c.1140-c.1215, encountered by Dante in hell). NED, 158

Beswick, Ethel (author of *Jataka Tales*, 1956). OCC, 780

Betteredge (character in Collins's *The Moonstone*). P, 48

Bevilacqua, Alfredo (tango composer and pianist, 1874-1942, author of *Venus*, *Apolo*, *Independencia*, *Emancipación* and other works). OC, 165

Bezla (character in the *Elder Edda*). OCC, 928

Bhils (people of Indostan who believe that there are hells for tigers). OCC, 701

Bianchi, Alfredo A. (Argentine writer and journalist, 1882-1942). OCC, 320

Bianchi (scholar of Dante). NED, 107

Bibiloni (supposed poet from Catamarca, character in Bustos Domecq story). OCC, 38-43, 46, 47

Bibiloni Webster de Bullrich, Beatriz (friend of Borges). OC, 861

Bicho Feo. See Bustos Domecq, Honorio

Bicicleta, Lungo (character in Bustos Domecq and Suárez Lynch stories). OCC, 156, 157, 173, 183, 396

Bifronte, el. See Jano

Bilbao, Manuel (Argentine journalist and writer, director of the newspaper *La República*, 1867-1881, author of *Buenos Aires*, 1902). OC, 82

Bilham, Miss (English governess, character in Bustos Domecq story). OCC, 54-58

Billy the Kid (famous outlaw in the American West, d. 1881, whom Borges calls Bill Harrigan though his real name may have been Henry McCarty or William H. Bonney). OC, 316-19. BC, 33, 41. P, 113

Bimbo (cartoon character in the *Talkcartoons* with Betty Boop). OC, 224. BC, 33

Bion (Bion the Borysthenite, Greek philosopher, c.325-c.255). OC, 661. P, 120

Bioy Casares, Adolfo (Argentine novelist, b. 1914, author of *La invención de Morel*, *El sueño de los héroes*, numerous other novels, stories, and essays, and collaborator with Borges in the creation of Bustos Domecq and Suárez Lynch and in the edition of the several anthologies of detective stories, the fantastic and Argentine poetry). OC, 166, 431, 432, 433, 612. OCC, 200, 823-24, 977. BC, 77-79. BO, 79. P, 22-24. PB, 167

Bischoff, Erich (German scholar, 1865-1936, author of *Die Elemente der Kabbalah* as well as writings on the Talmud, the Yiddish language, etc.). TE, 67

Bishop, Edmund (English divine, author of *The Genius of the Roman Rite* and other works on religion). CONJ, 37

Bismarck, Otto Eduard Leopold (German politician and statesman, 1815-1898). OCC, 834. P, 36

Bjarni Thorkelsson (character in Borges story). LA, 116, 118-19

Black, John (character in Bradbury's *Martian Chronicles*). P, 27

Blair, Hugh, Dr. (Scottish Presbyterian divine and professor of rhetoric and literature, 1718-1800, author of a laudatory *Dissertation on Macpherson's Ossian*). OCC, 830

Blakamán (here used as a nickname for Dr. Bernardo Castillo). OCC, 80

Blake, Guillermo (English rancher in Chubut, character in Bustos Domecq story). OCC, 365, 366

Blake, Sexton (detective in a long series of anonymous novellas for boys). OCC, 181, 347

Blake, William (English poet and artist, 1757-1827, author of *Songs of Innocence and of Experience*, *The Book of Urizen*, *The Marriage of Heaven and Hell* and many other works). OC, 135, 216n., 694, 719, 722, 1081, 1139. OCC, 498, 574, 699, 774n., 840, 848, 851. A, 48, 75, 80. BO, 51, 54, 55, 60, 87. C, 47. LA, 26. OP, 365, 415, 521. P, 13n., 156, 158, 159. PB, 124, 145, 171. VA, 27

Blanco Fombona, Rufino (Venezuelan writer and politician, 1874-1944). OCC, 471, 502, 503, 504

Blanqui, Louis Auguste (French revolutionary, 1805-1881, author of a work on astrology, *L'Eternite par les astres*, 1872). OC, 393, 651. BO, 14. P, 23-24

Blemies (monsters with their faces on their chests, mentioned by Lane). OCC, 672

Blok, Alexander (Russian
symbolist poet, 1880-1921).
OC, 224.   BC, 32

Blomberg, Héctor Pedro
(Argentine poet, 1890-1955).
PB, 133

Bloom, Leopold (character in
Joyce's *Ulysses*).   OC, 591.
BC, 48

Blosio (perhaps Gaius Blosius,
Stoic philosopher of Cumae,
2nd century B.C.).   OCC, 68

Blougram, Sylvester (character
in Browning's poem "Bishop
Blougram's Apology").   PB,
139

Bloy, Léon (French writer,
1846-1917, author of *Le
Désesperé, La Femme pauvre,
Le Mendiant ingrat* and other
works).   OC, 395, 483, 553,
692, 711, 716, 720-22.   A,
58.   P, 33, 34n., 101, 161

Bluntschli, Captain (character
in Shaw's *Arms and the Man*).
OC, 749

Bluntschli (character in
Bustos Domecq story).   OCC,
330-31

Bo (character in Bustos Domecq
story).   OCC, 400

Boabdil (Abu Abdullah, last
Moorish king of Granada,
ruled 1482-1492).   OC, 306

Boccaccio, Giovanni (Italian
writer, 1313-1375, author of
the *Decameron*).   OC, 406,
746.   OCC, 312, 815.   NED,
100.   P, 46n.   PB, 183

Boccioni, Umberto (Italian
futurist painter and
sculptor, 1882-1916).   OCC,
79

Bodendrucker (animal rather
like a cross between an
elephant and a steam roller,
lives on the planet Neptune).
OCC, 584

Bodhidharma (legendary founder
of Zen Buddhism, who came to
China from India in the late
5th century A.D.).   OCC,
766, 772-73.   PB, 196.   SN,
93-95

Bodhisattva (here used to
refer to Siddhartha, Gautama

Buddha before he received
enlightenment).   OC, 740-43.
OCC, 721-23, 757, 759, 762,
765

Bodoni, Giambattista (Italian
printer, 1740-1813).   OCC,
336

Boecio (Anicius Manlius
Severinus Boethius, Roman
philosopher and scholar, 480-
524, author of *De
consolatione philosophiae*).
OC, 282, 283, 361, 745, 770,
976.   OCC, 799, 814-15, 894,
907, 956.   SN, 36

Boehme, Jakob (German mystic,
1575-1624, author of *De
signatura rerum* and
*Mysterium magnum*).   OC,
508, 509, 704n.

Bogle, Ebenezer (character in
Borges story about Tom
Castro, based on Ezra Bogle,
Tichborne family servant).
OC, 301-5

Boiardo, Matteo Maria (Italian
poet, 1441?-1494, author of
the *Orlando Innamorato*).
OCC, 920

Boileau, Nicolas (French
critic and poet, 1636-1711).
OC, 265.   OCC, 826, 828.   A,
83-84.   BO, 85.   P, 13.
SN, 62, 71, 157

Boitano (character in Bustos
Domecq story).   OCC, 402

Bolívar, Simón (Venezuelan
soldier and statesman, 1783-
1830).   OC, 729, 872, 1048,
1062-67

Bolli (character in the
*Laxdoela Saga*).   OCC, 939

Bolthorn (character in the
*Elder Edda*).   OCC, 928

Bombal, Susana (Argentine
writer, author of *Tres
domingos, El cuadro de
Ennseke Loors* and other
works).   OC, 1039, 1094.
OP, 374, 465, 506.   SN, 48

Bompiani, Valentino (Italian
compiler of several
encyclopedias of world
literature, b. 1898).   OCC,
321

Bonaparte.   See Napoleón

Bonastre (author of *Almafuerte*, 1920).   P, 12

Bonavena, Ramón (character in various Bustos Domecq stories).   OCC, 306-10, 315, 348, 422, 423

Bone, Gavin (translator of *The Seafarer*).   OCC, 796, 975

Bonfanti, Mario (character in Bustos Domecq and Suárez Lynch stories, also mentioned once in a Borges story).   OC, 627.   OCC, 62, 63, 66, 67, 70, 72-80, 129n., 154, 156-57, 161-70, 184, 185

Bonfirraro (character in Bustos Domecq story).   OCC, 400, 401, 402

Bonifacio V (pope, d. 625).   OCC, 888

Bonney, Anne (pirate).   OC, 306

Bonorino, Agustín R. (butcher in Belgrano murdered by the Pata Santa gang, crime for which Isidro Parodi is imprisoned).   OCC, 22

Bontempelli, Máximo (Italian novelist and poet, 1878-1960).   OCC, 13

Boole, George (English logician and mathematician, 1815-1864).   OC, 445

Borametz (plant of Tartary that resembles a sheep, described by Thomas Browne in *Pseudodoxia Epidemica*).   OCC, 597, 661

Borelius, Axel (Swedish theologian in Borges story).   OC, 515, 516n.

Borges family.   OC, 831, 839

Borges, Elsa Astete Millán de (woman to whom Borges was married from 1967 to 1970).   OC, 1010

Borges, Francisco (Argentine colonel, 1833-1874, Borges's grandfather).   OC, 68, 558, 559, 828, 941, 1106, 1138.   A, 88.   OP, 384, 445, 490, 491, 549.   PB, 136

Borges, Guillermo Juan (Argentine poet, cousin of Borges, 1906-1966).   OCC, 497.   P, 54

Borges, Jorge Guillermo (Borges's father, 1873-1938, author of *El caudillo*).   OC, 9, 117, 152, 156, 433, 870, 1009, 1010, 1081, 1133, 1138, 1143.   A, 37, 88.   BO, 39.   C, 37, 51.   CONJ, 35, 63.   I, 129-30.   LA, 13, 14, 89.   OP, 409, 439, 445, 454, 470, 471, 490, 492, 501, 558.   P, 52, 53, 90, 138.   SN, 144, 145

Borges, Jorge Luis (Argentine writer, 1899-1986).   OC, 9, 13, 15, 32, 55, 73, 79, 101, 103, 117, 122n., 130, 164-65, 166, 169, 171, 177, 181, 195, 233, 238, 280, 289, 291, 293, 301n., 304, 334, 351, 371n., 429, 431-43, 464, 495, 589, 595, 624, 626, 657, 764-66, 771, 790, 805, 808, 809-10, 814, 833, 854, 857-58, 861-62, 870, 872, 880, 933, 936-37, 941, 953, 975-76, 1009-10, 1014, 1016, 1017-18, 1021-23, 1034, 1044, 1047, 1081, 1129, 1132, 1138, 1143-45.   OCC, 199-200, 455, 457, 497, 513-514, 569, 719, 787-788, 807, 861-862, 977.   A, 7-8, 15, 17, 25, 32, 37, 38, 40, 41, 44-45, 46, 47-48, 50, 51, 54, 60, 67, 70, 73-74, 75-76, 77, 81, 82, 83-84, 85, 86, 88, 89.   BC, 35-37, 42, 46-47, 57-58, 65, 68, 73, 77-79.   BO, 9, 10, 13, 15, 16, 21, 22, 23, 27-29, 33, 35, 38, 39, 40, 79-80, 84, 96.   C, 9, 11-12, 19, 23, 25-26, 27, 29, 35, 37-38, 50, 51-52, 53, 54-55, 77-78, 89-90, 91, 96.   CONJ, 11, 12-13, 33, 35-36, 51, 59, 63, 67, 69-71, 87, 93.   I, 5, 74, 81, 85, 97, 99, 109, 126, 152, 153, 158, 160.   IA, 7-8, 101-3, 147-51.   ILN, 8.   LA, 9-21, 36, 89, 179-82, back cover.   NED, 95, 96, 107, 123, 158.   OP, 365-66, 376, 377-78, 379, 382, 391, 409-10, 412-13, 419-20, 445, 449-50, 452, 454, 456, 458, 469-70, 471-72, 488, 492, 493,

501, 508, 511, 537, 539, 542–
43, 545, 546, 547, 549–50,
558.    P, 7–9, 11, 12, 22–24,
27, 28, 34, 40, 47, 49, 52–
54, 58, 60, 76, 87, 88, 101,
104, 112–15, 117, 128, 130,
138, 139, 162, 168, 173, 174.
PB, 117, 119, 122, 125–26,
130, 136, 137, 141, 155, 156,
157, 158, 159, 167, 168, 171–
73, 174–75, 181–82, 223, 238,
242, 243–44, 245–48.  PJ, 57–
58, 61–62.    SN, 11–13, 26,
27, 31–32, 36–39, 43, 44, 46,
47–48, 53, 59, 64, 67, 79,
90, 93, 95, 97, 102, 106,
107, 108, 109, 111, 117–18,
120, 128, 138, 143–60.    TE,
22, 24, 112, 145–53, 154.
VA, 11–18

Borges, Norah  (Argentine
painter, b. 1901, Borges's
sister).    OC, 9, 1009, 1145.
A, 28.    BO, 21, 28.    LA,
13.    OP, 521.    SN, 143

Borgia, Cesare  (Italian duke
and politician, 1476–1507).
OC, 277

Borrow, George  (English
traveler, adventurer and
writer, 1803–1881, author of
*The Bible in Spain*).    TE, 32

Borzage, Frank  (American film
director, 1893–1962).    OC,
223.    BC, 28

Boscán, Juan  (Spanish poet
and translator, 1487?–1542).
IA, 104.    TE, 51, 71

Bosco, don  (Salesian
missionary to the Argentine
Indians).    OCC, 48

Bossuet, Jacques Bénigne
(French theologian, moralist
and orator, 1627–1704, author
of *Discours sur l'histoire
universelle, Elévations a
Dieu sur les mysteres* and
other works).    OCC, 826.
IA, 22, 94.    P, 69

Boswell, James  (Scottish
writer and biographer, 1740–
1795, author of a  *Journal of
a Tour to the Hebrides*, a
*Life of Samuel Johnson* and
extensive diaries and

letters).    OC, 276, 693,
735.    OCC, 828–29.    P, 56

Bousset, Wilhelm  (Biblical
scholar, author of articles
for the  *Encyclopaedia
Britannica* on the Antichrist,
Basilides, Gnosticism, and
Valentinus).    OC, 213, 552

Bouvard  (copy clerk,
character in Flaubert's
*Bouvard et Pécuchet*).    OC,
259–62

Bradamante  (character in
Ariosto).    OCC, 920

Bradbury, Ray  (American writer
of science fiction, b. 1920).
ILN, 60.    P, 25–27

Bradford, Eduard S.  (clothing
designer of Necochea,
character in Bustos Domecq
story).    OCC, 351–53

Bradford, William  (American
historian and governor, 1590–
1657, author of *History of
Plimmoth Plantation*).    ILN,
10

Bradley, Andrew Cecil (English
scholar of Shakespeare, 1851–
1935, author of *Shakes-
pearean Tragedy* and  *Oxford
Lectures*, brother of F. H.
Bradley).    BO, 24.    P, 145

Bradley, Francis Herbert
(English idealist
philosopher, 1846–1924,
author of *Ethical Studies,
Principles of Logic,
Appearance and Reality*, and
*Essay on Truth and Reality*).
OC, 257, 280, 353, 354, 462,
510, 647, 718, 745, '766, 770.
A, 83.    BO, 90, 93.    I, 111.
IA, 5.    SN, 106

Bradley, James  (English
astronomer, 1693–1762; the
references suggest that
Borges actually has in mind
F. H. Bradley).    BO, 90, 93

Bragi  (Scandinavian god of
poetry and eloquence, son of
Odin).    OC, 371

Brahma  (Hindu god).    OC, 251,
394, 740n.    OCC, 733, 734,
735, 741, 743, 751.    ILN,
22.    SN, 89–90

Brahms, Johannes (German composer, 1833–1897). OC, 577, 591. OCC, 277. OP, 488

Bramah, Ernest (British writer of detective fiction, 1869?–1942, creator of Max Carrados). OCC, 18, 105

Brandán, San (St. Brendan, Irish saint and traveller, c.484–c.578, hero of the *Navigatio Sancti Brendani*). OCC, 628, 711, 712, 892

Brandimarte (Bradamante, character in Ariosto's *Orlando Furioso*). OC, 837

Brandán Caraffa, Alfredo. See Caraffa, Alfredo Brandán

Braque, Georges (French painter, 1882–1963). ILN, 40

Brawne, Fanny (Keats's beloved). OC, 1095. OP, 375

Bréhier, Emile (French philosopher, 1876–1952, author of an *Histoire de la philosophie*). OCC, 581

Brémond, Henri (French priest, historian and critic, 1865–1933, author of *Histoire littéraire du sentiment religieux en France, Priere et poésie, La Poésie pure* and other works). OCC, 325

Breno (Brennus, leader of the Gauls who invaded Italy and sacked Rome in 390 B.C.). OC, 1087. A, 56. OP, 371

Breslauer (name of shopkeeper in Borges story). OC, 608

Brewster, Earl Henry (author of *The Life of Gotama the Buddha*, 1926). OCC, 780

Bridges, Robert (English poet, critic and physician, 1844–1930). OC, 718

Briján. OCC, 187

Brissac, Tonio (character in Bustos Domecq stories). OCC, 278–81, 296

Brock, Lynn (author of *The Two of Diamonds*, 1926, and other detective stories). OCC, 17

Brockhaus, Friedrich Arnold (German publisher and editor, 1772–1823, editor of the *Konversations-Lexikon* and of literary periodicals). BO, 23. C, 23. LA, 48. SN, 146

Brod, Max (Austrian-Israeli writer, 1884–1968, friend and editor of Kafka). OCC, 655. BO, 29. P, 103, 104n. SN, 134

Brodeur, Arthur Gilchrist (translator of Snorri Sturluson). OC, 381. OCC, 951

Brodie, David (character in Borges story). OC, 1073–78

Brodir (Viking warrior from the Isle of Man who conspired against king Brian of Ireland). OC, 379

Bromfield, Louis (American novelist, 1896–1956, author of *Early Autumn, Mrs. Parkington* and other works). ILN, 49

Brooke, Rupert (English poet, 1887–1915). OCC, 365. BO, 30. ILN, 46

Brooke, Stopford (English writer and divine, 1832–1916, author of a *History of Early English Literature, English Literature from the Beginnings to the Norman Conquest* and other works). OCC, 877, 884

Brooks, Van Wyck (American biographer and critic, 1886–1963, author of *The Ordeal of Mark Twain, The Flowering of New England* and other works). OC, 685. BO, 65. PB, 121, 122

Brouwer (perhaps Adrian Brouwer, Dutch painter, 1608–1640). OC, 276

Brown, Father (priest and detective, character in Chesterton stories). OC, 694, 696. OCC, 46, 191n., 851. BO, 72, 79. CONJ, 95. PB, 140–42. SN, 74

Brown, Padre (character in Bustos Domecq and Suárez

Lynch stories who stole his identity from Chesterton). OCC, 39-47, 53, 149, 159, 191

Brown, John (American abolitionist leader, 1800-1859). OC, 250. ILN, 48. P, 172

Brown, John (American literary scholar, 1830-1922, author of *The Pilgrim Fathers and Their Puritan Successors*). ILN, 25, 28

Browne, Edward G. (British Orientalist, author of a *Literary History of Persia,* 1902-1906). OC, 382n.

Browne, Thomas (English writer and physician, 1605-1682, author of *Urn Burial, Religio Medici* and other works). OC, 203, 277n, 393, 443, 553, 650, 704, 716, 1103. OCC, 318, 573, 594, 597, 661, 822, 823-24, 833, 891, 948. I, 30-38. OP, 381. P 117, 166. PB, 229. SN, 36, 45

Brownies (creatures in Stevenson's dreams). OCC, 598

Browning, Elizabeth Barrett (English poet, 1806-1861). OCC, 710, 853. NED, 138

Browning, Robert (English poet, 1812-1889, author of *The Ring and the Book* and numerous other poems). OC, 111, 151, 241, 496, 711, 712, 858, 1081. OCC, 15, 710, 835, 841-42, 851, 853, 880. C, 11. I, 73, 107. IA, 61. ILN, 43, 46, 52. NED, 138. OP, 365, 366, 424-25, 469. P, 47-48, 79n., 141, 148, 149, 150, 165. PB, 139, 156. SN, 117. TE, 32, 78, 102, 114, 152

Brujas (the witches in *Macbeth*). See Weird Sisters

Brull, Mariano (Cuban poet, 1891-1956, in the first reference here used as the name of a cigar). OCC, 158. PB, 160

Brunhild (character in the *Nibelungenlied,* sometimes spelled Brynhild). OCC, 912-13, 920, 939, 966, 968-70. LA, 30

Bruno, Giordano (Italian writer and philosopher, 1548-1600, burnt as a heretic, author of *De la Causa, Cena de le Ceneri, De l'Infinito* and other works). OC, 637, 638, 703, 704n. OCC, 579, 817. P, 26

Brunschvicg, Léon (French philosopher, 1869-1944, author of numerous works and editor of Pascal). OC, 638, 703

Bruto (Marcus Junius Brutus, Roman nobleman, c.78-42 B.C., one of the conspirators against Julius Caesar). OC, 793, 853. LA, 181

Brynhild. See Brunhild

Bube. See Fingermann

Buber, Martin (German-Jewish philosopher, 1878-1965, author of numerous philosophical works, of the novel *Gog und Magog,* and collector and translator of the tales of the Hasidim). OC, 522, 696n., 751. OP, 559. P, 85

Buchan, John (English writer, 1875-1940, author of *The Thirty-Nine Steps* and other works). BC, 39

Buchanan, Daisy (character in Fitzgerald's *Great Gatsby*). ILN, 41

Buchanan, Tom (character in Fitzgerald's *Great Gatsby*). ILN, 41

Buchner, Friedrich Karl Christian Ludwig (German physician and philosopher, 1824-1899, author of *Kraft und Stoff* and other works). P, 15

Buckley (translator of Homer). OC, 241

Buckley, Ezra (character in Borges story). OC, 440, 441

Buckley, Silas (alias of Lazarus Morell in Borges story). OC, 300

Buddha or Buda (here used to refer mostly to Gautama

Buddha, c.568–c.488).    OC,
281, 738n., 740–43, 758n.
OCC, 387, 495, 602, 606, 623,
634, 658, 671, 719–81, 936,
977.    A, 38.    BO, 16, 35.
C, 87, 95.    I, 94.    P, 50,
53–54, 80, 153.    PB, 195,
196.    SN, 77–97
Buen Ladrón (the Good Thief
crucified with Jesus, who
repented at the last).    OCC,
35
Buenaventura, San (St.
Bonaventura, Franciscan
theologian, 1221–1274, author
of the *Breviloquium,
Itinerarium Mentis ad Deum,
De Reductione Artium ad
Theologiam* and other works).
OC, 775
Bufano (perhaps a reference to
the Argentine poet Alfredo R.
Bufano, 1895–1950).    OCC,
160
Buffon, Georges-Louis Leclerc
(French naturalist, 1707–
1788, author of an *Histoire
naturelle* in 44 vols.).
OCC, 320
Bugard (minor character in
Bustos Domecq story).    OCC,
367
Buitrago (priest, friend of
Zúñiga).    OCC, 447
Bull, John (symbol of
Englishman and of England).
OC, 791
Bullrich, Silvina (Argentine
novelist, short-story writer,
essayist and journalist, b.
1915).    OC, 863
Bunge, Carlos Octavio
(Argentine novelist,
playwright, critic, lawyer,
businessman and educator,
1875–1918).    OCC, 565
Bunge, Margarita (Argentine
writer, b. 1913, author of
*Fisonomías de la muerte* and
other works).    OC, 156
Bunyan, John (English writer
and preacher, 1628–1688,
author of *Grace Abounding to
the Chief of Sinners, The
Pilgrim's Progress* and other
works).    OC, 236, 671, 696,

735.    BC, 41.    ILN, 44.
LA, 180.    PB, 145, 146
Buonconte da Montefeltro
(Ghibelline leader, d. 1289,
character in Dante's
*Purgatorio*).    OC, 867.
OCC, 902
Burak (beast which sped
Mohammed from Mecca to
Jerusalem to heaven in a
single night).    OCC, 599
Buratti (owner of a granary).
OCC, 139
Burckhardt, George Edward
(German scholar, author of
*Gilgamesch, Eine Erzahlung
aus dem alten Orient,* 1920).
OCC, 652
Burger, Gottfried August
(German poet and novelist,
1747–1794, author of
*Munchhausen* and other works).
OP, 542–43
Burgos, Juliana (character in
Borges story).    OC, 1025–28
Burnet, John (classical
scholar, 1863–1928, editor of
Heraclitus).    OP, 502
Burnouf, Eugene (French
Orientalist scholar, 1801–
1852).    OC, 743n.    OCC, 752
Burns, Kit (a gangster in New
York who bit off the heads of
rats).    OC, 311
Burns, Robert (Scottish poet,
1759–1796).    OC, 773.    IA,
108.    LA, 173
Burns, Walter Noble (author of
*The Saga of Billy the Kid,*
1925).    OC, 345
Burton, Isabel Arundell, Lady
(Richard Burton's wife and
biographer).    OC, 401, 403
Burton, Richard (British
traveler, diplomat, writer
and translator, 1821–1890,
author of *The Pilgrimage to
Al-Medinah and Meccah, Goa
and the Blue Mountains, The
Highlands of the Brazil,
Letters from the Battle-
Fields of Paraguay, Ultima
Thule, The Book of the Sword*
and countless other works, as
well as translations of
Camoes and of the *Arabian*

*Nights*). OC, 152n., 341, 343, 397–406, 407, 408, 418n., 588, 627, 736. OCC, 569, 599, 600, 695, 837, 968. P, 8. PB, 241. SN, 64, 65, 66, 67, 71, 72, 73. TE, 32

Burton, Robert (English scholar and writer, 1577–1640, author of *The Anatomy of Melancholy*). OC, 278n., 389. OCC, 312, 569, 656, 977. I, 125. OP, 558

Bustos, Francisco (Borges's great-great-grandfather, whose name he used as a pseudonym in the original publication of "Hombre de la esquina rosada"). OC, 291

Bustos, Juan Bautista (Argentine caudillo, 1779–1830). OC, 1001. P, 64, 138

Bustos Domecq, Honorio (Argentine writer, b. 1893, author of *Seis problemas para don Isidro Parodi*, *Dos fantasías memorables*, *Nuevos cuentos de Bustos Domecq*, perhaps only comparable at his worst to his disciple B. Suárez Lynch). OCC, 13, 15–19, 69, 112n., 145–47, 299n., 300n., 311, 316, 336, 341–42, 348n., 360–62, 365–68, 375, 379, 391n., 421, 426, 433–37, 447, 450n., 451n., 977

Butcher, S. H. (British classical scholar who, with Andrew Lang, made prose translations of Homer). OC, 241

Buti, Francesco da (14th century commentator on Dante). NED, 93, 136, 148, 152n.

Butler, Samuel (English poet, 1612–80, author of *Hudibras*). OC, 401. OCC, 602

Butler, Samuel (English writer, 1835–1902, author of *Erewhon*, *The Fair Haven* and other works). OC, 197, 203, 240, 242, 243, 281, 429, 748. OCC, 67, 355, 848. A, 27. I, 46. P, 15. PB, 164, 229

Byron, George Gordon, Lord (English poet, 1788–1824, author of *Beppo*, *Don Juan*, *Childe Harold's Pilgrimage* and other works). OC, 250, 256, 266, 402. OCC, 48, 474, 830–31, 835, 837. A, 23. ILN, 55. NED, 136, 154. OP, 424. P, 79n., 82, 142, 172. SN, 61

Cabal, Oswald (character in Wells). BC, 43, 44

Caballero Blanco. See White Knight

Caballo Celestial (Chinese monster which looks like a black-headed flying dog). OCC, 630

Caballo del Mar (horse which lives in the sea, mentioned in the *Arabian Nights* and other sources). OCC, 600–1

Cabezas, A. (Buenos Aires tailor mentioned in Bustos Domecq story). OCC, 409

Cabral, Pedro Alvares (Portuguese navigator, c.1460–c.1518, who discovered Brazil in 1500). PB, 244

Cabrera family (ancestors of Borges, a family of early Spanish settlers in South America). OC, 863. OP, 483

Cabrera, Alonso de (priest who accompanied Mendoza at the time of the first foundation of Buenos Aires). PB, 125, 175

Cacciaguida (character in Dante's *Paradiso*). NED, 116

Cáceres, Fabio (narrator and character in Guiraldes's *Don Segundo Sombra*). BO, 72. PB, 188. SN, 19

Cachafaz (here a cat, but also the nickname of a tango musician). OCC, 378

Cachaza, Lungo (character in Bustos Domecq story). OCC, 125

Caedmon (early English poet, fl. 670). OC, 643. OCC, 881–82, 903. OP, 419. P, 108

Cagliostro, Alessandro (pseud. of Giuseppe Balsamo, Italian alchemist, adventurer, physician and impostor, 1743–1795).    OC, 716

Cagnazzo.    See Tonelada

Cain (brother and slayer of Abel in the Bible).    OC, 154, 763, 794, 853, 898, 934, 948, 956, 1014, 1027, 1092, 1113.    OCC, 533n., 658, 659, 801, 871, 874, 904. BC, 57.    BO, 36.    CONJ, 17, 23, 95.    NED, 93.    OP, 387, 436.    SN, 139

Cain, James (American novelist and journalist, b. 1892). P, 82

Calandria, ño.    See Cardoso, Servando

Calas (victim of the Argentine judicial system defended by Gerchunoff).    P, 67

Calderón de la Barca, Pedro (Spanish playwright, 1600–1681, author of *La vida es sueño* and countless other plays).    OC, 688, 755. OCC, 330, 463, 842, 911. BO, 20.    I, 74, 128.    SN, 39

Caldwell, Erskine (American writer, b. 1903, author of *Tobacco Road*, *God's Little Acre* and other works). ILN, 50.    P, 82

Calfucurá, Juan (Argentine Indian leader, d. 1873). OCC, 153

Caliban (character in Shakespeare's *Tempest*). OCC, 821, 841.    OP, 425. P, 149.    TE, 32

Calígula (nickname of Caius Caesar Germanicus, Roman emperor, 12–41).    OC, 1114. OCC, 686.    OP, 390

Calipso (nymph, daughter of Atlas, who figures as a character in the *Odyssey*). OC, 250.    OCC, 501

Calogero, Guido (Italian philosopher, b. 1904, author of *Estetica, semantica, istorica* and many other works).    OC, 636

Calou, Juan Pedro (Argentine poet, d. 1923, author of *Humanamente*, 1918).    PB, 164

Calpurnia (Roman noblewoman, wife of Julius Caesar).    OC, 497

Calvino (Jean Calvinus or Cauvin, Swiss religious leader, 1509–1564, author of *Institution de la réligion chrétienne* and many other works).    OC, 362.    OCC, 825.    A, 38, 56.    BC, 47. ILN, 9, 10, 11, 17, 20. LA, 70.    NED, 123.    P, 33, 35, 69, 86.    PB, 121.    SN, 78

Camaña, Raquel (Argentine writer, 1883–1915, author of *Pedagogía social* and *El diletantismo sentimental*). OCC, 137

Camargo (minor character in Bustos Domecq story).    OCC, 361

Camba, Julio (Spanish humorist, 1882–1962, author of *La rana viajera* and other works).    OCC, 428

Cambaceres de Alvear, Mariana. OC, 620

Cambours Ocampo, Arturo (Argentine poet and dramatist, b. 1908, author of *El problema de las generaciones literarias*). OCC, 497

Camerarius, Gaspar (editor of the apocryphal *Deliciae Poetarum Borussiae*, perhaps based on Joachim Camerarius, German classical scholar, 1500–1574).    OC, 852

Camila (character in *El curioso impertinente*, the exemplary novel Cervantes included in the first part of *Don Quijote*).    OC, 218

Camino, Miguel Andrés (Argentine poet, 1877–1944, author of *Chacayaleras, Chaquiras, El paisaje, el hombre y su canción* and other works, mostly remembered for the poem "El tango" in *Chaquiras*).    IA, 115–16, 119

Camoes, Luis de (Portuguese poet and adventurer, 1524–1580, author of the epic poem *Os Lusíadas* as well as sonnets and other lyrics). OC, 249. P, 8, 112. PB, 225, 234–45

Campana (nickname of a thug in Buenos Aires). OC, 1046

Campanella, Tommaso (Italian philosopher, 1568–1639, author of the *Civitas Solis, De sensu rerum, De Monarchia Hispanica* and other works). OC, 638

Campbell, Pedro (Argentine caudillo). OC, 1001

Campbell, Roy (South African poet, 1902–1957, translator of Camoes, Juan de la Cruz and Calderón). PB, 241

Campillo y Rodríguez, José (Spanish professor of literature and philosophy, author of *Lecciones de calotecnia para un curso de principios generales de literatura y literatura española,* 1879). I, 116n.–117n.

Campo, Estanislao de (Argentine poet, 1834–1880, author of *Fausto* and other poems). OC, 141, 154n., 181, 186–88, 232, 267, 268, 656. OCC, 18, 513, 516, 520–21, 527, 531, 543, 548, 558. A, 58. C, 37. I, 55, 56, 63–64, 134. OP, 471. P, 18, 28–31, 65, 91–93, 97, 98. PB, 123. TE, 6, 13, 16, 17, 57, 71

Campos, Rubén (Mexican writer, 1876–1945, author of *El folklore y la música mexicana*). OC, 150

Can Grande della Scala (Italian nobleman, Ghibelline leader of Verona and protector of Dante). OCC, 199. BC, 77. NED, 92. P, 157. SN, 10

Canal Feijóo, Bernardo (Argentine poet and essayist, b. 1897, author of *Ensayo sobre la expresión popular artística en Santiago del Estero, Proposiciones en torno al problema de una cultura nacional argentina* and other works, here ridiculed as Padre Feijoo ¿Canal?, author of *Tratado del epíteto en la Cuenca del Plata*). OCC, 336–37

Canby, Henry Seidel (American critic, teacher and editor, 1878–1961). OC, 250n.

Cancela, Arturo (Argentine dramatist, novelist and short-story writer, 1892–1957). OC, 410

Cáncer (a crab that bit Herakles's ankle during his battle with the Hydra, now a zodiac sign). OCC, 645

Cancerbero (Cerberus, monstrous dog that guards the underworld in classical mythology). OCC, 602

Candelaria (character in Hudson's *Purple Land*). TE, 35

Candelas, Luis. OCC, 965n.

Candide (character in Voltaire's *Candide*). OC, 259

Cané, Miguel (Argentine writer and journalist, 1851–1905, author of *Juvenilia* and other works). OCC, 558. IA, 170

Cangrande della Scala. See Can Grande della Scala

Cangrejo, don (nickname used by Bustos Domecq). OCC, 146

Cano Maestro. See Frogman

Cansinos Assens, Rafael (Spanish poet, novelist, translator and critic, 1883–1964). OC, 401, 641, 652, 915. CONJ, 81. I, 15–17, 46–50, 75, 77. IA, 157. OP, 470. P, 53, 79n., 107. SN, 65, 72, 73, 117. TE, 21, 95–99

Canto, Estela (Argentine novelist, journalist and translator, b. 1919, author of *El muro de mármol, El retrato de la imagen* and other works). OC, 628

Cantor, Georg (German
  mathematician, 1845–1918,
  known for his work on set
  theory and transfinite
  numbers). OC, 258, 385,
  387. OCC, 775. BO, 35
Cantu, Cesare (Italian
  historian and politician,
  1804–1895, author of a
  universal history). OCC,
  25, 413
Cao (caricaturist who worked
  for *Caras y Caretas*, here
  illustrator of Loomis's
  *Catre*). OCC, 320
Capdevila, Arturo (Argentine
  poet and essayist, 1889–1967,
  author of *Melpómene*, *La
  fiesta del mundo* and other
  works). OC, 410. IA, 163.
  PB, 164, 166
Capella, Marciano (Latin
  encyclopedist, 5th century
  A.D., author of *De Nuptiis*)
  OC, 627. OCC, 972
Capelle, Wilhelm (author of
  *Die griechische Philosophie*,
  1922, *Das alten Germanien*,
  1937, and other works). OC,
  155, 254
Capitano, César (character in
  Bustos Domecq story). OCC,
  375–79
Capo. See Caponsacchi
Capone, Al (American gangster,
  born in Italy, 1899–1947).
  OC, 297, 313
Caponsacchi (character in
  Bustos Domecq story). OCC,
  376, 378, 379
Capote, Truman (American
  novelist, 1924–1985). ILN,
  51–52
Caraballo, Gustavo (Argentine
  dramatist, friend of
  Carriego). OC, 117
Caraffa, Alfredo Brandán
  (Argentine lawyer and poet,
  b. 1898, one of the editors
  of *Proa*). TE, 85–87
Carbajal (family of early
  Spanish settlers in
  Argentina). OP, 483
Carbajal, Simón (hunter and
  gaucho in Antelo). OP, 439–
  40

Carbone. OCC, 226
Carbone, Rodolfo (priest,
  character in Bustos Domecq
  stories). OCC, 88, 127,
  420, 440
Cárcano, Miguel Angel
  (Argentine lawyer and writer,
  1860–1946). P, 138
Cárdenas, Julio (character in
  Bustos Domecq story). OCC,
  405, 406, 408–17, 419, 420
Cardoso (landowner in
  Tacuarembó, character in
  Borges story). OC, 491
Cardoso, Manuel (character in
  Borges story). OC, 1058–61
Cardoso, Servando (gaucho
  outlaw and knife-fighter,
  nicknamed Calandria). OC,
  971. P, 113
Carducci, Giuseppe (Italian
  poet and critic, 1835–1907).
  SN, 104–5
Carlo (Emily Dickinson's dog).
  ILN, 32
Carlomagno (Charlemagne,
  Frankish emperor, 742–814).
  OCC, 827, 903, 921, 936.
  OP, 431, 466. SN, 60
Carlos. See Anglada, Carlos
Carlos I (Charles I, English
  king, 1600–1649). OC, 944,
  1069. OCC, 824, 825.
  CONJ, 21. ILN, 10. OP,
  553. SN, 154, 155
Carlos II (English king, 1630–
  1685). OCC, 824. SN, 155
Carlos Luis (Palatine prince).
  OC, 706
Carlos V (king of Spain and of
  Germany, 1500–1558). OC,
  295
Carlos XII de Suecia (Swedish
  king, 1682–1718). OC, 562,
  908, 1087. BO, 45, 47, 59.
  OP, 371. P, 153, 154
Carlos el Calvo (Charles II of
  France, 823–877). OC, 363
Carlyle, Thomas (British
  essayist and historian, 1795–
  1881, author of *Sartor
  Resartus*, *The French
  Revolution*, *On Heroes* and
  many other works). OC,
  216n., 641, 668, 669, 689,
  716, 725, 726, 729, 756n.,

Cazamian, Louis (French
literary historian and
English scholar, 1877-1965,
co-author with Emile Legouis
of a history of English
literature). OCC, 857
Ceard, Henry (French
naturalist novelist, 1851-
1924). OC, 260
Cebolla Tibetana. See Frogman
Cejador y Frauca, Julio
(Spanish critic and
historian, 1864-1927, author
of *Fraseología y estilística
castellana, Tesoro de la
lengua castellana, Historia
de la lengua y literatura
castellana* and other works).
OCC, 75, 319, 326
Celestino V (pope and saint,
d. 1296). NED, 121
Céline, Louis Ferdinand
(French physician and
novelist, 1894-1961, author
of *Voyage au bout de la
nuit*). OC, 450. ILN, 44
Cellini, Benvenuto (Italian
artist and writer, 1500-1571,
author of famous autobio-
graphy). OCC, 690
Cendrars, Blaise (French-Swiss
novelist and poet, 1887-
1961). ILN, 44
Centauro (in Greek mythology,
a race of creatures, half-
horse, half-man). OC, 226-
229. OCC, 604-5. OP, 524
Cepeda y Ahumada, Teresa.
See Teresa de Jesús, Santa
Cerbero. See Cancerbero
Cerf, Bennett (American writer
and publisher). OC, 403
Cerintho. OC, 213
Cervantes, Miguel de (Spanish
writer, 1547-1616, author of
*Don Quijote*, the *Entremeses*,
the *Novelas ejemplares*,
*Persiles y Segismunda*, the
*Galatea* and other works).
OC, 115, 202, 203, 218, 219,
233, 239, 277, 409, 446-50,
461, 660, 667, 668, 713, 733,
794, 799, 890, 892, 1092,
1096, 1143. OCC, 129n.,
145, 156, 551, 820, 841, 851,
880, 942. BO, 20, 67.

C, 15. I, 44, 74, 128.
IA, 11-13, 68, 73, 107, 139-
46, 174, 182. NED, 121n.
OP, 436-37, 441, 460, 528.
P, 8, 23, 32, 43-46, 53, 54,
67, 70n., 90, 93, 111, 112,
119, 137, 147, 155, 164.
PB, 147, 148, 149, 175-77,
203-12, 230, 231, 235, 240.
SN, 12, 51, 60. TE, 33,
43, 108-14, 136, 139, 140,
152
César (title used in a general
sense). OC, 634, 683.
OCC, 84, 285. IA, 18.
LA, 60. NED, 99, 102. P,
71. PB, 183, 184, 235
César (Greek king in the
*Widsith*). OCC, 876
César, Julio (Gaius Julius
Caesar, Roman emperor, 100-
44, author of *De Bello
Gallico* and *De Bello Civili*).
OC, 156, 167n., 249, 402n.,
486, 496, 497, 533, 555,
1097. OCC, 741, 848. A,
9, 13, 56. C, 41, 44, 53,
69. CONJ, 19, 21. OP,
442, 552. P, 63. PB,
219, 224. SN, 88, 111, 150
Cesarotti, Melchiore (Italian
poet and critic, 1730-1808,
translator of Ossian and
Homer). OCC, 830
Chacho, el. See Peñaloza
Chamberlain, Neville (British
statesman, 1869-1940, known
for his monocle). OCC, 78
Chang Seng-Yu (6th century
Chinese painter). OCC, 620
Chano, Jacinto (overseer of a
ranch in Tordillo, character
in Hidalgo). OC, 180, 188.
OCC, 517, 522
Chano, Jacinto (pseud. of
Ascasubi). OCC, 520
Chanut, Pierre (French
ambassador, correspondent of
Descartes). OC, 544
Chaplin, Charles (English
film actor, director,
producer and writer, 1889-
1977). OC, 222, 223, 224.
BC, 28-29, 33, 48, 55. ILN,
52. PB, 176

Chaplin, Oona O'Neill
(daughter of Eugene O'Neill,
wife of Charlie Chaplin).
ILN, 52
Chapman, George (English
playwright, scholar and
translator, 1559?-1634, best
known for his translations of
Homer).    OC, 239, 240, 242,
243, 377, 729, 732.    OCC,
833.    OP, 459.    P, 163, 174
Chartier, Emile-Auguste.    See
Alain
Chateaubriand, Francois-René
(French writer, 1768-1848,
author of *Atala* and *Le Génie
du Christianisme*).    OC, 652
Chatterton, Thomas (English
poet and forger, 1752-1770).
OC, 921.    P, 144
Chaucer, Geoffrey (English
poet, c.1340-1400, author of
the *Canterbury Tales* and
other works).    OC, 274, 406,
411, 719, 746, 976.    OCC,
593, 814-16, 851, 896.
NED, 105, 139.    OP, 538,
559.    P, 8, 147.    PB, 177
Chelsum (rival of Gibbon).
P, 72
Chengo, el (knife-fighter,
rival of Ezequiel Tabares).
OP, 536
Chesterton, Gilbert Keith
(English short-story writer,
essayist, novelist, poet and
journalist, 1874-1936, author
of five volumes of Father
Brown stories, *The Man Who
Was Thursday*, *The Man Who
Knew Too Much*, biographies of
Blake, Dickens, Stevenson,
Watts and countless other
works).    OC, 231, 261, 262,
289, 414, 483, 496, 629, 662,
672, 689, 692, 693, 694-96,
709, 745.    OCC, 172, 175,
189, 191n., 500, 597, 816,
832, 835, 845, 851, 857, 948.
A, 48.    BC, 65.    BO, 68,
78-79.    ILN, 20, 56.    LA,
180.    NED, 95, 141, 158.
P, 23, 35, 45, 47, 48, 59,
83, 116, 122, 129, 166.
PB, 138-42, 178, 181.    SN,
73-74.    VA, 27

Ch'i (Chinese prince).    OCC,
678
Chiang-liang (Chinese monster).
OCC, 629
Chica de Rafaela, Maffia
(character in Bustos Domecq
story).    OCC, 125
Chichón, Condesa de (subject
of a story by Ricardo
Sangiácomo).    OCC, 65
Chiclana, Alberto (character
in Borges-Levinson story).
HE, 59, 69
Chiclana, Jacinto (knife-
fighter in Buenos Aires).
OC, 959-60
Chiclana, Raúl (character in
Borges-Levinson story).
HE, 59, 63
Chileno, el (knife-fighter,
character in early Borges
story).    IA, 152-54
Ching (Chinese admiral).
OC, 306, 307
Ching (widow and pirate in
Borges story).    OC, 306-10
Chio-tuan (Chinese unicorn).
OCC, 705
Chippendale, Thomas (English
cabinetmaker, d. 1779).
OCC, 193
Chirico, Giorgio di (Italian
painter, 1888-1978).    OC,
222.    BC, 28
Chirino, Andrés (character in
Borges story).    LA, 96
Chlodwing.    See Clovia
Cho Chod, Louis (translator to
French of a prayer from
Annam).    OCC, 701
Chocano, José Santos (Peruvian
poet, 1875-1934).    OC, 422
Chopin, Frédéric (Polish
composer, 1810-1849).    OCC,
208, 223, 236
Ch'ou-t'i (two-headed monster
in China).    OCC, 629
Chrétien de Troyes (French
poet, fl. late 12th century,
author of *Yvain*, *Lancelot*,
*Perceval* and other works).
OCC, 908n.
Christie, Agatha (British
detective writer, 1891-1976).
OC, 461

Chrysólogo (mentioned by
Gracián). OC, 370

Chu (Chinese prince in the
*Analects* of Confucius).
OCC, 632

Chuang Tzu (Chinese Taoist
writer, c.369–c.286). OC,
255n., 256n., 633, 768, 769.
OCC, 610, 766. C, 87. OP,
506, 552, 559. P, 54

Chumbiao, el (gaucho soldier
in the forces of López
Jordán). OC, 152

Ch'ung-Hsin (master in Zen
fable). OCC, 774

Church, Richard William
(English religious figure and
writer, 1815–1890). OC, 418

Chuzzlewit, Jonas (character
in Dickens novel). OCC 835

Cibeles (great mother-goddess
of Anatolia). OC, 234

Cicerón (Marcus Tullius Cicero,
Roman orator and politician,
106–43, author of *De
divinatione, De natura
deorum, De fato, In Pisonem*
and many other works). OC,
282, 283, 393, 394, 551, 661,
704n. OCC, 304, 305, 308,
690, 956. P, 120

Cíclopes (the Cyclops, one-
eyed monsters of classical
myth). OCC, 666–67

Cid, el (Ruy Díaz de Vivar,
Spanish hero, 1040–1099).
ILN, 25. P, 171

Cide Hamete Benengeli (Arabic
historian, character in
Cervantes). OC, 794. P,
32

Cien Cabezas (Chinese monster,
a fish with a hundred heads,
born of invective). OCC,
606

Ciervo Celestial (Chinese
monsters of the darkness).
OCC, 607

Cipriano de Valera. See
Valera, Cipriano de

Circe (sorceress in Greek
myth). OC, 228n. OCC,
626, 662, 696. ILN, 45.
NED, 113

Cirilo de Jerusalén (Cyril of
Jerusalem, bishop and orator,

c.315–386, author of twenty-
four catechetical lectures).
OCC, 588

Ciro (Cyrus, Persian king,
ruled 559–529). OC, 488

Clack, Miss (character in
Collins's *The Moonstone*).
P, 48

Clair, René (French film
director, 1898–1981). OC,
420

Clara (character in Borges
story, Avelino Arredondo's
fiancée). LA, 152, 155,
157, 159

Claro, Epifanio (character in
Hudson's *Purple Land*). TE,
35

Claudel, Paul (French poet,
dramatist and diplomat, 1868–
1955). OCC, 461. NED, 89.
P, 166. PB, 128. SN, 9

Claudiano (Claudius Claudianus,
Alexandrian-Greek writer, d.
404, author of Latin panegy-
rics, invectives, epistyles,
epigrams and an unfinished
epic). OCC, 588, 650

Claudio (Tiberius Claudius,
Roman emperor, 10–54).
OP, 453

Clausewitz, Karl von (Prussian
general and writer, 1780–
1831, author of *Vom Kriege*
and other works). OC, 494

Clavdia Fiodorovna (Russian
princess turned madam,
character in Bustos Domecq
and Suárez Lynch stories,
later married to Gervasio
Montenegro). OCC, 41–42,
44, 46, 48, 52, 79, 108, 149,
161–64

Clemencia. See Juárez,
Clemencia

Clemens, Samuel Langhorne.
See Twain, Mark

Clemente, José Edmundo
(Argentine librarian, b.
1918, director of the
Biblioteca Nacional in Buenos
Aires and author of the
*Estética del lector* and other
works). OC, 351

Clemente de Alejandría
(Clement of Alexandria or

Titus Flavius Clemens,
Christian theologian and
writer, c.150–c.200, author
of the *Protrepticus, Stromata*
and other works). OC, 636,
713, 714. NED, 114. P, 66

Clementina. See Traversi,
Clementina

Clementine (housekeeper in
Bustos Domecq story). OCC,
381, 386

Clemm, Virginia (Poe's cousin
and wife, 1822–1846). ILN,
18

Clerice, Carlos (illustrator
of the 1894 edition of the
*Martín Fierro*). OCC, 565

Clive, Robert (British
statesman and general, 1725–
1774, founder of the empire
of British India). OC, 200.
OCC, 836. OP, 463

Cloots, Jean-Baptiste du Val
de Grace or Anacharsis
(French revolutionary
politician of Prussian
origin, 1755–1794, author of
*Adresse d'un Prussien a un
Anglais, L'Orateur du genre
humain* and *La République
universelle*). LA, 43, 49–50

Clotilda de Borgoña (princess
of Burgundy and Frankish
queen, wife of Clovis,
married in 493). PB, 199

Clough, Arthur Hugh (English
poet, 1819–1861, author of
*The Bothie of Tober-na-
Vuolich, Dipsychus, Amours
de Voyage* and *Mari Magno*).
P, 148

Clovis or Clovia (Frankish
king, c.466–511). OC, 217.
PB, 199

Cocteau, Jean (French poet,
novelist and dramatist, 1889–
1963, author of *La Machine
infernale, Les Parents
terribles* and numerous other
works). I, 18. TE, 132

Codicia (personification of
envy). NED, 128

Codovilla (district attorney
in Necochea, character in
Bustos Domecq story). OCC,
352

Coifi (Northumbrian pagan
priest mentioned in Bede's
history). OCC, 888

Coleridge, Samuel Taylor
(English poet and
philosopher, 1772–1834,
author of *The Rime of the
Ancient Mariner, Dejection,
Christabel,* the *Biographia
Literaria* and numerous other
works). OC, 226, 256, 397,
401, 639, 640, 642–45, 718,
719, 738, 745, 805. OCC,
561, 819–20, 831, 832, 869,
882. A, 37, 46. BO, 24.
C, 89. ILN, 20, 21. LA,
19. OP, 419. P, 72, 84,
95, 108, 145, 146. PB, 205,
230. SN, 17, 45, 47, 61,
71, 153. TE, 48

Coliqueo (Argentine Indian
chief, 19th century). OCC,
153. P, 113

Colleville (French scholar,
co-editor with Tonnelat of an
edition of the *Nibelungenlied*
in 1944). OCC, 915, 967n.

Collins, Wilkie (English novel-
ist, 1824–1889, author of *The
Moonstone* and *The Woman in
White*). OC, 414. OCC, 835.
BO, 78, 80. P, 47–48

Colombina (stock role in the
*commedia dell' arte*, maid of
the Inamorata and beloved of
the Harlequin). OCC, 17

Colombres (Argentine neo-
idealist artist, character in
Bustos Domecq story). OCC,
317–18

Colón, Cristóbal (Cristoforo
Colombo, Italian explorer,
c.1446–1506). OCC, 317,
326, 357, 367. BO, 59.
IA, 112. ILN, 16

Coluccio, Félix (Argentine
writer, author of the
*Diccionario folklórico
argentino*, 1948, and other
works on folklore and
language). OCC, 612

Columela, Lucio (Lucius Junius
Moderatus Columella, Latin
writer on agriculture, author
of *De Re Rustica*, written
c.60–66). OCC, 661

Colvin, Sidney (English critic and writer, 1845–1927). OC, 717

Compson (family, characters in Faulkner). ILN, 36

Conde, José Antonio (Spanish historian, 1765–1820, author of *Historia de la dominación de los árabes en España*). OC, 231

Condé, Le Grand (Louis II, prince of Condé, 1621–1686). PB, 159

Condillac, Etienne Bonnot de (French philosopher, 1715–1780, author of *Essai sur l'origine des conaissances humaines*, *Traité des systemes*, *Traité des sensations* and other works). OC, 758, 769. OCC, 581, 699

Condorcet, Antoine-Nicolas de (French mathematician and philosopher, 1743–1794, author of *Tableau historique des progres de l'esprit humain*). OC, 394, 497

Confucio (Confucius or Kung Fu-tzu, Chinese philosopher and politician, 551–479, author of the *Annals of Lu*, *Spring and Autumn*, and the *Analects*). OC, 589, 633, 680, 772. OCC, 263, 617, 619, 632, 678, 705, 728, 766. ILN, 42. P, 84

Coni, Emilio A. (Argentine publisher). OC, 233, 421. OCC, 514

Conn (Irish king, d. 157 A.D.). PB, 222

Connelly, Marc (American playwright, 1890–1980, author of *The Green Pastures*). BC, 57–58

Conrad, Joseph (Polish-English novelist, born Teodor Josef Konrad Korzeniowski, 1857–1924, author of *Victory*, *Chance*, *Lord Jim*, *Heart of Darkness*, *Youth*, *The Shadow-Line*, *The Nigger of the "Narcissus," The Secret Agent* and numerous other works). OC, 55, 64, 182, 572, 667, 675, 681, 1062, 1143. OCC, 839, 842, 848–49. A, 38, 62. BC, 48, 51, 52, 64. C, 77. CONJ, 95. ILN, 26. LA, 15. P, 117. PB, 230

Conrado de Regensburg (Konrad, German priest and writer, translator of the *Chanson de Roland*). OCC, 908

Conselheiro, Antonio (Antonio Vicente Mendes Maciel, Brazilian messianic leader, d. 1897). OC, 516n. P, 15

Constantino (Constantine the Great, Flavius Valerius Constantinus, Roman emperor, 288?–337). NED, 143. P, 68. PB, 179

Consuelo (maid of the Muñagorris, character in Bustos Domecq story). OCC, 57

Contreras, Ramón (gaucho, character in Hidalgo's poems). OC, 180, 188. OCC, 517, 522

Contursi, Pascual (Argentine tango composer and dramatist, 1888–1932, author of "Mi noche triste," "Bandaneón arrabalero" and many other works). OC, 127, 653

Conze, Edward (author of *Buddhism, Its Essence and Development* and *The Buddha's Law among the Birds*). OCC, 729, 780

Coolidge, Calvin (American president, 1872–1933). ILN, 64

Cooper, James Fenimore (American novelist, 1789–1851, author of *The Prairie*, *The Last of the Mohicans*, *The Spy* and other works). OC, 670. ILN, 14–15. P, 134

Copernico (Nicolaus Copernicus, Polish astronomer, 1473–1543, author of *De revolutionibus orbium coelestium*). OC, 637, 703. OCC, 817. A, 7

Corbiere, Tristan or Edouard-Joachim (French poet, 1845–1874, author of *Gens de mer*). ILN, 43

Corday, Charlotte (French woman, 1768-1793, murderer of Marat). LA, 181

Cordone (Alberto Cardone, Argentine writer of detective fiction under the pseudonym Jacinto Amenábar, author of *El crimen de la noche de bodas*). OCC, 23

Cordovero, Nahum (author of *The Coat of Many Colours*). OC, 544

Corelli, Marie (pseud. of Mary Mackay, English novelist, 1864-1924). P, 82

Coriolano (Gnaeus Marcius Coriolanus, legendary Roman general, d. c.490 B.C., subject of a play by Shakespeare). P, 144

Corneille, Pierre (French playwright, 1606-1684, author of *Le Cid, L'Illusion comique* and other works). OCC, 330

Cornejo (Spanish playwright, author of *A buen toro mejor buey*). OCC, 451

Cornelio Agripa. See Agrippa von Nettesheim

Corralero, el. See Real, Francisco

Correas, Edmundo (Argentine historian, b. 1901). OCC, 67, 345

Cortejón, Clemente (Spanish priest and writer, author of *Duelos y quebrantos, Diccionario de todas las palabras usadas en el "Quijote"* and *La iglesia católica es la protectora y mejor amiga de la agricultura*). PB, 230

Cortés, Hernán (Spanish conqueror of Mexico, 1485-1547). OCC, 331, 344, 604, 959-60. PB, 191

Cosmas (Cosmas Indicopleustes, Alexandrian merchant, fl. 6th century A.D., author of *Topographia Christiana*). OC, 552

Costa Alvarez, Arturo (Argentine linguist, author of *Nuestra lengua* and *El castellano en la Argentina*).

OC, 654n. OCC, 514. IA, 170, 179. TE, 44

Cotone (character in Bustos Domecq story). OCC, 164, 165

Cottone, Giuseppe (Italian writer, editor of Mussolini's writings on fascism and author of studies of the *commedia dell' arte*, Dante and other subjects). OCC, 328

Coty (French perfume manufacturer). OCC, 158

Couto, Diego de (Portuguese historian, 1542-1616, author of *Décadas* about the annexation of Portugal by Spain). OC, 741

Covarrubias, Sebastián (Spanish lexicographer, 1539-1613, author of *Tesoro de la lengua castellana o española*). OCC, 545n. I, 33

Cowley, Abraham (English poet and dramatist, 1618-1667, author of *Love's Riddle, The Guardian, Pindarique Odes, The Mistress* and other works). OC, 461. P, 154

Cowley, Malcolm (American critic, editor and poet, b. 1898). OC, 678

Cowper, William (English poet, 1731-1800, author of *The Task*). OC, 241, 243

Cox, William T. (author of *Fearsome Creatures of the Lumberwoods*, 1910). OCC, 698

Craigie, Alexander (character in Borges story). VA, 27-42

Craigie, W. A. (British scholar, assistant to the editor of the *New English Dictionary* and editor of some of the sagas). OCC, 933

Crane, Stephen (American novelist and poet, 1870-1900, author of *The Red Badge of Courage, The Open Boat* and other works). ILN, 33-34

Crawford, Joan (American film star, 1906-1977). OC, 230

Creador. See Dios

Crenshaw (accomplice of
Lazarus Morell in Borges
story). OC, 297
Criseida (Chryseyde or
Cressida, daughter of
Calchas, whose tragic love
for the Trojan prince Troilus
is the subject of a poem by
Chaucer and a play by
Shakespeare). OCC, 815
Crisipo (Chrysippus, Greek
Stoic philosopher, c.280–
207). OC, 394
Crisóstomo (character in
pastoral segment of the first
part of *Don Quijote*). IA,
142
Cristiana (character in
Stevenson's *Weir of
Hermiston*). OC, 384
Cristilo (character in
Gracián's *Criticón*). TE,
146
Cristina de Suecia (Christina,
queen of Sweden, 1626–1689).
OC, 284n. BC, 73n.
Cristo. See Jesucristo
Croce, Benedetto (Italian
philosopher and critic, 1866–
1952, author of *La estetica
come scienza dell' espressione
e linguistica generale, La
poesia, Storia dell' eta
Barocca in Italia* and other
works). OC, 217, 382, 557,
558, 635, 672, 673, 744.
OCC, 911, 957. BO, 66.
IA, 15, 16, 17, 70, 83.
NED, 100, 106–7, 120, 121.
PB, 183. SN, 13, 102, 106
Croce, Giovanni (character in
Bustos Domecq story, also
known as Juan Cruz). OCC,
65, 66, 68, 76, 77, 78, 80,
83, 84
Crocota (wolf-dog of India,
described by Pliny). OCC,
608
Cromwell, Oliver (English
Puritan leader and statesman,
1599-1658). OC, 680, 726,
822. OCC, 824, 834. LA,
25. P, 36. PB, 132. SN,
155
Cronos (Kronos, Greek god,
father of Zeus and other

Olympian gods). OC, 355.
OCC, 609
Cronyn, George (editor of an
anthology of American Indian
poetry). ILN, 61
Cross, Cipriano (Jesuit,
character in Bustos Domecq).
OCC, 315
Crusoe, Robinson (character in
Defoe romance, based on
Alexander Selkirk). OC,
356n., 416. NED, 110.
PB, 123
Cruz (gaucho and soldier,
character in the *Martín
Fierro*, in Borges story given
the first names Tadeo
Isidoro). OC, 131–32, 154,
196, 561–63. OCC, 538–40,
552, 561. P, 94, 99. PB,
231. SN, 19. TE, 144
Cruz, doctor (character in
Borges story). LA, 52, 55
Cruz, Irene (character in
Borges–Bioy filmscript).
OCC, 199, 254–55, 259–61,
272–73, 275–84, 288, 291–92,
295–96. BC, 77
Cruz, Isidora (mother of Tadeo
Isidoro Cruz in Borges
story). OC, 561
Cruz, Juan. See Croce,
Giovanni
Cruz, Laura (character in
Borges–Bioy filmscript).
OCC, 255, 261, 262, 275–76,
296
Ctesias (Greek physician and
historian, 4th century B.C.,
author of the *Persica* as well
as works on geography and on
India). OCC, 608, 663, 703
Cuarenta Ladrones (characters
in the *Arabian Nights*). OC,
397
Cueto (old Argentine family).
P, 78
Cuff, Sergeant (character in
Collins's *The Moonstone*).
P, 48
Cullen, Countee (American poet
and novelist, 1903–1946,
author of *The Black Christ,
Copper Sun* and other works).
ILN, 48–49

Cummings, Edward Estlin
(American poet, novelist and
nonlecturer, 1894–1963).
ILN, **44**.   PB, 119
Cunda   (blacksmith in Buddhist
legend).   OCC, 726
Cunha, Euclydes da   (Brazilian
military engineer, journalist
and writer, 1866–1909, author
of *Os Sertoes*).   OC, 516n.
P, 15n.
Cunninghame Graham, Robert
Bontine   (Scottish writer and
traveler, 1852–1936, author
of *Mogreb-el-Acksa, The
Horses of the Conquest* and
other works).   OC, 736.
OCC, 839
Cura   (priest, character in
*Don Quijote*).   C, 15.   PB,
207, 209
Curchod, Suzanne   (Swiss
pastor's daughter, beloved of
Gibbon, mother of Mme. de
Stael).   P, 69
Curcio   (character in
Hawthorne's Marble Faun).
OC, 682
Cuttini   (friend of Borges).
A, 48
Cuvier, Georges   (French
zoologist and paleontologist,
1769–1832, author of *Lecons
d'anatomie comparée* and other
works).   OCC, 320, 603
Cynewulf   (Old English poet,
late 8th or early 9th
century, author of *St.
Juliana, Elene*, and the *Fates
of the Apostles*).   OCC, 878,
879–81, 895, 918
Cyrano de Bergerac, Savinien
(French writer of romances,
1619–1655, author of *Le
Pédant joué, La Mort
d'Agrippine, Histoire comique
des états et empires de la
Lune* and other works).   OC,
697
Czepko, Daniel von   (German
poet, 1605–1660, author of
*Sexcenta monodisticha
sapientum*, 1655, and other
poems).   OC, 757
D., S.   (angelical Englishwoman
to whom Borges dedicated

*Historia universal de la
infamia*).   OC, 293
Dabove, Julio César   (brother
of Santiago Dabove).   OC,
1009.   P, 51, 52, 58
Dabove, Santiago   (Argentine
writer, 1889–1949, author of
*La muerte y su traje*).   OC,
1025.   P, 24, 49–51, 52, 58
Dahlmann, Friedrich Christoph
(German historian and
politician, 1785–1860, author
of *Politik, Geschichte
Danemarks, Quellenkunde der
deutschen Geschichte* and
other works).   OCC, 959
Dahlmann, Johannes   (German
pastor who arrived in
Argentina in 1871, character
in Borges story, grandfather
of Juan Dahlmann).   OC, 525
Dahlmann, Joseph   (German
priest, author of *Buddha*,
1898, *Die Sprachkunde und die
Missionen*, works on the
*Mahabharata*, Nirvana, etc.).
OCC, 752
Dahlmann, Juan   (character in
Borges story).   OC, 525–30
Dalai-Lama   (leader of Tibetan
Buddhism).   OCC, 761, 762
Dalgarno, George   (British
writer, c.1626–1687, author
of *Didascalocophus, or the
Deaf and Dumb Man's Tutor*,
1680, and *Ars Signorum*,
1661).   OC, 440
Dalinda   (character in Ariosto).
OC, 837
Dama de las Camelias.   See
Gautier, Marguerite
Damasceno, Juan   (John of
Damascus or Johannes
Damascenus, eminent
theologian of the Eastern
Church, d. c.754, author of
*The Fountain of Knowledge*).
OC, 552–53
Damascio   (Damascius,
Neoplatonist philosopher,
480–c.540, author of
*Difficulties and Solutions of
First Principles*).   OCC, 609
Damián, Pedro   (character in
Borges story).   OC, 571–75

Damiani, Pietro (St. Peter Damian, Italian monk and theologian, Doctor of the Church, c.1007–1072, author of *Liber Gomorrhianus, Officium Beatae Virginis* and other works). OC, 574–75, 629. C, 33

Dandolo, Vincenzo (Italian chemist and agronomist, 1758–1819, author of *Les Hommes nouveaux, ou moyen d'opérer une régéneration nouvelle*). A, 23

Daneri, Carlos Argentino (Argentine poet, author of *La tierra*, character in Borges story). OC, 617–28

Daniel (cousin of Baltasar Espinosa, character in Borges story). OC, 1068, 1069, 1070

Daniel (character in Jewish story about truth and falsehood). OC, 146. IA, 32

Dannay, Frederick (American writer, b. 1905, co-author with his cousin Manfred Lee of the detective novels of Ellery Queen, and co-editor of *Ellery Queen's Mystery Magazine*). ILN, 57

Dantas, Julio (Portuguese writer, 1876–1962). OCC, 39. P, 58

Dante Alighieri (Italian poet, 1265–1321, author of the *Divina Commedia,* the *Vita Nuova, De Monarchia* and other works). OC, 79, 168, 193, 210, 227n., 235, 275, 384, 462n., 514, 558, 574, 610, 637, 666, 667, 672, 744, 745, 747, 795, 800, 807, 867. OCC, 69, 305, 316, 317, 328, 471, 475, 530, 573, 588, 602, 637, 639, 640, 658, 664, 669, 680, 801, 836, 837, 856, 880, 883, 902, 907, 933. A, 60. BC, 77. BO, 32, 39, 48, 60. C, 73. CONJ, 61. ILN, 41, 43. NED, 85–161. OP, 540, 549. P, 44, 110, 119, 157, 166. PB, 128, 177, 178, 181–85, 191, 213, 226, 228–30, 247. SN, 9–32, 48–49, 63. TE, 78

Dante, Iacopo di (Dante's son, author of commentary on the *Divina Commedia*). NED, 92

Dante, Pietro di (Dante's son, a Verona lawyer, d. 1364, author of a commentary on the *Divina Commedia*). NED, 148. SN, 10

Darío (Darius or Darayavaush, Persian king, 521–486). PB, 194

Darío, Rubén (pseud. of Félix Rubén García Sarmiento, Nicaraguan poet, short-story writer and critic, 1867–1916, author of *Prosas profanas, Cantos de vida y esperanza, Canto a la Argentina* and numerous other works). OC, 122n., 384n., 858, 1081. OCC, 449, 464, 466, 467, 477, 478. I, 26, 97, 99, 122, 153. ILN, 9. LA, 16. OP, 365. P 40, 41, 57, 86. PB, 221, 232–33, 240. SN, 88–89. TE, 42, 72, 105

Darracq, Juan F. (restaurateur in Geneva, character in Bustos Domecq story). OCC, 326

Darwin, Charles (English natural scientist, 1809–1882, author of *The Origin of Species*). OC, 277, 1113. OCC, 367. OP, 387. TE, 20

Dasent, George Webbe (English writer, 1817–1896, author of an Icelandic grammar and translator of the *Njals Saga,* the *Prose Edda,* the *Gisli* and other works). OC, 381

Dass, Bhagwan (character in Borges story). VA, 34, 35

Daudet, Alphonse (French novelist and playwright, 1840–1897, author of *Lettres de mon moulin, L'Arlésienne* and other works). OC, 446. ILN, 38

David (Biblical king of Israel, c.1012–c.972). OC, 337, 362, 383, 384, 1063, 1081. OCC, 709, 904. NED, 143, 144. OP, 365. PB, 179, 180. TE, 78

David-Neel, Alexandra (Anglo-French writer on Buddhism, 1868-1969, author of *Voyage d'une Parisienne a Lhassa, Puissance du néant* and *Mystiques et magiciens du Thibet*).   OCC, 780

Davids, Thomas William Rhys (British scholar, 1843-1922, author of *Buddhist India* and *Dialogues of the Buddha*).   OC, 743n., 758n.   OCC, 752, 761.   PB, 195

Davidson, M. (author of *The Free Will Controversy*).   OC, 282-83

Davies, John (English classical scholar, 1679-1732, editor and commentator on Cicero).   P, 72

Davis, Bette (American film star, b. 1908).   BC, 69-70

De Filipo (character in Bustos Domecq story).   OCC, 361

De Gubernatis, Bruno (character in Bustos Domecq and Suárez Lynch stories).   OCC, 146, 160, 164-66, 168, 186, 444, 445

De Kruif, Bimbo (character in Suárez Lynch novella).   OCC, 149, 163, 170, 172, 173, 175, 176

De Mille, Cecil B. (American film director, 1881-1959).   OC, 224, 408, 754.   BC, 32, 73

De Quincey, Thomas (English writer, 1785-1859, author of *Confessions of an English Opium Eater, On Murder as one of the Fine Arts, Autobiographic Sketches, On the Knocking at the Gate in Macbeth* and other works).   OC, 52, 99, 211, 263, 275, 279, 375n., 397, 423, 433, 483, 514, 544, 641, 651, 682, 700, 702n., 720, 731, 744, 750, 762, 870, 991.   OCC, 627, 832, 833.   I, 24.   IA, 102, 130.   LA, 28, 139.   NED, 144.   P, 23, 29, 45, 50, 73, 87, 117, 144, 161.   PB, 139, 169, 180, 190, 229.   SN, 42, 50, 72, 73, 153.   TE, 152.   VA, 19

De Sanctis, Francesco.  See Sanctis, Francesco De

De Vedia.   See Vedia, de

De Vore, Nicholas (American musician, b. 1882, author of *Familiar Organ Classics* and numerous other collections of organ music as well as *New Frontiers of Psychology* and an *Encyclopedia of Astrology*).   OCC, 643

De Voto, Bernard (American critic and novelist, 1897-1955, author of *Mark Twain's America, The Course of Empire, Across the Wide Missouri* and other works).   OC, 345.   P, 81.   PB, 122, 123

Dédalo (Daedalus, architect in Greek myth).   OC, 877.   OCC, 664, 699

Dedalus, Stephen (character in Joyce's *Portrait of the Artist* and *Ulysses*).   BC, 48

Defoe, Daniel (English writer, c.1660-1731, author of *Robinson Crusoe, Moll Flanders* and other works).   OC, 220.   CONJ, 14.   IA, 88.   PB, 123.   VA, 31

Demeter (Greek earth goddess).   P, 71

Demiurgo or Artífice (Neoplatonic creator).   OCC, 579.   NED, 90

Demócrito de Abdera (Democritus, Greek philosopher, c.460-c.360, author of the *Mikros Diakosmos* and other works, almost completely lost).   OC, 276-77, 393-94, 661, 749, 1017.   BO, 31.   P, 120.   SN, 157-58

Demonio (the devil).   OCC, 679, 722, 813, 892, 907.   ILN, 26.   P, 32.   SN, 139

Demonios (devils of various kinds).   OCC, 585, 614.   BO, 50, 51, 52, 56.   P, 160

Demóstenes (Demosthenes, Greek orator and statesman, c.384-322).   OC, 553.   OCC, 730

Dempsey, Jack (American boxer, b. 1895). P, 53. TE, 102

Deor (minstrel, character in the Old English poem *Deor*). OCC, 794, 889-90

Desargues, Girard (French mathematician, 1591-1661). OC, 276

Descartes, René (French philosopher, 1596-1650, author of *Discours de la Méthode, Traité des passions de l'ame, Meditationes de prima philosophia, Principia philosophiae* and other works). OC, 258, 444, 445, 544, 706. OCC, 364, 581, 649. BO, 32, 46. C, 17. I, 116, 117n. P, 154. PB, 159

Descharmes, René (French scholar, author of *Flaubert, sa vie, son caractere et ses idées*). OC, 262

Desdemona (character in Shakespeare's *Othello*). OCC, 820-21

Destino (personification of fate or destiny). OC, 304

Deussen, Paul (German philologist and philosopher, 1845-1919, whose chief work was *Allgemeine Geschichte der Philosophie*, with sections on the India, Bible, and Western philosophy from the Greeks to Schopenhauer). OC, 354, 367, 392, 646. OCC, 721, 727, 730, 745, 749, 751. A, 80. P, 70. SN, 90, 118

Deva (Godhead in Buddhism). OCC, 722, 747, 757

Devadatta (Buddha's cousin). OCC, 725-26

Devorador de las Sombras (monster in the *Book of the Dead* of the ancient Egyptians that eats the souls of liars). OCC, 615

Dewey, Christopher (official of British consulate in Buenos Aires). OC, 612

Dhyam Buddha (celestial buddha, of whom the historical buddha was just a projection, according to Mahayana Buddhism). OCC, 757

Diablo (the devil). OC, 642, 1007. OCC, 622, 712, 873, 893. BC, 57. IA, 182

Diablotin. OCC, 159

Diácono, Pablo el. See Pablo el Diácono

Diágoras (Greek poet and sophist of Melos, 5th century B.C.). OC, 661. P, 120

Diana (Roman goddess of the hunt and of the moon, associated with the Greek Artemis). OC, 504, 550, 820. OCC, 224, 585. A, 9. I, 35. OP, 524-25. PB, 197

Diávolo, Fra (popular nickname for Michele Pezza, famous Italian brigand, 1771-1806). OCC, 965n.

Díaz, José (local thug in Buenos Aires). OC, 129n.

Díaz, Juan (Juan Díaz de Solís, Spanish navigator, d. 1516, discoverer of the River Plate for Spain, captured and killed by Indians somewhere on the Uruguayan coast). OC, 81

Díaz de Beyral (Spanish translator of St. Augustine). OC, 392

Dickens, Charles (English novelist, 1812-1870, author of *David Copperfield, Oliver Twist, Martin Chuzzlewit, Pickwick Papers* and numerous other works). OC, 9, 196, 197, 689, 695, 698, 733, 734. OCC, 563, 834-35, 847. BO, 68, 70, 80. CONJ, 44. I, 131. IA, 102. ILN, 20, 56. P, 48, 83, 117, 127

Dickinson, Edward (lawyer in Amherst, Massachusetts, father of Emily Dickinson). ILN, 31

Dickinson, Emily (American poet, 1830-1886). BO, 65. ILN, 31-32

Dickson, Carter (writer of detective fiction, 1906-1977). OCC, 17

680, 689, 698, 703, 704n.,
705, 708, 711, 714–716, 720–
722, 737–739, 750–753, 760,
767, 775, 787, 800, 804, 807,
809, 813, 830, 835, 840, 854,
865, 868, 875, 882, 883, 885–
887, 890, 893, 896, 909, 910,
927, 929, 930, 934, 977–978,
983, 993, 996, 997, 1006,
1011, 1023, 1069, 1076, 1103,
1105–6, 1114, 1138.    OCC,
317, 318, 365, 396, 451,
534n., 563, 574, 590, 595,
599, 616, 637, 640, 655, 810,
813–14, 822, 824, 825, 827,
840, 841, 848, 870, 876, 879,
880, 881, 882, 885–86, 887,
888, 891, 895, 897, 900–1,
903, 906, 909, 914, 919, 924,
939, 952, 956.    A, 14, 27,
70, 80.    BC, 57, 58, 72.    BO,
17, 27, 49, 50–53, 55, 56,
88, 94.    C, 13, 15, 63, 67.
CONJ, 37, 57, 76, 83, 91.
I, 13, 27, 31, 32, 34, 35,
69, 93, 114, 116, 119.    IA,
38, 49, 51, 62, 74, 128, 154,
160, 164.    ILN, 9, 11, 12,
20, 44.    LA, 58, 71, 82,
104, 117, 173.    NED, 88, 90,
93, 99, 103, 115, 121, 142,
143, 149, 159.    OP, 369, 381,
384, 385, 389, 447, 465, 491,
497, 498, 499, 502, 505, 507,
511, 512, 513, 517, 527, 528,
545, 551, 559.    P, 13–15,
27, 32, 34, 43, 70, 76, 82,
86, 120, 121, 140, 141, 154,
155, 158–62, 172.    PB, 119,
141, 145, 178, 179, 183, 184,
190, 199, 200, 244, 246.    SN,
11, 20, 22, 25, 26, 31, 36,
37, 50, 52, 68, 80, 90, 91,
101, 117, 128–39, 147.    TE,
5, 18, 23, 51, 64, 65, 67,
87, 102, 111.    VA, 19, 24,
41
**Dioscuros** (Dioscuri, the sons of Zeus, the twins Castor and Pollux).    OCC, 699
**Dioses** (gods).    OC, 805–806, 985, 1120.    OP, 398–99
**Dirae** (devils).    OCC, 585
**Discordia** (personification of discord).    OCC, 690.    NED, 128

**Discórides** (Dioscorides Pedanius, army physician at the time of Claudius and Nero).    OCC, 662
**Disney, Walt** (American commercial artist, animator and executive, 1901–1966, creator of Mickey Mouse and Donald Duck).    OCC, 59
**Doblas** (minor character in Borges-Bioy filmscript).    OCC, 226
**Doblas, Alfredo** (co-worker with Borges in the public library in Almagro).    OC, 630
**Doce Pares** (twelve English knights in *Os Lusíadas*, canto 6, who fight a tournament with twelve Portuguese knights).    PB, 238, 239
**Dodds, Eric Robertson** (b. 1893, author of *Pagan and Christian in an Age of Anxiety* and editor of *Select Passages Illustrating Neo-platonism*, 1923).    OC, 367
**Dodgson, Charles Lutwitdge.** See Lewis Carroll
**Dodsworth** (character in Lewis's *Dodsworth*).    ILN, 35
**Dolan, Johnny, el Dandy** (New York gangster, character in Borges story also mentioned in Asbury's *Gangs of New York*).    OC, 311
**Dolly Sister** (character in Bustos Domecq story).    OCC, 70, 82, 84
**Domiciano** (Domitian or Titus Flavius Domitianus, Roman emperor, 51–96).    OC, 700
**Dominga, la china** (character in a *sainete* set in Palermo).    OC, 110
**Domingo, Santo** (Domingo de Guzmán, Spanish monk and reformer, 1170–1221).    NED, 148
**Donne, John** (English poet and divine, 1572–1631, author of *The Progress of the Soul*, *Hymn to God the Father*, the *Pseudo-Martyr*, *Biathanatos*, and numerous sermons, letters and poems).    OC, 209, 210,

Dudgeon, Richard (character in Shaw). OC, 748

Duhau, Alfredo (Argentine dramatist, author of *La dote* and *Príncipe que mató al dragón*). OCC, 146

Dujardin, Edouard (French writer, 1861-1949, author of *Les Lauriers sont coupés*, an early example of stream-of-consciousness narrative). I, 25

Dujovne, León (Argentine lawyer and man of letters, b. 1899, author of *Teoría de los valores y filosofía de la historia* and works on Hegel and Buber, and translator of the *Sefer Yetsirah*). SN, 138

Dulcinea (Dulcinea del Toboso, Don Quijote's lady, also known as Aldonza Lorenzo). C, 33. PB, 204, 208, 210

Dumas, Alexandre (Dumas *pere*, French novelist and dramatist, 1802-1870, author of *Le Comte de Monte-Cristo*, *Les Trois Mousquetaires* and other works). OC, 116, 157, 158. ILN, 61. NED, 121n. P, 40, 41

Dumas, Alexandre (Dumas *fils*, French novelist and dramatist, 1824-1895, author of *La Dame aux Camélias* and other works). ILN, 55

Dumas, Vito (nickname for a character in Bustos Domecq story, also known as "el Navegante Solitario"). OCC, 395

Dumesnil, René (French literary critic, author of numerous studies of Flaubert). OC, 260

Dunbar, William (Scottish poet, c.1460-c.1520). OC, 773, 1014

Duncan (character in Borges story). OC, 1039-43

Duncan (Scottish king, d. 1040, character in Shakespeare's *Macbeth*). OCC, 819. OP, 437. P, 143, 145, 146

Dunne, J. W. (British philosopher, author of *An Experiment with Time* and *Nothing Dies*). OC, 279, 462, 646-49. SN, 36, 37, 61

Dunraven (poet, character in Borges story). OC, 600-6

Dunsany, Edward John Moreton Drax Plunkett, Lord (Irish dramatist, poet and short-story writer, 1878-1957). OC, 711, 712

Dupin, Auguste (amateur detective, character in Poe's "Purloined Letter," "Mystery of Marie Roget" and "Murders in the Rue Morgue"). OC, 499, 686, 694, 746. OCC, 18, 849. BO, 72, 76, 77. ILN, 56. P, 47. PB, 140

Dupont de Montpellier (artistic chef, perhaps based on Pierre Dupont, French writer, 1821-1870, author of *Les Boeufs* and other songs). OCC, 326

Durero, Albert (Durer, German painter and engraver, 1471-1528). OC, 811, 1007-8, 1054. C, 52. OP, 522, 541

Duroc-Jersey. OCC, 126

Durtain, Luc (pseud. of André Nepveu, b. 1881, French writer and physician, author of a sequence of novels, *Les Conquetes du monde*, and numerous other works). OC, 445. OCC, 320, 381, 386

Duvernois. See Puffendorff-Duvernois

Dux (the Venetian Dogo). A, 23

Dymant, Dora (woman with whom Kafka lived in 1923-1924). P, 103

Eald (character in Borges story, also known as Alt). OC, 1032

Earle, John (translator of *Beowulf*, 1892). OC, 381. OCC, 871, 893

Eastman, Monk (Edward Ostermann, New York gangster). OC, 311-15

Ebión. OC, 213

Eca de Queiroz, José Maria (Portuguese novelist, 1845-

and other works).    OC, 223.
BC, 28, 32–33, 73

Ekkenhard  (Ekkehard I, German
monk and poet, d. 973, author
of the *Waltharius*).    OCC,
919, 920

Eleata.    See Zenón

Eleazar de Worms  (Eleazar ben
Jehudah, rabbi of Worms, d.
c.1225, author of the *Sefer
Rokeah*).    OCC, 637, 638

Electra  (Greek mythological
princess of Mycenae, daughter
of Agamemnon).    ILN, 53

Elefante blanco  (white
elephant of Buddhist legend).
OCC, 623

Eléfantis  (author of erotica).
OCC, 139

Elena.    See Rojas, Elena

Elena de Troya  (Greek
mythological figure, daughter
of Zeus and Leda, sometimes
Helena de Troya).    OC, 215,
265n., 674, 763, 796, 936,
1128.    OCC, 818, 841.    BC,
28.    C, 45.    CONJ, 17.
OP, 540

Elfgar  (son of Elfric,
mentioned in the *Anglo-
Saxon Chronicle*).    OCC, 895

Elfos  (elves).    OCC, 624,
702.    SN, 41

Elfric  (character in the
*Anglo-Saxon Chronicle*).
OCC, 895

Eliano  (Johannes Baptista
Elianus, d. 1589, supposed
author of *Mohommedis
imposturae*).    OCC, 665, 679

Elías  (angel who fights the
Antichrist in the *Muspilli*).
OCC, 902

Elías  (in the Bible, prophet
who fought the idolatry of
Jezabel and Ahab).    OC, 517

Eliezer.    See Eleazar de Worms

Eliot, Thomas Stearns  (Anglo-
American poet and critic,
1888–1965, author of *The
Waste Land, Four Quartets,
Tradition and the Individual
Talent, Murder in the
Cathedral* and other works).
OC, 249, 418, 544, 686, 712n,
772, 1015.    OCC, 304, 679,

817, 835, 838, 846, 854, 855–
56, 892.    BC, 41, 60.
ILN, 41, 42–43, 46.    NED,
118.    P, 8, 18, 48.    PB,
144, 156, 157

Elizabeth I.    See Isabel de
Inglaterra

Elizabeth de Bohemia  (Bohemian
queen, 1596–1662, wife of
Frederick V).    C, 17

Elizalde, Rufino de  (Argentine
lawyer and statesman, 1822–
1887, author of *Bolivia,
origen de su nacionalidad*).
P, 18

Ellis, Havelock  (British
psychologist and writer,
1859–1939, author of *Studies
in the Psychology of Sex, The
Soul of Spain, Affirmations*
and other works).    OC, 642

Ellis, Hilda Roderick  (author
of *The Road to Hel*, 1945).
OCC, 931, 954n., 965–66.
PB, 201

Ellis, Stewart Marsh  (author
of *Wilkie Collins, Le Fanu
and Others*, 1931).    P, 48

Elohim  (plural name of the one
god in Hebrew).    OC, 737.
OCC, 595.    I, 74

Eloi  (monsters in Wells's *Time
Machine*).    OCC, 625

Elphinston, James  (British
scholar of Anglo-Saxon
England, 1721–1809).    LA,
140

Else, Doctor  (Swedish doctor,
character in Horacio
Quiroga's story "Los
destiladores de naranja,"
also a character in the film
*Prisioneros de la tierra* by
Soffici).    BC, 62

Elton  (translator of *Historia
Danica*).    OCC, 975

Eluard, Paul  (French writer
and poet, 1895–1952).    OCC,
189, 325

Ema.    See Fingermann, Ema

Emerson, Ralph Waldo  (American
poet and philosopher, 1803–
1882, author of
*Representative Men, The
American Scholar, Brahma,
Self-Reliance, History* and

numerous other works). OC,
79, 168, 206, 251, 252, 364,
395, 571, 573, 639, 679, 684,
911, 1018, 1114.    OCC, 333,
735.    BO, 21–22, 46, 47, 48,
57, 65, 67, 77.    C, 9.
CONJ, 69, 71.    ILN, 20, 21–
22, 24, 27, 28, 32, 38, 46.
OP, 389.    P, 34–39, 81, 112,
133, 153, 171.    PB, 167,
172.    SN, 101, 106

Empédocles (Greek philosopher,
poet, statesman and religious
teacher, c.490–430, author of
*On Nature, Purifications* and
other works, mostly lost;
Borges calls him "Empédocles
de Agrigento," but no
connection with Agrigentum is
mentioned in the reference
works).    OC, 636, 661, 704n.
OCC, 690, 740.    P, 120.
SN, 88

Emperador (Japanese emperor).
C, 95

Emperador Amarillo (legendary
first emperor of China,
reigned 2698–c.2600).    OC,
633, 801–2.    OCC, 105, 580.
C, 41

Emperador Chino (Chinese
emperor).    OCC, 701

Empírico, Sexto.    See Sexto
Empírico

En soph (the hidden or
infinite God, according to
the *Zohar*).    SN, 132–33

Endimión (Endymion, beautiful
young man of Greek myth).
OC, 1104.    OP, 382, 524

Eneas (Aeneas, Roman
mythological hero).    OC,
265n., 640.    ILN, 25.    LA,
101.    NED, 102, 116.    P,
71, 171.    SN, 28, 41, 105

Enemigo del Hombre (cook in
Bustos Domecq story).    OCC,
91, 100

Engelhart, Baron (character in
Bustos Domecq story).    OCC,
330

Engstrom, Lars Peter (Swedish
theologian, adversary of Nils
Runeberg, character in Borges
story).    OC, 515

Enitharmon (figure in Blake's
prophetic books, the giver of
a rigid morality).    OCC, 840

Enkidu (character in *Gilgamesh*,
Sumerian mythic hero).    OCC,
652

Ennio (Quintus Ennius, Latin
poet, 239–169, author of
*Annalium*).    IA, 173

Enrique I (English king, 1068–
1135).    OC, 252

Enrique II (Henry II, 1154–
1189, English king at the
time of Layomon).    OCC, 897

Eormanric or Ermanaric (king
of the East Goths, fl. 350–
376, mentioned in the *Widsith*
and *Deor*).    OCC, 876, 889–90

Epicarmo (Epicharmus, Sicilian
writer of comedy, c.530–
c.440).    OCC, 746

Epicteto (Epictetus, Greek
Stoic philosopher, c.55–
c.135).    OC, 591, 700.
OCC, 279

Epicuro (Epicurus, Greek
philosopher, 341–270).    OC,
394.    OCC, 733n.

Equidna (Echidna, Greek
monster).    OCC, 645

Er (soldier whose dream is
discussed in the tenth book
of Plato's *Republic*).    SN, 88

Erasmo, Desiderio (Desiderius
Erasmus, Dutch philosopher
and writer, 1466–1536, author
of *Encomium Moriae, Novum
Instrumentum, Enchiridion
Militis Christiani* and other
works).    OC, 151, 641.    P,
29.    PB, 139, 230

Erato (Muse of love-poetry).
I, 41, 142

Ercilia.    See Larramendi,
Ercilia

Erfjord, Erik (Danish Hebrew
scholar, author of
*Christelige Dogmatik*).    OC,
516, 517n., 553

Erfjord, Gunnar (correspondent
of Herbert Ashe in Borges
story).    OC, 440, 441

Erfjord, Nora (character in
Borges story).    LA, 40, 44,
55, 57, 58, 59, 62

Erico (bishop of Greenland).
OCC, 940. PB, 190

Erico el Rojo (Eric or Eirik
the Red, Norwegian discoverer
and settler of Greenland).
OC, 1087, 1118. OCC, 940.
A, 7. LA, 139. NED, 118.
OP, 371, 395. P, 153. PB,
190

Erigena, Juan Escoto (Duns
Scotus, Irish theologian, fl.
850, author of De Divisione
Naturae). OC, 211n., 261,
280, 351, 363, 727, 728, 737,
738, 746, 749, 751, 830.
OCC, 637, 848. A, 14.
PB, 190. SN, 10, 101, 132

Erman, Johann Peter Adolf
(German Egyptologist, b. 1854,
author of Neuagyptische
Grammatik and other works).
OCC, 587

Ernoul (putative author of the
Chronique d'Ernoul, a history
of the kingdom of Jerusalem
from its foundation to 1229).
P, 141

Erostrato (Erostratus, who set
fire to the Temple of Artemis
at Ephesus). I, 35

Es-Sindibad del Mar. See
Simbad el Marino

Escaldos or Escaldas (Icelandic
hermetic poets). OCC, 942–
49, 958. P, 107

Escaligero, Joseph Justus
(Joseph Justus Scaliger,
Italian Renaissance scholar,
1504-1609, author of De
Emendatione Temporum,
Thesaurus Temporum and other
works). OC, 641. P, 69

Escaligero, Julius Caesar
(Julius Caesar Scaliger,
Italian critic and physician,
1484-1558, author of
Exercitationes and other
works). OC, 641

Escila (Scylla, a sea-monster
that lives in a cave opposite
Charybdis in the Odyssey).
OC, 250. OCC, 299, 626

Escipión el Africano (Publius
Cornelius Scipio Africanus
Major, Roman general and
statesman, 236–183). OCC,
504, 683. NED, 149

Escorpio (Scorpio, the zodiac
sign). OCC, 643

Escorzo (pseud. of Bustos
Domecq). OCC, 341

Escoto, Juan. See Erigena,
Juan Escoto

Escudero, Doctor (perhaps
Ernesto Escudero, a prominent
physician of Buenos Aires, b.
1909). OCC, 93

Esculapio (Asclepius or
Aesculapius, Greek hero and
god of healing). OCC, 474,
605. BO, 37

Esfinge (sphinx, mythological
monster with human head and
the body of a lion). OC,
228n., 275, 830, 929. OCC,
627, 643, 696. C, 44. OP,
522. P, 138

Esfinge Tebana (Theban sphinx,
the sphinx which ravaged
Thebes until killed by
Oedipus). NED, 144. PB,
162, 180

Esmerdis (magician of Uqbar,
perhaps based on Smerdis,
evil Persian king mentioned
by Ctesias, Xenophon,
Aeschylus and others). OC,
432

Esopo (Aesop, Greek teller of
fables, d. c.564 B.C.). OC,
1021. P, 68. PB, 245.
SN, 65

Esparbes, Georges-Thomas D'
(French author of patriotic
and historical novels, 1864–
1944). OC, 116

Espinel, Vicente (Spanish
novelist and poet, 1550-1624,
author of Marcos de Obregón).
I, 45. TE, 143

Espinosa, Baltasar (character
in Borges story). OC, 1068–
72

Espinosa, Daniel (character in
Borges-Bioy filmscript).
OCC, 264, 267, 277–78, 280,
292–95

Espinosa, Irma (character in
Borges-Bioy filmscript).
OCC, 263, 278–82

Espíritu (the spirit,
sometimes Espíritu Santo).
OC, 283. OCC, 628, 704,
882. A, 70. BC, 64, 72.
BO, 17, 18, 19, 68-69. LA,
107. NED, 116, 140. OP,
469. P, 137. PB, 144,
225, 227, 236. SN, 126,
129, 131

Espronceda, José de (Spanish
poet, 1808-1842, author of *El
estudiante de Salamanca*).
IA, 101

Esquilo (Aeschylus, Greek
tragic poet, 525-456). OC,
206, 754. OCC, 330. A,
44. IA, 105-6

Esquimales (Eskimos, called
Skraelings by the Norsemen).
OCC, 940

Essex, Robert Devereux
(English earl, 1566?-1601).
OCC, 822

Esteban, San (St. Stephen, the
first Christian martyr,
stoned to death in
Jerusalem). OC, 551

Estiércol (god of the Yahoos
in Borges story). OC, 1076

Estomba (Argentine military
leader in the wars of
independence). PB, 132-33,
152

Estrabón (Strabo, Greek
historian and geographer, 64
B.C.-c.21 A.D., author of
*Historical Sketches* and
*Geography*). OC, 228n. OCC,
665, 696

Ethelred (Aethelred the
Unready, English king, 979-
1016). OCC, 936, 948

Etzel. See Atila

Euclides (Euclid, Greek
mathematician, c.300 B.C.,
author of the *Elements* and
other works). OCC, 831,
838. A, 59. LA, 181.
SN, 52

Eudemo (Eudemus of Rhodes,
Greek philosopher, fl. c.350-
300). OC, 387

Euforbo (Euphorbus, a
Dardanian warrior in Greek
mythology; Pythagoras said he
was Euphorbus in a previous

incarnation). OC, 456.
OCC, 740. C, 33

Euforbo (prophet of the
Eternal Return in Borges
story; the name is surely
drawn from the Euphorbus
discussed above). OC, 552

Eurípides (Greek tragic poet,
c.485-407). OCC, 495, 842.
ILN, 49. P, 85. SN, 117

Eusculapio. See Esculapio

Eusebio de Nicodemia (Eusebius
of Caesarea, Palestinian
bishop, theologian and
historian, d. c.342, author
of an *Ecclesiastical
History*). OCC, 863

Eva (first woman in the Bible,
wife of Adam). OC, 650,
1131. OCC, 659, 801, 813,
823, 904. BO, 36. C, 43,
73. NED, 138. OP, 408

Evangelistas (Biblical
evangelists, Matthew, Mark,
Luke and John). NED, 148

Evans, Amy (American business-
woman associated with
Gervasio Montenegro in an
enterprise exporting women
from Buenos Aires to Salt
Lake City). OCC, 76, 84

Evans-Wentz, W. Y. (British
Orientalist, 1878-1965,
author of works on Celtic
fairy tales, yoga and other
subjects, and editor of the
*Tibetan Book of the Dead*).
OCC, 615, 737n., 764, 780

Ewers, Hans Heinz (German
novelist, 1871-1943, author
of *Alraune, Vampir* and other
works). OCC, 661

Eyvind Skáldaspillir
(Icelandic poet, author of
the *Hákonarmál*). OC, 376.
OCC, 949, 955

Ezequías (Hezekiah, Biblical
king of Judah). NED, 143.
PB, 179

Ezequiel (Ezekiel, Biblical
prophet). OC, 625, 695.
OCC, 642. P, 156

Fa Hien. OC, 741

Fa Hsien (Chinese Buddhist
monk, fl. 399-414). OC,
741. OCC, 671

Fader, Fernando (Argentine
painter, 1882–1935).    TE, 83
Fafnir (dragon in the *Volsunga
Saga*).    OC, 380, 592.    OCC,
675, 966–68
Faguet, Emile (French literary
historian and critic, 1847–
1916).    OC, 259, 260
Fainberg, Simón (character in
Bustos Domecq and Suárez
Lynch stories, also known as
"el Gran Perfil" and "el
padre Fainberg").    OCC, 86,
89, 90, 92, 95, 96–100, 104,
127, 156, 423
Fair, A. A. (pseud. of Erle
Stanley Gardner).    ILN, 57
Fairbanks, Douglas (American
film actor, 1883–1939).
OCC, 63
Falak (cosmic serpent
mentioned in the *Arabian
Nights*).    OCC, 590
Falcao Espalter, Mario
(Uruguayan literary critic
and historian, 1892–1941).
OCC, 517
Falsirena (allegorical female
figure in Gracián's
*Criticón*).    PB, 162
Falso Artajerjes.    A, 37
Falstaff (character in
Shakespeare's *Henry IV*,
parts I and II, and *The Merry
Wives of Windsor*).    OC, 738.
OCC, 821
Falucho (nickname for Antonio
Ruiz, a black Argentine
soldier in the wars of
independence, d. 1824).    OC,
295.    OCC, 146, 174
Fama (personification of Fame,
also called Escándalo and
Rumor).    NED, 139.    PB, 177
Fang (character in Ts'ui Pen's
novel).    OC, 478
Fang She (character in Bustos
Domecq story).    OCC, 109–21
Farach (character in Borges
story).    OC, 583, 585, 586,
587
Farfarello (character in
Bustos Domecq story).    OCC,
403–8, 419–21
Fargo.    OCC, 396

Farías (Sephardic surname).
OC, 876
Farid ud-din Attar (Abu Talib,
Persian poet and mystic,
c.1150–1230, author of the
*Mantiq al-Tayr* or *Coloquio de
los pájaros* and countless
other works).    OC, 251, 286,
414, 418n, 594, 695n.    OCC,
695.    BC, 68.    NED, 141–44.
OP, 465.    PB, 178, 179
Farrel, James T. (American
novelist, b. 1904, author of
*Studs Lonigan* and other
works).    P, 82
Farrel du Bosc (character in
Bustos Domecq stories, author
of *La línea Paladión-Pound-
Eliot* and studies of Loomis).
OCC, 304, 321
Farinata degli Uberti
(Ghibelline leader, mentioned
in the *Divina Commedia*).
OCC, 561
Fastitocalon (whale in Old
English bestiary).    OCC,
628, 892
Fata Morgana (Morgay le Fay,
sister of King Arthur, a
sorceress).    OCC, 299, 317,
381, 641
Fatone, Vicente (Argentine
writer, 1902–1962, author of
*El Budhismo nihilista*, 1962).
OCC, 780
Faucigny Lucinge (princess,
friend of Borges).    OC, 441,
533
Faulkner, William (American
novelist, 1897–1964, author
of *The Sound and the Fury,
Absalom, Absalom!, As I Lay
Dying, The Wild Palms* and
other works).    OC, 684, 756.
BC, 48.    ILN, 36, 50, 55.
P, 48, 109
Faunos (fauns, wood sprites
associated with Pan).    OCC,
692
Fausset, Hugh Ianson (British
critic, b. 1895, author of
numerous studies of Donne,
Cowper and other British
poets).    OC, 701
Faustino (character in Borges-
Bioy filmscript).    OCC, 206

Fausto (Faust, German conjurer, c.1488-1541, who according to later legend sold his soul to the devil, subject of literary works by Marlowe, Goethe, Mann and del Campo). OC, 260, 262, 577, 730, 755. OCC, 817, 818.    TE, 12, 152

Favaro, Antonio (Italian scholar, 1847-1922, editor of numerous works of Galileo). OC, 716n.

Favonio (character in Góngora sonnet).    TE, 128

Febo (Phoebus Apollo, sun god in classical mythology). CONJ, 83

Fechner, Gustav Theodor (German scientist and philosopher, 1801-1887, author of *Zend-Avesta oder uber die Dinge des Himmels und des Jenseits, Elemente der Psychophysik* and other works).    OC, 704n. OCC, 579.    BO, 32

Federico I (Friedrich I, first king of Prussia, 1657-1713). OCC, 911

Federico II (Kaiser Friedrich II, Holy Roman emperor, 1194-1250).    OC, 726

Federico el Grande (Friedrich II, der Grosse, Prussian king, 1712-1786).    OCC, 834, 911.    P, 36

Fedro (Phaedrus, Latin writer, c.15 B.C.-c.50 A.D., author of five books of verse fables).    OP, 550

Feijoo, Benito Jerónimo, Fray (Spanish scholar and monk, 1676-1764, and in the second instance also refers to the Argentine poet Bernardo Canal Feijoo).    OC, 277n.    OCC, 336-37

Fein (resident of Rio Grande do Sul who communicates to Emma Zunz the news of her father's death, perhaps Fain). OC, 564, 565

Fein, Carlos (Uruguayan judge who condemned Avelino Arredondo).    LA, 181

Felipe, don (character in Borges story).    LA, 72

Felipe II (Spanish king, 1527-1598).    ILN, 16.    PB, 225. SN, 156

Felipe III (Spanish king, 1578-1621).    P, 45

Felipe IV, el Hermoso (Philippe IV, "the Fair," French king, 1285-1314). NED, 152n.

Felton, John (assassin of the first duke of Buckingham, c.1595-1628).    LA, 181

Fénelon, Francois de Salignac de la Mothe- (French writer and archbishop, 1651-1715, author of *Traité de l'éducation des filles, Télémaque* and other works). SN, 62

Feng (Horvendil's brother and Amlodi's uncle in Saxo Grammaticus's version of the Hamlet story).    OCC, 972-73

Fénix (phoenix, mythological bird).    OCC, 587-88, 619, 632, 689-90, 695, 892.    C, 53.    PB, 161

Fenrir (Scandinavian mythological wolf).    OCC, 707, 927, 953

Fermat, Pierre de (French mathematician, 1601?-1665). OC, 600.    C, 53

Fermín (minor character in Borges-Bioy filmscript). OCC, 268

Fernandes, Padre (character in Borges story).    OC, 1077

Fernández, Juana.    BC, 73n.

Fernández, Macedonio (Argentine philosopher, poet and novelist, 1874-1952, author of *Papeles de recienvenido, No todo es vigilia lo de los ojos abiertos, Museo de la novela de la eterna, Adriana Buenosayres* and other works).    OC, 13, 21, 139, 420, 773, 784, 796, 1010.    OCC, 499, 563.    A, 57.    BC, 65.    C, 37, 77.    I, 29, 74, 94, 122, 160.    OP, 459, 470.    P, 8, 49-51, 52-61.    SN, 93.    TE, 7, 40, 86, 147.    VA, 15

Fernández Guerra, Aureliano
(Spanish scholar and
politician, 1816–1894). OC,
661. P, 120, 121

Fernández Irala, José
(character in Borges story,
sometimes Irala). LA, 35,
37–39, 41, 45, 47–54, 57–59,
63

Fernández Latour, Enrique
(Argentine writer, friend of
Macedonio Fernández). P,
52, 57, 59

Fernández Moreno, Baldomero
(Argentine poet, 1886–1950).
OCC, 479. I, 137. PB, 128,
164, 165. TE, 14

Fernández Saldaña, José M.
(Uruguayan critic, author of
a *Diccionario uruguayo de
biografías*, 1945). OCC, 311

Ferrabás (radio announcer in
Bustos Domecq story). OCC,
361

Ferrari, Antonio (character in
Borges–Levinson story). HE,
51, 52, 56, 57, 58–65, 67–69

Ferrari, Eloísa (character in
Borges–Levinson story). HE,
51–55, 57–59, 60–71

Ferrari, Francisco (character
in Borges story). OC, 1029–
33

Ferrari, Gladys (character in
Borges–Levinson story). HE,
55–56, 59, 61–62, 69

Ferrari, Irma (character in
Borges–Levinson story). HE,
53–56, 61–63, 67–71

Ferrarotti, el Tullido
(character in Bustos Domecq
story). OCC, 29

Ferrex (character in *Gorboduc*,
one of the earliest of
English tragedies, by Norton
and Sackville, first
performed in 1561). OC, 803

Ferri, Alejandro (character in
Borges story). LA, 35–63

Festo (Festus, a favorite of
the emperor Domitian). OC,
700

Fichte, Johann Gottlieb
(German philosopher, 1762–
1814, author of *Versuch einer
Kritik aller Offenbarung*,

*Uber den Begriff der
Wissenschaftslehre* and other
works). OC, 658, 725.
OCC, 832, 834

Ficino, Marsilio (Italian
philosopher and scholar,
1433–1499). OCC, 579

Fidias (Phidias, Greek
sculptor, d. c.431 B.C.).
OCC, 604

Fielding, Henry (English
novelist and playwright,
1707–1754, author of *Tom
Jones*, *Joseph Andrews*,
*Shamela* and other works).
P, 47

Fierro, Martín (main character
in Hernández poem). OC,
131, 134, 154, 163, 179, 180,
182, 183, 192, 196, 269, 295,
519–21, 563, 572, 658, 659,
735, 797, 966, 1023, 1040.
OCC, 518, 530, 531–40, 542,
548–50, 552–55, 563–64. I,
135. IA, 134. P, 29, 64,
93, 94, 95, 98, 99, 136.
PB, 134–35, 186, 230, 231.
SN, 19. TE, 34, 35, 144,
152

Figari, Pedro (Uruguayan
painter and lawyer, 1861–
1938). OC, 295. OCC, 440

Figueroa, señora de (minor
character in Borges story
"La señora mayor," perhaps
to be identified with Clara
Glencairn de Figueroa in "El
duelo"). OC, 1051

Figueroa, Isidro (doctor,
character in Borges story).
OC, 1053, 1054, 1056

Filiberto, Juan de Dios
(Argentine musician and
historian of the tango, 1885–
1964). IA, 134–36

Filón de Alejandría (Philo,
Alexandrian philosopher, 20
B.C.–54 A.D.). OC, 720.
OCC, 957

Fingal (hero of Macpherson's
Ossianic poems). OCC, 830

Fingermann, Ema (character in
Suárez Lynch novella). OCC,
165, 180, 193

Fingermann, Kuno (character in
Bustos Domecq and Suárez

Fonseca (sergeant, character in Bustos Domecq story). OCC, 443–45

Foppens, Francisco (17th century publisher in Brussels). TE, 123

Ford, Myriam Allen de. See Allen, Myriam

Forkel (character in Bustos Domecq story). OCC, 286

Forkel, Johannes (German theologian, 1799–1846, an ancestor of Otto Dietrich zur Linde in Borges story, perhaps based on the German musician of the same name, 1749–1818). OC, 576

Forkel, Ulrich (ancestor of Otto Dietrich zur Linde, d. 1870). OC, 576

Formento, José (character in Bustos Domecq stories). OCC, 48–61, 120n.

Forster, Edward Morgan (English novelist, 1879–1970, author of Passage to India, Howard's End, Aspects of the Novel and other works). OCC, 856. P, 116

Forster, John (English biographer and critic, 1812–1876, author of a Life of Charles Dickens). P, 83

Fort, Paul (French poet, 1872–1960, author of Ballades francaises). OC, 618. OCC, 470n.

Fortinbras (character in Shakespeare's Hamlet). OCC, 819

Fosco, Isidoro (Italian noble-man, consul in Buenos Aires, character in Bustos Domecq story). OCC, 64, 65, 81

Foucher, Alfred (French writer on Buddhism). OC, 741, 742. OCC, 780

Fouillée, Alfred (French philosopher, 1838–1912, author of La Liberté et le Déterminisme and other works). OC, 367

Foxe, John (English religious figure, 1517–1587, author of the Book of Martyrs). OP, 426

Fragueiro (old Buenos Aires family). P, 78

Frambuesa, Nano (character in Bustos Domecq story). OCC, 184

France, Anatole (pseud. of Jacques-Anatole-Francois Thibault, French writer, 1844–1924, author of La Vie littéraire, L'Ile des pingouins, Les Dieux ont soif and other works). OCC, 39, 78, 496, 847

Francesca da Rimini (Italian noblewoman whose love for Paolo is narrated in Dante's Inferno). C, 73. NED, 88, 100, 119–23, 153, 158. PB, 183. SN, 21–25

Francia, Gaspar Rodríguez de (Paraguayan dictator, 1766–1840). OC, 726. OCC, 834. P, 36, 132

Francisco de Asís, San (Italian monk and reformer, 1182–1226). OC, 937. OCC, 765, 851. NED, 148

Francisco de Sales, San (French priest, bishop and doctor of the church, 1567–1622). OC, 446n.

Francisco de Vitoria. See Vitoria, Francisco de

Frank, Waldo (American writer, 1889–1967, author of numerous novels and travel books and a co-founder of Sur). P, 117. PB, 124

Frauwallner, Erich (Austrian scholar of Buddhism, b. 1898, author of Philosophie des Buddhismus and other works). OCC, 753

Fray Mocho. See Alvarez, José Sixto

Frazer, James George (British anthropologist and scholar, 1854–1941, author of The Golden Bough). OC, 230. OCC, 569

Fredegario de Tours (St. Gregorius Fredegarius, bishop of Tours, 538–594, author of a history of the Franks). OC, 574

Freeman, John (American
literary critic, 1880–1929,
author of a book on Robert
Frost).    P, 117, 118
Frégoli.    OCC, 49, 209
Freud, Sigmund (Austrian
psychoanalyst and writer,
1856–1939).    OC, 464, 687,
727.    OCC, 840.    OP, 419.
P, 137.    PB, 122, 236
Freyja (Scandinavian goddess
of love and of the night).
OCC, 930, 955
Freyr (Scandinavian god of
fertility, rain and
sunshine).    OCC, 699n.
Frías, Carlos (editor
at Emecé, publisher of
Borges).    OC, 975
Friedrich, Hugo (German
literary critic, b. 1904,
author of *Die Rechts-*
*metaphysik der Gottlichen*
*Komodie* as well as studies
of Flaubert, Stendhal,
Abbé Prevost, Balzac and
and other French writers).
NED, 114–15
Frigg (Frigga, Scandinavian
goddess of the hearth, wife
of Odin).    OCC, 928
Frithjof (hero of a 14th
century Icelandic saga).
OCC, 965
Frogman, Marcelo N. (character
in Bustos Domecq and Suárez
Lynch stories, editor of *El*
*malón,* also called by
numerous aliases and
nicknames).    OCC, 149, 157,
163–65, 169–70, 173–79, 181,
183, 184, 188, 189, 190, 195,
402
Frost, Beatriz (character in
Borges story).    LA, 54, 55,
56, 60, 62
Frost, Robert (American poet,
1874–1963, author of *North of*
*Boston* and other works).
OC, 1014.    C, 11.    OP, 459.
P, 147
Froude, James Anthony (English
scholar and writer, 1818–
1894, author of the
miscellaneous essays of *Short*
*Studies on Great Subjects* as

well as works on Australia,
the West Indies and Ireland
and studies of Erasmus and
Carlyle).    SN, 134
Frugoni, Emilio (Uruguayan poet
and drama critic, 1880–1969).
OCC, 471, 502
Frute (Danish hero in the
*Gudrun*).    OCC, 917
Frutos, don (character in
*Paulino Lucero*).    OC, 184
Fu-Man-Chu.    OCC, 396
Fuego (god of fire in Borges
story).    OC, 453
Fuehrer.    See Hitler
Fulano (somebody or another,
the first member of the
Spanish trio of Fulano,
Mengano and Sutano).    OCC,
350, 369
Fuller, Margaret (American
feminist, social reformer and
writer, 1810–1850).    OC, 684
Fumasoli.    OCC, 94
Funes, Gregorio (Argentine
politician and historian,
1740–1829).    P, 131
Funes, Ireneo (character in
Borges story).    OC, 483,
485–90.    PB, 167–68
Funes, María Clementina
(character in Borges story,
mother of Ireneo Funes).
OC, 486, 489
Fung Yu-Lan (author of *A*
*Short History of Chinese*
*Philosophy,* 1948).    C, 105
Furias (the three Furies of
classical mythology, also
called Erinyes or Parcae).
OCC, 585
Fursa (Irish monk whose
visions are narrated in
Bede's history).    OCC, 883–
84.    NED, 128
Furt, Jorge M. (Argentine
historian, critic and
folklorist, editor of a two
volume *Cancionero popular*
*rioplatense* and author of
works on Hernández,
Echeverría, Tejeda and
others).    I, 63.    TE, 75
Fuseli, Henry (English painter
and writer of Swiss-German
origin, 1741–1825, painter of

"Nightmare," "Hamlet Breaking
from his Attendants to follow
the Ghost" and numerous other
works).   SN, 42

Fussell, Ronald  (author of *The
Buddha and his Path to Self-
Enlightenment*, 1955).   OCC,
780

Fustel  (black knife-fighter
mentioned by Ernesto T.
Marcó).   OC, 169

Fylgia  (Norse monster which
takes the form of an animal
and appears in dreams).   PB,
200

Fyris  (fire in Scandinavian
mythology).   OCC, 955

G., C.  See Guerrero, Concepción

Gaboriau, Emile  (French writer
of detective novels, 1835–
1873, author of *Monsieur
Lecoq* and *L'Affaire Lerouge*).
OCC, 15.   P, 47

Gabriel  (archangel).   OC, 325

Gabriel, José  (Argentine
novelist and critic, b. 1896,
author of *Evaristo Carriego,
su vida y su obra*, 1921).
OC, 103, 115, 122, 128.   TE,
27

Gabriel y Galán, José María
(Spanish poet, 1870–1905).
IA, 60

Gabrielle  (character in the
film *The Petrified Forest*,
1936).   BC, 42

Gache, Roberto  (Argentine
dramatist and essayist, 1891–
1966, author of *Glosario de
la farsa urbana, Baile y
filosofía* and other works).
OCC, 78

Gaiferos  (kinsman of Roland
and husband of Charlemagne's
daughter Melisenda, subject
of many Spanish ballads).
OCC, 80, 357

Gaitero de Hamelin  (Pied Piper of
Hamelin, legendary figure who
became the subject of a
Browning poem).   P, 141

Galahad  (knight in Arthurian
legend).   OCC, 200.   BC, 78

Galatea  (in Greek mythology, a
nymph beloved of the cyclops
Polyphemus).   OCC, 666

Gale, Gabriel  (character in
Chesterton story).   PB, 140

Galeano, Avelino  (knife-fighter
in Buenos Aires).   OC, 128n.

Galileo Galilei  (Italian
astronomer and philosopher,
1564–1642).   OC, 716n.
OCC, 824.   C, 51

Gallach.   OCC, 135

Gallach y Gasset.   OCC, 328

Galland, Antoine  (French
Orientalist, 1646–1715,
translator of the *Arabian
Nights*).   OC, 397–401, 406,
407, 412, 413, 629, 731.   P,
68.   SN, 61, 66, 71, 72, 73

Gallegani.   OCC, 174

Gallo Celestial  (Chinese
creature).   OCC, 633

Gallostra y Frau, José  (Spanish
jurist and orator, 1833–
1888).   OCC, 190

Galsworthy, John  (British playwright and novelist, 1867–
1933, author of the *Forsyte
Saga* and other works).   OCC,
936

Gálvez, Manuel  (Argentine
novelist, 1882–1962, author
of *El mal metafísico, Nacha
Regules* and dozens of other
works).   TE, 23, 152

Gama, Vasco da  (Portuguese
navigator, c.1469–1524).
PB, 239, 242, 243, 244

Gandharvas  (Vedic mythological
figures).   OCC, 604

Gandhi, Mohandas Karamchand
(Indian politician and
writer, 1869–1948).   OC,
222.   OCC, 745.   BC, 28.
ILN, 22.   SN, 90

Gandía, Enrique de  (Argentine
historian, b. 1906, author of
*Historia de la conquista del
Río de la Plata y del
Paraguay* and the ten volumes
of *Historia de las ideas
políticas en la Argentina*).
OCC, 65, 357

Gangleri  (assumed name of
Gylfi in the *Gylfaginning*,
part of the *Prose Edda*).
OCC, 953

Gannon, Patricio  (Argentine
writer, journalist and

cattleman, b. 1901, author of
*Poets of the Rhymers Club* and
editor of the *Argentine
Anthology of Modern Verse*).
OC, 571, 573

Gantry, Elmer (main character
in Sinclair Lewis novel).
ILN, 35

Garay, Antártido A. (architect,
character in Bustos Domecq
story). OCC, 340–43

Garay, Clemente (thug in Buenos
Aires). OC, 1126

Garbe, Richard von (German
scholar, 1857–1927, author of
works on the *Bhagavadgita,*
the *Mahabharata,* and of
*Contributions of Buddhism to
Christianity*, 1911). OCC,
730, 731, 733

Garbo, Greta (Swedish film
actress, b. 1905). OC, 222,
284. BC, 28, 72

García Calderón, Ventura
(Peruvian critic and writer,
1885–1959). OCC, 480

García Lorca, Federico (Spanish
poet and playwright, 1898–
1936). OCC, 45. PB, 122

Garcilaso de la Vega (Spanish
poet, 1501?–1536, important
for popularizing the new
Italian style in Spanish).
OC, 268, 858. OCC, 467,
468. I, 74, 97. PB, 232.
TE, 71, 119–20

Garcin de Tassy (French translator of Farid ud-din Attar's
*Mantiq al-Tayr*). OC, 418n.

Gardel, Carlos (Argentine
tango singer, composer and
film actor, 1887–1935).
OCC, 189, 357, 400

Gardner, Erle Stanley (American
novelist, 1889–1970, writer
of detective novels about
Perry Mason). ILN, 57

Gardner, Martin (American
mathematician and writer, b.
1914, editor of Lewis
Carroll). P, 108

Garduña (pseud. of Zúñiga).
OCC, 449

Garfunkel (character in Bustos
Domecq story). OCC, 395,
396

Garibaldi, Giuseppe (Italian
patriot, 1807–1882, of whom
there is a statue in Plaza
Italia in Buenos AIres).
OC, 108. OCC, 179

Garmendia (character in Borges
story). OC, 1034, 1035,
1036

Garmendia, doctor (character
in Bustos Domecq story).
OCC, 307

Garmr (Scandinavian
mythological dog). OCC, 602

Garnier (French publisher of
Spanish works). OC, 113.
OCC, 471. LA, 11

Garófalo (singer). OCC,
400

Garrett (sheriff who befriended
and later killed Billy the
Kid). OC, 318–19

Garrido. OCC, 448

Garrod, Heathcote William
(British literary critic, b.
1878, author of studies of
Keats, Collins, Housman and
others). OC, 717, 718

Garuda (Hindu mythological
bird). OCC, 634

Garulf (Frisian prince). OCC,
792

Garzón (Spanish lexicographer).
OCC, 156. TE, 137

Gastambide, doctor. OCC, 318

Gatsby, Jay (character in
Fitzgerald novel *The Great
Gatsby*). ILN, 41

Gauss (maiden name of Aarón
Loewenthal's wife). OC, 567

Gautama (family name of
Siddhartha, called the Buddha
after his enlightenment).
OC, 1093. OCC, 722, 729,
730, 757, 775. OP, 437.
SN, 77, 79

Gautier, Marguerite (the "dame
aux camélias," character in
Dumas novel). ILN, 55

Gauweloose. OCC, 57

Gawain (knight in Arthurian
legend, hero of Middle
English poem *Sir Gawain and
the Green Knight*). OCC,
814

Geirrod (king in the *Elder
Edda*). OCC, 929

Gelio, Aulo (Aulus Gellius, Roman writer, c.130-180, author of *Noctes Atticae*). OC, 277. P, 25-26

Gemisto (Georgius Gemistus Pletho, Greek Platonic philosopher and scholar, c.1355-1450). OC, 766

Genghis Khan (Mongol emperor of China, 1162-1227, also called Jenghiz, Jingis or the Gran Khan). OC, 153, 155, 418n. OCC, 589, 705. NED, 142. PB, 179

Genio (genie in *Arabian Nights*). SN, 68-69

Gentle Maggie (woman in New York gang). OC, 312

Genzmer, Felix (German scholar, 1878-1959, translator of *Elder Edda*). OCC, 975

Geoffrey of Monmouth (English chronicler, c.1100-1154, author of *Historia Regum Britanniae*). OCC, 936

George, Stefan (German poet, 1863-1933). OC, 251, 280, 666, 686, 691. OCC, 974. P, 125

Geraldine, Colonel (character in Stevenson's *New Arabian Nights*). SN, 73

Gerardo (Benedictine monk of St. Gall, later bishop). OCC, 919

Gerardo de Gales (Giraldus Cambrensis, medieval Welsh historian, c.1146-1220, author of *Topographia Hibernica, Expugnatio Hibernica* and *Itinerarium Cambrense*). OCC, 949

Gerbillon, Jean (French Jesuit missionary in China, 1654-1707). OC, 644

Gerchunoff, Alberto (Argentine writer, 1884-1950, author of *Los gauchos judíos* and other works). OC, 259. P, 66-67

Gerhardt, Johann (German Lutheran divine, 1582-1637, author of numerous polemical and exegetical works). IA, 51

Gering, Hugo (19th century German translator of the Eddas). OC, 381, 851. OCC, 965n., 966n., 975

Gerión (Geryon, monster with three bodies or three heads, slain by Hercules). OCC, 700

Gernot (character in the *Nibelungenlied*). OCC, 912, 914

Gernsback, Hugo (American science fiction writer, 1884-1967). ILN, 58

Gerónimo, San. See Jerónimo.

Gertrude or Geruth (Danish queen, Hamlet's mother). OCC, 820, 972-73

Geseminus (here a misprint for Heinrich Friedrich Wilhelm Gesenius, German orientalist and Biblical critic, 1786-1842, author of numerous works on the Hebrew and Maltese languages, on the Samaritans and Syrians, as well as commentaries on the Pentateuch and Isaiah). OC, 576n.

Gesner, Konrad von (German-Swiss writer and naturalist, 1516-1565, author of *Enchiridion historiae plantarum, Bibliotheca universalis, Historia animalium* and other works). OCC, 622

Ghazad Mahmud. See Mahmud

Ghazali, al- (Persian theologian and mystic, sometimes called Algazel, 1058-1111, author of the *Tahafut-ul-Tahafut* or *Incoherence of the Philosophers*). OC, 582, 705, 715

Gibbon, Edward (English historian, 1737-1794, author of the *Decline and Fall of the Roman Empire* and other works). OC, 107n., 211, 217, 219, 235, 236, 270, 557n., 629, 692. OCC, 357, 826-27, 868, 872-73, 899, 969-70. A, 24. ILN, 15. LA, 81. NED, 126. P, 37, 68-74, 141, 157. PB, 139. SN, 16

Gide, André (French writer, 1869-1951, author of *Les Faux-Monnayeurs*, *L'Immoraliste*, a *Journal* and other works). OC, 281, 398, 410, 674. OCC, 468. A, 68

Gigante, Tatú (nickname for character in Bustos Domecq). OCC, 125

Giganti-Tomassoni (singer). OCC, 400

Gigena, Rufino (character in Bustos Domecq story). OCC, 59

Gigon, Olof (philosopher, b. 1912, author of *Ursprang der griechischen Philosophie*). OC, 636

Gilbert, Stuart (British writer, author of *James Joyce's Ulysses, a Study*, 1930). OC, 232. OCC, 854. PB, 161, 168

Gilchrist, Arthur (translator of the *Elder Edda*). OCC, 975

Gildas (British historian, called "The Wise," d. 570, author of *De Excidio et Conquestu Britanniae*). OCC, 868

Giles, Herbert Allen (British scholar of China, 1845-1935, author of *Chuang Tzu, a Short History of Chinese Literature* and other works). OC, 255, 634, 679, 768, 772. OCC, 580

Gillygaloo (fabulous bird of North America). OCC, 631

Gilson, Etienne (French philosopher and scholar, b. 1884, author of studies of medieval philosophy, Descartes, Aquinas and other subjects). OC, 775

Ginebra (Guinevere, British queen of Arthurian legend). OCC 814. C, 73

Ginsburg, Christian David (English Hebrew scholar, born in Warsaw, 1831-1914, author of a critical study of the *Massorah*, as well as *Facsimiles of Manuscripts of the Hebrew Bible* and *The Text of the Hebrew Bible in Abbreviations*). OC, 1029

Ginzberg or Ginsburg (alias of Scharlach in Borges story, the name being derived from that of Christian David Ginsburg). OC, 501, 507

Ginzberg, Santiago (character in Bustos Domecq story). OCC, 336-39, 349

Gioberti, Vincenzo (Italian philosopher and politician, 1801-1852, author of *Del primato morale e civile degli italiani* and other works). NED, 102n. PB, 182n.

Giorello (Carriego's mother's maiden name). OC, 114

Giotto di Bondone (Italian painter, c.1226-1337). OC, 1055

Girón, Pedro. See Téllez Girón

Girondo, Eduardo. P, 52

Girondo, Oliverio (Argentine poet, 1891-1963, author of *Veinte poemas para ser leídos en el tranvía*, *Calcomanías* and other works). OCC, 497, 499. I, 11, 126. TE, 92-95

Girri, Alberto (Argentine poet, b. 1918). A, 7, 84

Giselher (character in the *Nibelungenlied*). OCC, 912, 914

Gitanilla, la (character in a Cervantes exemplary novel). P, 46

Giusti, Roberto F. (Argentine essayist and critic, 1887-1978, co-founder and editor of the periodical *Nosotros*). OC, 113, 116. OCC, 320

Gizur Thorvaldsson (Snorri Sturluson's son's father-in-law). OCC, 951

Gjuki (German prince in the *Volsunga Saga*). OCC, 968

Glam (character in the *Egils Saga*). OCC, 938

Glanvill, Joseph (British divine and writer, 1636-1680, author of *The Vanity of Dogmatizing, Lux Orientalis* and *Saducismus Triumphans*). OC, 638

Glatzer, Nahum (Jewish scholar, author of *In Time and Eternity* and other works). OC, 696n.

Glauco (Glaucus of Anthedon in Boeotia, a Greek mythological figure who wooed Scylla in vain). OCC, 626

Glauco (Glaucus of Corinth, son of Sisyphus and father of Bellerophon). OCC, 685

Glencairn (general, ancestor of Clara Glencairn de Figueroa in Borges story). OC, 1056

Glencairn, David Alexander (Scottish military man in India, character in Borges story, perhaps descended from the earls of Glencairn). OC, 612-16

Glencairn de Figueroa, Clara (character in Borges story). OC, 1053-57

Glencoe, Alejandro (character in Borges story, president of the "Congreso"). LA, 39-63

Glendening (author of *Teach Yourself Icelandic*). OCC, 974

Glora (Lorikus's wife in the *Prose Edda*). OCC, 953

Gloriana (name for Elizabeth I in *The Faerie Queene*). OC, 418. See also Isabel de Inglaterra

Glums (winged race in Paltock's *Peter Wilkins*). OCC, 710

Glus, Molly. OCC, 430

Gnomos (race of diminutive spirits that live in the earth, described by Paracelsus). OCC, 636, 694

Godel, Roberto (Argentine poet, author of *Nacimiento del fuego*). OC, 1044. P, 75-76

Godofredo (Godfrey of Bouillon, character in Tasso's *Gerusalemme* poems). OC, 265n.

Godric (Saxon warrior in the *Battle of Maldon*). OCC, 887

Goebbels, Paul Joseph (Nazi propagandist, 1897-1945). OC, 724

Goering, Hermann Wilhelm (Nazi leader, 1893-1946). OC, 723. PB, 158

Goethe, Johann Wolfgang von (German poet and writer, 1749-1832, author of *Faust, Egmont, Iphigenie auf Tauris, Wilhelm Meisters Lehrjahre* and other works). OC, 186, 279, 280, 420, 473, 577, 666, 698, 754, 762, 773, 1116. OCC, 300, 303, 333, 818, 819, 829, 830, 837, 911, 918, 965. BC, 60. BO, 20, 24, 33, 34, 57, 83, 95. CONJ, 29. I, 43, 94, 137, 144, 146, 149. IA, 13, 15. ILN, 21. OP, 392. P, 38, 45-46, 50, 84, 112, 126, 171. PB, 146, 168, 197, 229. SN, 125, 137, 159-60. TE, 12, 31. VA, 15

Gog (prince of Meshech and Tubal in the Bible who, with Magog, represents the nations of the earth deceived by Satan). OC, 585

Goldoni, Carlo (Italian writer of stage comedies, 1707-1793). OC, 619. OCC, 330

Goldsmith, Oliver (Anglo-Irish writer, 1730?-1774, author of the *Vicar of Wakefield* and other works). OCC, 301, 304

Golem (being of Jewish legend created from a magic combination of letters). OC, 885-887. OCC, 637-38

Gólgota (nickname). See Marpurgo

Goliádkin (character in Bustos Domecq story). OCC, 35-47

Gollancz, Victor (British writer, b. 1893, author of numerous works on religion, education and politics). OC, 414

Golosa (character in unfinished novel of Nierenstein Souza). OCC, 313

Golpe de Furca (character in Suárez Lynch). OCC, 174

Gomensoro (minor character in Borges-Bioy filmscript). OCC, 226

Gomensoro (family, characters in Nierenstein Souza's historical novel *El feudo de los Gomensoro*). OCC, 311

Gomensoro, Ernesto (character in Bustos Domecq story, author of "En camino!," "En Belén," "Yo alecciono," "La alfombra de esmeralda," "Pan de centeno" and other poems collected in *Antología*). OCC, 433-37

Gómez (old Buenos Aires family). P, 78

Gómez, Juan Carlos (Uruguayan politician, journalist and romantic poet, 1820-1884, author of *El cedro y la palma*). P, 133. PB, 129, 213

Gómez de Huerta, Geróimo (Spanish poet and translator, 1568?-1643, who translated Pliny in 1599). OCC, 686n.

Gómez de la Serna, Ramón (Spanish writer, 1888-1963, author of *greguerías*, an autobiography, *Automoribundia*, numerous biographies, novels and plays). I, 15-17, 24, 73, 93, 124-26. IA, 150. PB, 142. TE, 86, 95

Gómez Pereira, Antonio (Spanish physician and philosopher, 1500-1558, author of *Antoniana Margarita*. I, 117n.

Gomperz, Theodor (German philosopher and classical scholar, b. 1832, author of numerous studies of Herodotus, Plato, Epicurus, Heraclitus and others). OC, 258, 713. OCC, 691

Goncourt (here a reference to both brothers, Edmond and Jules Alfred). OCC, 319. P, 26n. PB, 160, 218

Goncourt, Edmond (French novelist and man of letters, 1822-1896). OCC, 850

Goncourt, Jules Alfred (French novelist and man of letters, 1830-1870). OCC, 850

Goneril (evil daughter in *King Lear*). P, 144

Góngora, Luis de (Spanish baroque poet, 1561-1627, author of the *Soledades*, *Fábula de Polifemo y Galatea* and other works). OC, 122n., 151, 204, 219, 243, 249, 384, 660, 670. OCC, 66, 75, 467, 468, 480, 666, 818, 936, 952. CONJ, 13, 81, 83. I, 11, 25, 36, 37, 44, 45, 75. IA, 56, 61, 66, 68-73, 84-85, 87, 92, 123-24, 131, 174. NED, 86, 120n., 136n. P, 53, 75, 76, 78, 79, 86, 110, 120, 124, 171. PB, 147, 230, 232. SN, 45, 47, 104. TE, 40, 68, 70, 123-30, 146

Gongu-Hrolf (hero of an Icelandic saga). OCC, 971

González, Juan (knife-fighter in Buenos Aires). OC, 129n.

González, Juana. OC, 284n.

González, Justo (knife-fighter in Buenos Aires). OC, 129n.

González Baralt (lawyer in Bustos Domecq). OCC, 422, 425, 437

González Blanco, Andrés (Spanish novelist and critic, 1886-1924, author of *Los contemporáneos*). OCC, 77

González de Salas, José (Spanish humanist, 1588-1651, author of *Nueva idea de la tragedia antigua* and other works). P, 123

González Lanuza, Eduardo (Argentine poet and critic, b. in Spain in 1900, author of *Prismas*, *Aquelarre* and other works). OCC, 497. I, 96-99, 160. PB, 166

González Tuñón, Raúl (Argentine poet, 1905-1974, author of *El violín del diablo*, *La calle del agujero en la media* and *La rosa blindada*). OC, 653

Goofang (strange fish of North America). OCC, 631

Goofus Bird (bird of North America which flies backwards). OCC, 631

Gordon, E. V. (British medieval scholar, 1896-1938, author of an *Introduction to Old Norse*

and editor of various Old and
Middle English poems). OCC,
976

Gordon, Robert Kay (British
scholar, editor of *Anglo-
Saxon Poetry*). OC, 381.
OCC, 975

Gorgias (Greek sophist
philosopher, c.483–376).
BO, 15

Gorgonas (Medusa and her
sisters Sthenno and Euryale
in Greek mythology). OCC,
603

Gosse, Edmund (English writer
and biographer, 1849–1928,
author of *Father and Son,
Northern Studies* and other
works). OC, 250, 259, 650.
OCC, 932

Gosse, Philip (British writer,
1879–1959, author of *The
History of Piracy, The
Pirates' Who's Who* and other
works). OC, 345

Gosse, Philip Henry (English
scientist, father of Edmund
Gosse, 1810–1888). OC, 650–
52

Gottfried de Estrasburgo
(Gottfried von Strassburg,
German poet, d. c.1210,
author of *Tristan*). OCC,
908

Gotuso (singer). OCC, 400

Goudron, Padre (Jesuit, alias
of Bogle in Borges's account
of the story of the Tichborne
Claimant). OC, 304

Gounod, Charles Francois
(French composer for the
opera, 1818–1893, composer of
*Faust*). OC, 186

Gourmont, Remy de (French
critic and novelist, 1858–
1915, author of *Le Livre des
masques, Promenades
littéraires* and other works).
OC, 240, 259. OCC, 562.
IA, 57. PB, 169. TE, 50

Gouvea (singer). OCC, 400

Goya y Lucientes, Francisco
José de (Spanish painter,
1746–1828). OCC, 450

Goyena, Pedro (Argentine
literary critic, 1843–1892,

author of *Crítica literaria*).
OCC, 137

Grabher, Carlo (Italian
scholar, editor of Dante's
*Divina commedia* ). SN, 13

Gracián y Morales, Baltasar
(Spanish writer, 1601–1658,
author of *El criticón,
Oráculo manual y arte de
prudencia, Agudeza o arte de
ingenio* and other works).
OC, 150, 202, 203, 249, 291,
370, 748, 881–82. OCC, 319,
943, 956–57. I, 13, 37, 43,
132, 146. IA, 73, 157, 174.
NED, 107. P, 53, 110, 112,
126. PB, 117, 162, 232

Graebner, Fritz (German
anthropologist, author of
*Anthropologie, Methode der
ethnologie* and other works).
IA, 12. TE, 18, 47

Graffiacane (minor character
in Bustos Domecq story).
OCC, 402

Grajales, la (character in the
*Buscón*). TE, 142

Gran Khan. See Genghis Khan

Gran Perfil. See Feinberg

Granada, Daniel (Uruguayan
lexicographer, 1849–1929,
author of *Vocabulario
rioplatense razonado*, 1889).
OCC, 156

Grande, Chicho (subject of Bustos Domecq's *Vida y muerte de
don Chicho Grande*). OCC, 13

Grandvilliers-Lagrange, Alexis
(baron, character in Bustos
Domecq story). OCC, 384,
389, 390

Grandvilliers-Lagrange, Chantal
(character in Bustos Domecq
story). OCC, 384, 385, 388,
391

Grandvilliers-Lagrange, Gaston
(character in Bustos Domecq
story). OCC, 384, 385, 387,
388

Grandvilliers-Lagrange,
Jacqueline (character in
Bustos Domecq story). OCC,
384, 385, 387–91

Grandvilliers-Lagrange (family,
characters in Bustos Domecq
story). OCC, 382–90

Grani (name in runic inscription). OCC, 924. PB, 190

Grant, Ulysses S. (U. S. general and president, 1822–1885). ILN, 63

Graves, Robert (English poet, novelist and critic, 1895–1985, author of *The White Goddess, I, Claudius* and other works). OCC, 855. A, 51–53. ILN, 41. SN, 59

Gray, Dorian (character in Oscar Wilde novel). OCC, 977

Gray, Thomas (English poet, 1716–1771). OCC, 928

Greco, Vicente (tango composer, 1888–1924, author of "El cuzquito," "Rodríguez Peña," "La viruta" and other works). OC, 139, 159, 165, 889

Green, Julien (French writer, b. 1900, author of *Léviathan, Epaves, Minuit* and other works). OC, 464

Green Knight (Bercilak de Hautdesert, character in *Sir Gawain and the Green Knight*). OCC, 814

Greene, Graham (English novelist and dramatist, b. 1904, author of *The Heart of the Matter, A Burnt-Out Case* and numerous other works). P, 102

Gregorio de Valencia (Jesuit theologian). OC, 701

Gregorio Magno (Gregory the Great, saint and pope, c.540–604, author of various epistles, dialogues and homilies). OC, 737

Gregorio Nazianzeno, San (St. Gregory of Nazianzus, Theologus, one of the four great fathers of the Eastern Church, 329–389). OCC, 956

Gregorovius, Ferdinand (German historian and writer, 1821–1891, author of *Geschichte der Stadt Rom im Mittelalter, Lucrezia Borgia* and other works). OC, 522. OCC, 321

Grendel (monster in *Beowulf*). OCC, 811, 871–72, 874

Grettir (Grettir the Strong, hero of the Icelandic saga *Gretla* or *Grettir Saga*). OC, 368. OCC, 934, 938. P, 113

Greve, Felix Paul (German translator of the *Arabian Nights*). OC, 410, 411

Grey, Zachary (British writer, 1688–1766). OCC, 602

Grey, Zane (American novelist, 1875–1939, author of *Desert Gold* and numerous other works). ILN, 61

Griffith, D. W. (American film director, 1874–1948, director of *Birth of a Nation* and many other films). BC, 65

Grifo (griffin or gryphon, fabulous animal). OCC, 639–40, 666–67, 917. NED, 149–50, 158. OP, 522

Grimal, Pierre (French classical scholar, b. 1912, author of a *Diccionnaire de la mythologie grecque et romaine*). OC, 228n. OCC, 696

Grimm, George (German Orientalist, 1868–1945, author of *Die Lehre des Buddha, Buddhistische Weisheit* and other works). OCC, 780. I, 94, 95

Grimm, Jakob (German linguist and folklorist, 1785–1863, author of *Deutsche Grammatik* and *Deutsche Mythologie*, and compiler with his brother Wilhelm, 1786–1859, of the *Kinder- und Hausmarchen* and *Deutschen Sagen*). OC, 695. OCC, 312, 598, 963, 966

Grimmelshausen, Johann Hans Jakob Christoffel von (German writer, 1622–1676, author of *Der abenteurliche Simplicissimus Teutsch* and other works). OCC, 591

Grisebach, Eduard (German diplomat and writer, 1845–1906, author of *Der neue Tanhauser, Der Tanhauer in Rom* and a biography of

Schopenhauer). OC, 367, 1064. IA, 81. TE, 118

Grisebach, Johannes (character in Borges story). VA, 19-25

Grondona (warden of prison where Isidro Parodi is held). OCC, 23, 44-45, 51, 71

Grondona, Mariana (Argentine writer, author of *El chal violeta y otros relatos*). OC, 1098

Gropius, Walter (German-American architect, 1883-1969). OCC, 333. BC, 55

Grosso Grant, José C. (Argentine historian, author of *La constitución debe regirnos: Alberdi, Estrada, Bas*). OC, 1029. OCC, 65

Groussac, Paul (Argentine writer, born in France, 1848-1929, author of *El viaje intelectual* and other works and editor of *La Biblioteca*). OC, 105, 106, 132n., 177, 186, 203, 233-34, 419, 421, 655, 667, 682, 810, 1010, 1022, 1144. OCC, 80, 485, 500, 558, 801, 892-93, 933, 943. IA, 141, 170. P, 26n., 28, 38, 44, 67, 89-90, 91, 98, 113, 132, 139, 147. PB, 125, 131, 160, 169, 170, 175, 176, 192, 228, 245. SN, 18, 35, 40, 146, 147, 150, 156, 157. TE, 7

Grousset, René (French Orientalist and historian, 1885-1952). OC, 153

Grunberg, Carlos M. (Argentine poet, 1903-1968, author of *Mester de judería* and other works). P, 77-80. PB, 166

Grundtvig, Nikolai Frederik Severin (Danish poet, statesman and divine, 1783-1872, author of works on the Eddas and Norse mythology as well as hymns and pamphlets for the Danish church). OCC, 871

Gryphius (alias of Scharlach in Borges story, derived from Andreas Gryphius, German lyric poet and dramatist, 1616-1664, author of *Absurda Comica, Horribilicribrifax* and other works). OC, 502, 507

Gudrun (hero of the *Volsunga saga*). OCC, 915, 916-18, 924, 934, 939, 949, 966, 968-69. PB, 197

Guedalla, Phillip (British historian and biographer, 1889-1944). OC, 414, 464

Guemes, Martín Miguel de (Argentine general, 1785-1821). P, 64, 136, 138

Guérin, Maurice de (French poet, 1810-1839, author of *Le Centaure*). OCC, 837

Guermantes (family in Proust's *Recherche*). OCC, 440

Guerrero, Concepción (woman to whom Borges dedicated various poems, later reduced to her initials, C. G.). OC, 46

Guerrero, Margarita (friend and collaborator of Borges). OC, 631. OCC, 514, 569

Guevara, José (Spanish priest who lived for a time in Argentina and Paraguay, 1719-1806). OCC, 485

Guido, José Tomás (Argentine military man and diplomat, 1788-1866). OCC, 559

Guido y Spano, Carlos (Argentine poet and journalist, 1827-1918). OCC, 338, 347, 502. P, 29

Guillén, Alberto (Peruvian poet, 1897-1935). I, 126

Guillermo I (William the Conqueror, English king, 1027?-1087, also called Guillermo el Bastardo and Guillermo de Normandía). OC, 689, 726, 1140. OCC, 834, 895, 937. OP, 546. P, 36

Guillermo de Occam. See Occam, Guillermo de

Guillermo el Bastardo. See Guillermo I

Guillermo Juan. See Borges, Guillermo Juan

Guillermone, Virgilio (scholar cited in Bustos Domecq's preface to Suárez Lynch, a reference to Homero

Guglielmini, Argentine professor, essayist, poet, dramatist and journalist, 1903-1968). OCC, 146

Guillinbursti (boar in Scandinavian mythology). OCC, 699n.

Guiraldes, Ricardo (Argentine novelist and poet, 1886-1927, author best known for *Don Segundo Sombra*). OC, 114, 132n., 155, 194, 196, 271, 620, 733, 735, 746, 833, 988, 1069. OCC, 321. I, 57. IA, 78, 117, 177. ILN, 9, 28. P, 7, 42, 60, 63, 91, 98, 130. PB, 124, 134, 154, 166, 170, 186-88. TE, 7, 24, 85-87, 112

Gullinkambi (rooster in Norse mythology that awakes the heroes at Ragnarok). OCC, 926

Gulliver, Lemuel (character in Swift romance). OC, 422, 1022. LA, 125. VA, 45

Gundolf, Friedrich (pseud. of Friedrich Gundelfinger, German writer, 1880-1931, disciple of Stefan George and author of studies of Goethe, George, and *Shakespeare und der deutsche Geist*). OC, 280

Gunnar (character in the *Volsunga Saga*). OCC, 924, 966, 968-70, 970. PB, 197

Gunnar de Hlitharen (character in the *Njals Saga*). OCC, 932-33

Gunnlaug (character in the *Gunnlaugssaga Ormstungu*). OCC, 936-37

Gunnlaug (Icelandic skald and warrior). OCC, 948. PB, 190

Gunnlaug (king in Borges story). LA, 113, 114-15, 119

Gunnlaug (warrior mentioned in runic inscription). OCC, 924

Gunther (character in the *Nibelungenlied*). OCC, 912-14, 919, 920

Gustavo Adolfo (Gustavus II Adolphus of Sweden, Swedish king, 1594-1632). OC, 853

Guthrie family (characters in Borges story). See Gutre

Guthrum (also known as Godrum, king of East Anglia, d. 890, conquered by Alfred the Great and then baptized). CONJ, 15

Gutiérrez, Carlos (brother of Eduardo). PB, 153

Gutiérrez, Eduardo (Argentine popular novelist, 1851-1889, author of *Juan Moreira, Hormiga Negra* and other works). OC, 79, 115, 165, 670, 684, 735, 1042. OCC, 558. BC, 57. BO, 73. IA, 101. ILN, 60. P, 31, 40, 64, 82, 113. PB, 134, 152-55, 187, 231. TE, 8, 26

Gutiérrez, Ricardo (Argentine poet, 1838-1896, author of *La fibra salvaje*, "El Misionero," "La oración" and other works, brother of Eduardo). OC, 188

Gutiérrez Nájera, Manuel (Mexican poet, 1859-95). OC, 119. OCC, 465, 466, 468, 478. OP, 479

Gutiérrez Solana, José (Spanish poet and painter, 1886-1945). I, 126

Gutre family (characters in Borges story). OC, 1068-72

Guttorm (Gunnar's half-brother). OCC, 969

Guyau, Marie-Jean (French philosopher, 1854-1888, author of *L'Irréligion de l'avenir, La Genese de l'idée de temps* and other works). OC, 278. TE, 121

Gylfi (Swedish king who disguises himself as an old man named Gangleri in the *Gylfaginning*, part of the *Prose Edda*). OCC, 953, 954

Gynt, Peer (Norwegian peasant, character in Ibsen play). OC, 260. OCC, 702. NED, 110

Gyp (pseud. of Marie-
Antoinette de Riquetti de
Mirabeau, French comic and
satirical novelist, 1850–
1932). P, 83
H. B. D. See Bustos Domecq
Habicht (German translator of
part of the *Arabian Nights*
for the Breslau edition of
1835–1843).
Hackmann, Heinrich Friedrich
(German scholar of China,
1864–1935, author of
*Chinesische Philosophie, Der
Buddhismus* and other works).
PB, 196n.
Hadas (fairies). OCC, 641
Hades (Greek god of the under-
world). OCC, 602. OP,
455. P, 71
Hado (Fate or Destiny). OC,
883. C, 63. CONJ, 24.
OP, 505
Hadubrand (son of Hildebrand
in the *Hildebrandslied*).
OCC, 901–2
Haeckel, Ernst Heinrich
(German biologist and
philosopher, 1834–1919,
author of *Der Kampf um den
Entwicklungsgedanken,
Anthropogenie* and other
works). OC, 283
Haedo, Bernardo Juan Francisco
(cousin of the narrator in
Borges story "Funes el
memorioso"). OC, 485, 486
Haedo, Gregorio (uncle of the
narrator in Borges story
"Funes"). OC, 486
Haedo, Julio Platero
(Uruguayan poet, author of
*Inscripciones*, 1923). OC,
849
Haedo, Villegas (friend who
gave Beatriz Viterbo a
pekinese). OC, 617
Hagen (character in the
*Nibelungenlied*). OCC, 913–
15, 917, 919
Hahn, Werner (German expres-
sionist poet). I, 151–52
Hákim de Merv (Al-Moqanna, the
Veiled Prophet of Khorasan,
d. 779). OC, 101, 324–28,
402n., 594. PB, 172

Hakon, Jarl (count in the
*Heimskringla*). OCC, 961
Hakon Hakonarson (Haakon IV,
"the Old," Norwegian king,
1204–1263). OC, 741.
OCC, 950, 951, 957, 964
Halevi, Yehudá (Jehudah
Halevi, Jewish rabbi, poet
and philosopher, born in
Spain, c.1075–1141, sometimes
Judah ha-Levi or Judah
Halevy). I, 13. TE, 96
Half (legendary king in the
*Halfssaga*). OCC, 965
Hall (character in the *Njals
Saga*). OCC, 888
Hall, J. R. Clark (scholar of
Old English poetry and author
of *A Concise Anglo-Saxon
Dictionary*). OCC, 871, 974
Hall Thorarinsson (Icelandic
poet, co-author with Rognvald
of the *Hattalykill*). OCC,
957
Halldor Snorrason (oral bard
of Iceland). OCC, 935
Halleck, Henry Wager (Union
general in the U. S. Civil
War, 1815–1872). LA, 145
Halley, Edmund (English
astronomer, 1656–1742). IA,
156. ILN, 28
Hallfred (Icelandic skald who
died in Scotland). OCC, 949
Hallgerd la Hermosa (character
in the *Njals Saga*). OCC,
932
Hamadriadas (tree nymphs of
classical mythology). OCC,
673
Hamilton, Anthony or Antoine
(French classical author born
in Ireland, 1646–1720, author
of *Mémoires du comte de
Gramont, Zénéyde, Les Quatres
facardins* and other works).
OC, 731
Hamlet (prince of Denmark,
character in Shakespeare,
called Amleth or Amlodi in
earlier accounts). OC, 383,
446, 668, 669, 675, 700, 703,
755, 788. OCC, 330, 563,
569, 819, 820, 936, 972–73.
BO, 24. CONJ, 33, 44, 50.
IA, 142. LA, 36. NED,

110-11. OP, 496. P, 138, 142. PB, 154, 226. SN, 17

Hammer Purgastall, Joseph, Freiherr von (Austrian orientalist, 1774-1856, author of *Geschichte des osmanischen Reiches* and other works). SN, 64

Hammett, Dashiell (American detective novelist, 1894-1961, author of *Red Harvest, The Maltese Falcon* and other works). ILN, 57-58

Han (dynasty that ruled China from 202 B.C. to c. 220 A.D.). PB, 196

Han Yu (9th century Chinese writer cited in the *Anthologie raisonée de la littérature chinoise*). OC, 710

Handy, William Christopher (American jazz and blues musician and composer, 1873-1958, editor of *Blues: An Anthology* and author of *Father of the Blues*). OC, 295

Haniel (one of the monsters in Ezekiel's dream). OCC, 642-43

Hanna (Maronite who aided Galland in his translation of the *Arabian Nights*). OC, 397

Hannon (Hanno, Carthaginian explorer sent to West Africa before 480 B.C., of whose report a Greek version survives). OCC, 504

Hansen, Juan (owner of a restaurant, the "3 de febrero," known in the mythology of the tango as "Lo de Hansen," in the Palermo neighborhood in Buenos Aires, from 1874 to 1892). OCC, 18

Hanuman (monkey god in the *Ramayana*). OCC, 743

Haokah (Sioux god of thunder). OCC, 644

Harald, son of Tula (on runic inscription). OCC, 924. PB, 190

Harald Hardrada Sigurdarson (Harold III, Norwegian king,

d. 1066 at Stamford Bridge). OC, 542, 689, 755, 756, 798, 812. OCC, 935, 949, 958-59, 960-61, 961-62. OP, 370.

Harald Harfagar or Harfagr (Harold I, first king of Norway, c.850-c.933). OCC, 923, 960, 964

Harding, Warren G. (U. S. president, 1865-1923). ILN, 64

Hardy, Edmund (German scholar of Buddhism, author of *Der Buddhismus nach alteren Pali-Werken*, 1890, and numerous other works on Indian religions). OC, 741

Hardy, Oliver (American film actor, 1892-1957, worked in team with Stanley Laurel). BC, 47

Harnack, Adolf (German theologian, b. 1851, author of *Lehrbuche der Dogmengeschichte, Geschichte der altchristlischen Litteratur* and other works). OC, 552

Harold (English king, son of Godwin, earl of Wessex, 1022?-1066, defeated by the Normans at the battle of Hastings). OC, 542, 689, 755, 756. OCC, 896, 961-62. OP, 370

Harold Diente Azul (Harold Bluetooth, Danish king, d. c.985). OCC, 971

Harrap, Colonel (character in Bustos Domecq and Suárez Lynch stories). OCC, 37-47, 53, 149, 191

Harrigan, Bill. See Billy the Kid

Harris, Frank (American writer, born in Ireland, 1856-1931, author of *My Life and Loves*, biographies of Shakespeare, Shaw and Wilde, and numerous novels and collections of short stories). OC, 697, 749

Hart, Liddell. See Liddell Hart, Basil Henry

Harte, Francis Bret (American writer, 1836-1902, author of *The Luck of Roaring Camp and Other Sketches* and many other works). ILN, 27, 28–29. P, 81–83

Harun ar-Rashid (fifth Abbasid caliph, c.764–809, sometimes Arrasid, al-Raschid, Emir de los Creyentes, even Aarón el Ortodoxo; figures as a character in the *Arabian Nights*). OC, 397, 893. SN, 59

Harún Benalmotásim, Vatiq Bila. See Vathek

Harvarth (in Icelandic saga). See Havarth

Harvey, Paul (author of the first three editions of the *Oxford Companion to English Literature* and co-author of the *Oxford Companion to French Literature*). OCC, 857

Haslam, Fanny or Frances (Borges's English grandmother, d. 1936). OC, 558–60, 937. CONJ, 44. LA, 13. SN, 144.

Haslam, Silas (author of *History of the Land Called Uqbar*, 1874, and *A General History of Labyrinths*). OC, 432

Haslam family (ancestors of Borges through Fanny Haslam). OC, 839. OP, 549

Hassan ben Sabbah (Hassan ibn Sabbah, founder of the Assassins at the end of the 11th century). OC, 688

Hasting (Viking warrior in Etruria). PB, 190

Hastings, Warren (first governor general of British India, 1732–1818). OC, 200

Hathaway, Anne (Shakespeare's wife, 1557?–1623). OC, 803

Hathor (Egyptian goddess of love and festivity). OCC, 675

Havarth or Harvarth (character in Icelandic saga). OCC, 940, 949

Havilland, Olivia de (British film actress, b. 1916). OCC, 63

Hawkwood (perhaps Sir John Hawkwood, English condottiere, d. 1394 in Florence). CONJ, 11

Hawthorne, Nathaniel (American writer, 1804–1864, author of *The Scarlet Letter, The Marble Faun, The Blithedale Romance, Wakefield* and other works). OC, 670–85. OCC, 616. ILN, 17–18, 26, 27, 58. P, 100, 143

Hawthorne family (ancestors of Nathaniel Hawthorne, including Major William Hathorne, early Puritan settler in Salem). OC, 671

Hayoth (four angelic beings in Jewish tradition). OCC, 642–43

Hazlitt, William (English essayist, 1778–1830, author of countless essays on drama, poetry and history, as well as travel books and letters). OC, 522, 687, 738. IA, 130

Heard, Gerald (English writer on religion and psychology, 1889–1971, author of *Pain, Sex and Time*). OC, 277–79, 394

Hearn, Lafcadio (American writer, 1850–1904, author of various books on Japan). A, 38. TE, 32

Hebbel, Christian Friedrich (German tragic dramatist, 1813–1863). I, 146–47

Hebe (minor Greek goddess, daughter of Hera and Zeus). OC, 242n.–243n.

Hecate (in Greek mythology, goddess of ghosts and witchcraft). OCC, 585

Hechicero (God). OCC, 734

Héctor (Trojan hero, son of Priam). OC, 781. PB, 242

Hedinn (character in the *Prose Edda*). OCC, 916

Hegel, Georg Wilhelm Friedrich (German philosopher, 1770–1831, author of *Wissenschaft der Logik, Philosophie der Geschichte* and numerous writings on logic, history, politics and aesthetics). OC, 162, 252, 497, 576n., 658, 698, 766. I, 107, 111,

OC, 627, 655, 805, 1129.
OCC, 465, 468.    P, 44, 45,
84–88

Henry, O.   See O. Henry

Heorrenda  (rival of Deor in
the *Deor*).   OCC, 794

Hepburn, Katharine  (American
film actress, b. 1907).   OC,
284.   BC, 72

Hera  (goddess in Greek
mythology).   OCC 604

Heracles  (hero in Greek
mythology).   See Hercules

Heraclides Pontico  (Heraclides
Ponticus the Younger, Greek
grammarian and poet, fl.
c.30–60).   OC, 456

Heráclito el Oscuro (Heraclitus
of Abdera or Ephesus, Greek
philosopher, c.535–c.475).
OC, 30, 158, 251, 394, 541,
652, 718, 745, 748, 763, 811,
843, 852, 924, 979, 1093.
OCC, 319, 688, 707, 728, 734,
746, 751.   A, 63.   BO, 24,
85, 96.   C, 49.   CONJ, 27,
35.   I, 88.   LA, 9.   NED,
100.   OP, 422, 437, 495,
502–3, 508, 554.   PB, 194.
SN, 77, 85, 102, 127

Herbelot de Moulainville,
Barthelemy D' (French
orientalist, 1625–1695,
author of a *Bibliotheque
orientale*).   OC, 731

Herbert, George  (English poet,
1593–1623, author of *The
Temple*).   LA, 167

Hercules  (Heracles, hero in
Greek mythology).   OC,
242n.-243n., 362, 382, 701,
728.   OCC, 602, 605, 609,
622, 645, 700, 873, 899,
900n., 930, 948.   I, 88.
NED, 113.   OP, 455, 514,
559.   PB, 200

Herder, Johann Gottfried von
(German philosopher and
critic, 1744–1803, author of
*Uber die neuere deutsche
Literatur, Uber den Ursprung
der Sprache, Ideen zur
Philosophie der Geschichte
der Menschheit* and other
works).   OC, 280

Heredia, José María (French
Parnassian poet born in Cuba,
1842–1905, author of *Les
Trophées*).   OCC, 468.   IA,
76

Hereward the Wake  (English
leader of the resistance to
William the Conqueror).   P,
113

Heriman  (Hermann of Reichenau
or Herimannus Augiensis,
German scholar and
chronicler, 1013–1054, author
of a *Chronicum ad annum
1054*).   OC, 746

Hermes  (Greek god).   OC, 504.
OCC, 740

Hermes Trismegisto  (Hermes
Trismegistus, Greek
translation of name of
Egyptian god of wisdom,
Thoth, to whom the hermetic
books were attributed).   OC,
636, 704

Hermótimo  (one of Pythagoras's
previous incarnations, a
soldier in the Trojan War).
OCC, 740

Hernández, José  (Argentine
politician and gauchesque
poet, 1834–1886, author of
the *Martin Fierro* as well as
*Instrucción del estanciero,
Vida del Chacho* and other
prose collected in *Prosas
del Martín Fierro*).   OC, 114,
135, 153, 154, 165, 181, 182,
187, 188, 190, 191, 192, 193–
97, 233, 267–69, 654, 684,
734, 735.   OCC, 18, 431,
482, 487, 516, 517, 520, 521,
522, 524, 525, 525–29, 530,
531, 533, 534, 537, 539, 541,
542, 548, 551, 554, 556, 557,
558–61, 564, 565, 977.   BC,
59.   BO, 20.   I, 55, 137.
IA, 56.   LA, 50.   P, 18–20,
29, 64, 65, 81, 82, 89–99,
112, 113.   PB, 122, 133–35,
152, 153, 154.   TE, 6, 34,
71, 88, 143

Hernández, Pedro  (public
scribe, stock figure).   PB,
125

Hernández, Rafael  (brother and
biographer of José Hernández,

author of *Pehuajó*.    OC,
187.    OCC, 520, 525, 527n.,
528, 548.    P, 29-30, 89, 90,
96
Hernández, Rafael   (father of
José and Rafael Hernández).
P, 89
Hernández   (soldier at
Paysandú).    OC, 968
Herodes   (Herod Antipas,
tetrarch of Galilee mentioned
in New Testament, d. c.39
A.D.).    OCC, 903
Herodes el Grande   (king of
Judea who ordered the
massacre of the innocents,
reigned 40-4 B.C.).    OC, 633
Heródoto   (Greek historian,
484?-425?).    OC, 522.    OCC,
587, 588, 627, 639, 667.
SN, 57
Héroe del Desierto   (name for
Juan Manuel de Rosas after
the campaign of 1833 against
the pampas Indians).    P, 131
Herrera, Fernando de   (Spanish
poet, 1534-1597).    I, 37.
PB, 240
Herrera, Tulio (character in
Bustos Domecq story, author
of *Hágase hizo*, *Madrugar
temprano* and other works).
OCC, 344-46, 347
Herrera y Reissig, Julio
(Uruguayan modernist poet,
1875-1910, author of *Los
parques abandonados*, *Los
éxtasis de la montaña* and
other works).    OC, 748, 841.
OCC, 303, 304, 338, 471, 472,
502-4.    I, 72, 75, 107, 137,
139-45.    P, 40, 41, 86.
TE, 42, 54, 55, 61, 147, 148
Herrero, Antonio   (Argentine
literary scholar, author of
*El poeta del hombre:
Almafuerte y su obra*, 1918).
P, 12
Herrigel, Eugen (author of *Zen
in the Art of Archery*, 1953).
OCC, 780
Herrigel, Gustiel (author of
*Zen in the Art of Flower
Arrangement*, 1958).    OCC,
780

Herrmann, Paul (German scholar,
author of *Nordische
Mythologie* and *Danische
Geschichte des Saxo
Grammaticus*).    OCC, 699n.
PB, 198, 201n.
Hesiodo   (Greek poet, 8th
century B.C., author of *Works
and Days* and the *Theogony*).
OC, 394, 497, 619.    OCC,
585, 602, 673, 685, 707
Hettel   (king of the
Hegelings in the *Gudrun*).
OCC, 917
Hidalgo, Alberto   (Peruvian
avant-garde poet, 1897-1967).
OC, 857.    TE, 113
Hidalgo, Bartolomé (Uruguayan
poet, creator of gauchesque
poetry, 1788-1822).    OC,
154n., 180-81, 188, 267, 268.
OCC, 516, 517, 520, 522, 558.
P, 18, 91, 92, 94, 95, 97,
113.    PB, 133, 187.    TE, 61
Hidalgo, Juan   (author of a
*Vocabulario de germanía*,
1609).    TE, 140
Hidebehind   (strange
creature of North America).
OCC, 631
Hidra   (Hydra, water serpent in
Greek myth).    OC, 254, 363,
413.    OCC, 645, 675.    I, 34
Hierocles   (Greek Stoic
philosopher, fl. c.120 A.D.,
author of *Elements of
Ethics*).    C, 85
Hight, G. Ainslie   (translator
of the *Grettir Saga*). OC, 381
Hijo   (in the Trinity, Christ
the Son).    OCC, 863
Hijo de Hombre.   See Jesucristo
Hild de Streoneshal (St. Hilda,
abbess of Whitby, 614-680).
OCC, 881
Hilde   (princess of India in
the *Gudrun*).    OCC, 917
Hildebrand   (hero of the German
poem *Hildebrandslied*).    OCC,
901-2, 910, 914, 917
Hildeburh   (Danish princess in
the *Finnsburh* fragment).
OCC, 875
Hildegund de Borgoña   (French
princess in the *Waltharius*).
OCC, 919, 920

Hildr (daughter of Hogni, character in the *Prose Edda*). OCC, 916

Hilgenfeld, Adolf Bernhard Christoph (German Protestant divine and scholar, 1823–1907, author of numerous works on the early Christians). OC, 214

Hinton, Charles Howard (British philosopher, 1853–1907, author of *The Fourth Dimension, A New Era of Thought* and other works). OC, 276, 440, 510. LA, 67, 68, 69. PB, 168

Hipocampos (seahorses). OCC, 650

Hipócrates (Hippocrates, the Asclepiad of Cos, Greek physician, father of medicine, 469–399). OCC, 815

Hipogrifo (cross of griffins with horses). OCC, 647–48. OP, 382

Hipólita, doña (ranch owner mentioned in *Evaristo Carriego*). OC, 171

Hirsch, Maurice (German-Jewish baron, financier and philanthropist, 1831–1896). OCC, 430

Historia (personification of history). OC, 317

Hitchcock, Alfred (Anglo-American film director, 1899–1980, director of *The Thirty-Nine Steps, Spellbound* and dozens of other films). BC, 39, 51, 52

Hitler, Adolf (Nazi dictator, 1889–1945, author of *Mein Kampf*). OC, 580, 723, 724, 725, 727–28. BC, 45. LA, 14, 133. P, 37n., 77. PB, 158–60, 225. VA, 51

Hjadnings (group of warriors in the *Prose Edda*). OCC, 916

Hjalprek (Danish king in the *Volsunga Saga*). OCC, 967

Hladík, Jaromir (character in Borges story, author of the verse drama *Los enemigos*, perhaps kin to the Czech novelist and dramatist Václav Hladík, whose work *Evzen Voldan* the *Encyclopaedia Britannica* judges "a very striking representation of the life of modern Prague"). OC, 508–13, 517n.

Hler (character in the *Prose Edda*, also called Aegir). OC, 371

Hoare, Samuel John Gurney, Viscount Templewood (English statesman, 1880–1959). OC, 723

Hobbes, Thomas (English philosopher, 1588–1679, author of *Leviathan*). OC, 244, 258. IA, 79

Hochigan (god of the bushmen). OCC, 649

Hodler, Ferdinand (Swiss painter, 1853–1918). A, 38

Hoelderlin, Friedrich. See Holderlin

Hoffmann, Ernst Theodor Amadeus (German romantic novelist and composer, 1776–1822). OC, 682

Hofman, Luther (literary critic). P, 144

Hofmannsthal, Hugo von (Austrian dramatist and poet, 1874–1929, author of *Brief des Lord Chandos* and numerous other works, and editor of *Die osterreichische Bibliothek*). I, 148

Hogarth, William (English painter and engraver, 1697–1764). OC, 164. PB, 146

Hogben, Lancelot (literary critic, author of *Dangerous Thoughts*, 1939). OC, 706

Holderlin, Friedrich (German lyric poet, 1770–1843, author of *Hyperion* and other poems). OC, 1116. I, 73, 144. OP, 392. PB, 159. TE, 100

Holinshed, Raphael (English chronicler, d. c.1580, author of *The Historie of England* and editor of the *Chronicle*). P, 138, 143, 144. PB, 226

Holland, Philemon (British physician, writer and translator, 1552–1637). OC, 625

Holmes, Oliver Wendell
(American author and
physician, 1809-1894, author
of *The Autocrat at the
Breakfast-Table*, "The
Chambered Nautilus" and other
works).  ILN, 28
Holmes, Sherlock (character in
detective stories by Arthur
Conan Doyle).  OCC, 15, 41,
849.  BO, 72, 73.  CONJ,
49-50.  ILN, 56.  P, 47.
PB, 176
Hombres Azules (blue men,
Viking name for the
Saracens).  LA, 117
Hombres-Escorpiones (scorpion-
men in *Gilgamesh*).  OCC, 652
Hombres Marinos (mermen of
China).  OCC, 629
Homero (Greek poet to whom the
*Iliad* and *Odyssey* are
traditionally ascribed).
OC, 161, 177, 206, 215n.,
228n.,  239-43, 263, 264,
265, 268, 383, 540-44, 619,
660, 667, 700, 738, 781-82,
795, 881, 918, 1128.  OCC,
304, 314, 357, 471, 489,
491,558, 562, 604, 621, 626,
666, 669, 685, 696, 707, 824,
830, 833, 837.   A, 27.  BC,
48.  BO, 16, 18.  C, 42.
ILN, 45.  NED, 98, 103, 133.
OP, 459, 526.  P, 26, 68,
94, 119, 174.  PB, 168, 182,
184, 189, 225, 230, 235, 242,
243.  SN, 14, 21, 22, 28,
49, 126, 127, 152, 153.  TE,
50, 116
Hope, Mrs. (character in
James's *Abasement of the
Northmores*).  P, 101
Hope, Warren (character in
James's *Abasement of the
Northmores*).  P, 101
Hopkins, Edward (Tichborne
family lawyer).  OC, 304
Hopkins, Gerard Manley
(English poet, 1844-89).
OCC, 318, 842
Hopkins, Miriam (American film
actress, 1902-1972).  OC,
285, 356.  BC, 67
Horacio (Quintus Horatius
Flaccus, Latin poet, 65-8,

author of satires, odes and
epodes, epistles and an "Ars
Poetica").  OC, 127, 253.
OCC, 504, 836.  A, 62.
ILN, 12.  NED, 98, 103, 133.
P, 138.  PB, 182, 184.  SN,
49, 126.  TE, 87
Hormiga Negra (semi-mythical
gaucho, based on Guillermo
Hoyo, subject of a novel by
Eduardo Gutiérrez).  OC,
659, 735, 1021.  OCC, 444.
P, 31, 64, 113.  PB, 153,
154
Horn, Paul (German Orientalist
and philologist, author of
*Grundriss der iranischen
Philologie*, 1895, and other
works).  OC, 324
Horsa (Jutish warrior, brother
of Hengist; together they led
conquest of England by Jutes
in 5th century).  OCC, 809
Horst, George Conrad (German
writer, 1769-1832, author of
the *Zauber-Bibliothek*).
OCC, 637n.
Hotchkis de Estephano (architect, character in Bustos
Domecq story).  OCC, 335
Houdin, Jean Eugene Robert
(French conjurer and
magician, 1805-1871).  OCC,
78
Hourcade, Carolus (French
lithographer).  OC, 445,
446n.
Housman, Alfred Edward (English
poet and classical scholar,
1859-1936, author of *A
Shropshire Lad, Last Poems*
and *More Poems*).  OC, 756
Howells, William Dean (American
novelist, critic and editor,
1837-1920, author of *The Rise
of Silas Lapham* and other
works).  ILN, 28.  P, 82
Hoyo, Guillermo (gaucho outlaw,
known as Hormiga Negra).  P,
114.  PB, 153, 154
Hrabano Mauro (Rabanus Maurus
Magnentius, German scholar
and theologian, c.780-856,
author of *De universo* and *De
institutione clericorum*).
OC, 522

Hsi P'eng (character in Borges story). OC, 475

Hsiang (in Borges poem, the guardian of the book). OC, 999-1000

Hsiang-Lien (character in the *Hung Lu Meng* or *Dream of the Red Chamber*). PB, 197

Hsiao (Chinese monster). OCC, 629

Hsin, Madame (character in Bustos Domecq story). OCC, 105, 106, 110-17

Hsing-hsing (Chinese monster). OCC, 629

Hsing-t'ien (Chinese monster). OCC, 629

Hsuang Tsang (Chinese Buddhist monk and traveler, c.605-664, author of the *Ta-T'ang-Si-Yu-Ki* or *Memoirs on Western Countries*). OCC, 731, 760

Hua (Chinese monster). OCC, 629

Hudson, William Henry (English writer, born in Argentina, 1841-1922, author of *The Purple Land, El Ombu, Far Away and Long Ago, Green Mansions* and numerous other works). OC, 106, 194, 733-36, 1069. OCC, 543, 838-39. I, 137. P, 65, 136. PB, 187. TE, 21, 32-36

Huergo, Camilo N. (author of *El elegido*, character in Bustos Domecq story). OCC, 365, 366

Huésped del Oceano (Old English name for the whale). OCC, 712

Hughes, Langston (American poet, 1902-1967, author of *Dear Lovely Death, Shakespeare in Harlem* and other works). ILN, 48

Hugo, Victor (French poet, dramatist and novelist, 1802-1885, author of *Hernani, Notre-Dame de Paris, Les Misérables* and countless other works). OC, 116, 161, 207, 265, 496, 673, 682, 684, 705, 738, 754, 756, 820. OCC, 151, 463, 466, 468, 471, 472, 474, 557, 558, 732, 818, 835. A, 14, 44. BO, 20, 37. I, 62, 128. ILN, 14. LA, 18. NED, 93. OP, 420, 469, 521, 522, 546, 547. P, 7, 40, 53, 75, 82, 86, 87, 89-90, 112, 144, 172. PB, 218, 226, 228, 232. SN, 43, 61, 116, 139. TE, 110, 133

Hugo (French general under Napoleon, father of Victor Hugo). OCC, 450

Hui (Chinese monster). OCC, 629

Hui Tzu (Hui Shih, Chinese logician, c.380-c.300). OC, 255n.

Huidobro, Vicente (Chilean avant-garde poet and novelist, 1893-1948, author of *Poemas árticos, Altazor* and other works). I, 29, 96, 98

Hull, Edna Mayne (American science fiction writer, author of *Out of the Unknown, The Winged Man* and other works). ILN, 60

Hulme, Thomas Ernest (iconoclastic English writer, 1883-1917, author of *Speculations* and *The Complete Poetical Works of T. E. Hulme*). ILN, 41

Hume, David (Scottish philosopher and historian, 1711-1766, author of a *Treatise of Human Nature, Dialogues concerning Natural Religion* and numerous other works). OC, 217, 253n., 285, 394, 584, 708, 718, 719, 745, 757, 760, 761, 762, 766, 767, 768, 770, 863. OCC, 151, 742, 746, 751, 758. BC, 65, 67. BO, 14, 31. IA, 11. LA, 173. P, 61, 72, 164. SN, 93, 118

Humphreys, Christmas (English writer on Buddhism, b. 1901, author of *Zen Buddhism, The Middle Way* and other works). OCC, 744, 780

Humpty Dumpty (egg in Mother Goose rhyme, later a character in Lewis Carroll). PB, 160

Hunain ibn-Ishaq (Arabian philosopher of Hira, called Johannitius in Latin, known for his translations of Aristotle). OC, 583

Hunt, Leigh (English poet, critic and journalist, 1784-1859, author of *The Story of Rimini*). OCC, 833

Hurtado sisters (characters in Borges-Levinson story). HE, 65

Hurtado y Mendoza, Diego de (Spanish humanist, historian, poet and diplomat, 1503-1575). IA, 73

Hus, Jan (Czech religious reformer and theologian, 1369?-1415). OP, 495

Huxley, Thomas Henry (English biologist and educator, 1825-1895, author of *The Physical Basis of Life, Man's Place in Nature* and other works). OC, 647, 757. ILN, 34

Huysmans, Joris Karl (French novelist, 1848-1907, author of *A rebours* and other works). OC, 731

Hyde, Edward (character in Stevenson novel). OC, 285. OCC, 598, 845. BC, 67-68. BO, 75. P, 108

Hylas (character in Berkeley dialogue). OC, 767, 768

Hystaspes (ruler of ancient Persia, 6th century B.C., father of Darius the Great). PB, 194

Iago (villain in Shakespeare's *Othello*). OC, 803. OCC, 820. P, 144

Ibarbourou, Juana de (pseud. of Juana Fernández Morales, Uruguayan poet, 1895-1979). TE, 61

Ibarra, Néstor (Franco-Argentine writer and translator, b. 1908, French translator of Borges and author of *La nueva poesía argentina: ensayo crítico sobre el ultraísmo*). OC, 335, 390n., 434. P, 164

Iberra, Daniel (knife-fighter in Buenos Aires). LA, 72

Iberra, Juan (Daniel's brother, knife-fighter in Buenos Aires). OC, 888, 955-56, 957, 1025, 1027

Ibn abi Tair Tarful or Taifur (Arabian historian, d. 894, author of works on the Abbasid caliphs). OC, 324, 325

Ibn Qutaiba (Arabian historian, 828-889, author of a *Kitab ul-Ma'arif* or *Handbook of History* and other works). OC, 583, 584

Ibn-Sháraf de Berja. OC, 586, 587

Ibrahim (brother of Abderrahmen El Masmudi, 19th century Sudan). OC, 341

Ibrahim (character in the *Arabian Nights*). OC, 358n.

Ibrahim (Druse character in Bustos Domecq story). OCC, 26, 27, 30, 33

Ibsen, Henrik (Norwegian poet and dramatist, 1828-1906, author of *Peer Gynt, Hedda Gabler* and other works). OC, 260, 695. OCC, 300, 702, 847, 923, 939. ILN, 52. LA, 29, 55. P, 100, 112. PB, 146, 226, 247. SN, 17, 157

Icaza, Jorge (Ecuadorian novelist, 1906-1978, author of *Huasipungo*). OCC, 157

Ictiocentauros (sea-horses). OCC, 650

Idiarte Borda, Juan (Uruguayan politician and president, 1844-1897). OC, 853, 1086. LA, 157, 158-59. OP, 371

Ignacio de Loyola, San (Spanish religious leader, founder of the Society of Jesus, 1491-1556). TE, 68

Ildico (beautiful virgin who married Attila the night of his death). OCC, 969-70

Illán de Toledo, don (character in the *Conde Lucanor*). OC, 339-40

Indio. See Ubalde, Félix

Indra (Vedic warrior and thunder god). OCC, 726

Infanta (princess of Spain in 1910). OC, 1050

Infantes de Aragón (in the
Romancero). IA, 48
Ingenieros, Cecilia (friend of
Borges). OC, 544, 629.
OP, 459
Ingenieros, José (Argentine
positivist philosopher and
sociologist, born in Spain,
1877–1925). OP, 459. P,
52. TE, 7
Inglés, el (character in Borges
story). OC, 330, 333
Ingrato (merchant in legend of
Buddha). OCC, 726
Ingvar (in runic inscription).
OCC, 924. PB, 190
Inocencio, San (Innocent I,
pope, reigned 401–417).
OCC, 824
Inry, Iris (actress in Bustos
Domecq story). OCC, 421
Ipuche, Pedro Leandro
(Uruguayan poet, 1889–1976,
author of Tierra honda and
other works). OC, 485. I,
56, 57–60. TE, 61
Irala (character in "El
Congreso"). See Fernández
Irala
Irala, Luis (character in
Borges story). OC, 1035,
1036
Ireneo (Irenaeus, Greek
theologian, c.130–202). OC,
210, 213, 214, 354, 359, 360,
750n. OCC, 743. SN, 133
Iriarte y Oropesa, Tomás de
(Spanish fabulist, poet and
playwright, 1750–1791).
OCC, 435
Irigoyen (almost certainly a
reference to Hipólito
Yrigoyen, who does indeed
form part of an Argentine
mythology along with the
tango and truco). OC, 187
Irigoyen, Bernardo de
(Argentine politician and
educator, 1822–1906). OCC,
526
Irma. See Espinosa, Irma
Ironside, William Edmund
(British general, 1880–1959).
OC, 723
Irving, Washington
(American author and

diplomat, 1783–1859, author
of The Sketch–Book, Legends
of the Alhambra and other
works). OC, 670. ILN, 15–
16
Isa (name for Jesus in the
Arabian Nights). OCC, 590
Isabel de Inglaterra (Elizabeth
I, queen of England, 1533–
1603, called Gloriana by
Spenser). OC, 418. OCC,
856. BO, 36. NED, 111n.
P, 8, 149. PB, 227. SN,
110
Isaías (Isaiah, Biblical
prophet). OC, 517, 639
Isidoro de Sevilla (Spanish
encyclopaedic writer and
Church father, c.560–636).
OCC, 639, 703
Iskandar. See Alejandro de
Macedonia
Issota. See Abd-el-Issota
Ivan el Terrible (Ivan IV,
Russian tsar, 1530–1584).
OCC, 68
Ixaqui, El (Arabian historian
cited in the Arabian Nights).
OC, 338
Ixión (mythical king of
Thessaly). OC, 551. OCC,
604
Izedin (Druse character in
Bustos Domecq story). OCC,
24–34
Jackson, Andrew (American
general and president, 1767–
1845). ILN, 48, 63
Jacob (Biblical patriarch).
OC, 737. TE, 64
Jacob, Max (French writer and
painter, 1876–1944, author of
Le Cornet a dés, La Défense
de Tartufe and other works).
I, 125
Jacobo I (James I of England
and VI of Scotland, 1566–
1625). OCC, 819. P, 146
Jacoibo (stock name for a Jew
in Bustos Domecq story).
OCC, 172
Jafez (Persian poet). SN,
117–18
Jaimes Freyre, Ricardo
(Bolivian–Argentine poet,
1868–1933, author of Castalia

bárbara).    OCC, 467–68.    C,
11.    P, 40, 76.    TE, 72
Jalálu'd-Dīn Rúmī (the
greatest of the Persian Sufi
poets, 1207-1273, author of
*The Spiritual Mathnawi*).
OC, 695n.    OCC, 735
Jalifa.    See Mahdi, Mohammed al
Jalil    (al-Khalil ibn Ahmed,
Arab philologist from Oman,
718-791, author of the first
Arabic dictionary, the *Kitab-
ul-'Ain*).    OC, 583
Jalil    (Druse character in
Bustos Domecq story).    OCC,
27
Jalil    (Khalil or Malik al-
Ashraf Salah al-din, leader
of the Moslem forces that
drove the Franks from Syria
and Palestine and took Acre
in 1291).    P, 140
Jamblico (Iamblichus, Syrian
Neoplatonic philosopher,
c.250-c.325, author of the
*Protrepticus, De mysteriis*
and other works).    OC, 636,
715
Jamboneau.    See Fingermann
James, Henry (American novelist
and critic, 1843-1916, author
of *The American, The
Ambassadors, The Turn of the
Screw, The Figure in the
Carpet* and many other works).
OC, 266, 351, 461, 640, 641,
667, 681, 683, 685, 691, 714,
1021, 1053, 1128.    OCC, 835,
842, 846, 850-51, 853, 855.
A, 23.    BO, 58, 65.    ILN,
38-40.    NED, 110.    P, 23,
43, 100-2.    PB, 167, 187
James, Henry, Sr. (American
student of religious and
social problems, 1811-1882,
father of William and Henry).
BO, 58.    ILN, 38.    P, 100
James, Will (American Western
writer and artist, 1892-1942,
author of *Horses I've Known,
Lone Cowboy: My Life Story*
and other works).    OC, 179
James, William (American
philosopher and psychologist,
1842-1910, author of *The
Principles of Psychology, The

*Varieties of Religious
Experience, Some Problems in
Philosophy, A Pluralistic
Universe* and other works).
OC, 246-48, 257n., 258, 282,
283, 449, 718, 745.    OCC,
579, 850.    BO, 27, 28, 58,
65, 92.    ILN, 11, 38, 40.
P, 100.    PB, 123.    SN, 146
James I.    See Jacobo I
Jan, Zingis.    See Genghis Khan
Jannings, Emil (stage name of
Theodor Emil Janenz, German
film actor, 1882-1950).
OCC, 66-67.    BC, 62
Jano (Janus, Roman god of time,
often pictured with two
faces, sometimes called "el
Bifronte").    OC, 505, 805, 879,
1110, 1136.    C, 49, 53.
CONJ, 44.    OP, 412, 446,
502, 518
Jantzen, Hermann (German
medievalist, author of
numerous works on Germanic
medieval literatures and
translator of *Historia
Danica*).    OCC, 975
Jarnés, Benjamín (Spanish
novelist, essayist and
biographer, 1888-1949).    IA,
86
Jaroslavski (Jaromir Hladik's
mother's maiden name in
Borges story).    OC, 508
Jasconye (fish in Irish
mythology).    OCC, 712
Jasodhara.    See Yasodhara
Jasón (hero in Greek mythology
who travels to Colchis with
the Argonauts, obtains the
Golden Fleece with the help
of Medea, then deserts her).
OC, 220, 226, 228, 1093,
1128.    OCC, 699, 843.    OP,
438
Jaspers, Karl (German
philosopher, 1883-1969).
OC, 749
Jáuregui, Bernardo (character
in Borges story).    OC, 1048
Jáuregui, Juan de (Spanish
poet, 1583-1641, author of
*Rimas, Discurso poet ico
contra el hablar culto y
oscuro, Antídoto contra la*

*pestilente poesía de las Soledades* and *Orfeo*, and translator of Tasso, Lucan and others). OCC, 593. IA, 71-72. P, 174. TE, 68, 129

Jáuregui, Mariano (character in Borges story). OC, 1049

Jazmín. See Frogman

Jazmín (Clemencia Juárez's dog). OCC, 205

Jean Paul. See Richter, Jean Paul

Jefe. See Morgan

Jefferson, Thomas (U. S. president, 1743-1826). ILN, 12, 41, 63

Jehová (modern reconstruction of the ineffable Hebrew name of God). OC, 715, 737. OCC, 752, 928. SN, 133, 134

Jekyll, Henry (doctor in Stevenson novel *The Strange Case of Dr. Jekyll and Mr. Hyde*). OC, 285. OCC, 598, 845, 977. BC, 67-68. BO, 75. P, 44, 108

Jenófanes de Colofón (Xenophanes of Colophon, Greek philosopher, c.570-c.480, author of some satires that are still extant). OC, 636, 704n. NED, 90

Jenyns, Soame (English writer, 1704-1787, author of *The Art of Dancing*, *Free Inquiry into the Nature and Origin of Evil* and *View of the Internal Evidence of the Christian Religion*). OC, 138. PB, 145

Jerónimo, San (St. Jerome or Eusebius Sophronius Hieronymus, Christian scholar, Father of the Church, c.347-420?, translator of the Bible into Latin, author of *De viris illustribus sive de scriptoribus ecclesiasticis* and numerous other works of Christian history, commentaries on the Bible, polemical works, etc.). OCC, 609, 643, 680, 883. NED, 148

Jerrold, Douglas (English dramatist, humorist and man of letters, 1803-1857). PB, 191

Jerusalem, David (poet, character in Borges story, author of "Tse Yang, pintor de tigres" and "Rosencrantz habla con el Angel"). OC, 578-81

Jespersen, Otto (Danish philologist, 1860-1943, author of histories and grammars of the English language). OCC, 868. PB, 160

Jesucristo (the Christian Messiah, c.4 B.C.-c.29 A.D., sometimes called Jesús, Cristo, Redentor, Hijo, Cristo Blanco). OC, 88, 210, 214, 215n., 235, 236, 281, 283, 296, 343, 362n., 368, 369, 388, 441, 446, 506, 514-18, 551, 553, 578, 580, 641, 650, 661, 701, 702, 714, 727, 769, 796, 800, 840, 853, 870, 881, 917, 918, 970, 977-98, 996, 1010, 1070-72, 1078, 1129. OCC, 496, 574, 590, 639, 643, 657, 658, 679, 701, 705, 710, 726, 728-29, 740, 755, 756, 757, 759, 761, 763, 774, 789, 801, 809, 810, 813, 818, 827, 840, 867, 874, 879-80, 882, 888, 891, 892, 903-4, 905, 928, 943, 952, 956. BC, 72. BO, 14, 15-16, 28, 39, 48, 54, 60. C, 41, 45, 63, 81, 95. CONJ, 15-16, 17. IA, 26. ILN, 12, 20. LA, 13, 60, 82-85, 106, 112, 130, 165. NED, 116, 126, 140, 141, 148, 150n. OP, 462, 493, 494, 505, 540. P, 14, 15, 35, 50, 69, 73, 121, 140-41, 155, 160, 166, 171. PB, 173, 178, 197, 199, 200, 201. PJ, 71. PB, 199, 200, 201. SN, 20, 26, 50, 77, 80, 82, 85, 86. TE, 100-101

Jichlinski, Simón (childhood friend of Borges in Geneva). LA, 19

Jim (fugitive slave, character in *Huckleberry Finn*). ILN, 28

Jimena (mentioned in Alfonso
Reyes's *Reloj del Sol*). IA,
128

Jiménez (character in Borges–
Levinson story). HE, 51–53,
55–56

Jiménez, Juan Ramón (Spanish
poet and essayist, 1881–
1958). OCC, 162. P, 78–
79. TE, 68–69, 103, 127

Jinshin-Mushi (Japanese
monster, "Escarabajo de los
Terremotos"). OCC, 651

Jinshin-Uwo (Japanese monster,
"Pez de los Terremotos").
OCC, 651

Jiriczek, Otto Luitpold (German
literary scholar, 1867–1941,
author of *Deutsche Heldensage*
as well as works on Victorian
poetry, Wagner and so on).
OCC, 915. PB, 200

Joachim du Bellay. See Du
Bellay, Joachim

Job (in Bible, just man who
suffers). OC, 209, 661,
701. OCC, 451. LA, 60.
P, 15, 120. SN, 25, 134

Jodwin (father of Harold, Saxon
king of England). OCC, 961

John of the Rood. See Juan de
la Cruz, San

Johnson, Jack (American boxer,
1878–1946). OCC, 169

Johnson, Lionel (English poet
and critic, 1867–1902, author
of *Postliminium* and other
works). OC, 691

Johnson, Lyndon B. (U. S. president, 1908–1973). ILN, 64

Johnson, Samuel (English
scholar, critic, poet and
lexicographer, 1709–1784,
editor and writer for the
*Rambler*, author of the famous
*Dictionary*, *Lives of the
Poets* and countless other
works). OC, 234, 249, 406,
417, 419, 422, 461, 638, 680,
682, 692, 748, 803, 975,
1113, 1138. OCC, 503, 825,
827–29, 830, 836. BC, 59–
60. BO, 19. C, 89. ILN,
32. LA, 68. OP, 387, 445.
P, 56, 62, 66, 147. PB,
226. SN, 42

Jolivet, Emile (French scholar
of old Germanic literatures).
OCC, 974

Jonas (Biblical prophet).
ILN, 12

Jonas, Gas Houser (New York
gangster). OC, 316

Jonson, Ben (English dramatist
and poet, 1572–1637, author
of *Every Man in his Humour*,
*The Poetaster*, *Sejanus* and
numerous other works). OC,
544, 641, 738. OCC, 817,
818. I, 32, 125. IA, 127.
ILN, 42. OP, 508. P, 86,
143, 144. TE, 24, 74.

Jordán, Luis María (Argentine
writer, author of *La túnica
del sol*, 1909, *Cavalcanti*,
1907, and other works).
OCC, 431

Jordanes (6th century historian
of the Ostrogoths, author of
*De rebus Geticis*). OCC,
863, 910, 969. PB, 189

Jorge, San (St. George, prince
of Capadocia, legendary saint
who killed a dragon). OC,
592. OCC, 622

Jormungandr (Scandinavian
mythological serpent). OCC,
707

Josafat (character in legend
of Barlaam and Josafat, a
Christianized version of the
Buddha legend). OC, 741.
OCC, 936

José, San (St. Joseph, in New
Testament, husband of Mary).
OC, 343. OCC, 658

José de Arimatea, San (Joseph
of Arimathaea, wealthy man
who buried Jesus). OCC,
908n.

Josué (Joseph, in Bible the
successor of Moses as leader
of Israel). I, 143. TE,
64

Joubert, Joseph (French
moralist, 1754–1824, author
of *Pensées, essais, maximes
et correspondance*). IA, 22

Jove. See Júpiter

Jovellanos, Baltasar Melchor
Gaspar María de (Spanish
statesman and polymath, 1744–

1811, author of *El delin-
cuente honrado* and other
works).   OCC, 448
Joyce, James   (Irish writer,
1882-1941, author of
*Dubliners, Portrait of the
Artist as a Young Man,
Pomes Penyeach, Ulysses*
and *Finnegans Wake*).   OC, 232,
249, 266, 363, 418, 450, 641,
650, 666, 686, 714, 983,
1004-5, 1022.   OCC, 301,
461, 853-54, 948.   A, 15,
16, 76.   BC, 48.   BO, 21.
CONJ, 13.   I, 20-25.   ILN,
36, 53.   P, 126, 129, 134,
146, 171, 173.   PB, 160-62,
167-69, 230, 239.   SN, 79,
157.   VA, 15
Juan   (king don Juan, in the
*Romancero*).   IA, 48
Juan, Don   (heartless libertine
of legend and literature,
sometimes surnamed Tenorio).
OCC, 831
Juan, San   (St. John the
Evangelist).   OC, 702, 893.
OCC, 878, 885.   IA, 60.
TE, 110
Juan Bautista, San   (St. John
the Baptist).   OCC, 333, 934
Juan de Afuera   (stock
character in saying).   OCC,
205, 376
Juan de la Cruz, San   (Spanish
poet, mystic and doctor of
the Church, 1542-1591).   OC,
524.   OCC, 771, 879.   BO,
56.   I, 156.   P, 156.   PB,
232.   TE, 112
Juan de Mena. See Mena, Juan de
Juan de Panonia   (theologian,
character in Borges story).
OC, 550-56
Juan de Viterbo   (famous
sorceror).   OC, 517
Juan el Teólogo, San   (St. John
the Divine or John of Patmos,
author of the *Apocalypse* or
*Book of Revelation*).   OC,
360, 800, 819, 823.   OCC,
591, 622, 642, 643, 873.   A,
30.   CONJ, 17.   NED, 150.
P, 159.   PB, 145, 199n.
Juan Manuel, don.   See Rosas

Juan Manuel, infante don
(Spanish prose writer, 1282-
1348, author of the *Conde
Lucanor* or *Libro de Patronio*
and other works).   OC, 340.
OCC, 312
Juana de Arco   (Jeanne d'Arc,
French saint and national
heroine, 1412?-31).   OCC,
848, 853.   CONJ, 16.   OP,
546.   TE, 100, 101
Juárez   (soldier in Indian
wars).   See Suárez
Juárez   (stock figure in
saying).   OCC, 83
Juárez, Clemencia   (character
in Borges-Bioy filmscript).
OCC, 201, 203, 205-6, 210-11
Juárez, Clementina   (character
in Borges story).   OC, 1034
Juárez, Rosendo   (character in
Borges story).   OC, 329-34,
1034-38
Juda León   (rabbi in Prague,
creator of Golem).   OC, 885-
87
Judas Iscariote   (disciple who
betrayed Jesus).   OC, 395,
495, 514-18, 551, 591, 766.
OCC, 53, 320.   BC, 35.   LA,
85-86.   NED, 94.   PB, 173.
OP, 425, 497.   TE, 101
Judas Tadeo, San   (St. Jude,
one of twelve disciples,
perhaps brother of St. James
the Less).   OC, 1100
Judío Errante   (Wandering Jew
of legend).   OC, 591.   TE, 101
Judith   (Jewish widow in Bible
who kills Holofernes, the
subject of an Anglo-Saxon
poem).   OCC, 810
Juez de las Sombras   (in
Buddhist theology).   OCC,
747-48
Julia   (character in brief
Borges story).   OC, 786
Julia la Lujanera   (character
in Borges story).   OC, 329-
34, 1036, 1038
Julia, Santa   (martyred in
439).   OCC, 880
Juliana   (character in Borges
story).   OC, 1030
Julieta   (heroine in Shakespeare).
OC, 803.   OCC, 820.   OP, 432

Karlinski (character in Borges story). LA, 57

Kasner, Edward (mathematician, co-author of *Mathematics and the Imagination*). OC, 276–77

Kaspar von der Roen (of Runnerstadt, German printer of the 15th century). OCC, 910

Katibi (of Nishapur, Persian poet, d. 1434, author of the *Majma'-ulbahrain* or *Confluence of the Two Seas*). NED, 141n. PB, 178n.

Katz, Leopoldo (character in Bustos Domecq story). OCC, 405, 407, 408

Kautzsch, Simon (Pittsburgh financier, character in Borges story). OC, 444

Keaton, Buster (American movie actor, 1895–1966). OC, 223, 224. BC, 28, 33

Keats, John (English romantic poet, 1795–1821, author of "On a Grecian Urn," "To a Nightingale," "On First Looking into Chapman's Homer," "Endymion," "Lamia" and other poems). OC, 356, 642, 682, 717–19, 1095. OCC, 463, 484, 656, 833. ILN, 31, 49. OP, 375, 432. P, 41. TE, 40. VA, 15

Keegan, Father. OCC, 301

Keins, Paulino (friend of Borges). OC, 1073

Keller, Gottfried (Swiss novelist and poet, 1819–1890). OC, 1116. OP, 392

Kelly, Paul (New York gangster). OC, 313–15

Kemnitz, Martin (or Chemnitz, German Lutheran theologian, 1522–1586). OC, 517

Kempis, Thomas a. See Thomas a Kempis

Kennedy, Charles W. (scholar, author of *The Earliest English Poetry*, 1943). OCC, 857

Kennedy, John Fitzgerald (U. S. president, 1917–1963). OC, 853. ILN, 64

Kenyon (character in Hawthorne's *Marble Faun*). OC, 682

Kepler, Johann (German astronomer, 1571–1630, author of *Astronomia nova* and other works). OC, 703. OCC, 579. A, 36. P, 25, 26

Ker (Greek death-bringer). A, 28

Ker, William Paton (scholar of medieval literature, author of *Epic and Romance*, *Essays on Medieval Literature* and other works). OCC, 857, 861, 873, 874, 926, 934, 941, 974. PB, 187, 192

Kern, Jan Hendrik (Dutch Orientalist, b. 1833, author of *Geschiedenis van het Buddhisme in Indie*, a *Manual of Indian Buddhism* and a translation of the *Saddharma Pundarika*). OCC, 671, 749, 780

Keteh Meriri (medieval Jewish demon). OCC, 613

Keyserling, Hermann, Graf (German writer and philosopher from the Russian Baltic provinces, 1880–1946, author of *Europas Zukunft*, *Politik, Wirthschaft*, *Weisheit, Philosophie als Kunst, Amerika, Das Buch vom personlichen Leben* and other works). P, 63n.

Khayyam. See Omar Khayyam

Khumbaba (Babylonian monster). OCC, 652

Kia-King (Chinese emperor, ruled 1795–1820). OC, 307, 308, 309

Kierkegaard, Soren (Danish philosopher and religious thinker, 1813–1855, author of *Frygt og Baevan* and other works). OC, 710, 711. OCC, 180. P, 36, 105. SN, 136

K'i-lin (Chinese unicorn). OCC, 705–6

Kilpatrick, Fergus (Irish traitor and hero, character in Borges story). OC, 496–98

Kim (character in Kipling novel *Kim*). OC, 733. BO, 72. OP, 463, 511. SN, 19

Kingsley, Charles (English novelist, writer and clergyman, 1819-1875, author of *Westward Ho!, Hereward the Wake, Water Babies, The Saint's Tragedy* and numerous other works). OC, 652

Kipling, Rudyard (English author, born in India, 1865-1936, author of *Kim*, the *Jungle Books, Just So Stories, Barrack-room Ballads, Plain Tales from the Hills, Many Inventions, Puck of Pook's Hill* and other works). OC, 114, 160, 185, 220n., 221, 271, 273, 377, 418, 612, 659, 691, 694, 733, 975, 976n., 1021. OCC, 722n., 794, 812, 831, 836, 845, 846-47, 877, 910, 948. A, 48. I, 46. ILN, 28, 38. OP, 419, 463. P, 83, 100, 110-11, 137, 149. PB, 124, 142, 224, 246. SN, 62, 119-20. VA, 27, 29

Kir, Abu (executioner mentioned by Richard Burton). OC, 342

Kirk, Robert (18th century Scottish ecclesiastic, author of *The Secret Commonwealth of Elves, Fauns and Fairies*). OCC, 641

Kirón, César (painter in Bustos Domecq story). OCC, 318

Kjartan (name of Sigurd in the *Laxdoela Saga*). OCC, 939

Klaeber, P. (scholar and editor of the *Beowulf*). OCC, 974. LA, 140

Klaingutti (character in Borges-Levinson story). HE, 61, 63, 67-71

Klee, Paul (Swiss painter, graphic artist and art theorist, 1879-1940). A, 80. CONJ, 97

Klemm, Wilhelm (German expressionist poet). OC, 383. OCC, 948. I, 152

Knickerbocker, Dietrich (pseud. of Washington Irving). ILN, 15

Knorr von Rosenroth, Christian (German mystic, 1636-1689, author of *Kabbalah denudata*). OC, 1029

Knox, John (Scottish religious reformer, founder of Presbyterianism, 1514?-1572, author of *First Blast of the Trumpet against the Monstrous Regiment of Women, Treatise on Predestination* and other works). OC, 726. LA, 68. P, 36

Koch, Max (author of a highly nationalistic history of German literature). OC, 280

Kodama, María (second wife Borges, married 1986). OCC, 788. A, 7, 8, 32, 41, 51, 58, 60, 84. C, 9, 87. CONJ, 11, 35. OP, 487, 511. SN, 93

Koeppen, Karl Friedrich (German scholar of Norse mythology and Buddhism, author of *Die Religion des Buddhas*, 1857, and *Literarische Einleitung in die nordische Mythologie*, 1837). OC, 742, 743. OCC, 724, 750

Koerner (character in Soffici film *Prisioneros de la tierra*). BC, 63

Koheleth (name of the speaker in *Ecclesiastes*). BC, 64

Kohler, Fred (American movie actor, 1889-1938, often seen as the bad guy in cowboy films). BC, 63. CONJ, 75

Kolbein el Fuerte (subject of St. Olaf, king of Norway). PB, 200

Konrad, Karl (German editor of Snorri Sturluson's *Prose Edda*). OC, 371

Koppen. See Koeppen

Korda, Alexander (Hungarian film director and producer, 1893-1956). BC, 28, 44, 46, 47

Kormak Ogmundarson (Icelandic skald). OCC, 948

Korzeniowski, Jozef. See Conrad, Joseph

Korzybski, Alfred (philosopher
of language, 1879–1950,
author of *The Manhood of
Humanity*). OC, 198–99

Kosher (name of kosher butcher
in Bustos Domecq story).
OCC, 376, 377

Kotsuké no Suké, Kir (uncivil
master of ceremonies of
Japanese legend, subject of
an early Borges story). OC,
320–23

Kraken (Scandinavian sea
monster, subject of a poem by
Tennyson). OCC, 653

Kranz, Walther (German scholar,
author of *Die Kultur der
Griechen*, 1943, *Die Fragmente
der Vorsokratiker*, 1934 and
other works). OCC, 609

Krazy Kat (George Herriman
cartoon character, subject of
numerous animated films from
1916 to 1960). OC, 224.
BC, 33

Kreegan (character in Shaw
play). OC, 748

Kriemhild (character in the
*Nibelungenlied*). OC, 383.
OCC, 910, 912–15

Krishna (Hindu deity, the
eighth avatar of Vishnu).
OCC, 736

Kroner (translator of
*Nibelungenlied*). OCC, 975

Kronfuss, Perla (friend of
Emma Zunz, character in
Borges story). OC, 565

Kroo (primitive tribe similar
to the Yahoos, mentioned in
Brodie's report). OC, 1074

Kropotkin, Piotr Alekseyevich
(Russian prince and
anarchist, 1842–1921). P,
13, 49

Kuan Yin (Chinese goddess of
mercy). OCC, 767

Kubin, Eliseo (character in
Borges–Bioy filmscript).
OCC, 199, 260, 266–67, 270–
71, 282, 284–87, 290–95.
BC, 77

Kubin, Jaroslav (character in
Jaromir Hladík's verse drama
*Los enemigos*). OC, 510

Kublai Khan (Mongol emperor of
China, founder of the Yuan
dynasty, 1215?–1294). OCC
832, 882. SN, 61, 71

Kuhlmann, Ulrike von (friend
of Borges). OC, 560, 574

Kuhn, Franz Felix Adalbert
(German philologist and
folklorist, 1822–1881, author
of numerous works on
comparative mythology, Indo-
Germanic peoples and
languages, German folktales
and early literature, etc.).
OC, 708

Kuranosuké, Oishi (character in
Japanese legend of the forty
seven Ronins). OC, 321, 323

Kutb (upright men of Islam
whose mission is to justify
the world to God). OCC, 655

Kuyata (Islamic monster, bull
with four thousand eyes).
OCC, 654

Kvo-Lang (Chinese admiral,
character in Borges story).
OC, 308, 309

Lab (queen in the *Arabian
Nights*). OC, 412

Labruna (Argentine politician).
OCC, 13

Lachmann, Karl (German
philologist, 1793–1851,
author of important treatises
on Old High German metrics
and poetics, editor of the
first critical edition of the
*Nibelungenlied* in 1826 and of
an important edition of
Lessing's works, and
translator of Shakespeare's
sonnets and *Macbeth*). OCC,
911

Lactancio (Lucius Caelius
Firmianus Lactantius,
Christian author and
apologist, born in Africa,
c.260–340, author of *De
Opificio Dei*, *Divinae
Institutiones*, *Phoenix* and
other works). OCC, 588,
733n.

Laderecha (ranch foreman,
character in Reyles). OC,
1058

Ladner, Max (German or Swiss
    scholar of Buddhism).    OCC,
    780
Lady Macbeth (character in
    Shakespeare's *Macbeth*).
    OCC, 819.    P, 145, 146
Laercio, Diogenes (Diogenes
    Laertius, Greek biographer,
    early 3rd century, author of
    *Lives of Eminent
    Philosophers*).    OCC, 740
Laertes (king of Ithaca,
    father of Ulysses).    OC,
    250, 1117.    OCC, 15.    NED,
    113.    OP, 394, 526.    P,
    144
Lafayette, Marie Joseph,
    marquis de (French general
    and political leader, 1757–
    1834).    ILN, 15
Laferrer (character in Borges
    story).    OC, 1036
Lafinur, Juan Crisóstomo
    (Argentine poet, 1797–1824).
    OC, 619, 757, 1054.    OP,
    501.    P, 135
Lafinur (Borges's cousin).
    See Melián Lafinur, Alvaro
La Fontaine, Jean de (French
    poet and fabulist, 1621–
    1695).    OC, 204, 412.    P,
    110
Laforgue, Jules (French poet,
    1860–1887, author of
    *L'Imitations de Notre-Dame la
    Luna, Les Complaintes* and
    other works).    OC, 122.
    OCC, 468, 473, 474.    CONJ,
    33.    I, 137.    ILN, 43.
    PB, 160, 162, 166, 231
Lagrange (family in Suárez
    Lynch story).    See
    Grandvilliers-Lagrange
Lais (Greek courtesan of
    Sicily, carried to Corinth
    after the Athenian expedition
    to Sicily).    OC, 591
Lajouane (bookseller in Buenos
    Aires).    OCC, 320
Lalou, René (French critic and
    historian of French
    literature).    P, 141
Lamartine, Alphonse Marie Louis
    de (French poet, novelist
    and statesman, 1790–1869).
    OCC, 502.    NED, 119

Lamb, Charles (English
    essayist, 1775–1834).    OC,
    660.    P, 87, 120
Lamb, Richard (character in
    Hudson's *Purple Land*).    OC,
    734, 735, 736.    TE, 33–36
Lambkin Formento, Hilario
    (character in Bustos Domecq
    stories).    OCC, 300, 315–17
Lamed Wufnik (thirty-six
    upright men of Jewish
    legend).    OCC, 655
Lamias (Greco-Roman monsters,
    half-woman, half-serpent).
    OCC, 656
Lamprecht von Regensburg
    (German preacher, early 13th
    century, author of a *Sanct
    Francisken Leben* and the
    poetic allegory *Die Tochter
    Syon*).    OCC, 907–8
Lampridius, Aelius (one of
    several authors known as
    *Scriptores historiae
    Augustae*, whose work includes
    an account of the life of
    Heliogabalus).    OC, 459
Lamy, Bernard (French
    rhetorician, 1640–1715,
    author of *La Rhétorique; ou,
    l'Art de parler*, 1701, and
    numerous other works on
    rhetoric).    I, 65
Lana, Jacopo della (14th
    century commentator on Dante,
    author of *Commento alla
    Divina Commedia*).    NED, 92
Lancelote (knight in Arthurian
    legend, sometimes Lanzarote).
    C, 73.    SN, 24
Landi (engineer, character in
    Borges-Bioy filmscript).
    OCC, 256–57, 295
Landor, Walter Savage (English
    poet and essayist, 1775–
    1864).    ILN, 21.    SN, 155
Lane, Edward (British
    Orientalist, 1801–1876,
    author of *Account of the
    Manners and Customs of the
    Modern Egyptians* and trans-
    lator of *Selections from
    the Kur-an* and the *Arabian
    Nights*).    OC, 397, 398, 399,
    400, 401, 403, 404, 405, 406,
    407, 408, 409, 588, 1073.

OCC, 590, 672, 695. LA,
11. SN, 64, 65, 71, 73.
TE, 65

Lane, Theophilus (Edward Lane's
clergyman father). OC, 398

Lang, Andrew (British scholar
and man of letters, 1844–
1912, author of *Myth, Ritual
and Religion,* a *History of
Scotland, Essays in Little,
Letters to Dead Authors,*
translations of Homer and
Theocritus, numerous
collections of fairy tales,
etc.). OC, 215n., 240, 241,
291, 405, 693, 731, 998.
OCC, 844, 857, 895. ILN,
15. NED, 118, 121n. P,
83, 117

Langdon, Harry (American film
actor, 1884–1944, known for
his portrayals of clowns).
OC, 223, 224. BC, 28, 33

Lange, Haydee (Argentine
writer, author of *Gigante
americano: Walt Whitman y su
época,* 1944, and translator
of *The Abasement of the
Northmores*). OC, 42. A,
67. CONJ, 75

Lange, Norah (Argentine poet
and novelist, b. 1906, author
of *La calle de la tarde, 45
días y 30 marineros,
Cuadernos de infancia* and
other works). OC, 380.
OCC, 497. I, 73, 76–78,
160. P, 106–7

Langland, William (putative
author of *Piers Plowman,*
c.1332–c.1400). OCC, 814,
840, 896

Lanier, Sidney (American poet
and musician, 1842–1881,
author of *Tiger Lilies*).
ILN, 30–31

Lanuza, José Luis (Argentine
poet, short–story writer and
essayist, 1903–1976). P, 62

Lao Tse or Lao Tzu (Chinese
philosopher, reputed founder
of Taoism and putative author
of the *Tao Te King,* b. c.604
B.C.). OC, 265, 633.
OCC, 619, 701, 728, 766

Lapitas (Lapiths, in Greek
myth the enemies of the
centaurs). OCC, 604

Laplace, Pierre Simon, marquis
de (French astronomer and
mathematician, 1749–1827,
author of *La Méchanique
celeste, Exposition du
systeme du monde* and other
works). OC, 279, 282, 651.
BO, 46. NED, 122. P, 154

Lappenberg, Johann Martin
(German historian, 1794–1865,
author of *Geschichte von
England* and many works on
the history of Germany and the
Netherlands). LA, 111

Laprida, Eusebio (sergeant in
Argentine army in 1856,
mentioned in Borges story).
OC, 562

Laprida, Francisco Narciso de
(Argentine politician, 1780–
1829, president of the
Congress of Tucumán of 1816).
OC, 863, 867–68, 1111. OP,
385. PB, 132, 152

Laquedem, Isaac (Flemish name
for the Wandering Jew). OC,
591

Larbaud, Valery (French writer,
1881–1937, author of *A. O.
Barnabooth, Fermina Marquez,
Ce vice impuni, la lecture*
and other works). I, 20,
25. ILN, 9. P, 7, 118

Larco, Jorge (Argentine painter
and writer, author of *La
pintura española moderna y
contemporánea,* 1964, and
other works). OC, 984

Lares (in Roman religion,
guardian spirits of home).
OCC, 657

Larousse, Pierre (French
grammarian and lexicographer,
1817–1875). LA, 48

Larrain, Pedro (character in
Borges–Bioy filmscript).
OCC, 266–69, 273, 274, 282–
84, 288–90, 292, 294–96

Larramendi, Ercilia (character
in Borges–Bioy filmscript).
OCC, 224, 225, 229–30, 232–
37, 239, 244, 248–49

Larramendi, Israel (character in Borges-Bioy filmscript). OCC, 135, 140, 217, 221, 224–29, 231–37, 245, 248–50

Larrañaga (perhaps refers to Dámaso Antonio Larrañaga, Uruguayan naturalist, 1771–1848). OCC, 448

Larrea, Benito (character in Bustos Domecq story). OCC, 375–80

Larreta, Enrique (Argentine novelist, 1875–1961, author of *La gloria de don Ramiro, Zogoibi* and other works; Borges sometimes mockingly calls him "el doctor Rodríguez Larreta"). OC, 220, 448. P, 55

Larsen (author of German encyclopedia). LA, 48

Las Casas, Bartolomé de (Spanish Dominican monk and missionary in the New World, 1474–1566, author of *Historia general de las Indias* and *Brevíssima relación de la destruyción de las Indias*). OC, 295

Las Heras, Juan Gregorio (Argentine general and politician, 1780–1866). PB, 132

Lasso de la Vega, Rafael (Argentine writer who collaborated in *Caras y Caretas*) I, 159

Lasswitz, Kurd (German writer, 1848–1910, author of *Geschichte der Atomistik vom Mittelalter bis Newton* and other works). OC, 429, 747

Last Reason (pseud. of Máximo Sáenz, Argentine journalist and humorist, 1886–1960). OC, 655. TE, 137

Latini, Brunetto (Italian man of letters, d. 1294?, author of the first vernacular encyclopedia). OCC, 573

Latour. See Fernández Latour

Lauhirat, Juan B. (Argentine grain merchant, b. 1889, here a correspondent of Borges about Wenceslao Suárez). OC, 172

Laura. See Cruz, Laura

Laurel, Stan (British film actor, 1890–1965, worked in team with Oliver Hardy). BC, 47

Laurencena (part-owner of a meat packing plant). OC, 169

Lavalle, Juan (Argentine general, leader of Unitarian forces against Rosas, 1797–1841). OC, 184, 561, 1048. P, 17, 18, 28, 131, 138. PB, 133, 152

Lavardén, Manuel José de (Argentine dramatist and poet, 1754–1809, author of "Oda al majestuoso río Paraná"). A, 73

Lavater, Johann Kaspar (Swiss theologian and mystic, student of human physiognomy, 1741–1801). PB, 229

Lavinia (character in Shaw play). OC, 749

Lavinia (character in Dante). NED, 102. PB, 184

Lawrence, David Herbert (English novelist, 1885–1930, author of *Sons and Lovers, The Rainbow, The Plumed Serpent, The White Peacock, Lady Chatterley's Lover* and other works). OC, 186, 685. OCC, 49, 852. P, 117

Lawrence, Frieda von Richthofen Weekley (German noblewoman married to D. H. Lawrence). OCC, 852

Lawrence, Thomas Edward (British adventurer, soldier, writer and scholar, also known as Lawrence of Arabia and T. E. Shaw, 1888–1935, author of *Seven Pillars of Wisdom* and a translation of the *Odyssey*). OC, 514, 756. OCC, 852. P, 15n., 117, 174. PB, 145, 215

Layamon (Anglo-Saxon poet, 13th century, author of *Brut*). OCC, 897–98

Lázaro (in Bible, man of Bethany resurrected by Jesus). OCC, 827, 841, 903. C, 66. LA, 20. TE, 101

Le Bon.  See Lebon

Le Corbusier  (pseud. of
Charles Edouard Jeanneret,
Swiss-French architect, 1887–
1965).    OCC, 109, 301, 333

Le Fanu, Tonio  (character in
Suárez Lynch novella).    OCC,
149, 155–57, 159, 161, 163,
165, 167–73, 175–76, 178–80,
185, 193–95

Le Parc, Julio  (Argentine
painter, b. 1928).    OCC, 423

Lead, Jane Ward  (English
mystic, 1623–1704, leader of
the Philadelphians, author of
a diary entitled  A Fountain
of Gardens).    OCC, 637n.

Leadbeater, Charles Webster
(writer on theosophy, 1847–
1934, author of  The Astral
Plane).    OC, 279

Leandro  (Leander, in Greek
myth, lover of Hero,
priestess of Aphrodite in
Sestos, who swam the
Hellespont nightly to visit
her).    OCC, 831

Lear  (legendary king of
Britain, subject of
Shakespeare play).    OC, 738.
P, 165.    TE, 147

Lear, Edward  (English humorist
and artist, 1812–1888, author
of  The Book of Nonsense).
PB, 160

Leatherstocking (main character
in Cooper's  Leatherstocking
Tales, also known as Natty
Bumppo, Pathfinder and
Deerslayer).    ILN, 14

Leavis, Frank Raymond  (English
critic and teacher, 1895–
1978, author of  The Great
Tradition, New Bearings in
English Poetry and other
works).    OC, 717, 718

Lebon, Phillippe  (French
chemist, 1769–1804).    OC,
393

Leconte de Lisle, Charles Marie
(French Parnassian poet,
1818–1894, author of  Poemes
antiques, Poemes barbares and
other works).    BO, 33.    LA,
53

Lecoq, Monsieur  (detective in
Gaboriau novel  Monsieur
Lecoq, 1869).    OCC, 15

Leda  (in Greek mythology,
queen of Sparta seduced by
Zeus, who visited her in the
form of a swan).    OC, 1128.
HE, 58

Lee, Robert E.  (Confederate
general during the U.S. Civil
War, 1807–1870).    OC, 942.
C, 33

Lee, Manfred  (American writer,
1905–1917, co-author with his
cousin Frederick Dannay of
the detective novels of
Ellery Queen, and co-editor
of  Ellery Queen's Mystery
Magazine).    ILN, 57

Legouis, Emile  (French
literary historian and
critic, 1861–1937, co-author
with Cazamian of a  History of
English Literature).    OCC,
857, 887

Leguisamo  (famous Argentine
jockey).    OCC, 159

Leguizamón, Martiniano
(Argentine writer, 1858–1935,
author of  Montaraz, Calandria
and other works).    OC, 114.
OCC, 429, 517.    PB, 153

Lehmann-Nitzsche, Roberto
(Argentine ethnologist and
linguist, 1872–1938, author
of a book on Santos Vega).
OC, 132

Lehmgrubner, Wilhelm  (German
scholar, b. 1910, author of
Die Erwecknung der Valkyrie,
1935).    OCC, 967n.

Lehnert, Martin (German scholar
of Anglo-Saxon poetry, author
of  Altenglisches
Elementarbuch and other
works).    OCC, 974

Leibniz, Gottfried Wilhelm,
Baron von  (German
philosopher, mathematician,
historian and scientist,
1646–1716, author of  Essais
de Théodicée sur la Bonté de
Dieu, la liberté de l'homme
et l'origine du mal).    OC,
256, 258, 276, 280, 434, 444,
445, 496, 647, 692n., 704,

705, 707n., 759, 772. A, 72. BC, 60, 93. NED, 139n. PB, 159. SN, 135

Leif Arnarson (mentioned in runic inscription found by Black Sea). LA, 117

Leif Ericsson or Eiriksson (Norse discoverer of America, fl. c.1000). OCC, 940. C, 32. NED, 118. PB, 190

Leisegang, Hans (German philosopher, 1890-1951, author of *Denkformen*, *Einfuhrung die Philosophie, Die Gnosis* and other works). LA, 81

Lempriere, John (English classical scholar, born in Jersey, c.1765-1824, author of a classical dictionary, *Bibliotheca Classica*, and of a *Universal Biography of Eminent Persons in all Ages and Countries*). OC, 228n., 264. OCC, 645, 696

Lemures (in Roman religion, vampire-like ghosts of the dead). OCC, 657. OP, 442

Lenin, V. I. (pseud. of Vladimir Ilyich Ulyanov, Russian revolutionary, 1870-1924). OC, 725

Leodila (character in Boiardo's *Orlando Innamorato*). OCC, 920

Leonardo da Vinci (Italian painter, architect, musician, scientist, 1452-1519). OCC, 679, 680, 691, 704. BO, 46

Leone (character in Ariosto's *Orlando Furioso*). OCC, 920

Leonor (Eleanor of Aquitaine, 1122?-1204, queen of Louis VII of France and later of Henry II of England). OCC, 897

Leonore (character in Poe's poem "The Raven"). BO, 70

Leovenath (Layamon's father). OCC, 897

Lepe. OCC, 186

Leroux, Gaston (French writer of crime fiction, 1868-1927, author of *Le Mystere de la chambre jaune, Le Parfum de la dame en noir* and other works). BO, 75

Lesage, Alain-René (French writer, 1668-1747, author of *Gil Blas de Santillane*). SN, 71

Lessing, Gotthold Ephraim (German philosopher, dramatist and critic, 1729-1781, author of the *Laokoon* and numerous other writings on aesthetics). OC, 280, 383. BC, 44. P, 95. PB, 169

Letellier, Charles Louis Augustin (French linguist and language philosopher, b. 1801, inventor of an artificial language and author of *Cours complet de langue universelle, Etablissement immédiat de la langue universelle* and other works). OC, 707

Leucipo (Leucippus, Greek philosopher, 5th century B.C.). OC, 429

Leumann, Carlos Alberto (Argentine critic, novelist and journalist, 1882-1952, scholar of the *Martín Fierro*). OCC, 565

Leusden, Johannes (German theologian and Hebraist, 1624-1699, author of *Philologus Hebraeo-Graecus* and other works). OC, 502, 507

Levene, Ricardo (Argentine historian, 1885-1959, author of *Lecciones de historia argentina, La Revolución de Mayo* and *Mariano Moreno*). OCC, 65

Levi (third son of Jacob in the Bible). A, 35

Leviatán or Leviathan (Biblical aquatic monster). OCC, 646. OP, 484. SN, 25, 134. VA, 38

Lewes, George Henry (English critic and author, 1817-1878, author of a *Biographical History of Philosophy* and other works). OC, 244, 276, 745

Lewis, Clive Staples (English author, 1898-1963, author of

*The Problem of Pain, Out of the Silent Planet, Perelandra, The Allegory of Love* and numerous other works). OC, 764. OCC, 576–77, 687

Lewis, Sinclair (American novelist, 1885–1951, author of *Main Street, Babbitt, Elmer Gantry, Dodsworth* and other works). ILN, 35. P, 27

Lewisohn, Ludwig (American novelist and critic, born in Berlin, 1882–1955, author of *The Story of American Literature*). OC, 681, 685. P, 81, 101

L'Herbier, Marcel (French film director, 1888–1979). BC, 36

Lhomond, Charles-Francois (French abbot, grammarian and writer, 1727–1794, author of *De viris illustribus Romae* and *Elements de la grammaire latine*). OC, 486

Li Su (minister of the so-called First Emperor of China, Shih Huang Ti). OC, 679

Liang (dynasty of the Tu-Bat family in southern China, fl. early 5th century A.D.). PB, 196

Licofronte (Lycophron of Chalcis, Alexandrian Greek poet and playwright, 3rd century B.C.). OC, 375n., 382. OCC, 650, 948

Liddell, Alice (little English girl who became Alice in Wonderland). OCC, 838

Liddell Hart, Basil Henry (English military strategist and writer, 1895–1970, author of *A History of the World War, 1914–1918, A History of the Second World War* and other works). OC, 276, 472

Liebre Lunar (Chinese equivalent of the man in the moon). OCC, 658

Liliencron, Detlev, Freiherr von (German lyric poet, 1844–1909). OC, 158. C, 43. P, 21

Lilith (Jewish female demon). OCC, 659. ILN, 45

Lima, Félix (Argentine humorist and writer, author of *Con los nueve . . .* and *Pedrín*). OC, 103, 117, 118, 653. TE, 22

Limardo, Tadeo (character in Bustos Domecq stories). OCC, 85, 87, 90–104, 360, 362

Linares, Jorge (character in Bustos Domecq story). OCC, 427

Lincoln, Abraham (U. S. president, 1809–1865). OC, 295, 498, 853, 1132. ILN, 28, 45, 47, 48, 63

Linde, Christoph zur (ancestor of Otto Dietrich zur Linde). OC, 576, 580

Linde, Dietrich zur (ancestor of Otto Dietrich zur Linde). OC, 576

Linde, Friedrich zur (ancestor of Otto Dietrich zur Linde). OC, 580

Linde, Otto Dietrich zur (character in Borges story, perhaps related to his namesake, Otto zur Linde, German poet, 1873–1938, author of poetry inspired by Nietzsche). OC, 576–81

Lindsay, Vachel (American poet, 1879–1931). ILN, 48

Liniers, Santiago de (Jacques de Liniers, French officer in Spanish service, 1753–1810, viceroy of the Río de la Plata, 1807–1810). I, 133. P, 136

Linnig, Samuel (Uruguayan writer of tango lyrics, author of "Milonguita"). TE, 23

Lipsio, Justo (Justus Lipsius or Joest Lips, Flemish scholar of Latin literature, 1547–1606). OC, 641

Lisi (woman in Quevedo sonnet). I, 41, 142. IA, 75

Littmann, Enno (German scholar and archeologist, translator of the *Arabian Nights*). OC, 401, 405, 407, 408, 409, 410–13. SN, 72, 73

Llambías, Hector (Argentine essayist, a conservative nationalist). OCC, 176

Llanderas, Nicolás de las (Argentine dramatist, co-author with Malfatti of *Así es la vida* and *Los tres berretines*). OC, 653

Llull, Raimón (sometimes Lull, Lulio or Lullius, Mallorcan theologian, novelist and poet, 1235?-1316?, author of *Ars compendiosa inveniendi veritatem* or *Ars magna*, *Llibre de contemplació*, *Arbre de Filosofia d' Amor* and other works). OC, 262, 445, 692, 747, 748. OCC, 327. A, 70-72. IA, 26. PB, 213

Lobatto, Carlos J. (provincial poet, Bustos Domecq character). OCC, 429, 430

Lobezno. See Ulfilas

Lobo, Jerónimo (Portuguese Jesuit missionary, 1593-1678, author of a *Viagem a Abissinia*). OCC, 828

Locarno, María Esther (character in Bustos Domecq story). OCC, 438-45

Locke, Herbert (character in Borges story). LA, 138, 140, 141, 145

Locke, John (English philosopher, 1632-1704, author of two *Treatises on Government*, a treatise *On Education* and other works). OC, 489, 718, 719, 745, 758. BO, 31. ILN, 11, 20. OP, 501

Loco Calcomanía (nickname for a character in Bustos Domecq). OCC, 400

Loew den Bezabel, Judah (Jehudah Loewe den Bezalel, rabbi of Prague, c.1520-1609, later a character in Meyrink's *Der Golem*). OCC, 638

Loewenthal, Aarón (character in Borges story). OC, 564, 566-68

Loiácomo, Leonardo L. or Pardo (character in Bustos Domecq stories). OCC, 165, 174, 393

Loki (Scandinavian god of mischief and evil, sometimes Utgarda-Loki). OCC, 707, 929, 930, 954, 966

Loman, Willy (character in Miller play *Death of a Salesman*). ILN, 55

Lombardi, Francesco Bonaventura (commentator on Dante, author of *La Divina Commedia di Dante Aleghieri*, 1822). NED, 148

Lombroso, Cesare (Italian criminologist and physician, 1835-1909, author of *La Donna delinquente*, *Genio e follia*, *L'Uomo di genio* and other works). OCC, 25

Lomuto (perhaps refers to Francisco Lomuto, the tango musician). OCC, 65, 393

London, Jack (John Griffith London, American novelist, 1876-1916, author of *The Sea Wolf*, *The Call of the Wild*, *Before Adam* and other works). ILN, 26, 29-30, 57

Long, Gilbert (character in James's *Sacred Fount*). P, 101

Longfellow, Henry Wadsworth (American poet, 1807-1882, author of *Hiawatha*, *Evangeline* and numerous other works, and translator of Dante, various Spanish poets and early Germanic poetry). OC, 671, 980. OCC, 799, 801, 896. ILN, 17, 18, 21, 23, 27, 28, 31, 41, 52. NED, 118, 161. P, 82, 170. SN, 30. TE, 57

Longobardi (painter). OCC, 347, 375

Longuet, Maximilien (character in Bustos Domecq story). OCC, 331-32

Lonnrot, Erik (detective in Borges story). OC, 499-507

Lonnrot, Elias (Finnish philologist, compiler of the *Kalevala*, 1802-1884). P, 170

Loomis, Federico Juan Carlos (character in Bustos Domecq, author of *Boina*, *Catre*, *Luna*,

*Nata* and *Oso*). OCC, 319–22, 340

Lope de Vega Carpio, Félix. See Vega Carpio, Félix Lope de

López, Estanislao (Argentine caudillo, 1786–1838, governor of Santa Fe). OC, 561, 655, 1001, 1121. OP, 400. P, 64

López, Francisco Solano (Paraguayan general and president, 1826?–1870). A, 74

López, Juan (character in Borges poem). CONJ, 95

López, Luis Carlos (Colombian poet, 1883–1950). I, 26

López, Vicente Fidel (Argentine novelist and historian, 1815–1903). IA, 177. PB, 125, 167

López de Ayala, Pedro (Spanish historian and poet, 1332–c.1407, author of *El rimado de palacio*). IA, 70

López de Sigura, Ruy (Spanish writer, author of *Libro de la invencion liberal y arte del juego de axedrez*, 1561). OC, 445

López Jordán, Ricardo (Argentine military leader and caudillo, 1822–1889). OC, 152, 1001. OCC, 432, 526. P, 97. PB, 132 CONJ, 43

López Merino, Francisco (Argentine poet, 1904–1928, author of *Canciones interiores*, *Tono menor* and *Las tardes*). OC, 93, 985.

López Velarde, Ramón (Mexican poet, 1888–1921, author of "Suave patria" and numerous other works). OCC, 462, 501

Lorber, Jakob (German musician and educator, 1800–1864, author of *Johannes das grosze Evangelium*). OCC, 584

Lord Jim (character in Conrad novel *Lord Jim*). OC, 572

Lorente, Severiano (friend of Carriego). OC, 115

Lorenzo, Aldonza (peasant woman on whom Don Quijote based his Dulcinea). OC, 284. BC, 72

Lorikus (duke in Norse myth). OCC, 952–53

Lorusso, Arturo (Argentine playwright). OCC, 96

Los (mythical figure in Blake's prophetic books). OCC, 840

Lotario (character in Cervantes's exemplary novel *El curioso impertinente*, inserted in the *Quijote*). OC, 218

Lotze, Rudolf Hermann (German philosopher and psychologist, 1817–1881, author of a *Metaphysik, Logik, System der Philosophie* and other works). OC, 256, 257. OCC, 582

Louverture, Toussaint (Haitian general and politician, leader of the black slave revolt, 1743–1803). OC, 295

Lovecraft, Howard Philip (American writer of science fiction, 1890–1937). ILN, 58–59. LA, 65, 180. P, 27

Lowell, Amy (American poet, 1874–1925). OC, 717

Lowes, John Livingston (American scholar, 1867–1945, author of well-known work on Coleridge, *The Road to Xanadu*). OC, 644n.

Lowrie, Walter (author of *Kierkegaard*, 1938). OC, 711

Loyson, Charles Hyacinthe (French preacher, 1827–1912, author of a work on clerical celibacy). OCC, 187

Lozano, Isidro (doctor in Coronel Pringles, character in Borges story). OC, 1126

Lubbock, Percy (British critic, historian, and biographer, 1879–1965, author of *The Craft of Fiction* and other works). P, 102

Lubitsch, Ernst (German film director, 1892–1947, director of *Trouble in Paradise* and many other films). OCC, 199. BC, 46, 77

Lucano (Marcus Annaeus Lucanus, Latin poet, born in Spain, 39–65, author of the *Bellum Civile* or *Pharsalia*). OC, 249, 662, 667, 937. OCC,

writer, 1504–1566, author of
*Introducción del symbolo de
la Fe, Guía de pecadores* and
other works). I, 65

Luis de León, Fray (Spanish
poet, Biblical translator and
didactic writer, 1527?–1591,
author of *La perfecta casada,
De los nombres de Cristo,*
"La vida retirada" and other
works). OC, 737, 1113.
OCC, 595–96, 758n. C, 11–
12. IA, 46–47, 73, 182.
OP, 387, 555. P, 7. SN,
158, 159. TE, 51, 52, 63

Lujanera. See Julia la
Lujanera

Lulio, Ramón. See Llull,
Raimon

Lumbeira (character in Bustos
Domecq). OCC, 125, 128,
134, 135, 350

Lun, Luigi (Italian scholar of
Ariosto). OCC, 920

Luna (character in Borges–Bioy
filmscript). OCC, 212–14,
216, 220–21, 225, 228, 231–
33, 238, 242, 245–47, 250

Luna family (in San Cristóbal
Norte neighborhood in Buenos
Aires). OC, 134

Lung (Chinese dragon). OCC,
619

Luria, Isaac, el León (Jewish
cabalist, 1534–1572). OC,
418, 690. OCC, 741. OP,
481

Luso (in Greek mythology,
brother of Bacchus). PB, 239

Lussich, Antonio D. (Uruguayan
gauchesque poet, 1848–1928).
OC, 154n., 188–93. OCC,
513, 521–24, 532n. P, 92.
PB, 231

Lutero, Martín (Luther, German
leader of the Protestant
Reformation, 1483–1546,
translator of the Bible).
OC, 580. OCC, 864. BO,
45, 46. LA, 170. OP,
495. P, 77, 154, 162. PB,
145. SN, 78

Lutf Ali Azur (supposed Persian
author of an encyclopedia
called *Templo del Fuego*).
OC, 593

Luther, Martin. See Lutero

Lydia. OC, 127

Lyell, Charles (English
geologist, 1797–1875). OC,
651

Lynch, Benito (Argentine
novelist and short-story
writer, 1885–1951). OC, 654

Lynch, Ventura R. (Argentine
folklorist, 1851–1853, author
of *Cancionero bonaerense*).
IA, 115, 135

Lyons, Blind Danny (New York
gangster). OC, 311, 312

Lytton–Bulwer, Edward George
Earle (British novelist,
1803–1873, author of the *Last
Days of Pompeii* and other
works). OC, 464, 697.
OCC, 963

Ma–Tsu (Zen Buddhist monk in
fable). OCC, 773

Macario. See Romero, Macario

Macaulay, Thomas Babington
(English essayist and
historian, 1800–1859, author
of *Lays of Ancient Rome,* a
*History of England* and
numerous *Essays*). OC, 113,
735. OCC, 829, 836.
NED, 86. P, 77. PB, 138,
151, 165

Macaulay, Zachary (Thomas
Babington Macaulay's father,
a philanthropist). OCC, 836

Macbeth (Scottish king, d.
1057, subject of Shakespeare
play). OC, 755, 803, 1093.
OCC, 819, 949. C, 49.
OP, 437. P, 26, 138, 142–
47, 172, 174. PB, 226

Macedonio (Macedonius, bishop
of Constantinople from 342 to
360, heterodox theologian
associated with the
Homoiousians and
Pneumatomachi). OC, 210

Mach, Ernst (Austrian physicist
and philosopher, 1838–1916).
BC, 65. IA, 11

Machado, Benito (Argentine
colonel). OC, 562

Machado, Judith. OP, 476

Machado y Ruiz, Antonio
(Spanish poet, 1875–1939,
author of *Campos de Castilla,*

*Juan de Mairena* and other
works).    OC, 667.    PB, 165
Machado y Ruiz, Manuel
(Spanish poet and playwright,
1874-1947, author of
*Caprichos, Cante hondo* and
other works).    PB, 165, 189
Machen, Arthur  (British author,
1863-1947, author of *The
London Adventure*).    OC, 720.
ILN, 59
Maciel, Antonio.    See
Conselheiro, Antonio
Maciel, María de los Dolores
(Uruguayan woman, first
person to be buried in
Recoleta cemetery in Buenos
Aires).    OC, 92
Macnaghten, W. H.  (Calcutta
editor, publisher of an
edition of the *Arabian Nights*
in 1839).    OC, 407
Macpherson, James  (Scottish
poet, 1736-1796, author of
Ossianic poems).    OCC, 826,
830, 837.    PB, 229, 232
Macy, John (scholar of American
literature, 1877-1932, author
of *The Spirit of American
Literature*).    P, 82.    PB,
123
Mad Hatter  (character in
*Alice's Adventures in
Wonderland*).    P, 109
Madden, Richard  (character in
Borges story).    OC, 472-80
Madre de Grendel  (monster in
*Beowulf*).    OCC, 872, 874
Maenneken Pis  (statue in
Brussels).    OCC, 182
Maeterlinck, Maurice  (Belgian
author, 1862-1949, author of
*Pelléas et Mélisande* and
other works).    OCC, 470.
TE, 110
Maggid de Mesritch   (Rabbi Dov
Baer, the Maggid of Mesritch
or Mezeritz, second leader of
Hasidim, d. 1772).    OC, 751.
P, 85
Magnien   (translator of Homer).
OC, 239.    P, 163
Magnus I  (Magnus the Good, son
of Olaf, Norwegian king,
subject of a saga by Sturla
Thordarson).    OCC, 958, 964

Magnus Barfod or Berfoett
(Viking warrior, died in
Dublin).    OC, 851.    OCC,
959
Magnusson, Eirikr (with William
Morris, translator of the
*Volsunga Saga*).    OC, 381
Magnusson, Finnur  (Icelandic
historian and antiquarian,
scholar of the sagas, 1781-
1847).    OCC, 966
Magog  (warrior who will attack
the people of Israel, perhaps
a Scythian).    OC, 585
Magrebi, Mohamed El.   OC, 328
Mahamut  (character in
Cervantes).    P, 46
Mahavira  (Vardhamana or Jina,
Jain god, perhaps based on a
historical figure who
organized the Jain religion).
OC, 615
Mahdi  (Muhammad Ahmad, Muslim
religion leader in the Sudan,
1844-1885).    OC, 589
Mahdi, Mohamed al-  (caliph,
son of Mansur).    OC, 326,
327, 328
Mahmud, Ghazad  (Mahmud of
Ghazni, Afghan conqueror,
971-1030, who ordered the
compilation of *The Surviving
Monuments of Past
Generations, The Canon
dedicated to Mas'ud,* and
*India*).    OC, 644
Mahmúd Shabistarí  (Persian
Sufi poet, author of the
*Gulshan i Raz* or *The Mystical
Rose Garden,* c.1320). OC, 594
Mahoma  (Mohammed or
Muhammad, the prophet of
Islam, 570?-632).    OC, 270,
343, 361n., 405, 584, 618,
680, 799.    OCC, 62, 349,
574, 599, 709, 827.    IA, 52.
ILN, 16.    NED, 152n.    OP,
514, 527.    P, 15, 34, 68,
159-60.    SN, 68, 80
Maiakovski, Vladimir  (Russian
poet and dramatist, 1893-
1930).    OCC, 319, 948.    P,
173
Maier, Manuel (in Borges story,
alias of Emmanuel Zunz).
OC, 564

Maimónides (Moses ben Maimon, Jewish rabbi, physician and philosopher, 1135–1204, author of the *Guide for the Perplexed*). OC, 511

Mainlander, Philipp (Philipp Batz, German philosopher, 1841–1876). OC, 702

Maistre, Xavier de (French novelist, 1763–1852, author of *Voyage autour de ma chambre*). OC, 619

Maitreya (next Buddha). OCC, 760

Mak (character in *Grettirs Saga*). OC, 368

Malatesta (nickname of Guelf leader, the lord of Verucchio, d. 1312). C, 73

Malcolm (Malcolm III, Scottish king, 1057–1093, character in Shakespeare's *Macbeth*). P, 147

Malebranche, Nicolas (French philosopher, 1638–1715, author of *La Recherche de la vérité*). OC, 766

Malfatti, Arnaldo M. G. (Argentine playwright, co-author with Nicolás de las Llanderas of *Así es la vida* and *Los tres berretines*, 1932). OC, 653

Malherbe, Francois de (French poet and critic, 1555–1628). OC, 383

Mallarmé, Stéphane (French poet, 1842–1898, author of *Hérodiade* and other works). OC, 122, 151, 177, 229, 249, 250, 266, 447, 660, 666, 691, 713, 714, 716, 730, 732, 1022. OCC, 313, 936. P, 7, 59, 120, 125, 129, 146. PB, 147, 230. SN, 14. TE, 125

Mallea, Eduardo (Argentine novelist, b. 1903, author of *La ciudad junto al río inmóvil, Historia de una pasión argentina* and numerous other works). A, 62. OP, 543

Mallea, Fermín (Sarmiento's uncle, whose story is told in *Recuerdos de provincia*). P, 130

Pedro de Chaide, Pedro, Fray (Spanish Augustinian ascetic writer and preacher, 1530?–1589). OC, 356

Malvezzi. NED, 107

Mamberto, Josefa (character in Bustos Domecq story). OCC, 94–103

Mamoulian, Rouben (American film director, b. 1897). OC, 285. BC, 46, 67

Mandeville, John (putative author of the *Voiage of Sir John Maundeville*). OCC, 639

Maneglia (baker, character in Bustos Domecq story). OCC, 377

Mani (Scandinavian moon god). OCC, 926n.

Manilio (Marcus Manilius, Roman poet, fl. 20 A.D, author of a didactic poem on astrology). OCC, 588

Manno (Germanic god). OCC, 899

Mannteufel, Reverendo (character in Borges–Levinson story). HE, 57

Manntoifel, Otto Julius (reverend, character in Bustos Domecq story). OCC, 334

Manoel I (Portuguese king, 1469–1521). PB, 244

Manrique, Jorge (Spanish poet, 1440–1479, author of the *Coplas a la muerte de su padre*). OC, 404n. OCC, 13, 865. A, 73. I, 32. IA, 70, 82, 93–99. ILN, 23. TE, 78

Manrique, Rodrigo (Jorge Manrique's father, the Count of Paredes). I, 32, IA, 82

Mansilla, Lucio V. (Argentine writer, colonel and diarist, 1831–1931, author of *Excursión a los indios ranqueles, Mis memorias* and other works). IA, 177. PB, 167. TE, 6

Mantee (character in film *The Petrified Forest*). BC, 42

Manticora (monster described by Pliny and Flaubert). OCC, 663

Maples Arce, Manuel (Mexican
poet and essayist, b. 1898).
I, 98, 120-23
Maquiavelo, Niccolo
(Machiavelli, Italian author
and statesman, 1469-1527,
author of the *Principe*,
*Discorsi*, *Arte della guerra*
and *Mandragola*). OC, 641
Mara (Nepalese god of love).
OCC, 723-24, 726
Mara (character in Henry
Miller's *Tropic of
Capricorn*). ILN, 45
Mara (demon). SN, 84
Marcela (character in *El
curioso impertinente*, the
exemplary novel Cervantes
inserted in the first part of
the *Quijote*). IA, 142
Marchand, Jean Baptiste (French
explorer and general, 1863-
1934). OC, 408
Marciano Capella. See Capella
Marcó, Ernesto T. (given the
context this would seem to be
an invented name, but there
is a Teodoro Ernesto Marcó
listed in *Quien es quien en
la Argentina*, a politician in
Entre Ríos, b. 1911). OC,
169-70
Marco Antonio (Marcus Antonius,
Roman politician and soldier,
83-30). OC, 402n. OCC,
686
Marco Aurelio (Marcus Aelius
Aurelius Antoninus, Roman
emperor and writer, 121-180).
OC, 359, 395, 396. P, 13
Marco Bruto (Marcus Junius
Brutus, assassin of Julius
Caesar, 85?-42). I, 43
Marco Polo. See Polo, Marco
Marcos, San (St. Mark the
Evangelist). OCC, 643, 878
Marcul or Marculfo (in medieval
dialogues between Solomon and
Saturn, the name given to
Saturn). OCC, 801, 892
Marcus el Jurista. See Markus
Mardrus, Joseph-Charles-Victor
(French physician, 1868-1949,
translator of the *Arabian
Nights*). OC, 398, 400, 406-
413. SN, 72, 73

Marechal, Leopoldo (Argentine
poet, novelist, essayist and
playwright, 1900-1970, author
of *Adán Buenosayres* and
numerous other works). OCC,
497. P, 85. PB, 166.
TE, 86
Marforio (character in Bustos
Domecq story). OCC, 392
Margarita (Margaret of Navarre,
queen of Navarre, 1492-1549,
author of *Heptameron*). OCC,
312. P, 165
Margarita (character in
Goethe's *Faust*). TE, 12
Margolin, Jean-Claude (French
scholar of Flaubert). OCC,
672
Margoulies, Georges (French
scholar of China, author of
an *Anthologie raisonnée de la
littérature chinoise*,
*Histoire de la littérature
chinoise*, *Evolution de la
prose artistique chinoise* and
other works). OC, 710.
OCC, 706
Margulis, doctor (pharmacist,
character in Bustos Domecq
story). OCC, 137, 140
María, Virgen (in New
Testament, mother of Jesus
Christ). OCC, 426, 658,
880, 905, 907, 936, 948.
BC, 57. NED, 116
María Magdalena (in New
Testament, repentant
courtesan). OCC, 726.
TE, 101
Mariana. See Ruiz Villalba
de Anglada, Mariana
Mariani (character in Borges
story). LA, 69, 73-74
Marigargajo. OCC, 185
Marinetti, Filippo Tommaso
(Italian futurist poet,
novelist and critic, 1876-
1944). OCC, 48, 55
Marino, Giambattista (Italian
poet, 1569-1625, author of
*Adone*). OC, 731, 744, 795,
829, 881. OCC, 948. OP,
432
Maritornes (prostitute mistaken
for damsel in distress by Don
Quijote). OCC, 186

Markus (12th century Icelandic poet, known as Markus the Lawman). OC, 376. OCC, 949

Marlowe, Christopher (English dramatist and poet, 1564–1593, author of *Doctor Faustus, Tamerlane, The Jew of Malta* and other works). OC, 678, 1140. OCC, 817–18, 820. OP, 416. P, 144. TE, 12

Mármol, Jose (Argentine poet, novelist and politician, 1817–1871, author of *Amalia, Cantos del peregrino* and other works). P, 28. PB, 131. SN, 147, 148

Marquand, John Phillips (American novelist, 1893–1960, author of *The Late George Apley* and other works). ILN, 49

Marquardt, Herta (scholar of Norse poetry, author of *Die Altenglischen Kenningar,* 1938). OC, 351. LA, 143

Marryat, Frederick (English sea-captain and novelist, 1792–1848). I, 46

Marsham, John (British historian, 1602–1685, author of *Canon chronicus aegyptiacus, ebraicus, graecus*). P, 69

Marte (Mars, Roman god of war). OC, 241, 242, 533, 822. OCC, 900n. CONJ, 83. I, 46. PB, 243. SN, 111

Martensen, Hans Lassen (Danish theologian, 1808–1884, author of works on Christian ethics and dogma, and of a life of Jakob Boehme). OC, 361, 517

Martí, José (Cuban poet, novelist, journalist and political figure, 1853–1895, author of *Versos sencillos, Ismaelillo, Versos libres* and other works). OCC, 38, 464, 466, 468

Martín, Gaspar (Argentine writer, author of *Una mujer fronteriza,* 1924). OC, 199

Martínez Estrada, Ezequiel (Argentine poet and essayist, 1895–1964, author of *Radiografía de la pampa, Muerte y transfiguración de Martín Fierro* and other works). OC, 434, 440, 734. OCC, 462, 513, 561, 565, 707, 838. BO, 24. P, 89, 90, 96. PB, 164, 166, 167

Martínez López, Ramón. LA, 138

Martínez Sierra, Gregorio (Spanish playwright, poet, novelist, actor and journalist, 1881–1948). OCC, 75. I, 158

Maruts (wind gods in the *Vedas*). OCC, 585

Marvell, Andrew (English metaphysical poet, 1621–1678). OCC, 853. ILN, 51

Marx, Karl (German social philosopher, 1818–1883). OC, 404, 725. ILN, 22

Mas y Pi, Juan (Argentine critic and writer, d. 1916, author of studies of Almafuerte, Ghiraldo, Herrera y Reissig, and of Spanish literature). OC, 117. IA, 35, 36

Mascarenhas, don (character in Bustos Domecq, perhaps related to Horacio Alberto and Raúl Mascarenhas, prominent Argentine businessmen). OCC, 128, 135

Masefield, John (English poet, 1878–1967). OCC, 877

Masmudi, Abderrahmen El. OC, 341

Mason, Perry (detective, character in Gardner novels). ILN, 57

Maspons y Camarasa, J. OCC, 186

Masters, Edgar Lee (American poet and biographer, 1868–1950, author of the *Spoon River Anthology*). ILN, 45–46, 48. P, 173

Mastronardi, Carlos (Argentine poet, 1901–1976, author of *Luz de provincia, Tierra amanecida, Conocimiento de la* noche and other works). OC, 163, 433. OCC, 497. PB, 166

Masudi (Arab historian, geographer and philosopher, d. 956, author of *The Golden Meadows*). OC, 406

Mata y Fontanet, Pedro (Argentine scholar, 1810?-1877, author of *Curso de lengua universal*, 1861). OC, 707

Matecito, don. See Larramendi, Israel

Mateo, San (St. Matthew the Evangelist). OC, 362. OCC, 643, 878

Math (wizard in *Mabinogion*). OC, 383

Mather, Cotton (American Puritan clergyman and writer, 1663-1728, author of *The Wonders of the Invisible World*). ILN, 10

Mather, Increase (American Puritan clergyman, 1639-1723). ILN, 10

Matilde. OP, 536

Matisse, Henri (French painter, sculptor and lithographer, 1869-1954). ILN, 40

Mattaldi. OCC, 169

Maturana, José de (Argentine playwright and writer, 1884-1917). OCC, 137

Matusalén (Methuselah, in Bible, man who lived 969 years). OC, 638. I, 35

Maude, Frederic Natusch (British writer on military strategy, author of *Notes on the Evolution of Infantry Tactics, War and the World's Life* and other works). OC, 494

Maupassant, Guy de (French short-story writer and novelist, 1850-1893). OC, 260, 684. ILN, 38. P, 50, 51

Mauriac, Francois (French writer, 1885-1970). I, 18

Mauro, Hrabano. See Hrabano Mauro

Mauthner, Fritz (German novelist and philosopher,

1849-1923, author of *Woerterbuch der Philosophie, Berlin W* and other works). OC, 199, 276, 278, 279, 380, 389, 392, 483, 706, 707, 750. A, 72. IA, 28. P, 110

Maya (Nepalese queen, Buddha's mother). OCC, 623, 721, 722. SN, 81

Mayo, Archie (American film director, 1891-1968, director of *The Petrified Forest* and many other films). BC, 41-42

Mazo, Marcelo del (Argentine writer, author of *Los vencidos*, 1907). OC, 103, 113, 116, 117, 118. IA, 117. LA, 40. P, 26n., 52. PB, 160. TE, 23

McCarthy (translator of Omar Khayyam). NED, 120n.

Mead, George Robert Stow (philosopher, 1863-1933, author of *Fragmente eines verschollenen Glaubens*, 1902). OC, 213

Meccano. OCC, 99

Medea (in Greek mythology, princess of Colchis, skilled in magic and sorcery). OC, 227. OCC, 699, 843. CONJ, 61

Medeiro, Nicasio (character in Bustos Domecq story). OCC, 311, 312, 314

Medoro (character in Ariosto). OC, 837

Medrano, Tomás (knife-fighter in Buenos Aires). OC, 128n.

Medusa (in Greek mythology, most famous of the three monstrous Gorgon sisters). OCC, 593

Mefistófeles (personification of the devil in Faust legend). OCC, 149, 193, 818

Mehring, Sigmar (German literary scholar, 1856-1915, author of *Der Reim* and works on German and French poetry). P, 78

Meinong, Alexius (Austrian philosopher and psychologist, 1853-1920). OC, 435, 769. OCC, 129-33

Meissner, Rudolf (scholar of
Icelandic poetry, author of
*Die Kenningar der Skalden*,
1921). OC, 351. LA, 143

Mejías, Laurentino (author of
*La policía por dentro*, 1913).
OC, 125n.

Mejuto (alleged author of the
*Vidas y obras del Molinero*,
though this article is
included in the *Nuevos
cuentos de Bustos Domecq*).
OCC, 447

Melanchthon, Philip (German
scholar and humanist, 1497–
1560, author of *Loci
communes rerum theologi-
carum*). OC, 335–36

Melaza, doctor (Argentine
ambassador in imaginary
Estado Occidental, character
in Borges story). OC, 1062

Melena (criminal in Buenos
Aires). OC, 1046

Meléndez Valdés, Juan (Spanish
poet and playwright, 1754–
1817). IA, 56

Melián Lafinur, Alvaro
(Argentine poet, writer, and
educator, 1889–1958, cousin
of Borges). OC, 103, 117,
622, 1039, 1042. LA, 10

Melián Lafinur, Luis (Uruguayan
lawyer and historian, b.
1850, author of *Semblanzas
del pasado*, relative of
Borges's father). OC, 152,
156, 489. LA, 181, 213.
P, 133

Meliso (Melissus, Greek
philosopher and admiral of
Samos, last important member
of the Eleatic school, 5th
century B.C.). OC, 704n.

Melkart ("king of the city,"
Carthaginian name for Baal).
CONJ, 37–38

Melpómene (one of Greek muses,
who presides over tragedy).
OCC, 330

Melville, Herman (American
novelist, poet and short-
story writer, 1819–1891,
author of *Moby Dick, Pierre,
Bartleby the Scrivener, Billy
Budd* and many other works).

OC, 229, 660, 677, 731, 1128.
OCC, 200, 561, 712, 892.
BC, 78. BO, 65. ILN, 12,
21, 26, 27. NED, 96, 167.
OP, 484–85, 508. P, 101,
112, 116–18, 119. PB, 181.
SN, 30–31

Memory, Mr. (character in
Hitchcock film *The Thirty-
Nine Steps*). BC, 39

Mena, Juan de (Spanish poet
and prose writer, 1411–1456,
author of the *Laberinto de
fortuna* and other works).
OC, 647. TE, 48

Menandro (Milinda of Buddhist
tradition, Bactrian king of
the Indo-Greeks, ruled 155–
130). OC, 758n. OCC, 746–
47. PB, 195, 196

Menard, Pierre (French
symbolist writer, character
in Borges story, author of
*Les problemes d'un probleme,
Don Quijote* and numerous
other works). OC, 444–50

Menchaca, Clinudo (gaucho).
P, 64

Mencken, Henry Louis (American
editor, author and critic,
1880–1956, author of *The
American Language* and other
works). ILN, 57

Mendax (a jeweler in Bustos
Domecq story). OCC, 78

Mendes, Catulle (French
Parnassian poet, critic and
novelist, 1841–1909). OCC,
311

Mendes, Fradique. OCC, 78

Méndez, Evar (pseud. of
Evaristo González Méndez,
Argentine avant-garde poet,
editor of the magazine *Martín
Fierro* and author of *Palacios
de ensueño*). OC, 117. I,
160

Méndez, Tulio (perhaps Ramón
Tulio Méndez, Argentine
lawyer, b. 1898). P, 90

Mendoza, Pedro de (Spanish
conquistador, founder of
Buenos Aires, 1487?–1536).
PB, 125, 127, 137

Menelao (Menelaus, brother of
Agamemnon and husband of

Helen in Homeric poems).
OCC, 591

Menéndez Pidal, Ramón (Spanish philologist, specialist on medieval Spanish language and literature, 1869-1968). IA, 128

Menéndez y Pelayo, Marcelino (Spanish literary historian, 1856-1912). OC, 149, 367, 741. OCC, 447, 451, 463, 560-61, 836. IA, 46, 72, 87, 93, 94, 96-97, 103, 174. P, 45. PB, 245. SN, 118

Meng Tseu (Chinese astrologist). OCC, 106

Mengano (second member of Spanish trio of Fulano, Mengano and Sutano). OCC, 350, 369

Mennon (Icelandic name for some figure in Trojan story, perhaps Agamemnon). OCC, 952

Mensajero (the White Rabbit in *Alice's Adventures in Wonderland*). P, 109

Mentira (personification of lying). NED, 128

Mercurio (Roman name for Hermes, god of commerce and messenger of the gods). OCC, 423, 928

Meredith, George (English novelist and poet, 1828-1909, author of *The Ordeal of Richard Feverel, The Egoist* and other works). OP, 420. P, 101

Merlín or Merlino (in Arthurian legend, magician, seer and teacher). OC, 627, 970. OCC, 118

Meroveo (Merovech, founder of the first Germanic-Frankish dynasty, king of France from 448 to 457). OC, 217

Merrill, Stuart (American author who wrote mostly in French, 1863-1915). OCC, 311

Mesa, Manuel (Argentine gaucho soldier). OC, 562

Mesonero Romanos, Ramón de (Spanish *costumbrista* writer, 1803-1882). OCC, 327

Messía de Leiva, Alonso (correspondent of Quevedo). IA, 13

Metrodoro (Metrodorus of Lampsacus, Epicurean philosopher, c.331-278, or Metrodorus of Scepsis, philosopher and writer, fl. c.70 B.C.). OC, 488

Meyer (original author of German encyclopedia, *Meyers enzyklopadisches Lexikon*). SN, 146

Meyer, Kuno (scholar of old Irish poetry). OCC, 971n.

Meyer, R. M. (German scholar of Norse literature, author of *Altgermanische Religionsgeschichte*). OCC, 963, 972

Meyrink, Gustav (Austrian writer, 1868-1932, author of *Der Golem*). OC, 1066. OCC, 638. SN, 137-39

Micawber, Mister (character in Dickens's *David Copperfield*). OCC, 835

Michelet, Jules (French romantic historian, 1798-1874, author of *Introduction a l'histoire universelle* and many other works). OCC, 357

Micheli, Pietro (Italian literary scholar, author of *Dal Boiardo all' Ariosto*, 1898, and other works). OCC, 647

Micifuz (name of a cat in Lope de Vega's *Gatomaquia*, 1634). OCC, 156

Mickey Mouse (cartoon character created by Walt Disney in 1928). PB, 122, 176

Midas (Phrygian king in Greek mythology whose touch turned things to gold). OC, 235

Midgardsorm or Midgarthormr (Icelandic monster). OCC, 651, 927. A, 49. CONJ, 53

Mieditis (personification of fear in Bustos Domecq story). OCC, 409

Migne, Jacques Paul (French priest and publisher of theological works, 1800-1875, compiler of *Patrologiae cursus completus*, a work in some 300 vols.). OC, 552

Miguel Angel (Michelangelo Buonarroti, Italian artist, architect and poet, 1475–1564). OC, 729

Miguel Arcangel, San. OCC, 304, 622, 888

Miguens, Zoilo (friend of José Hernández, who wrote him an important letter about the *Martín Fierro*). P, 92, 94

Mikhael, Ephraim (pseud. of Georges-Ephraim Michel, French Symbolist writer, 1866–1890, author of *L'Automne* and *Briséis*). OCC, 311

Miklosich, Franz von (Austrian philologist, 1813–1891, author of important works on the Slavic languages as well as on Romanian, Albanian, Greek and the gypsy language). OC, 522

Milinda. See Menandro

Mill, John Stuart (British philosopher and economist, 1806–1873, author of *System of Logic, Principles of Political Economy, Autobiography* and other works). OC, 244, 245, 258, 388, 650, 651, 747. A, 7. P, 137

Mille, Cecil B. De. See De Mille, Cecil B.

Miller, Arthur (American playwright, b. 1915, author of *Death of a Salesman, View from the Bridge, The Fall* and other works). ILN, 55–56

Miller, Henry (American writer, 1891–1980, author of *Black Spring, The Tropic of Cancer, The Rosy Crucifixion* and other works). ILN, 44–45

Miller, William (British soldier in South America, later a diplomat and writer, 1795–1861, author of a volume of *Memoirs*). OC, 736

Milner, Zdislas (author of a study of Gongora and Mallarmé and French translator of Gracián in 1937). TE, 125

Milton, John (English poet, 1608–1674, author of *Paradise Lost, Paradise Regained, Samson Agonistes* and other works). OC, 249, 264, 265, 281, 384n., 638, 658, 701, 719, 747n., 773, 779, 837, 857, 865, 890, 891, 975. OCC, 459, 484, 540, 588, 628, 688, 711, 814, 822, 824–25, 826, 828, 833, 836, 853, 856, 892. BO, 55. C, 90. CONJ, 47. I, 28, 32, 43. IA, 17. ILN, 10, 41, 42. LA, 141. NED, 86, 138. OP, 376, 380, 408, 419, 451, 522. P, 59, 79n., 154, 168. PB, 161, 225, 245. SN, 13, 18, 152–56. TE, 54, 115–22

Minerva (Roman goddess of the arts, identified with Athena). OCC, 69. A, 9. BO, 71. I, 23. PB, 195

Ming-Ti (Chinese emperor, ruled 58–76, during whose reign Buddhism was introduced to China). OCC, 766

Minnesinger (German medieval knights, poets and singers). OCC, 909

Minos (in Greek mythology, king of Crete, creator of labyrinth at Knossos). SN, 21

Minotauro (monster, half-bull, half-man, imprisoned in the labyrinth at Knossos, also called Asterión). OC, 569–70. OCC, 300, 345, 622, 664, 873. A, 60. CONJ, 61. LA, 73. OP, 436. P, 25. PB, 213. SN, 43

Mir y Baralt, Julio (character in Bustos Domecq story, author of *Acopio de pullas y de gracejos*, 1934). OCC, 450

Mir y Noguera, Juan (Spanish Jesuit writer, 1840–1917, author of *Prontuario de hispanismos y barbarismos, Rebusco de frases castizas* and other works). PB, 175

Miriam (character in Hawthorne's *Marble Faun*). OC, 682

Mirmecoleón (monster, half-lion, half-ant). OCC, 665

Miró, Gabriel (Spanish novelist and short-story writer, 1879-1930). OCC, 13. PB, 170

Mitchell (English bookseller in Buenos Aires). OC, 573

Mitford, A. B. (American diplomat in Japan, author of *Tales of Old Japan*). OC, 320, 345

Mitre, Bartolomé (Argentine military man, statesman and writer, 1821-1906, author of *Historia de San Martín*). OC, 268. OCC, 82, 557, 558. A, 88. BC, 59. P, 18, 94, 95. PB, 131

Mitridates Eupator (Mithridates VI, Eupator Dionysus, king of Pontus and enemy of Rome, 120-63). OC, 488. PB, 172

Mlch (imaginary primitive tribe in Borges story). See Yahoos

Moby Dick (white whale in Melville novel). OC, 229. ILN, 26. NED, 96. P, 116, 117, 119. PB, 181

Moctezuma (Moctezuma II, Aztec emperor, 1466-1520). OC, 261, 599. SN, 62

Moebius, August Ferdinand (German astronomer and mathematician, 1790-1868). OC, 276

Moffo (opera singer). OCC, 327

Mohamed. See Mahoma

Moisés (**Moses**, Hebrew lawgiver in Bible who led Jews out of Egypt in 13th century B.C.). OC, 296, 361, 402n., 496, 517, 651, 750, 751. OCC, 193, 752. I, 25, 143. IA, 38. OP, 559. P, 70

Moisés de León (Moses ben Shemtob de León, Spanish Kabbalist, d. 1305, author of *Zohar*). OC, 668

Mokurai (Zen master in fable). OCC, 773

Molina Massey, Carlos (Argentine nationalist short-story writer and critic). TE, 83-84

Molina Vedia, Mandie. OC, 499

Molina y Vedia, Julio (Argentine avant-garde writer). P, 52

Molinari (character in Borges story). OC, 1049

Molinari, Aquiles (character in Bustos Domecq stories). OCC, 21-34, 35, 53, 62, 85, 367

Molinari, Ricardo (Argentine poet, b. 1898, author of *El pez y la montaña* and other works). IA, 132-34. PB, 166

Moloch (Canaanite god of fire). OCC, 138

Momigliano, Attilio (Italian scholar, 1883-1952, author of *Dante, Manzoni, Verga*). OCC, 605. NED, 98. PB, 182, 238. SN, 13

Mommsen, Theodor (German historian of Rome, 1817-1903). OCC, 899

Momo (Momus, in Greek mythology, spirit of censure and mockery). OCC, 87. I, 88

Moncha. See Ruiz Villalba de Muñagorri

Mondolfo, Rodolfo (Argentine philosopher born in Italy). OC, 636

Monet, Isabelle (friend of Borges). CONJ, 35

Monica (character in Hudson's *The Purple Land*). TE, 35

Monmouth. See Geoffrey of Monmouth

Monner Sans, José María (Argentine scholar and educator, b. 1896, author of *Julián del Casal y el modernismo* and other works). OC, 133n., 423. OCC, 156

Mono (character in a Chinese Buddhist novel, *Journey to the West* or *Monkey*). OCC, 767-78

Moño (a cat in Bustos Domecq story). OCC, 130

Mono Pancho (character in Suárez Lynch novella and

Borges-Bioy filmscript).
OCC, 174–75, 273
Mono de la tinta (fabulous
black monkey that drinks ink,
mentioned by Wang Ta-Hai).
OCC, 668
Monóculos (one-eyed creatures
like the cyclops). OCC,
666–67
Monroe, Harriet (American poet
and editor, 1860–1936, editor
of *Poetry*). ILN, 47, 48
Monroe, James (U. S. president,
1758–1831). ILN, 63
Monroe, Marilyn (American film
actress, born Norma Jean
Baker, 1926–1962). ILN, 56
Monsen, Erling (translator of
the *Heimskringla*). OCC, 975
Monstruo (here an obvious
reference to Perón). OCC,
392–402
Montague (Verona family in
*Romeo and Juliet*). OC, 419
Montaigne, Michel Eyquem,
seigneur de (French
essayist, 1533–1592). OC,
167n., 203, 704, 911, 1103.
OCC, 823, 977. BO, 21, 22,
57. I, 9, 128. ILN, 21.
OP, 381, 546, 558. P, 8,
44, 144. PB, 230. TE,
152
Montalbán (perhaps the Spanish
dramatist and poet Juan Pérez
de Montalbán, 1602–1638).
OC, 799
Montalvo, Juan (Ecuadorian
essayist, 1832–1889, author
of the *Siete tratados*). P,
67
Monteavaro, Antonio (Argentine
journalist who wrote in the
periodical *Crítica*). OC,
117
Monteiro Novato (character in
Bustos Domecq story, an
allusion to the Brazilian
writer José Benito Monteiro
Lobato, 1883–1948). OCC,
311
Montenegro, Gervasio (character
in Bustos Domecq and Suárez
Lynch stories, member of the
Academia Argentina de Letras,
author of *Historia panorámica*

*del periodismo nacional* and
several odes to José Martí).
OCC, 15–19, 35–47, 48, 50,
51–57, 59–60, 71, 76, 78–80,
82, 84, 105, 108–11, 116,
82, 84, 105, 108–11, 116,
118n., 136n., 145, 149, 158–
63, 166, 167, 169–76, 187–91,
299, 300, 319–20, 340, 353,
360, 365, 421, 423
Montenegro, Hortensia
(character in Suárez Lynch
novella, cousin of Gervasio
Montenegro, nicknamed Pampa).
OCC, 149, 159, 160, 161–70,
181, 193
Montes, Eugenio (Spanish
writer, b. 1897, author of *El
viajero y su sombra*). I,
16, 75
Montesinos (in *Don Quijote*,
character in the Cave of
Montesinos). OCC, 187
Montesquieu, Charles Louis de
Secondat, baron de la Brede
et de (French political
philosopher, 1689–1755,
author of *Esprit des Lois* and
other works). P, 140
Montgolfier, Joseph Michel and
Jacques Etienne (French
inventors of the hot air
balloon, brothers, 1740–1810
and 1745–1799 respectively).
A, 33
Montgomerie, Margaret
(Boswell's wife and cousin).
OCC, 829
Montoliú, Manuel de (Spanish
critic, author of *El lenguaje
como fenómeno estético* and
*Manual d'historia crítica de
la literatura catalana
moderna*). IA, 15–16
Montúfar, marqués de (character
in Bustos Domecq story,
contemporary of Zúñiga el
Molinero; because of the
dates given, this perhaps
refers to the Ecuadorian
patriot Juan Pío de Montúfar,
marquis of Seiva Alegre,
1759–1818, who died in
Cádiz). OCC, 450
Moon, John Vincent (Irish
revolutionary and traitor,

character in Borges story).
OC, 491–95

Moore, George (Anglo-Irish author, 1852–1933, author of *Hail and Farewell, Memoirs of My Dead Life, Untilled Field* and other works). OC, 221, 266, 324, 544, 641, 660. OCC, 312. A, 15. P, 119, 148, 149. SN, 157

Moore, Henry (writer on the fourth dimension). See More, Henry

Moore, Henry (English sculptor, b. 1898). OCC, 341

Moqanna, Al. See Hákim de Merv

Mora, Lola. OCC, 340

Morales, Julio (character in Borges-Bioy filmscript). OCC, 199, 201–19, 220–23, 234–42, 243–44, 248, 250–53. BC, 77

Moran, Bugs (New York gangster). OC, 297

Morand, Paul (French diplomat, novelist and travel writer, 1888–1976, author of *Tendres Stocks, Ouvert la nuit, Fermé la nuit, France la doulce* and other works). OC, 402

More, Henry (English philosopher of the Cambridge Platonist school, 1614–1687, author of *Opera theologica, Opera philosophica, Philosophical Poems* and *Divine Dialogues*). OC, 276. P, 159

More, Paul Elmer (American critic, educator and philosopher, 1864–1937). P, 38–39

More, Thomas (English statesman, writer and saint, author of *Utopia*, 1478–1535). OC, 218. LA, 126. VA, 46

Moréas, Jean (French symbolist poet, born in Athens, 1856–1910, author of *Les Syrtes, Les Cantilenes* and *Le Pelerin passionné*). OC, 692

Moreau, Dr. (vivisectionist, character in Wells's novel *The Island of Dr. Moreau*). P, 24

Moreira, Juan (Argentine gaucho, 1819–1874, subject of a novel by Eduardo Gutiérrez and subsequent adaptations for the stage and screen). OC, 116, 127, 130, 659, 958, 1031, 1036, 1040, 1042. OCC, 357. IA, 41. LA, 94–97. P, 40, 64, 98, 113, 114. PB, 153, 154. TE, 8, 10, 26, 101

Morel (Argentine political boss). OC, 329

Morell, Lazarus (James Murrell, a thief of fugitive slaves and murderer, mentioned in Twain's *Life on the Mississippi* and the subject of a Borges story). OC, 295–300

Moreno (character in the *Martín Fierro*, a singer or *payador* and the brother of black killed by Fierro). OC, 179, 295, 269, 295, 519–21, 966. OCC, 552–56. IA, 134

Moreno, Mariano (Argentine jurist, political writer, editor and statesman, 1778–1811). P, 135

Moreto y Cabaña, Agustín (Spanish dramatist, 1618–1669, author of *El desdén con el desdén*). OC, 240

Morgan (character in Borges-Bioy filmscript). OCC, 254, 260–62, 264–67, 269, 274, 276, 278, 282–85, 288–94, 296

Morgan, Charles Langbridge (English dramatic critic and novelist, 1894–1958, author of *Portrait in a Mirror, The Fountain, A Voyage* and other works). OCC, 855

Morgan, Henry (Welsh buccaneer, 1635?–1688). ILN, 49

Morgan, Kenneth W. (author of book on Buddha, 1956). OCC, 780

Morgann, Maurice (English writer and diplomat, 1726–1802, author of an "Essay on the Dramatic Character of Sir John Falstaff," 1777). OC, 738

Muraña, Eulogio (knife-fighter in Buenos Aires, alias "Cuervito"). OC, 129n.

Muraña, Juan (thug in turn-of-the-century Buenos Aires). OC, 128n., 129, 157, 166, 167, 827, 957-58, 961, 1044-47. C, 55-56. CONJ, 85. P, 128. VA, 15

Murchison, Juan (Anglo-Argentine who was for a time Borges's secretary). OC, 994

Murdock, John (character in Borges story). OC, 989-90

Murgan or Murgen (mermaid sanctified in 6th century Wales). OC, 228n. OCC, 697

Murray, Gilbert (British classical scholar, born in Australia, 1866-1957). P, 85

Murrell, James. See Morell

Murry, John Middleton (English critic and editor, 1889-1957). OC, 263, 382

Musa (in Greek mythology, one of nine patronesses of the arts). OCC, 451. BC, 38. BO, 18, 19. OP, 419. P, 98, 137, 173. SN, 126

Musante (Argentine soccer-player). OCC, 360, 361

Musante, Juana (character in Bustos Domecq story). OCC, 86-104, 342

Muscari, Arturo (anarchist friend of Macedonio Fernández). P, 52

Muspell (giant in *Elder Edda*). OCC, 903

Musset, Alfred de (French romantic poet, dramatist and fiction writer, 1810-1857). OCC, 616

Mussolini, Benito (Italian dictator, leader of the Fascist movement, 1883-1945). PB, 158

Muza Bennuseir (character in the *Arabian Nights*). OC, 410

N.. N. (designation in Argentine law for someone whose identity is unknown). OCC, 314

Nadir Shah (shah of Iran, 1688-1747). OC, 589

Naga (Indian king converted to Buddhism). OCC, 671, 724, 725

Nagarjuna (Buddhist monk to whom were revealed the arcane doctrines of Mahayana Buddhism). OCC, 671, 755, 757, 758, 759, 762

Nagas (Indian cloud-serpents). OCC, 671, 727, 747, 755

Nagasena (Buddhist monk who converted Menandro, Bactrian king, according to the *Milinda Panho*). OC, 758n. OCC, 746. PB, 195

Namuncurá, Manuel (leader of the Araucanian Indians in Patagonia, surrendered in 1883 to the Argentine army). OCC, 530

Napoleon I, Bonaparte (French emperor, born in Corsica, 1769-1821). OC, 116, 154, 489, 578, 721, 725, 726, 729. OCC, 25, 94, 95, 166, 431, 444, 450, 830, 832, 834, 908n. BO, 57. ILN, 21, 36. P, 36, 40, 82, 135. PB, 225

Napoleon III (Louis Napoleon Bonaparte, French emperor, 1808-1873). OCC, 841. P, 28-29, 149

Narbondo, Raúl (gerontologist, character in Bustos Domecq stories). OCC, 360, 365-68

Natán (Nathan, Biblical prophet). NED, 144. PB, 180

Nathan, George Jean (American essayist and critic, 1882-1958, co-founder and editor of *The American Mercury* and contributor to *Smart Set*). ILN, 57

Naturaleza (personification of nature). ILN, 11

Nava, el pardo (stock character in Argentine melodramas). OC, 110

Navarrete, Martín Fernández de (Spanish historian and hydrographer, 1765-1844, author of a 5 vol. work on

Nicolás de Cusa (Nikolaus von Cues or Cusanus, German humanist, scientist, statesman and philosopher, 1401-1464, author of *De reparatione Calendarii*). OC, 254, 600-1

Nicolás el barbero (character in *Don Quijote*). C, 15. PB, 207

Nicoll, Allardyce (Yale professor of drama, b. 1894, author of *Film and Theatre*, 1937). BC, 46-48

Nicolson, Harold (English biographer, historian and diplomat, 1886-1968). OCC, 853

Niedner, Felix (German scholar of Icelandic sagas, author of *Islands Kultur zur Wikingerzeit*, 1913, and numerous other works). OC, 369, 381. OCC, 933, 958, 975

Nierenstein (character in Borges story). LA, 47, 52, 57, 58, 59, 63

Nierenstein Souza (Uruguayan poet, novelist and critic, 1897-1935, character in Bustos Domecq story, author of *Brisas de Fray Bentos*, *Pánica llanura* and numerous other works). OCC, 311-14

Nietzsche, Friedrich (German philosopher, 1844-1900, author of *Also Sprach Zarathustra*, *Die Geburt der Tragodie aus dem Geiste der Musik*, *Der Wanderer und sein Schatten*, *Der Wille zur Macht*, *Ecce homo* and other works). OC, 250, 253, 277, 280, 385, 386, 388, 389, 390, 391, 392, 393, 449, 577, 651, 734, 748. OCC, 49, 827, 840, 926n. BO, 14, 83. I, 147. IA, 36, 37, 159. ILN, 21. NED, 93. P, 15, 32, 39. PB, 146, 158, 164, 168, 229. SN, 25, 26, 103

Niflungar (Icelandic name for Nibelungen). OCC, 913

Nils (character in Borges story). LA, 132. VA, 50

Nilsen, Cristián (character in Borges story). OC, 1025-28

Nilsen, Eduardo (character in Borges story). OC, 1025-28

Nimbarka (Hindu mystic). OCC, 634

Ninfas (nymphs in Greek mythology). OCC, 673, 692, 694

Nithhad or Nithhard (in Anglo-Saxon poem, enemy of Welund). OCC, 794

Nizam ul-Mulk (vizier of the Seljuk sultan Alp Arslán, childhood friend of Omar Khayyam and Hassan ibn Sabbah). OC, 688

Njal (hero of Icelandic saga *Njals Saga*). OC, 369, 379. OCC, 939-40

Nobel, Alfred (Swedish chemist and inventor, founder of Nobel prizes, 1833-1896). OCC, 58, 847, 848, 855, 856. ILN, 35, 36, 37, 42

Noche (personification of night). NED, 136

Noé (Noah in Bible, chosen by God to save representative animals and the human race from the flood). OC, 280. OCC, 330, 817. BC, 58

Nolan, James Alexander (character in Borges story). OC, 497, 498

Nolan, Juan Patricio (character in Borges story). OC, 1058-61

Nordau, Max (Hungarian writer and physician, 1849-1923, author of *Entartung*). PB, 141. TE, 96, 121

Nordsee, Doctor (character in Cansinos Assens novel based on Max Nordau). TE, 96

Nornas or Nornir (in Scandinavian mythology, the Furies). OCC, 674, 926. P, 145. PB, 201

Norris, Frank (American novelist and essayist, 1870-1902, author of *McTeague* and other works). ILN, 30

Norris, John (English clergyman and philosopher, 1657-1711, author of *An Essay Towards the Theory of an Ideal and Intelligible World*). OC, 766

Notaris (part owner of the Sastrería Funcional, in Bustos Domecq story). OCC, 355

Notker Labeo (German monk and scholar, teacher at St. Gall, c.950-1022, author of a rhetoric and translator of Aristotle, Boethius etc.). OCC, 907

Novalis (pseud. of Friederich von Hardenberg, German poet, 1772-1801, author of *Hymnen an die Nacht* and other works). OC, 216, 258, 279, 280, 446, 721, 766. CONJ, 47. IA, 66-67, 106. PB, 159, 224, 229

Novarro, Ramón (Mexican film actor, born Ramón Samaniegos, 1899-1968). OCC, 327

Novato, Monteiro. See Monteiro Novato

Noy, el (knife-fighter in Buenos Aires). IA, 119

Nuncio (papal nuncio in Argentina). OCC, 125, 376

Núñez (landowners in Chacabuco in Borges story). OC, 1070

Núñez de Arce, Gaspar (Spanish poet, playwright and journalist, 1832-1903). OCC, 347

Nurmi, Paavo (Finnish track star, 1897-1973). OCC, 193

Nux, Nena (character in Bustos Domecq story). OCC, 421

O., H. OC, 1102

O'Connor (character in Borges story, father of Ireneo Funes). OC, 486

O'Neill, Eugene (American playwright, 1888-1953, author of *The Great God Brown*, *Mourning Becomes Electra*, *Strange Interlude* and other works). OC, 698. ILN, 52-53

Oakhurst, John (character in Bret Harte story). P, 83

Obieta, Elena de (Macedonio Fernáandez's wife, d. 1920). P, 52

Obligado, Rafael (Argentine poet, 1851-1920, author of a version of *Santos Vega*). OCC, 856. I, 56. LA, 50. TE, 8, 89

Ocampo, Angélica (sister of Victoria and Silvina Ocampo). OC, 324

Ocampo, Silvina (Argentine poet and short-story writer, b. 1906, co-editor with Borges and Bioy of the *Antología de la literatura fantástica* and the *Antología poética argentina*, and author of *Enumeración de la patria*, *Espacios métricos*, *La Furia* and other works). OC, 444. NED, 143n. PB, 166, 167, 179n.

Ocampo, Victoria (Argentine essayist, 1890-1979, founder of the magazine *Sur* in 1931). OC, 472. PB, 215-16, 247-48

Occam, Guillermo de (William of Occam or Ockham, English philosopher and theologian, c.1285-c.1349). OC, 214, 719, 745. OCC, 102n. C, 75. CONJ, 15. NED, 122. PB, 170

Oceánidas (ocean nymphs). OCC, 673

Oceano (god of ocean). IA, 106, 142. OP, 453

Ochoa (translator of Virgil's *Georgics*). OCC, 304

Octuple Serpiente (Japanese monster). OCC, 675

Odd (character in *Bandamanna Saga*). OCC, 939

Odín (Norse supreme god, also Othin, Othinus, Voden and Woden). OC, 134n., 371, 793, 796, 883, 903, 908, 980, 1105, 1128. OCC, 583, 593n., 708, 789, 861, 863, 867, 878, 900, 924, 925, 926, 927, 928, 929, 931, 953, 954, 955, 965n., 966, 966-68. A, 17. CONJ, 51. LA, 112, 165, 166. NED, 126. OP, 384, 493. PB, 197, 199, 224

Odín (cat). A, 58

Odiseo. See Ulises

Odoacro or Otacher (Odoacer, chieftain of the Heruli, Sciri and Rugii in the service of Rome, later king of Italy, c.435–493). OCC, 901, 909–10

Odradek (monster in Kafka fable). OCC, 676–77

Ofelia (Ophelia, character in Shakespeare's *Hamlet*). OCC, 820

Offa (king of Mercia, called *rex Anglorum*, also mentioned in the *Widsith*, d. 796). OCC, 876

O. Henry (pseud. of American short-story writer William Sydney Porter, 1862–1910, author of "The Four Million," "The Gift of the Magi" and other works). ILN, 33, 51

Olaf or Anlaf (king of the Danish kingdoms of Northumbria and of Dublin, d. 981). OCC, 885. OP, 448, 466

Olaf I or Olaf Tryggvason (Norwegian king, c.963–1000). OCC, 811, 885, 924, 958, 961. PB, 197, 201

Olaf II or Olaf Haraldsson (Olaf the Fat, St. Olaf, *Perpetuus rex Norvegiae*, Norwegian king, 995–1030). OCC, 961. PB, 198–202

Olaf de Geirstadr (Olaf Geirstadálfr, Norse king of Vestfold, died c.840). PB, 201

Olaf el Blanco (9th century king of Dublin). OCC, 949

Olao Magno or Olaus Magnus (Swedish ecclesiastic, 1490–1558, author of *Historia de Gentibus Septentrionalibus*, 1555). OCC, 711. OP, 495

Olavarría, Félix (military man, comrade in arms of Isidoro Suárez). A, 88

Olavarría, José Valentín de (Argentine patriot and military man, 1801–1845). OC, 1048

Olave, José (cited as expert on knife-fighters of Buenos Aires). OC, 103, 128n., 1042

Oldenberg, Hermann (German scholar of Buddhism, c.1855–1920, author of *Buddha: Sein Leben, seine Lehre, seine Gemeinde*). OCC, 728, 730, 753, 781. SN, 81

Oldenburg, Claes (Swedish-American artist, b. 1929). A, 43

Oldrado. OCC, 74

Olivares, Gaspar de Guzmán, conde-duque de (Spanish statesman, 1587–1645). I, 41

Olivera, Carlos (19th century Argentine writer and theatre critic, member of the Círculo Científico Literario, and translator of Poe). OCC, 526–27

Ollán (*ollam*, distinction given to leading poet in medieval Ireland). LA, 101–7

Omar (second caliph, born in Mecca, c.581–644, conqueror of Egypt). OCC, 682. C, 13. OP, 514, 559

Omar Khayyam (Persian poet and mathematician, d. c.1123, author of *Rubaiyat*, sometimes Jaiam). OC, 670, 688–90, 813. OCC, 842. I, 127–30. NED, 120n. P, 47. PB, 122, 231. SN, 118

Onagro (monster in Golden Legend). OCC, 646

Ongentheow (Swedish king mentioned in *Widsith*). OCC, 876

Onís, Federico de (Spanish critic, scholar and editor, 1886–1966). OCC, 185. P, 15

Oothoon (character in Blake's *Visions of the Daughters of Albion*, perhaps inspired by Ossian's Oithona). OCC, 840

Orczy, Emmuska, baroness (British detective and adventure novelist, 1865–1947, author of *Unravelled Knots*). OCC, 16

Orfeo (Orpheus, in Greek mythology, celebrated Thracian musician). OC, 228, 229. OCC, 474, 609, 696, 740-41, 917, 925. BO, 37. NED, 100. PB, 183. SN, 88

Oribe, Emilio (Uruguayan physician and poet, 1893-1975). OCC, 520. LA, 123. OP, 491, 497. P, 17, 64. TE, 61-62. VA, 43

Oribe, Manuel (Uruguayan general, politician and president, 1792-1857). OC, 1048

Origenes (Origen, Christian scholar and philosopher, 185?-254?). OC, 211n., 282, 551, 553, 704n. OCC, 579. P, 23. SN, 158

Orión (in Greek mythology, Boethian hunter). I, 35

Orlando (Roland or Rolando, legendary Carolingian knight, subject of French epic poem and character in later poems by Boiardo and Ariosto). OC, 836, 838. ILN, 25. OP, 431, 466. P, 171. SN, 60

Orloff. OCC, 226

Orm (mentioned in runic inscription). OCC, 924. PB, 190

Orm (character in Borges story, a blacksmith). LA, 113-19

Orosio (Orosius, 5th century Spanish historian, author of *Historia adversus paganos*). OCC, 799, 894

Ortega (character in Bustos Domecq story). OCC, 369-71

Ortega y Gasset, José (Spanish philosopher and essayist, 1883-1955, author of *Meditaciones del Quijote, La deshumanización del arte* and numerous other works). OC, 673, 1054. OCC, 157. I, 126. P, 22, 23. PB, 170, 187, 228, 245. TE, 18

Ortlieb (son of Attila the Hun). OCC, 914

Orton, Arthur (son of a butcher from Wapping, identified as the Tichborne Claimant). OC, 301-5

Osiris (Egyptian god of the underworld). I, 35. PB, 197

Osmán (Hákim de Merv's father). OC, 325

Ossian or Oisin (legendary 3rd century Gaelic poet, hero of a cycle of tales and poems; later, James Macpherson attributed to Ossian two poems that he had at least partly written himself). OCC, 826, 830, 911. PB, 229, 232

Ostermann, Edward. See Eastman, Monk

Osuna, duque de. See Téllez Girón, Pedro.

Otacher. See Odoacro

Otálora, Benjamín (character in Borges story). OC, 545-49, 629

Otálora, Javier (character in Borges story). LA, 25-31

Oteiza (minor character in Borges-Bioy filmscript). OCC, 226

Otelo (Othello, moor in Venetian service, subject of Shakespeare play). OC, 574. OCC, 820-21

Otfried de Weissenburg (Ottfried von Weissenburg, German monk and poet, c.800-870, author of *Liber Evangeliorum*). OCC, 904-5

Othin. See Odín

Othinus. See Odín

Otis, Elisha Graves (American inventor of elevator, 1811-1861). OCC, 409

Oton I (Otho, Holy Roman Emperor and German king, 912-973). OCC, 906

Otr (son of Hreidmar in the *Volsunga Saga*). OCC, 966

Ottar (Norwegian explorer, whose life was told by Alfred the Great). OCC, 799

Ottar el Negro (Icelandic skald). OCC, 949

Ottolengui, Rodrigues (dentist
and writer of detective
stories, author of *The Crime
of the Century*, 1896, *The
Artist in Crime*, 1892, and
various works on dentistry).
OCC, 13
Ovidio (Publius Ovidius Naso,
Latin poet, 43 B.C.-18 A.D.,
author of *Metamorphoses*).
OC, 228n., 717.    OCC, 588,
602, 604-5, 626, 657, 664,
669, 696, 920, 952, 956.
NED, 98, 103, 133.    OP, 508.
P, 68.    PB, 182, 184, 213.
SN, 49
Ovidio, Francesco D' (Italian
literary scholar, 1849-1925,
author of numerous studies
of Dante).    NED, 107
Oyuela, Calixto (Argentine
essayist, critic and poet,
1857-1935, author of an
*Antología poética hispano-
americana*).    OC, 103, 183,
186, 194.    OCC, 464, 560,
562, 563.    I, 55.    IA, 36.
P, 94, 96, 98.    PB, 169,
170.    TE, 15, 27, 134
Ozanam, Frédéric (French
critic and literary
historian, 1813-1853).    NED,
145, 156, 158
Ozep, Fedor (Russian film
director, 1893-1949).    OC,
222.    BC, 27
Ozeray, Madeleine (French
writer, author of *A toujours,
M. Jouvet*, 1966, and *La reve
et la vie de Gérard de
Nerval*, 1958).    OCC, 63
Pablo, San (Saul or St. Paul,
apostle to the Gentiles, d.
c.64).    OC, 297, 516, 517,
522, 551, 578, 698, 701, 703,
720-22, 775, 800.    OCC, 883.
BO, 96.    IA, 97, 183.    NED,
116.    P, 71, 133, 166.    PB,
150.    SN, 120
Pablo el Diácono (Paul the
Deacon, Lombard historian,
c.725-799?, author of a
continuation of the Roman
history of Eutropius).    OC,
557

Pablos de Segovia (main
character in Quevedo's
*Buscón*).    TE, 142
Pacheco, Carlos Mauricio
(Argentine dramatist and
writer, 1881-1924, author of
*El diablo en el conventillo,
Barracas, Los disfrazados* and
other works).    OC, 653
Pacheco (family name of early
settlers of Buenos Aires).
P, 78
Pactolus (decorator).    OCC,
164
Padma-Sambhava (8th century
master of Tibetan Buddhism).
OCC, 738
Padre (God the Father, first
person of the Trinity).    OC,
283.    OCC, 863
Pagés Larraya, Antonio
(Argentine critic and writer,
b. 1918, editor of the *Prosas
del Martín Fierro*).    OCC,
528-29
Pagola (character in Borges-
Bioy filmscript).    OCC, 211-
15
Painé (19th century Argentine
Indian chief).    SN, 73
Paja Brava (character in Bustos
Domecq stories).    OCC, 88,
89, 96, 99
Pájaro Rojo (in Chinese
cosmology, animal which marks
the south compass point).
OCC, 701
Palacios, Pedro Bonifacio.    See
Almafuerte
Paladión, César (character in
Bustos Domecq stories).
OCC, 303-5, 315, 320
Palas Atena (Greek goddess of
wisdom).    BO, 70, 71.    ILN,
19
Palau, Doctor (character in
Bustos Domecq story, director
of literary supplement of the
newspaper *La Opinión*).    OCC,
434, 435
Palau, Lucas (character in
Bustos Domecq story, poet,
nephew of doctor Palau).
OCC, 435
Palcos, Alberto (Argentine
scholar, author of studies of

Echeverría, Sarmiento etc.).
P, 137, 138

Palermo (some Argentine writer
mentioned by Américo Castro
in *La peculiaridad
lingüística*). OC, 653

Palermo, Domínguez (Doménico
de Palermo, Italian immigrant
to Buenos Aires from Sicily
in the 17th century, a
butcher). OC, 105, 106

Palgrave, Francis (English
historian, 1788-1861, author
of a *History of England,
Anglo-Saxon Period* and other
works). OCC, 864

Palgrave, Francis Turner
(English critic and poet,
1824-1897, editor of the
*Golden Treasury of English
Songs and Lyrics*). OC, 149

Palma, Ricardo (Peruvian
writer, 1833-1919, author of
countless *tradiciones
peruanas*). OCC, 558-59

Palomeque, el viejo (mentioned
in Bustos Domecq story).
OCC, 126

Paltock, Robert (English writer,
1697-1767, author of *Peter
Wilkins*). OC, 697. OCC, 710

Pampa (nickname for female
character). See Hortensia
Montenegro

Pampa (male child, character
in Bustos Domecq story).
OCC, 54, 55, 58, 60

Pan (Greek pastoral god of
fertility). OCC, 692. PB,
233

Pancho, don. See Fang

Pancita de Gelatina (nickname
used in Suárez Lynch novel).
OCC, 183

Pándaro (a Trojan warrior, a
major character in Chaucer's
*Troylus and Cryseyde*). OCC,
815

Pangloss (character in
Voltaire's *Candide*). OC,
259

Paniego, Pedro (character in
Bustos Domecq story, friend
and editor of Pedro Zúñiga,
el Molinero). OCC, 450

Pankhurst, Sylvia (British
feminist and political
writer, 1882-1960). OC, 706

Panormitano, Antonio (Antonio
Beccadelli of Palermo, called
Panormita, d. 1471, author of
*Hermaphroditus* and *De dictis
et factis magnanimi
Alphonsi*). OCC, 139

Pantchen-Lama (second to Dalai
Lama in hierarchy of Tibetan
Buddhism). OCC, 761

Pantera (the panther of
medieval bestiaries). OCC,
679, 891-92. NED, 150n.

Pantier, Benjamin (character
in Edgar Lee Masters' *Spoon
River Anthology*). ILN, 45

Pantoja, Doctor (character in
Bustos Domecq story). OCC,
427, 428, 431, 432

Panza, Sancho (the squire,
character in *Don Quijote*).
OC, 203, 259, 265, 660, 878.
OCC, 303, 550, 551, 892-93.
BO, 72. IA, 144. ILN,
55. P, 67, 119. PB,
176, 203, 209-11. SN, 19

Panzer, Friedrich (author of
*Hilde-Gudrun*, 1901). OCC,
931

Paoli, Pasquale (Paoli de
Corcega, Corsican patriot,
1725-1807). OCC, 829

Paolo (character in Dante's
*Inferno*, lover of Francesca
di Rimini). C, 73. NED,
88, 153. SN, 21-25

Papa (the Pope). OC, 340.
OCC, 94, 363, 602, 640, 842.
NED, 148

Papini, Giovanni (Italian
writer, 1881-1956). NED,
116n.

Paquín (French *couturier*).
OCC, 110

Paracelso (Philippus Aureolus
Parcelsus, born Theophrastus
Bombastus von Hohenheim,
Swiss physician and
alchemist, 1493?-1541).
OCC, 636, 673, 694. CONJ,
97. VA, 19-25

Parachú (part-owner of a meat-
packing plant, mentioned in
*Evaristo Carriego*). OC, 169

Paravicino, Hortensio Félix
(Spanish preacher and poet,
1580-1633).   I, 37
Parcas (the three Fates of
Greek mythology, also the
three weird sisters in
Macbeth and the Nornir of
Scandinavian mythology).
OCC, 437, 573, 585, 674, 924,
926, 929.   OP, 532, 555.
P, 144, 145.   PB, 201, 226.
SN, 14
Parda, la (minor character in
Borges story).   OC, 1037
Pardo (minor character in
Borges story).   OC, 1028
Pardo Bazán, Emilia (Spanish
novelist and short-story
writer, 1851-1921).   OCC, 77
Paredes, Nicolás or Nicanor
(old Buenos Aires knife-
fighter, a friend of Borges
in the 1920's).   OC, 103,
117, 118, 159, 329, 961-62,
1034, 1035, 1124-25.   C, 35,
77.    LA, 46.    OP, 404-6.
P, 128
Paredes, Diego García de
(Spanish captain and count,
1466-1530).   IA, 95
Parham (character in Wells).
OC, 698
Paris (Trojan prince, son of
Priam).   OC, 161, 1128
Parkman, Francis (American
historian, 1823-93).   ILN,
16-17, 62
Parménides (Greek philosopher
of Elea, b. c.515 B.C.).
OC, 52, 244, 253n., 280, 351,
510, 636, 704n., 718, 745,
766.    OCC, 733, 759.    A,
29.    NED, 90.    P, 32.
PB, 244
Parnell, Charles Stewart
(Irish nationalist leader,
1846-1891).   OC, 492
Parodi, Isidro (the first
imprisoned detective,
character in Bustos Domecq
and Suárez Lynch stories).
OCC, 16, 17, 18, 21-121, 140,
147, 149, 173, 175, 177, 181,
183, 185, 188-90, 192-95,
342n., 360, 426.    BO, 80

Parolles (soldier, character
in Shakespeare's All's Well
that Ends Well).   OC, 751,
753.    OP, 559
Parténope (a mermaid whose
name was later bestowed on
the city now called Naples).
OC, 228n.    OCC, 696
Pasado (personification of the
past).   OCC, 674
Pascal, Blaise (French
scientist and religious
philosopher, 1623-1662,
author of Pensées).   OC,
536, 638, 703-5.    OCC, 827.
A, 11, 24.    BO, 35.    OP,
555.    P, 105.    PB, 244
Pascal, Roy (literary scholar,
b. 1904, author of Shakespeare in Germany, 1740-
1815 and works on Marx,
Nazism, German history and
literature).    OC, 280
Pasifae (Pasiphae, in Greek
mythology, queen of Crete,
wife of Minos and mother of
the Minotaur).   OC, 569.
OCC, 664
Pasman, Tubiana (minor
character in Bustos Domecq
story).    OCC, 438
Passent (character in Layomon's
Brut).    OCC, 897
Pasternak, Boris (Russian poet,
novelist and translator,
1890-1960, author of Doctor
Zhivago).   OCC, 312
Pata Santa ("precioso elemento
electoral," a thug in Bustos
Domecq story).    OCC, 22
Patas (nickname in Bustos
Domecq story).    OCC, 130
Pater, Walter (English
essayist and critic, 1839-
1894, author of Studies in
the History of the
Renaissance, Marius the
Epicurean, Imaginary
Portraits, Plato and
Platonism, Appreciations and
other works).    OC, 249, 635.
P, 148
Pato Donald (Donald Duck,
cartoon character created by
Walt Disney in 1934).    OCC,
393

Patoruzú (gaucho cartoon character created by Lino Palacio). OCC, 178

Patou, Jean (French clothing designer). OCC, 54, 405

Patroclo (Patroclus, Greek warrior, friend of Achilles). OC, 240. TE, 50

Paulino, San (Italian missionary, bishop of York, d. 644). OC, 210, 360

Pausanias (Greek traveller and geographer, fl. c.150 A.D., author of the *Periegesis* or *Description of Greece*). OCC, 626

Pavesa (character in Bustos Domecq story). OCC, 415

Pavilliard (Swiss Calvinist minister). P, 69

Payne, John (translator of the *Arabian Nights*). OC, 407, 412

Payot (pharmacist, character in Bustos Domecq story). OCC, 324

Payró, Roberto (Argentine novelist and journalist, 1867–1928, author of *Pago Chico*, *El casamiento de Laucha* and other works). OCC, 40

Paz, José María (Argentine general, 1791–1854). P, 17

Peano, Giuseppe (Italilan mathematician and logician, 1858–1932, author of *Elementi di calcolo geometrico* and inventor of the artificial language *Interlingua*). OC, 706

Pearson, Hesketh (British literary critic, 1887–1964, author of studies of Shaw, Gilbert and Sullivan, Dickens and others). OC, 691, 692

Pecoso (minor character in Borges–Bioy filmscript). OCC, 258

Pécuchet (copy clerk, character in Flaubert's *Bouvard et Pécuchet*). OC, 259–63

Pecus (shoe designer). OCC, 192, 396

Pedro (character in Borges–Bioy filmscript). OCC, 278, 280, 281

Pedro, San (most prominent of twelve disciples, later bishop of Rome, d. c.64). OCC, 333. LA, 84

Pedro Juan. PJ, 61

Pedro Pascual. See Acevedo, Pedro Pascual

Pedro de Agrigento. BO, 35–36

Pedro el Labrador. See Piers Plowman

Pedro el Mentao (knife fighter in Borges story). IA, 152, 153

Peduto. OCC, 180

Peer Gynt (Norwegian peasant, character in Ibsen play). OC, 755

Pees, Jean or Juan P. OCC, 192, 331

Pegoraro, Q. (owner of a garage in Bustos Domecq story). OCC, 413

Peine-Arrozal (fabulous animal). OCC, 675

Pelagio (Pelagius or Morgan, British monk and theologian and heretic, c.355–c.425). OC, 362

Pelícano (pelican of myth and legend). OCC, 680

Pellegrini, Carlos (Argentine politician, jurist and president, 1846–1906). OC, 134n.

Pellicer de Ossau Salas y Tovar, José de (Spanish poet and presumed hoaxer, 1602–1679, author of *El Fénix y su historia natural*, 1630). OCC, 588. IA, 71

Peluda (French medieval monster). OCC, 681

Peluffo, Vicente (author of *El Jardinero Ilustrado*, 1909). OCC, 25

Peman, José María (Spanish poet and playwright, b. 1898, author of *Santa Virreina*, *Elegía a la tradición en España* and other works). OCC, 74, 80

Peñaloza, Angel Vicente (Argentine caudillo murdered

at behest of Sarmiento, also
known as "El Chacho," 1797–
1863, subject of a biography
by José Hernandez).    OC,
1001.    OCC, 486, 527
Pendrel, Ralph (character in
James's *The Sense of the
Past*).   OC, 640
Penélope (in Greek legend and
literature, the faithful wife
of Odysseus and queen of
Ithaca).   OC, 250.   NED,
113.   OP, 526.   SN, 29
Peralta, Atanasio (Buenos
Aires knife-fighter).    OC,
129n.
Percy, Thomas (English
antiquary and churchman,
1729–1811, editor of *Reliques
of Ancient English Poetry*).
LA, 53.   SN, 71
Pereda, José María de (Spanish
novelist, 1833–1906, author
of *Peñas arriba, Sotileza* and
other works).  OCC, 77.  P,
78
Pereira, Benito (Spanish
preacher, c. 1535–1610,
author of *De magia, de
observatione somniorum et
de divinatione astrologica*,
1593).  OC, 701
Pereira Rodríguez, José
(Uruguayan critic, b. 1893,
author of studies of Cruz y
Souza, Bilac and other
Brazilian writers, as well as
of Herrera y Reissig, Whitman
and so forth).   OCC, 502
Pereyra (of Pegotes Pereyra,
in Bustos Domecq).   OCC, 400
Pereyra (Argentine family).
P, 78
Pérez, Baulito (character in
Bustos Domecq amd Suárez
Lynch stories).   OCC, 149,
159, 160, 170, 171, 177, 438–
39
Perez, Máximo (Uruguayan
colonel, 1825–1872, mentioned
in *Los tres gauchos
orientales*, here a number in
Funes's system of
enumeration).   OC, 489
Pérez de Ayala, Ramón (Spanish
novelist, poet, essayist and

diplomat, 1880–1962, author
of *Troteras y danzaderas,
Belarminio y Apolonio* and
other works, here called
Ratón Perutz de Achala).
OCC, 164
Peréz Galdos, Benito (Spanish
novelist, 1843–1920, author
of *Fortunata y Jacinta,
Episodios nacionales* and
countless other works).
OCC, 77.   I, 46
Pérez Petit, Victor (Uruguayan
poet, novelist and play-
wright, 1871–1947).   OCC,
471, 502
Pérez Ruiz, Carlos (friend of
Macedonio Fernández). P, 58–59
Peri Banu (character in the
*Arabian Nights*).   OC, 397
Periandro (Periander, Greek
despot, tyrant of Corinth, d.
585 B.C.).   OCC, 605
Peritios (ancient monsters,
half-deer, half-bird).    OCC,
682–83
Perles, Alfred (French writer,
b. 1897, author of *Le quatuor
en ré majeur, Sentiments
limitrophes* and other works).
ILN, 44
Perón, Eva Duarte de (Argentine
political figure, 1919–1952).
OC, 789.   OCC, 347
Perón, Juan (Argentine
military man and president,
1895–1974).  OC, 789.  OCC,
392–402.  LA, 14.  PB, 174,
214.  SN, 145
Perosio.   OCC, 398
Perséfone or Proserpina
(Persephone, in Greek
mythology, goddess of
fertility and queen of the
underworld).   OC, 384n.
OCC, 585.   P, 71
Perseo (Perseus, Greek
mythological hero).   OC,
782.  OCC, 675
Persio (Persius Flaccus,
Etruscan knight and Stoic
satirist, 34–62).   OC, 665.
P, 125
Persky, Doctor (character in
Bustos Domecq stories).
OCC, 405, 407, 408, 421

Persons, Truman Streckfus.
See Capote, Truman

Perthes, Johan Georg Justus
(German publisher, 1749-1816,
publisher of Adolf Stieler's
*Hand-atlas* and numerous other
atlases and maps).    OC, 431.
LA, 47

Pertiné, Doctor (dietary expert
invoked in Bustos Domecq
story).    OCC, 98

Perutz de Achala, Ratón
(ironic reference to Ramón
Pérez de Ayala).    OCC, 164

Pestalozzi, Johann Heinrich
(Swiss educational reformer,
1746-1827, here used as a
nickname for Ladislao
Barreiro).    OCC, 183

Petavio (Dionysius Petavius or
Denis Petau, French Jesuit
theologian and philologist,
1583-1652, author of *Opus de
doctrina temporum* and *De
theologicis dogmatibus*).    P,
69

Petit (character in Edgar Lee
Master's *Spoon River
Anthology*).    ILN, 45

Petit de Murat, Ulises
(Argentine poet, novelist,
screenwriter and journalist,
b. 1907, author of *El balcón
hasta la muerte*, *Las islas*
and other works).    BC, 63.
PB, 166

Petitpain, Maxime (character
in Bustos Domecq story).
OCC, 331

Petrarca, Francesco (Italian
poet and humanist, 1304-
1374).    OC, 264.    OCC, 836.
A, 23.    IA, 76.    NED, 86.
P, 122.    TE, 71, 119

Petronio (Petronius Arbiter,
Roman satirist, d. c.66 A.D.,
author of *Satyricon*).    OC,
733.    SN, 45

Peuser, Jacobo (Argentine
publisher).    OC, 121

Pew, Blind (old buccaneer,
character in Stevenson's
*Treasure Island*).    OC, 101,
826.    PB, 172

Peyrou, Manuel (Argentine
novelist and short-story

writer, b. 1902, author of
*La espada dormida*, *La noche
repetida*, *El estruendo de las
rosas* and other works).    OP,
547-48.    P, 51

Pezzoni, Enrique (Argentine
critic, editor and teacher).
A, 7, 84

Phillpotts, Bertha (scholar of
old Norse literature, d.
1932, author of *Edda and
Saga*).    OCC, 927, 953, 965,
974

Phol (the Germanic god Balder).
OCC, 900

Pibe del Centro (character in
Bustos Domecq stories).    OCC,
405, 421

Picardía (character in the
*Martín Fierro*, son of Cruz).
OCC, 552, 561

Picasso, Pablo (Spanish
painter, sculptor, graphic
artist and ceramicist, 1881-
1973).    OCC, 50, 66, 301.
A, 80.    I, 92.    ILN, 40

Pickford, Mary (Canadian film
actress, born Gladys Smith,
1893-1979).    ILN, 48

Pico della Mirandola, Giovanni
(Italian philosopher and
humanist, 1463-1494, author
of the *Heptaplus*, *De omni re
scibili*, *Apologia* and other
works).    OCC, 407

Piedad (personification of
pity).    NED, 148

Pierce, Franklin (U. S.
president, 1804-1869).    ILN,
17, 18

Pierrot (character in French
pantomime).    OCC, 17, 40

Piers Plowman (character in
Langland poem).    OCC, 813

Pietro Damiani.    See Damiani,
Pietro

Pietrobono, Luigi (scholar of
Dante).    NED, 107, 108n.,
114, 148, 156

Pilatos, Poncio.    See Poncio
Pilatos

Pincén (19th century Argentine
Indian chief).    OCC, 153,
530.    CONJ, 89.    P, 113

Píndaro (Pindar, Greek lyric
poet, c.522-442, author of

*Epinicia* or triumphal odes).
OC, 263. OCC, 484. OP,
554. P, 37
Pinedo (Sephardic Jewish
family expelled from Spain).
OC, 876
Piñero (early settlers in
Buenos Aires). P, 78
Piñero, Francisco (Argentine
avant-garde poet, co-founder
of *Prisma*). OCC, 497
Piñero, Sergio (Argentine
avant-garde poet, an editor
of the magazine *Martín
Fierro*). OCC, 497. IA, 154
Piñero, doctor (victim of the
venom of Paul Groussac).
OC, 233, 421
Ping-feng (Chinese monster).
OCC, 630
Pinkerton, Allan (American
detective, 1819–1884). ILN,
57
Pinnacle Grouse (imaginary
one-winged bird of North
America). OCC, 631
Pinto (early settlers in
Buenos Aires). P, 78
Pirandello, Luigi (Italian
author, 1867-1936, author of
*Sei personaggi in cerca di
autore, Enrico IV, Il fu
Mattia Pascal* and other
works). OC, 674. OCC,
279. SN, 17
Piranesi, Giovanni Battista
(Italian engraver and
architect, 1720-1778). OC,
731. LA, 72
Piranesi, Alessandro (Italian
architect from Pisa,
character in Bustos Domecq
story). OCC, 333
Pirosanto (character in Bustos
Domecq story). OCC, 398,
402
Pirro (Pyrrhus, Molossian king
of Epirus, c.318-272). OC,
456
Pirrón (Pyrrhon, Greek
sceptical philosopher, c.365-
c.275). I, 88
Pisanello (Antonio Pisano,
Italian medalist and painter,
c.1395-1455?). OCC, 704

Pitágoras (Pythagoras, Greek
philosopher, c.582–c.507).
OC, 388, 456, 517, 553, 651,
688, 713, 715, 819, 863, 864.
OCC, 616, 661, 728, 736, 740,
745, 746, 755. BO, 14, 15,
34, 36. C, 33, 41. ILN,
40. P, 50, 66. PB, 201,
219, 221. SN, 77, 79, 88,
89, 127. VA, 40
Pizarro, Francisco (Spanish
conqueror of Peru, c.1476–
1541). OCC, 604, 960.
ILN, 16. PB, 191
Pizarro, Marta (character in
Borges story). OC, 1053-57
Pizarro, Nélida Sara
(character in Borges story,
Marta's sister). OC, 1053,
1054
Pizzurno (character in Bustos
Domecq story). OCC, 393
Pizzurno, Pablo (Argentine
inspector general of
education who resigned in
1903). OCC, 488
Planes (last name of Pedro
Salvadores' wife in Borges
story). OC, 994
Planes, Eduardo L. (character
in Bustos Domecq story,
author of *Gloglocioro,
Hrobfroga* and *Qul*). OCC,
322
Planes (priest mentioned in
Bustos Domecq story). OCC,
311
Platero, Ema Risso. See Risso
Platón (Plato, Greek
philosopher, 428-347, author
of the *Republic, Timaeus,
Cratylus, Parmenides,* and
numerous other dialogues).
OC, 215n., 228n., 253n.,
255n., 256n., 260, 263, 273,
277n., 278n., 280, 291, 351,
353, 354, 357, 358n., 393,
462n., 490, 496, 533, 580,
636, 637, 680, 688, 696, 699,
704, 705, 713, 718, 719, 745,
746, 770, 790. OCC, 299,
365, 489, 579, 588, 609, 616,
697, 730, 740-41, 745, 755,
840, 956. A, 11, 46, 48.
BO, 14, 15, 16, 29, 30, 34,
36, 86, 87, 96. C, 11, 19,

Polux (Pollux, a hero in Greek myth, the twin brother of Castor).    OCC, 699

Pomona (Roman goddess of fruit).    OCC, 154

Pompeyo (Gnaeus Pompeius Magnus, Roman general, rival of Julius Caesar, 106–48).    OC, 249, 555

Poncio, Ernesto.    See Ponzio, Ernesto

Poncio Pilatos (Roman procurator of Judaea, fl. 26 A.D.).    BC, 57.    LA, 84

Ponderevo, P. (character in Bustos Domecq accused repeatedly of plagiarism).    OCC, 344

Pons (character in Borges-Bioy filmscript).    OCC, 224, 225

Ponson du Terrail, Pierre-Alexis (French writer of romances, 1829–1871, author of the *Exploits de Rocambole*).    PB, 154

Pontiac (Ottawa Indian chief, fl. 1760–1766).    ILN, 16

Pontoppidan, Eric (Danish bishop of Bergen, 1698–1764, author of *Theatrum Daniae veteris et modernae, Det forste forsog Norges naturlige historie* and other works).    OCC, 653

Ponzio, Ernesto (Argentine musician, violinist and tango composer, 1885–1934).    OC, 159.    OCC, 81

Pope, Alexander (English poet and translator, 1688–1744, author of *The Dunciad, Essay on Man* and numerous other works, as well as famous translations of Homer).    OC, 240, 242, 243, 291, 533, 543, 633.    P, 68, 174.    TE, 50, 66

Poplavsky (jeweler mentioned in Bustos Domecq story).    OCC, 402

Porcel, Delia San Marco (a friend of Borges, mentioned in the company of Carlos Argentino Daneri and Beatriz Viterbo in the story "El Aleph").    OC, 617.    See also Delia San Marco

Porfirio (Porphyry, Greek scholar and Neoplatonic philosopher, c.232–304).    OC, 745, 829.    A, 11

Poro (Porus or Parvataka, Indian king, contemporary of Alexander the Great).    SN, 59

Porquero (swineherd, character in Homer's *Odyssey*).    OC, 250

Porras de la Cámara.    P, 45

Porten, Catherine (Gibbon's aunt).    P, 68

Porten, Judith (Gibbon's mother).    P, 68

Porter, William Sidney.    See O. Henry

Porthos (character in Dumas' *Trois mousquetaires*).    NED, 121n.

Portinari, Beatrice (Dante's Beatrice).    NED, 116, 159. SN, 18.    See also Beatriz

Porvenir (personification of the future).    OCC, 674

Poseidón (Greek god of the sea).    OC, 228n., 242n., 550.    OCC, 664, 696.    A, 27

Posnet, Blanco (character in Shaw play).    OC, 748.    OCC, 848

Postemilla (character in Borges-Bioy filmscript).    OCC, 202, 203, 206–8, 210–11, 223

Potasman (singer mentioned in Bustos Domecq story).    OCC, 397

Potranco.    See Ladislao Barreiro

Pound, Ezra (American poet, critic and translator, 1885–1972, author of *A Lume Spento, Cantos*, numerous essays, translations and other works).    OC, 249.    OCC, 304, 796, 856, 975.    ILN, 37, 40, 41–42, 43, 61

Powell (translator of *Historia Danica*).    OCC, 975

Poyarré (character in Bustos Domecq story).    OCC, 382, 383, 385–88

Praetorius, Frans (character in Bustos Domecq story,

author of *Les Saveurs*).
OCC, 323–24, 326
Pratyeka Buddha (solitary
saint who becomes a Buddha
without help from masters).
OCC, 759
Preetorius, Max (character in
Borges story). LA, 69, 70,
71, 74
Preller, Ludwig (German
philologist and antiquarian,
1809-1861, author of
*Griechische Mythologie,*
*Romische Mythologie,* and,
with H. Ritter, *Historia*
*philosophiae graecae et*
*romanae ex fontium locis*
*contexta*). OC, 389
Prescott, William (American
historian, 1796-1859, author
of a *History of the Conquest*
*of Mexico, History of the*
*Conquest of Peru* and other
works). OCC, 604. ILN,
16. OP, 480. SN, 156
Presente (personification of
the present). OCC, 674
Preste Juan (Prester John,
fabulous Christian monarch of
Asia). OCC, 585, 690.
OP, 462. SN, 64
Príamo (Priam, in Greek myth
and literature, the king of
Troy during the Trojan War).
OC, 161, 241, 660. OCC,
952. P, 119. PB, 189,
242
Priestley, John Boynton
(English novelist, dramatist
and critic, b. 1894). ILN,
57. P, 109
Pringles, Pascual (Argentine
colonel in wars of
independence, 1795-1831).
OC, 1054. P, 131
Procusto (in Greek mythology,
cruel highwayman who cut his
guests to fit the bed). OC,
550, 626. OCC, 185
Profeta. See Mahoma
Profeta Velado. See Hákim de
Merv
Profumo (here a brand of
soap). OCC, 361
Prometeo (Prometheus, titan in
Greek myth who sacrifices

himself to steal fire for
mankind). OC, 551. OCC,
485, 489. IA, 106, 141
Propercio (Sextus Propertius,
Latin elegiac poet, c.50–
c.16). OC, 664. OCC, 673.
P, 124
Prosciuto, Carlos Alberto
(poet in Bustos Domecq
story). OCC, 338
Proserpina. See Perséfone
Próspero (character in
Shakespeare's *Tempest*). OC,
694. OCC, 821. P, 49.
PB, 140
Protágoras (Greek philosopher
from Abdera, one of the more
distinguished of the sophists,
c.490-421). OC, 661. P,
120
Protector del Perú (honorific
title given to José de San
Martín). PB, 131
Proteo (Proteus, in classical
mythology, prophetic old man
of the sea who tended the
seals of Poseidon and could
change himself into any
shape). OC, 591, 803, 869,
916, 924, 925, 1108, 1109.
OCC, 591. OP, 421, 443,
444, 478, 485, 508. PJ, 58
Proust, Marcel (French
novelist, 1871-1922, author
of *A la recherche du temps*
*perdu*). OC, 186. OCC,
440, 836, 853. A, 23. P,
22-23. PB, 215
Provenzal, Dino (editor of
Dante, according to Bustos
Domecq). OCC, 316
Providencia (personification
of fortune). OCC, 195, 420.
SN, 31, 37
Prudencia (personification of
prudence). NED, 149
Prynne, Hester (character in
Hawthorne's *Scarlet Letter*).
OC, 681
Ptolomeo (Claudius Ptolemaeus,
Greco-Egyptian astronomer,
mathematician and geographer,
fl. 2nd century A.D.). NED,
89, 92. PB, 238, 244
Púa, Carlos de la (pseud. of
Carlos Muñoz del Solar,

Racine, Jean (French dramatist,
1639-1699, author of *Phedre*,
*Andromaque* and other works).
OC, 270.    IA, 176.    PB,
128, 229

Rackam, John (pirate).    OC,
306

Radaelli, Sigfrido (Argentine
poet, critic and editor,
author of *Hombre callado*,
editor of *Correspondencia*
and co-editor of anthology
*La novísima poesía
argentina*, 1931).    OCC, 65

Radamante (Rhadamanthus, in
Greek mythology one of the
judges in Hades).    OCC, 189

Radhakrishnan, Sarvepalli
(Indian philosopher, b.
1888).    OC, 770.    OCC,
744, 759

Raedwald (king of the Angles,
mentioned by Venerable Bede).
PB, 199

Rafael (Rafaello Sanzio,
Italian painter, 1483-1520).
OCC, 842

Rafael ("Rafael de la noche y
de las largas/ mesas de la
amistad").    See Cansinos-
Assens

Raft, George (American film
actor, 1895-1980).    OC, 285.
BC, 68

Raggio (of Aceite Raggio, in
Bustos Domecq story).    OCC,
28

Ragnarr Lodbrok (Viking hero
of Icelandic saga).    OCC,
965-66

Rahula (Gautama Buddha's son).
OCC, 725

Rains, Claude (British
character actor, 1889-1967).
BC, 69

Raleigh, Walter (Ralegh,
English soldier, explorer,
courtier and man of letters,
1554?-1618).    OCC, 817, 826

Rama (hero of *Ramayana*).
OC, 668

Ramanuja (Hindu religious
leader, devoted to Vishnu,
1017-1137).    OCC, 735

Rambaldi de Imola, Benvenuto
(Italian commentator on

Dante, d. 1390, author of
*Comentum super Dantis
Aligherii Comediam*).    OCC,
680.    NED, 106, 148, 152n.

Ramenti (composer of waltzes).
OCC, 224

Ramírez (character in Borges-
Bioy filmscript).    OCC, 254-
55, 270

Ramírez, Francisco (Argentine
*caudillo*, 1786-1821, governor
of Entre Ríos).    OC, 116,
655, 968, 1001.    P, 64, 132

Ramírez, Pedro Pablo
(Argentine general and
politician, 1884-1962).
OCC, 146

Ramírez Moroni, Hugo.    OC,
1022

Ramos Mejía, Francisco
(Argentine historian, 1847-
1893, author of *Historia de
la evolución argentina*).    P,
78.    SN, 147

Ran (Icelandic sea goddess).
OCC, 941

Rancherita (character in
Bustos Domecq story).    OCC,
398

Ranisch, Wilhelm (translator
of Eddas).    OC, 381

Rañó (printer mentioned in
Bustos Domecq story).    OCC,
345

Ransom (character in C. S.
Lewis's *Perelandra*).    OCC,
576

Ransom, John Crowe (American
poet, critic and editor,
1888-1974).    ILN, 46

Rapper, Irving (American film
director, b. 1898, director
of *The Now Voyager*).    BC,
69-70

Raquel (character in Borges-
Bioy filmscript).    OCC, 258

Rashid ed-Din (Rashídu'd-Din
Fadlu'lláh, Persian vizier
and historian, d. 1318,
author of the *Jámi'u't-
Tawárikh*, a history of the
Mongols which also includes
summaries of the history of
India, China and Europe).
OC, 644

Raskolnikov, Rodion Romanovich
(main character in
Dostoevsky's *Crime and
Punishment*). OC, 578. BC,
38. CONJ, 33. IA, 142.
NED, 121–22. P, 26, 36

Ratti, Horacio Esteban
(Argentine poet, b. 1903,
president of the SADE in the
1920's). OCC, 86

Rauch, Frederick (Prussian or
Alsatian soldier and Indian
fighter in Argentina, 1790–
1829). PB, 132, 152

Rav Zera (rabbi, mentioned in
*Talmud*). OCC, 637

Rava (rabbi, mentioned in
*Talmud*). OCC, 637

Razón (goddess Reason during
French Revolution). LA, 43

Razumov (character in Conrad's
*Under Western Eyes*). OC,
572

Razzano, José (Uruguayan folk
and tango musician, best
known for his work in
collaboration with Carlos
Gardel). OCC, 377

Read, Mary (English pirate).
OC, 306

Real, Francisco, el Corralero
(knife-fighter, character in
Borges stories). OC, 329–
34, 1034–38

Real, Tomás (knife-fighter).
OC, 128n.

Rebajino (mentioned in Bustos
Domecq story). OCC, 451

Reboul, Jacques (French writer,
author of *Un Grand précurseur
des romantiques, Ramond, M.
Bainville contre l'histoire
de France* and other works).
OC, 445, 449

Recabarren (character in
Borges story). OC, 483,
519–21

Reclam, Philipp (German
historian, author of *Erzherzog
Karl und Napoleon*, 1845, and
editor of the *Universal-
bibliothek*). OC, 411

Red King (character in Lewis
Carroll's *Through the Looking
Glass*). A, 14. C, 89.
P, 108, 111

Red Norah ("repetida viuda,"
widow of several gangsters).
OC, 312

Redentor. See Jesucristo

Redfern (designer). OCC, 54

Ref el Escaldo (Refr Gestsson,
Icelandic poet, son of
Steinunn). OC, 369

Regin (character in the
*Volsunga Saga*). OCC, 966,
967

Regules, Elías (Uruguayan
physician, poet and play-
wright, 1860–1929, author
of "El gaucho" and "La
tapera"). OC, 114, 1039.
OCC, 347. I, 64. LA, 10.
TE, 89

Regulo (Marcus Atilius Regulus,
Roman general in the First
Punic War who sacrificed
himself to the Carthaginians
for the sake of Rome, d.
c.250 B.C.). OC, 756.
OCC, 962

Reina Blanca. See White Queen

Reina Virgen. See Elizabeth I

Reinafé (four brothers, José
Vicente, 1782–1837, Francisco
Isidoro, 1796–1840, José
Antonio, 1798–1837 and
Guillermo, 1799–1837,
Argentine caudillos in
Córdoba in the time of Rosas
and Facundo Quiroga). OC,
791

Remarque, Erich Maria (German
novelist, 1897–1970, author
of *Im Westen nichts Neues*).
OC, 185. OCC, 492

Rembrandt Harmenszoon van Rijn
(Dutch painter and engraver,
1606–69). OC, 1054. SN,
135

Remo (Remus, in Roman legend,
twin brother of Romulus).
OCC, 657, 910. SN, 41

Rémora (fabulous fish
mentioned by Pliny). OCC,
686

Renan, Ernest (French
historian, philologist and
critic, 1823–1892, author of
*Averroes et l'Averroisme, Vie
de Jésus, Les Origines du
Christianisme* and numerous

other works).    OC, 234, 582,
588, 748.    OCC, 789, 837.
BC, 60.    PB, 217, 219
Renard, Jules  (French writer,
1864–1910, author of *Poil de
Carotte*, a *Journal* and other
works).    OCC, 482.  I, 125.
PB, 165
Renouvier, Charles  (French
philosopher, 1815–1903,
author of *Essais de critique
générale, Dilemme de la
métaphysique pure, Histoire
et solution des problemes
métaphysiques* and other
works).    OC, 258
Renovales  (soccer player,
character in Bustos Domecq
story).    OCC, 360, 361, 362
Renovales, Raimundo  (thug in
Buenos Aires).    OC, 128n.
Renovales, Vicente  (half-owner
of the Hotel El Nuevo
Imparcial in Bustos Domecq
stories).    OCC, 86, 87, 92,
93, 165
Repetto  (mentioned in Bustos
Domecq story).    OCC, 25
Reps, Paul  (author of *Zen
Flesh, Zen Bones*).    OCC, 781
Requena  (family in Balvanera
neighborhood).    OC, 134,
164.    PB, 118
Requena, Eliseo  (character in
Bustos Domecq story).    OCC,
65, 66, 69, 70, 74, 77, 79–83
Restaurador de las Leyes.
See Rosas
Reuch.    See Rauch
Rey Escalona  (Ecuadoran
historian, author of *Campaña
del Ecuador*).    PB, 132
Rey Rojo.    See Red King
Rey de la Muerte  (king of the
dead in Buddhism).    OCC, 778
Reyes, Alfonso  (Mexican man of
letters and diplomat, 1889–
1959, author of *Reloj de sol,
Visión de Anáhuac, Capítulos
de literatura española,
Simpatías y diferencias, El
suicida* and numerous other
works).    OC, 13, 175, 233,
434, 662n., 692n., 829–30,
998, 1144.    OCC, 846, 851.
I, 98.  IA, 124–31.    OP,

470.    P, 63n., 85, 121n.
PB, 215, 245.    SN, 156
Reyes Católicos  (Fernando II
de Aragón, 1452–1516, and
Isabel I de Castilla, 1451–
1504).    SN, 156
Reyles, Carlos  (Uruguayan
novelist, 1868–1936, author
of *El embrujo de Sevilla* and
numerous other works).    OC,
1058.    OCC, 468
Reyles, Carlos  (son of the
novelist).    OC, 1058
Reynoso  (a poultry farmer in
Bustos Domecq story).    OCC,
139
Ribecas.    OCC, 180
Ribera, Eudoro  (doctor in
Borges story).    OC, 1126
Ricardo I, Corazón de Leon
(Richard the Lion-Hearted,
king of England, 1157–1199).
SN, 60
Ricardo III  (king of England,
1452–1485, subject of a
Shakespeare play).    OC, 803.
OCC, 635
Ricci, Matteo  (Italian Jesuit
missionary to China, 1552–
1610, author of theological
and polemical works in
Chinese).    OCC, 701
Rice, Elmer  (American
dramatist, 1892–1967, author
of *Street Scene*).    OC, 224.
BC, 33
Richter.    OC, 216
Richter, Johann Paul Friedrich
(German novelist usually
called Jean Paul, 1763–1825,
author of *Hesperus* and other
works).    OCC, 834.  I, 157.
P, 32, 37
Ricketts, Charles S.  (British
critic, 1866–1931, author of
*Oscar Wilde, Recollections*,
1932).    OC, 691
Rienzi, Cola di  (Roman popular
leader, 1313?–1354).    OCC, 827
Rifeo  (Roman about whom little
is known, character in the
*Aeneid* and *Paradiso*).    NED,
141.    PB, 178
Riganti, Raúl  (character in
Bustos Domecq, "el hombre
torpedo").    OCC, 146

Rodó, José Enrique (Uruguayan essayist, 1871-1917, author of *Ariel* and *Motivos de Proteo*). OCC, 77, 185, 468

Rodrigo (Visigothic king of Spain at the time of the Moorish invasion in 711). OP, 516

Rodríguez, Florentino (knife-fighter in Buenos Aires). OC, 128n.

Rodríguez Larreta, Enrique. See Larreta, Enrique

Rodríguez Marín, Francisco (Spanish literary scholar, 1855-1943). I, 63, 68, 69-70. PB, 230. TE, 75

Rodríguez Monegal, Emir (Uruguayan scholar, d. 1985, author of *Jorge Luis Borges: A Literary Biography* and many other works). OC, 571

Rodríguez Navas y Carrasco, Manuel (Spanish writer, 1848-1922, author of a *Diccionario completo de la lengua española*, *Cría de gansos*, *Estudio de tecnología*, *Pedagogía social* and other works). TE, 109

Roemerstadt (baron, character in Jaromir Hladík's *Los enemigos*). OC, 510, 513

Roger, Mary (model for Poe's Marie Roget). BO, 76

Rogers, Samuel (English poet, 1763-1855, author of a volume of *Recollections*). P, 72

Roget, Marie (character in Poe story). BO, 77

Rognvald (seems to refer to Ari Thorgilsson, Icelandic writer, b. 1067, co-author with Hallr Thorarinsson of the *Háttalykill* or *Aettartala*). OCC, 957

Rojas, Elena (character in Borges-Bioy filmscript). OCC, 199, 223-25, 229-31, 234, 236, 242-44, 246-48, 250-53. BC, 77

Rojas, Eliseo (character in Borges-Bioy filmscript). OCC, 204-7, 213-14, 216, 220-21, 224, 227-33, 235, 239, 241-45, 247, 249, 251, 252

Rojas, Fernando de (Spanish writer, c.1465-1541, author of the *Celestina*). I, 125

Rojas, Ricardo (Argentine literary historian, critic and poet, 1882-1957, author of a much-maligned *Historia de la literatura argentina* and numerous other works). OC, 180, 183, 193, 194, 267, 268, 279, 421, 655. OCC, 336, 515, 516, 520, 526, 534, 540, 553, 559, 560, 565. I, 136. IA, 36, 157, 160. P, 91, 92, 98, 112. PB, 152, 153, 231

Rojas Paz, Pablo (Argentine poet and essayist, 1896-1956, author of *La metáfora y el mundo*, *El perfil de nuestra expresión* and other works). TE, 86

Roland or Rolando. See Orlando

Roldán, Belisario (Argentine poet, dramatist and orator, 1873-1922). OCC, 71

Rolf (leader of Norse invaders of Normandy). PB, 191

Romano, el (perhaps refers to Pliny's *Naturalis historia*). VA, 36

Romeo (character in Shakespeare's *Romeo and Juliet*). OCC, 820

Romero, Macario (a gunfighter mentioned in popular verses). OCC, 965n. P, 113

Rómulo (Romulus, in Roman legend, the founder of Rome and twin brother of Remus). OCC, 657, 910. SN, 41

Ronsard, Pierre de (French poet, 1524?-1585). OCC, 880. P, 112

Roosevelt, Franklin Delano (U. S. president, 1882-1945). ILN, 64

Roosevelt, Theodore (U. S. president, 1858-1919). ILN, 46, 64

Roperite (fabulous animal of North America). OCC, 631

Rosales, Luis (Spanish poet and literary critic, b. 1910). OC, 1143

Rosales, Porfirio (character in Borges-Bioy filmscript). OCC, 271, 272, 275, 276, 283

Rosalinda (Rosalind, character in Shakespeare's *Romeo and Juliet*). OCC, 820

Rosas, Juan Manuel (Argentine general and politician, governor of Buenos Aires and dictator of the Argentine confederation, 1793-1877, sometimes spelled Rozas, also known as "Héroe del Desierto" and "Restaurador de las Leyes"). OC, 9, 22, 28-29, 52, 61, 92, 106, 108, 145, 162, 183, 184, 196, 655, 791-92, 872, 899, 994, 1001, 1021, 1048, 1049, 1121, 1144. OCC, 487, 520, 526, 528, 533. A, 57, 65, 66, 74. I, 132, 137. IA, 29, 155. ILN, 33. LA, 14, 181. OP, 400, 477. P, 17, 28, 64, 65, 78, 96, 130, 131, 132, 136-38. PB, 130, 131, 246. SN, 147-48. TE, 8, 83

Roscelin, Jean (Roscellinus, French scholastic philosopher, c.1045-c.1120). OC, 745. NED, 122

Rosenberg, Alfred (German Nazi leader, 1893-1946). OC, 653

Rosenberg, Rosita (character in Bustos Domecq story). OCC, 100

Rosencrantz (character in Shakespeare's *Hamlet*). OC, 579

Rosenfeld, Sali (character in Nazi children's book). PB, 156

Rosenroth. See Knorr von Rosenroth

Rosenthal, Lee (character in Borges story). LA, 142, 145

Rosenzweig, Emma (pianist, character in Borges story). OC, 579n.

Rosney (writer of science fiction). OC, 697

Ross, Alexander (Scottish divine, one of the chaplains of Charles I, author of *Virgilius Evangelizans*, 1634). OC, 544

Rossetti, Christina (English poet, sister of Dante Gabriel Rossetti, 1830-1894). OCC, 842-43

Rossetti, Dante Gabriel (English poet and painter, 1828-1882, author of "The Blessed Damozel," "Eden Bower," "The House of Life," "Sudden Light" and other works). OC, 1128. OCC, 616, 659, 842-43, 844. BO, 28. I, 28. NED, 161n. P, 24. PB, 201n. SN, 89. TE, 132

Rossi, Attilio (Italian painter, author of *Buenos Aires en tinta china*, 1951). P, 127-28

Rossi, Mario (Italian critic, editor of the *Discorso di Giacopo Mazzoni in difesa della "Commedia" del divino poeta Dante*, 1898). NED, 102. PB, 182n., 184

Rossi, Vicente (Argentine critic and historian, author of *Cosas de negros*, 1926, and *Folletos lenguaraces*). OC, 103, 124n., 132n., 159, 162, 180, 295. OCC, 513, 544n., 565. IA, 111-14, 116, 117, 136. P, 30, 92

Rossmann, Karl (character in Kafka's *Amerika*). P, 104

Rostand, Edmond (French poet and dramatist, 1868-1918, author of *Cyrano de Bergerac*, *Chantecler* and other works). OC, 695

Rothe, Julius (character in Borges story). OC, 508, 509

Rothe, Richard (German Lutheran theologian, 1799-1867, author of *Theologische Ethik*, *Die Anfange der christlichen Kirche und ihrer Verfassung*, *Dogmatik* and other works). OC, 237, 367. IA, 51. TE, 66

Rousseau, Jean-Jacques (Swiss-French philosopher, author, political theorist and composer, 1712-1778, author of *Emile*, the *Nouvelle Héloise*, *Confessions* and many

other works).    OC, 734.
OCC, 304, 829.    A, 38.    I,
9.    IA, 90
Roverano   (pharmacist,
character in Borges-Levinson
story).    HE, 56
Roverano, Romualdo   (character
in Borges-Bioy filmscript).
OCC, 284-87
Roxlo, Carlos   (Uruguayan
writer, 1861-1926, author of
a vast *Historia de la
literatura uruguaya*).    OC,
180, 188.    P, 96
Royce, Josiah   (American
philosopher, 1855-1916,
author of *The World and the
Individual* and other works).
OC, 669, 764, 937.    OCC,
316.    LA, 74
Rozas, Prudencio   (character in
Hudson's *The Purple Land*).
TE, 34
Rubens, Peter Paul   (Flemish
painter, 1577-1640).    OCC,
605
Rubicante   (character in Bustos
Domecq story).    OCC, 403,
405, 421
Rubio, Mariano   (character in
Borges story).    OC, 1048,
1051
Rubio de Jáuregui, María
Justina   (character in Borges
story).    OC, 1048-52
Rubio de Molinaria, Julia
(character in Borges story).
OC, 1049-52
Ruckert, Friedrich   (German
Orientalist scholar and poet,
1788-1866, author of
*Liebesfruhling, Ostliche
Rosen, Ghaselen, Rostem und
Suhrab* and other works).
OC, 695n.    OCC, 902n.
Rudiger   (Ruedeger, character
in the *Nibelungenlied*).
OCC, 914
Ruegg, August   (German literary
scholar, author of *Jenseits-
vorstellungen vor Dante,
Dantes Divina Commedia*
and works on Cervantes, Homer
and Keyserling).    NED, 115
Rufino   (character in Borges
story).    LA, 90-97

Rufo, Marco Flaminio   (character
in Borges story).    OC, 536
Ruggieri degli Ubaldini
(character in Dante).    OC,
610.    NED, 106, 108
Ruggiero   (character in
Ariosto).    OCC, 920
Ruiz, Clodomiro   (character in
Bustos Domecq story).    OCC,
427-32
Ruiz, Francisco   ("el
Remiendo," character in
Bustos Domecq story).    OCC,
427
Ruiz, José Martínez.    See
Azorín
Ruiz Villalba, Julia   (Pumita,
character in Bustos Domecq
story).    OCC, 62-72, 74, 75,
77, 81-83
Ruiz Villalba de Muñagorri,
Mariana   (character in Bustos
Domecq and Suárez Lynch
stories, later Mariana Ruiz
Villalba de Anglada).    OCC,
50-60, 62-84, 149, 161-70,
405, 406, 408, 409, 412-15,
421
Runeberg, Nils   (Swedish
theologian, character in
Borges story, author of
*Kristus och Judas* and *Den
hemlige Fralsaren*, perhaps
kin to the Swedish poet Johan
Ludvig Runeberg, 1804-1877).
OC, 514-18
Runeberg, Viktor   (German
spy in Borges story, also
known as Hans Rabener).    OC,
472, 473
Ruperto   (character in Tulio
Herrera's novel *Hágase hizo*,
also known as Alberto).
OCC, 346
Rurik   (semilegendary Varangian
warrior, founder of the
princely dynasty of medieval
Russia, d. 879).    OC, 517.
PB, 190
Ruskin, John   (English critic
and social theorist, 1819-
1900, author of *The Stones of
Venice, Modern Painters, The
Political Economy of Art* and
other works).    OCC, 333,
836-37, 840, 843, 847.    A,

23. NED, 86. PB, 169.
SN, 157

Russell, Bertrand (British philosopher, mathematician, writer and social reformer, 1872-1970, author of *Introduction to Mathematical Philosophy*, *The Analysis of Mind*, *Free Thought and Official Propaganda*, *Let the People Think* and numerous other works). OC, 239, 246-48, 256n., 258, 277, 354, 392, 394, 437, 445, 449, 652, 673, 724-26. OCC, 746. BC, 60. BO, 89, 91. C, 101. IA, 165. P, 35, 163

Rustam (character in the Persian epic poem *Shah-nama* who fights against his son Suhrab). OCC, 902

Ruth (Moabite widow in Bible). OC, 357, 717, 718

Rutherford, Ernest (British physicist, 1871-1937). OC, 385, 386

Rutland, duke of (character in Herbert Quain's *The Secret Mirror*). OC, 463

Rutledge, Anne (American historical figure, alleged fiancee of Abraham Lincoln, 1813?-1835, later the subject of a poem in Edgar Lee Masters' *Spoon River Anthology*). ILN, 45

Ruysbrokio (Jan van Ruysbroeck or Ruusbroec, Roman Catholic mystic, born in Brabant, 1293-1381, author of *Seven Steps of the Ladder of Spiritual Love* and *The Spiritual Espousals*). OCC, 68

Ryan (character in Borges story). OC, 496-98

Saavedra Fajardo, Diego de (Spanish political writer and diplomat, 1584-1648, author of *Idea de un príncipe político christiano, Corona gótica, castellana y austríaca, Locuras de Europa* and other works). OCC, 686. I, 32, 38. IA, 73. OP, 459. P, 45. SN, 130

Sabat Ercasty, Carlos (Uruguayan poet, b. 1887). TE, 62

Sabato, Ernesto (Argentine novelist and essayist, b. 1911, author of *Sobre héroes y tumbas, Tres aproximaciones a la literatura de nuestro tiempo* and other works). OC, 543n.

Saborido, Enrique (Uruguayan composer, author of the tango "La Morocha," here mistakenly called José Saborido). OC, 81, 139, 159

Sachs, Hans (German poet, shoemaker and guild master, leading Meistersinger of Nuremberg, 1494-1576). OCC, 591

Sackmann, Morena (character in Borges story). OC, 594

Sackville-West, Victoria (English writer, 1892-1962, author of *The Earth, The Edwardians* and other works). OCC, 853

Saemund Sigfusson (Saemund "the Wise," Icelandic historian formerly thought to be the author of the *Elder Edda*, 1056-1131). OCC, 925, 958

Sáenz Peña, Carlos Muzzio (Argentine writer and journalist). OC, 159

Sáenz Peña, Roque (Argentine politician and president, 1851-1914). OC, 117

Sáenz Valiente (prominent family in 19th century Buenos Aires). P, 78

Safo (Sappho, Greek lyric poet, fl. early 6th century B.C.). OCC, 319

Sagitario (Sagittarius, centaur with bow and arrow, constellation in zodiac). OCC, 660

Sagrada Familia (Holy Family, St. Joseph, Virgin Mary and Jesus). OCC, 658

Saint Pe, Carlos or Carlota (character in Bustos Domecq story). OCC, 331-32

Sainte-Beuve, Charles-Augustin
(French literary historian
and critic, 1804-1869, author
of *Portraits littéraires,
Volupté* and numerous other
works).    OC, 772.   OCC, 837,
902n.    P, 72
Saintsbury, George (English
critic and historian, 1845-
1933, author of a *Short
History of English
Literature,* a *History of
Criticism* and numerous other
works).    OC, 692, 730, 731,
732.    OCC, 710, 857, 875.
P, 32, 117
Sakya family  (Gautama Buddha's
family).    OCC, 722
Saladino  (Saladin or Salah
ad-Din, Muslim warrior and
Ayyubid sultan of Egypt,
1137?-1193).   NED, 99.   PB,
183.   SN, 50
Salamandra  (fabulous
animal, a little dragon that
can live in fire).   OCC,
689-91, 694
Salas, José de  (friend of
Quevedo).   OC, 663
Salaverria, José María
(Argentine essayist, 1873-
1940, author of *Tierra
argentina* and *El Poema de la
pampa*).   OC, 131, 132
Salcedo y Coronel, José García
de  (Spanish poet, 1592?-
1651, author of *Rimas,
Ariadna* and other works).
IA, 71
Saldías, Adolfo  (Argentine
historian and politician,
1850-1914, author of *Historia
de la Confederación
Argentina*).   OCC, 559.
PB, 131
Sale, George  (English
Orientalist, c.1697-1736,
author of an English
translation of the *Koran*).
OC, 715.    NED, 123
Sales, San Francisco de.   See
Francisco de Sales, San
Salgari, Emilio  (Italian writer,
1863-1911, author of various
travel books and novels of
adventure).   OCC, 513

Salillas, Rafael  (Spanish
physician and criminologist,
1854-1923).   OC, 653
Salinas, Francisco  (blind
musician to whom Fray Luis
de León dedicated an ode).
SN, 159
Salivazo, Pardo  (character in
Bustos Domecq stories).
OCC, 18, 92, 259, 442
Salomón  (Solomon, Biblical
king of ancient Hebrews, d.
c.932 B.C.).   OC, 209, 533,
637.    OCC, 55, 709, 801,
892-94.   PB, 240.   SN,
68
Salomón de Constanza  (bishop
of Constance, to whom Otfried
dedicated his *De universo*).
OCC, 905
Salvadores, Pedro  (Argentine
Unitarian persecuted by
Rosas, mentioned in Mármol's
*Amalia* and the subject of a
Borges story).   OC, 994-95
Salvañac, Cristóbal  (Uruguayan
judge involved in the trial
of Avelino Arredondo).   LA,
181
Samain, Albert  (French poet,
1858-1900, author of *Au
jardin de l'infante* and other
works).   OCC, 471, 472, 502.
IA, 76
Samaniego, Félix María
(Spanish fabulist, 1745-
1801).   OCC, 185
Samet.    OCC, 336
Samkara.    See Sankara
Sampaio  (character in Bustos
Domecq story).   OCC, 127,
128, 129n.
Sampson  (minor character in
Shakespeare's *Romeo and
Juliet*).   OC, 419
Sampson, George  (author of
*Cambridge History of English
Literature*).   OCC, 857
Samr  (Gunnar's dog in the
*Njals Saga*).   OCC, 932
Sánchez, Florencio  (Uruguayan
playwright, 1875-1910).   OC,
117.    OCC, 330
Sancho Panza. See Panza, Sancho
Sanctis, Francesco De  (Italian
critic, 1817-1883, author of

a *Storia della letteratura italiana*). OC, 744. OCC, 561. NED, 107, 161

Sandburg, Carl (American poet and biographer, 1878-1967, author of *Chicago Poems, Good Morning America* and other works). OCC, 474. CONJ, 75. ILN, 9, 35, 47-48. P, 173

Sandrini, Luis (Argentine comic actor). BC, 62

Sangiácomo, Commendatore (character in Bustos Domecq story). OCC, 63-84

Sangiácomo, Ricardo (character in Bustos Domecq story, son of the Commendatore). OCC, 62-84

Sankara or Samkara (Sankara Acharya, Hindu theologian, c.789-820). OC, 738. OCC, 734, 752

San Marco, Delia Elena (friend of Borges). OC, 790. See also Porcel, Delia San Marco

San Martín, José de (Argentine general and statesman, liberator of Chile and Peru, 1778-1850, sometimes referred to as the *Libertador* or the *Protector del Perú*). OC, 727, 1029, 1052, 1062-67. I, 133. PB, 130, 131, 132. TE, 8

San Roque (dog in Borges-Bioy filmscript). OCC, 209

Sansón (Samson, judge of Israel in Bible). OC, 434, 701, 702, 997. OCC, 825. OP, 522. SN, 154, 155, 156

Santa Coloma (character in Hudson's *The Purple Land*). TE, 35

Santayana, George (American philosopher and poet, born in Spain, 1863-1952, author of *The Life of Reason, The Realms of Being* and other works). OC, 364

Santiago (policeman, character in Borges-Bioy filmscript). OCC, 178

Santos Dumont, Alberto (Brazilian aviator, 1873-1932). OCC, 189

Santos Pérez (a gaucho-outlaw, the murderer of Facundo Quiroga). OC, 791, 792, 1121, 1122. OP, 400-1

Santos Vega (legendary gaucho in 19th century Argentina only outsung by the Devil, subject of works by Obligado and Ascasubi). OC, 132. PB, 133, 187. TE, 8, 89, 144

Sapegno, Natalino (Italian literary critic and historian, author of a *Compendio di storia della letteratura italiana* and of a commentary on Dante). PB, 238

Saponaro, doctor (character in Bustos Domecq stories). OCC, 71, 82, 155

Sarah (Santiago Fischbein's aunt in Borges story). OC, 1030

Saranoff, Sergei (character in Shaw's *Arms and the Man*). OC, 749

Saravia, Aparicio (Uruguayan politician, 1855-1904). OC, 152, 188, 571, 572, 1001. OCC, 522. I, 133. LA, 152. OP, 426

Sarmiento, Domingo Faustino (Argentine writer, educator, politician and president, 1811-1888, author of the *Facundo, Recuerdos de provincia, Campaña del Ejército Grande* and many other works). OC, 899, 1066, 1106, 1121. OCC, 38, 486, 487, 527. BC, 59. BO, 20. IA, 177. ILN, 13. OP, 384, 401. P, 8, 16, 64, 91, 96, 112, 129-33, 134-39. PB, 130, 131, 154, 167, 187, 213-14, 247. TE, 6, 33

Saroyan, William (American author, b. 1908, author of *My Name is Aram* and other works). ILN, 54

Sartre, Jean-Paul (French philosopher, playwright and novelist, 1905-1980, author of *La Nausée, Huis-clos,*

*L'Etre et le Néant* and other works).   ILN, 35, 51

Saslavsky, Luis (Argentine film director and writer). BC, 54-55

Sastre, Marcos (Uruguayan writer, 1809-1887).   OCC, 40

Satán or Satanás (fallen angel, the adversary of man and God in Judaeo-Christian tradition). OC, 325.  OCC, 622, 711, 813, 824, 825, 873, 903.   NED, 152n.   PB, 141. TE, 12

Satanail (name given to Satan by Bogomil Manichean believers).   OC, 422

Sátiros (satyrs in classical mythology, half-man, half-goat).   OCC, 692

Satornilo (Satornil or Saturninus of Antioch, gnostic leader).   OC, 214, 514

Saturno (Saturn, in Roman religion, the god of harvests, later identified with the Greek god Cronos). OCC, 801, 892-94

Saul (San Pablo or St. Paul, apostle to the gentiles). OC, 517

Saulino (character in Bustos Domecq story).   OCC, 401

Saurat, Denis (Milton scholar). OCC, 825

Savastano, Tulio (character in Bustos Domecq and Suárez Lynch stories).   OCC, 18, 85-104, 149, 163-66, 170, 360-62, 438, 440-46

Savastano, Tulio, hijo (Argentine literary critic, author of a 1971 Harvard dissertation on Clodomiro Ruiz, evidently the son of the preceding).   OCC, 427-32

Savigny, Friedrich Karl von (German jurist and legal historian, 1779-1861).   OCC, 343

Saxo Gramatico (Saxo Grammaticus, Danish historian, c.1150-c.1220, author of the *Gesta Danorum* or *Historia Danica*).

OC, 756.   OCC, 819, 931, 954n., 958, 970-73, 975.   OP, 496.   P, 138.   PB, 199

Sayers, Dorothy (English writer, 1893-1957, author of numerous detective stories and polemical writings, translator of Dante, editor of anthologies of detective stories, etc.).   OC, 414

Sbarbi y Osuna, José María (Spanish priest and scholar, 1834-1910, author of a *Diccionario de refranes, Ambigú literario* and many other works).   PB, 230

Scaligero, Joseph Justus.   See Escaligero

Scarface Al (film gangster based on Al Capone).   OC, 222.   BC, 28

Scévola, Lucio (character in Bustos Domecq story, sometimes Sévola).   OCC, 355, 423

Scharlach, Dandy Red (gangster, character in Borges story). OC, 499, 504-7

Schelling, Friedrich Wilhelm Joseph von (German philosopher, 1775-1854, author of *Philosophie der Kunst, System des transzendentalen Idealismus, Ideen zur Philosophie der Natur* and other works). OCC, 832

Schering, Emil (supposed German translator of Runeberg's *Den hemlige Fralsaren*).   OC, 514

Schiaffino, Eduardo (19th century Argentine writer). OC, 106.   IA, 177

Schiaparelli, Giovanni Virginio (Italian astronomer, discoverer of the so-called canals on Mars, 1835-1910). OCC, 110

Schiavo (librarian who worked with Borges in library in Almagro Sur).   C, 19

Schiller, Friedrich von (German dramatist, poet and *historian, 1759-1805, author of Wallenstein, Uber das Pathetische, Uber naive und*

*sentimentalische Dichtung* and
numerous other works). OC,
280. OCC, 330. BO, 39,
83. I, 62. P, 45
Schlegel, Friedrich von
(German philosopher, critic
and writer, 1772-1829, author
of numerous plays, the novel
*Lucinde*, and critical works
on classical and Indian
literatures and on Goethe).
P, 145
Schlesinger (character in
Bustos Domecq story). OCC,
427
Schleyer, Johann Martin
(inventor of the artificial
language *Volapuk*, author of
numerous grammars and other
works about the language).
OC, 706
Schmidel, Ulrich (German
soldier, c.1510-c.1579, who
spent many years in the
River Plate in the employ of
a German bank, author of a
detailed diary of the
conquest of the River Plate
region from 1534 to 1554).
PB, 125
Scholem, Gershom (Jewish
scholar, born in Berlin in
1897, author of *Major Trends
in Jewish Mysticism* and other
works). OC, 886. OCC,
616. SN, 138-39
Schomberg, W. (character in
Conrad's *Victory*, hotelkeeper
in Sourabaya). OC, 674
Schopenhauer, Arthur (German
philosopher, 1788-1860,
author of *Die Welt als Wille
und Vorstellung* and *Parerga
und Paralipomena*). OC, 13,
38, 161, 199, 201, 258, 261,
275, 279, 280, 351, 356, 357,
367, 383, 395, 438, 463, 479,
483, 494, 577, 578, 594, 646,
648n., 649, 679, 700, 702,
717, 718, 737, 739, 744, 748,
752, 753, 760, 766, 767, 769,
770, 773, 854, 936, 1064,
1066, 1067, 1086. OCC,
637n., 729, 733, 735, 738,
742, 749, 752, 756, 820, 848,
911, 977. A, 38. BO,

38, 84, 88. CONJ, 93. I,
22, 63, 93, 95, 104, 116.
IA, 16, 53, 72, 80-81, 102,
126. LA, 27, 74. NED,
118, 120. OP, 371, 459.
P, 50, 55, 58, 61, 134, 148.
PB, 146, 159, 229. SN, 90,
92, 93, 135. TE, 47, 117-
18, 121
Schrader, Eberhard (German
Orientalist, 1836-1908,
author of numerous works on
Biblical, Assyrian and
Ethiopian studies). OCC,
703
Schultz, Alexander (the real
name of Borges's friend the
Argentine poet and painter
Xul-Solar, here the supposed
author of *Die Vernichtung der
Rose*). OC, 345
Schultz, Wolfgang (German
anthropologist, 1881-1936,
author of *Dokumente der
Gnosis* as well as works on
the *Popol Vuh*, myth and Nazi
ideology). OC, 213
Schwob, Marcel (French writer,
1867-1905, author of *Mimes,
Le Roi au masque d'or, Vies
imaginaires, La Croisades des
enfants, Monelle* and other
works). OC, 691. P, 140-41
Scio. OCC, 304n.
Scott, Walter (Scottish
novelist, 1771-1832, author
of *Waverley, Ivanhoe, Letters
on Demonology and Witchcraft*
and numerous other works).
OCC, 592, 641, 833, 835.
I, 128. ILN, 14, 15
Scotus, Duns. See Erigena
Scyld Sceaving (Danish king in
*Beowulf*). OCC, 790. LA,
141. OP, 453, 466
Sebastiao (king of Portugal,
killed at Alcacarquivir in
Morocco, 1554-1578). OC,
831
Segismundo (character in
Calderon's *La vida es sueño*).
OC, 755
Segovia, Lisandro (Argentine
lexicographer, b. 1842,
author of *Diccionario de
argentinismos, neologismos y*

*barbarismos*, 1911, and works
on law). OC, 133n. OCC,
156. IA, 180. TE, 137
Segovia, Pablos de.    See
Pablos de Segovia
Selenitas (inhabitants of the
moon in Lucian's *True
History*).    P, 25
Selkirk, Alexander (Scottish
sailor, 1676-1721, on whose
life Defoe based his Robinson
Crusoe).    OC, 857, 896
Sem Tob (Shem Tov Ardutiel,
Spanish rabbi and poet,
1290?-1369?).    P, 80
Séneca (Lucius Annaeus
Seneca or Seneca the younger,
Roman philosopher, dramatist
and statesman, born in Spain,
c.3 B.C.-65 A.D., author of
*Naturales quaestiones,
Epistulae Morales* and
numerous tragedies and
philosophical treatises).
OC, 200n., 278, 282, 362,
394, 544, 641, 662, 665, 700,
869, 928, 937.    OCC, 651,
856, 956.    BO, 16.    I,
31, 134.    OP, 557.    P,
121, 125.    SN, 18
Senet, Rodolfo (Argentine
novelist and critic, author
of *Evolución y educación,*
1901, *La derrota del genio,*
1914, *La psicología gauchesca
en el Martín Fierro,* 1927,
and other works).    IA, 114
Señor de la Muerte (in Tibetan
Buddhism, the judge of the
dead).    OCC, 764
Sephiroth (ten divine
emanations in the *Kabbalah*).
SN, 134
Seres Térmicos (previous
inhabitants of earth
according to Rudolf Steiner).
OCC, 693
Serpiente Musical (Chinese
monster, a serpent with four
wings).    OCC, 630
Servet, Miguel (Michael
Servetus, Spanish theologian
and physician, burned as a
heretic, 1511-1553).    OC,
423

Serviliana, la (character in
Borges story).    OC, 1059
Servio Honorato (Marcus
Servius Honoratus, 4th
century Latin grammarian and
critic, author of a
commentary on Virgil).    OCC,
585, 647, 685
Servus, baronesa de (character
in Bustos Domecq stories).
OCC, 73-75, 80, 82, 170, 345,
353, 354
Set (in Egyptian religion, god
of evil).    PB, 197
Setenta (the seventy
Hellenistic Jews who
translated the Hebrew Bible
into Greek).    OCC, 679
Seth (in Bible, third son of
Adam and Eve, father of
Enos).    OC, 701
Sevasco, doctor (character in
Bustos Domecq story).    OCC,
80
Sévola, Lucio.    See Scévola
Sexto Empírico (Sextus
Empiricus, Greek physician
and sceptical philosopher,
2nd and 3rd centuries A.D.,
author of *Adversus Mathe-
maticos* and *Outlines of
Pyrrhonism*).    OC, 256, 770
Shahrazad or Shahrazada
(Sheherazade, queen of
Shahriar in the *Arabian
Nights*).    OC, 281, 397, 407,
477, 527, 668, 669, 1073.
OCC, 441, 496.    C, 105.
OP, 516-18.    SN, 69
Shahriar (Schariar or Sharyar,
legendary king of Samarkand,
character in the *Arabian
Nights*).    OC, 413, 668, 669.
OP, 516-18.    SN, 69
Shakespeare, William (English
playwright and poet, 1564-
1616, author of *Hamlet,
Macbeth, The Tempest, Julius
Caesar* and some thirty other
plays, as well as sonnets and
narrative poems).    OC, 79,
109, 121, 135, 142, 150, 157,
180, 219, 233, 253, 270,
273, 280, 349, 383, 402, 412,
419, 438n., 447, 461, 494,
497, 498, 522, 577, 579,

649, 666, 667, 668, 673, 678,
687, 689, 717, 719, 738, 748,
751, 755, 762, 763, 773, 793,
803–4, 1066, 1093, 1105,
1116, 1131. OCC, 310, 330,
498, 557, 558, 617, 658, 661,
674, 756, 814, 817, 818–21,
822, 828, 831, 837, 847, 952,
970, 972–73. A, 23, 36,
44. BC, 48. BO, 19, 20, 24,
36, 39, 55, 57. C, 69.
CONJ, 23, 57, 93. I, 23,
33, 158. ILN, 10, 21, 24,
26, 31, 36, 43, 52. NED,
139. OP, 383, 392, 408, 437,
454, 496, 522, 531, 542,
550,559. P, 8, 23, 26, 45,
49, 76, 86, 90, 95, 102,
112, 117, 119, 126, 129, 134,
142–47, 154, 165, 174. PB,
120, 149, 159, 162, 168, 171,
177, 225–27, 228, 229, 230,
235, 247. SN, 13, 14, 17,
21, 38, 39, 40, 42, 43, 110,
117, 143–44. TE, 42, 54,
101, 127, 147
Shand, William (Anglo-Argentine
poet, author of *Ferment*).
P, 148–50
Shang (dynasty of China which
ruled from c.1766 B.C. to
c.1122 B.C.). OCC, 700
Shang Yang (legendary Chinese
bird which brings rain).
OCC, 678
Shaw, George Bernard (Irish
playwright and critic, 1856–
1950, author of *Major
Barbara*, *Saint Joan*, *Arms and
the Man*, *Man and Superman*,
*Back to Methuselah*, *Man and
Superman* and many other
works). OC, 134, 135, 180,
236n., 273, 277, 281, 291,
420, 483, 544, 698, 704n.,
713, 727, 747–49, 763, 1023.
OCC, 200, 330, 500, 749, 761,
770, 829, 839, 843, 847, 847–
48, 851. A, 14. BC, 60,
78. BO, 13, 17–18, 38, 51.
I, 21. ILN, 10, 52, 54.
LA, 130. P, 15, 57, 86,
101, 146–47, 157. PB, 143–
46, 158, 159, 236. SN, 92,
136. TE, 9, 99–102. VA,
49

Shaw, T. E. (pseud. used T. E.
Lawrence for his translation
of the *Odyssey*). OCC, 852
Shearer, Norma (Canadian film
actress, 1900–1983). OCC,
63. HE, 53
Sheffield, Lady (friend and
patron of Gibbon, along with
her husband, John Baker
Holroyd, 1st Earl of
Sheffield). P, 72
Shelley, Percy Bysshe (English
poet, 1792–1822, author of
*Adonais*, *Prometheus Unbound*,
*Defence of Poetry*, *The Revolt
of Islam* and other works).
OC, 394, 639. OCC, 463,
833. A, 44. ILN, 43, 50.
PB, 146
Shen-Kuan (disciple of
Bodhidharma). OCC, 772
Shere Khan (tiger, character
in Kipling's *Jungle Books*).
A, 48. OP, 521. SN, 19.
VA, 27
Sheriff. See Sherriff
Sherman, William Tecumseh
(Union general during the
U. S. Civil War, 1820–1891).
P, 82
Sherriff, Robert Cedric
(British playwright,
screenwriter and novelist,
1896–1975, author of
*Journey's End*). OC, 185
Shiel, Matthew Phipps (writer,
1865–1947, author of *The
Purple Cloud*, *Science*, *Life
and Literature* and other
works). OCC, 16
Shih Huang Ti (Shi Hwang-ti,
first universal emperor of
China, 246–210 B.C.). OC,
633–35. PB, 176
Shiva (Hindu god, sometimes
Siva). SN, 120
Shotover (character in Shaw).
OC, 748
Shu T'ung (character in Bustos
Domecq story). OCC, 105–21
Shulteshelvi (Danish king).
PB, 240
Shultz, Wolfgang. See Wolfgang
Schultz
Shulz (Schultz, Xul-Solar's
family). A, 77

Silveyra (owner of soap factory in Bustos Domecq story). OCC, 126

Simbad el Marino (Sinbad the Sailor, character in the *Arabian Nights*, sometimes Sindibad). OC, 403, 543, 733, 799, 829, 1118. OCC, 267, 589, 600, 703, 710, 965. A, 7. OP, 395, 516, 519. P, 23. SN, 29, 70

Simeon ben Azzai (rabbi, collaborator of Akiba in the Merkabah studies). OC, 517

Simón Pedro (in the New Testament, the disciple Peter). OCC, 903

Simón el Mago (Simon Magus, Samaritan sorceror who attempted to buy spiritual power from the apostles). OC, 215, 812

Simónides (Greek lyric and elegiac poet, inventor of a technique for remembering, c.556–468). OC, 488

Simorg Anka. See Simurg

Simrock, Karl (translator of the *Nibelungenlied* in 1827). OCC, 911, 975

Simurg or Simurgh or Simorg Anka (bird in Persian mythology and literature, a bird which is all birds, a symbol of the divinity). OC, 251, 418n., 689, 1128. OCC, 695. CONJ, 79. LA, 61. NED, 139–44. PB, 177–80

Sinagoga, Pibe (character in Bustos Domecq stories). OCC, 100, 180

Sinclair, Upton (American novelist and socialist leader, 1878–1968, author of *The Jungle* and other works). ILN, 35

Sindibad del Mar. See Simbad

Singer, Isaac Merritt (American inventor of sewing machine, 1811–1875). OCC, 363

Sinkiewicz, Henryk (Polish novelist, 1846–1916, winner of the Nobel Prize for Literature in 1905, author of *Quo Vadis?*). OCC, 327

Sirenas (mermaids). OC, 228n. OCC, 448, 696–97, 914

Sirmond, Jacques (French scholar and Jesuit, 1559–1651). OC, 705

Sirven, Pierre Paul (French Protestant accused of murdering his daughter to prevent her from converting to Catholicism, defended by Voltaire, 1709–1777). P, 67

Sisifo (Sisyphus, founder and king of Corinth, condemned to perpetual toil in Tartarus). OC, 551

Siva. See Shiva

Siward (Earl of Northumbria, a Danish warrior who probably came to Britain with King Canute, d. 1055). P, 143

Skarp-hedin (Njal's son in the *Njals Saga*). OCC, 939–40

Skraelings (old Norse name for the Eskimos or Inuit). OCC, 940

Slatin, Rudolf Carl, Freiherr von (Austrian adventurer in British and Egyptian service, 1857–1932). OC, 589

Sleipnir (Odin's eight-legged horse in Norse mythology). OCC, 583, 593n., 928

Slidrugtanni or Guillinbursti (boar in Norse mythology who draws the chariot of the god Freyr). OCC, 699n.

Smerdiakov (character in Dostoevsky's *Brothers Karamazov*). OC, 222. BC, 28

Smith, Norman Kemp (historian of philosophy, author of *The Philosophy of David Hume*). OC, 757

Smith, Margaret (Orientalist, author of *The Persian Mystics*). OC, 418n.

Smithers, Leonard C. (editor and expurgator of Burton's translation of the *Arabian Nights*). OC, 403

Snorri Sturluson (Icelandic chieftain, historian, critic and saga teller, 1178–1241, author of the *Prose Edda*). OC, 371, 376, 377, 381, 382, 755, 756, 907, 1016, 1086.

OCC, 674, 834, 916, 923, 925, 931, 935, 943, 949, 950–64, 972, 975. ILN, 23. NED, 126. OP, 459, 493. PB, 190–91, 198, 200

Soca, Susana (Uruguayan poet, essayist and editor). OC, 817

Sócrates (Greek philosopher, 469–399). OC, 260, 354, 358, 362, 790, 853, 936, 1086. OCC, 15. A, 29. BO, 15, 29, 30, 31, 34, 36, 37. C, 63, 81. CONJ, 43. OP, 370, 472, 505, 540. P, 50

Soergel, Albert (German critic, author of Dichtung der Zeit). OC, 578, 579n., 748

Sófocles (Sophocles, Greek tragic poet, c.496–c.406). OC, 660. I, 128. P, 119. TE, 59

Soiza Reilly, Juan José (Argentine novelist and journalist, author of El alma de los perros, Glosario del tango and other works). OC, 117

Sol (Scandinavian sun goddess). OCC, 926n.

Solano López, Francisco. See López, Francisco Solano

Solar. See Xul-Solar

Soler, Miguel Estanislao (Argentine general and politician, 1783–1814). OC, 295, 863, 965. P, 17. PB, 132. SN, 148

Soler Darás, José (Argentine writer). OCC, 497

Solimán (Arabic name for Solomon, used in Arabian Nights). OC, 337. P, 43. SN, 68, 69

Solino (Gaius Iulius Solinus, 3rd century Latin encyclopedist who drew most of his Collectanea Rerum Memorabilium from Pliny and Mela without acknowledgement). P, 38

Solomón. See Salomón

Sombra, Segundo (gaucho hero of Guiraldes novel Don Segundo Sombra, based on a

real figure named Segundo Ramírez). OC, 659, 1040. BO, 72. P, 63n., 113. PB, 186–88. SN, 19

Sombrerero Loco. See Mad Hatter

Sona (character in Buddhist fable). OCC, 778

Sonnecken. OCC, 145

Soothill (scholar of China and Confucianism). OCC, 705

Sorano. See Valverio Sorano, Quinto

Sordello (Italian troubadour, c.1180–1269?, mentioned by Dante and the subject of a poem by Browning). NED, 88–89

Soriano, Fermín (character in Borges–Bioy filmscript). OCC, 199, 200–5, 208–9, 215–17, 219–21, 224–33, 238, 242, 243, 245–48, 250. BC, 77

Sorolla y Bastida, Joaquín (Spanish painter, 1863–1921). OCC, 421

Sosa, Marcelino (Uruguayan colonel, 1811–1844, mentioned in Ascasubi's Paulino Lucero). OCC, 519

Soto, Andrés (knife-fighter in Buenos Aires). P, 63

Soto, Hernando de (Spanish soldier and explorer, 1500?–1542). OC, 295

Sotos Ochando, Bonifacio (inventor of an artificial language). OC, 707

Soussens, Carlos de (Swiss-French friend of Carriego). OC, 116

South, Robert (English clergyman and author, 1634–1716). OC, 638

Southey, Robert (English poet, biographer, historian and translator, 1774–1843, author of Thalaba, Roderick, the Last of the Goths, A Tale of Paraguay, a History of Brazil and many other works). OCC, 695

Souza (character in Bustos Domecq). OCC, 400

Spátola (character in Bustos Domecq story). OCC, 398–400

Spearman, Rosanna (character in Collins's *The Moonstone*). P, 48

Speciale, Vasco (character in Bustos Domecq story). OCC, 398

Spencer, Herbert (English philosopher, 1820-1903, author of *First Principles, The Principles of Psychology* and other works). OC, 200, 261, 651n., 659, 703, 767, 1068. I, 117-19. IA, 19. ILN, 34. P, 15, 33, 35, 49. PB, 171, 225

Spender, Stephen (English poet and critic, 1909-1986, author of *The Destructive Element, The Creative Element, The Struggle of the Modern* and other works). OC, 640n. OCC, 842. P, 102

Spengler, Oswald (German historian and philosopher, 1880-1936, author of *Der Untergang des Abendlandes*). OC, 394, 497, 577. OCC, 830. BO, 14. I, 44. IA, 106. P, 134. SN, 63, 125, 127-28. TE, 18, 31, 34

Spens, Patrick (character in Scottish ballad). LA, 62

Spenser, Edmund (English poet, 1552?-1599, author of *The Faerie Queene*). OC, 627, 660, 671. OCC, 703. P, 120, 154

Spiantujen, Gran (character in Bustos Domecq). OCC, 397

Spiller, Gustav (psychologist, author of *The Mind of Man*, 1902, *The Origin and Nature of Man* and other works). OC, 276, 647, 760. BO, 30. I, 22. IA, 17, 19. P, 87. SN, 35, 146. TE, 53

Spingarn, Joel Elias (American educator and literary critic, 1875-1939, who endowed the Spingard Medal for outstanding black Americans). ILN, 51

Spinoza, Baruch or Benedict (Dutch philosopher, 1632-1677, author of *Tractatus theologico-politicus* and *Ethica ordine geometrica demonstrata*). OC, 200, 257, 280, 436, 503, 634, 652, 698, 718, 738, 745, 751, 808, 925, 930, 997, 1029, 1143. OCC, 733. A, 41. C, 101, 105. CONJ, 44. IA, 26. ILN, 11. NED, 123. OP, 470, 498, 511, 542. P, 157, 172. SN, 131, 134. VA, 34

Spitzer (inventor of a balloon). PB, 117

Spitzer, Leo (German literary critic, author of *Linguistics and Literary Theory*). PB, 117, 229. VA, 28

Spoerri, Theodor (psychologist and literary scholar, author of *Genie und Krankheit*, 1952, as well as works on Trakl and other writers, necrophilia and so forth). NED, 148

Squonk (fabulous animal of Pennsylvania, *Lacrimacorpus dissolvens*). OCC, 698

Ssu-Ma Ch'ien (Chinese historian, c.145-c.90, author of the *Historical Record*). OCC, 619

Stacio (Publius Papinius Statius, Latin poet, c.45-96, author of the *Thebais, Achilleis* and *Silvae*). OCC, 956

Stael, Anne-Louis-Germaine Necker, Mme. de (Swiss-French woman of letters, 1766-1817, author of *De la littérature considerée dans ses rapports avec les institutions sociales, De l'Allemagne* and other works). NED, 122. P, 69

Stalin, Joseph Vissariionovich (Soviet leader, 1879-1953, originally named Dzhugavash-vili). OC, 723. PB, 158

Stapledon, Eric (doctor, character in Bustos Domecq story). OCC, 367

Stapledon, William Olaf (English writer, 1886-1950, author of *Star Maker*). P, 151-52

Stehelin, John Peter (British minister, editor of the

Stradivarius, Antonius
(Italian violin maker, 1644–
1737).   OCC, 35
Strauss, David Friedrich
(German theologian and
philosopher, 1808-1874).
OC, 216
Strether, Lambert   (character
in James's *The Ambassadors*).
ILN, 39
Strindberg, August   (Swedish
playwright and novelist,
1849-1912).   OCC, 923.   I,
9.   ILN, 52.   P, 112
Sturla Sighvatsson   (nephew of
Snorri Sturluson).   OCC, 951
Sturla Thordarson   (another
nephew of Snorri Sturluson,
author of part of the
*Sturlunga Saga*).   OCC, 964
Sturla el Jurista   (character
in *Grettirs Saga*).   OCC, 938
Sturlung   (family of Snorri
Sturluson).   OCC, 950
Sturluson.   See Snorri
Sturluson
Suárez   (family).   OC, 932
Suárez, Damasio   (Buenos Aires
thug, alias Carnaza).   OC,
128n.
Suárez, Isidoro   (Argentine
colonel in the wars of
independence, 1799-1846,
Borges's great-grandfather).
OC, 24, 762, 863, 872-73,
1064.   A, 74, 88.   LA,
11.   OP, 459, 473, 549.
P, 131.   PB, 130, 245
Suárez, Romualdo, el Chileno
(a knife-fighter, a character
in several Borges stories).
OC, 128n., 157-58.   P, 128
Suárez, Saverio, el Chileno
(knife-fighter).   OC, 961,
963
Suárez, Serapio   (young man
mentioned by Lugones in *El
Payador* who made a living
reciting the Martín Fierro).
OCC, 482
Suarez, Ulpiano   (character in
Borges story).   OC, 547-49
Suárez, Wenceslao   (knife-
fighter).   OC, 138, 166-68,
171-72

Suárez Calimano, Emilio
(Argentine literary
journalist, friend of
Carriego).   OC, 117
Suárez de Acevedo, Leonor
(Borges's maternal
grandmother, d. 1918).   A,
73-74
Suárez Lynch, B.   (Argentine
writer, disciple of H. Bustos
Domecq, author of *Un modelo
para la muerte*).   OCC, 145,
147
Suárez Miranda   (supposed 17th
century Spanish writer to
whom Borges attributes a
paragraph he elsewhere
attributes to Josiah Royce).
OC, 847
Suddhodana   (king of Nepal,
Buddha's father).   OC, 740.
OCC, 721, 728.   SN, 81
Sueño   (personification of
dreams).   OCC, 707
Suhrab   (character in the
*Shah-nama*, son of Rustam).
OCC, 902
Suleiman Bendaud   (character in
Beckford's *Vathek*).   OC, 730
Suleiman el Magnífico   (Suleiman
I, the Magnificent, sultan of
Turkey, 1494-1566).   A, 18
Sunday   (character in
Chesterton's *The Man Who
Was Thursday*).   OC, 629
Su Wu   (Chinese general,
mentioned in Bustos Domecq
story).   OCC, 114
Suzuki, Daisetz Teitaro
(Japanese Buddhist scholar
and writer, 1870-1966).
OCC, 781.   SN, 77
Svarfathardal or Svarfdoela
(subject of an Icelandic
saga).   OCC, 940
Svedberg, Gaspar   (name of
Emmanuel Swedenborg's father,
a bishop and professor at
Uppsala University).   P, 154
Sveinsson, Brynjolf or Brynjulf
(17th century Icelandic
bishop).   OCC, 925
Sverrir   (Norwegian king, 1152–
1215, subject of *Sverris
Saga*).   OCC, 958

Talia (Thalia, one of nine Greek muses, the muse of comedy). OCC, 330

Talib ben-Sahl (character in the *Arabian Nights*). OC, 409

Taliesen or Taliesi medieval Welsh bard). PB, 219, 221. SN, 88

Tallón, José Sebastián (Argentine poet and essayist, author of *Las torres de Nuremberg* and *El tango en su etapa de música prohibida*). TE, 22

Talos (monster of bronze, guardian of the island of Crete). OCC, 699

Tamberlick (tenor who played Otello). OC, 574

Tamerlán or Timur (Mongol conqueror, c.1336–1405, subject of a Marlowe play). OC, 155, 803, 1083–84, 1140. OCC, 817, 818, 827. C, 13. OP, 367–69, 416

Tamiris (Thracian bard who boasted that he could win a contest even if the Muses opposed him, whereat they blinded him and made him forget his skill). SN, 152

Tammuz (ancient nature deity of Babylonia). PB, 197

Tanith (face of Baal). CONJ, 37

Tanner, John (character in Shaw). OC, 727. BO, 51. P, 157

Tannhauser (13th century German Minnesinger). OCC, 844

Tántalo (in Greek mythology, king of Sipylos, condemned to suffer eternally in Tartarus). OCC, 340

Tapia (knife-fighter). LA, 46

Tarik Benzeyad (character in *Arabian Nights*). OC, 413, 627

Tartarin (main character in Daudet's novel *Tartarin de Tarascon*). OC, 446

T'ao-T'ieh (fabulous animal of China). OCC, 700

Tártaro (Tartarus, Greek god). OCC, 645

Tartini, Giuseppe (Italian violinist, 1692–1770). OC, 642, 643

Tarzan (character in novels by Edgar Rice Burroughs). PB, 176

Tasso, Torcuato (Italian poet, 1544–1595, author of *Gerusalemme liberata*). OC, 264, 265, 744. OCC, 825. PB, 225, 242. SN, 28

Taullard, Alfredo (Argentine scholar, author of *Historia de nuestros viejos teatros*, 1932). OC, 111n.

Tavolara, José Antonio (Uruguayan dramatist, author of *Cosas de todos los días*, 1858). OCC, 82

Taylor, Jeremyas (English bishop, theologian and devotional writer, 1613–1667, author of *Holy Living, Holy Dying* and other works). OC, 210, 277, 360

Taylor, Philip Meadows (British officer and journalist in India, 1808–1876, author of *Confessions of a Thug*). OC, 593, 594

Taylor, Thomas (British mathematician and philosopher, 1768–1835, translator of Plotinus). OC, 367

Te-Shan (character in Buddhist fable). OCC, 773–74

Teakettler (fabulous creature of North America). OCC, 631

Tegner, Elias or Esaias (Swedish poet and novelist, bishop of Vaxjo, 1782–1846, author of *Frithjofssaga*). OCC, 965. ILN, 23

Tegobi (nickname for Gervasio Montenegro). OCC, 170

Tejerina, Inés (character in Bustos Domecq story). OCC, 438, 439, 440

Tejedor, Carlos (Argentine jurist and politician, 1817–1903, author of the first Argentine Penal Code). IA, 114

Telémaco (Telemachus, son of Odysseus in the *Odyssey*). OC, 250. NED, 113

Telescopio (nickname). See Cárdenas

Téllez, Gabriel. See Tirso de Molina

Téllez Girón, Pedro, duque de Osuna (Spanish general and politician, 1579-1624, subject of a Quevedo sonnet). OC, 369, 664. IA, 75. P, 123. SN, 108-13

Temístocles (Themistocles, Athenian statesman, c.528-462). OC, 700

Temple, Shirley (American child film star, b. 1928). OCC, 160

Tenniel, John (English caricaturist and illustrator, 1820-1914). P, 109

Tennyson, Alfred (English poet, 1809-1892, author of *In Memoriam, Idylls of the King, Locksley Hall* and other works). OC, 211, 219, 397, 413, 594, 595, 686, 689. OCC, 653, 841, 844, 885-86, 963. BO, 53, 67, 84. ILN, 25, 45, 52. NED, 118. OP, 466. P, 37n., 148, 165. PB, 156. SN, 153. TE, 132

Tenorio, Juan (name for Don Juan in 1844 Zorrilla play). IA, 102. TE, 101

Teócrito (Theocritus, Hellenistic Greek poet, fl. c.270 B.C., author of pastoral idylls). OC, 871. OCC, 504

Teodorico (Theodoric the Great, king of the Ostrogoths, rival of Odoacer and conqueror of Italy, c.454-526, sometimes called Theodoric of Verona or Dietrich von Berne). OCC, 901, 909-10, 914

Teopompo (Theopompus, Greek historian and rhetorician, b. c.378 B.C., author of the *Hellenica* and the *Philippica*). OC, 462n., 554

Teresa de Jesús, Santa (Spanish Carmelite nun, Doctor of the Church and leading mystic writer, born Teresa de Cepeda y Ahumada in Avila, 1519-1582). OC, 800. OCC, 68, 853, 948

Terranova, Padre (character in Bustos Domecq story). OCC, 449, 450

Tertuliano (Quintus Septimus Florens Tertullianus, Roman theologian and Christian apologist, c.160-c.230, author of *Apologeticus*). OC, 235. OCC, 588. ILN, 12. PB, 219

Teseo (Theseus, in Greek mythology, hero of Athens, son of Aegeus and killer of the Minotaur). OC, 362, 570, 699. OCC, 664. CONJ, 61

Teste, Edmond (character in Valéry). OC, 250, 289, 447, 686, 748

Tetrarca de Galilea (character in Borges story). OC, 499, 500, 506

Teufelsdrockh, Diogenes (character in Carlyle's *Sartor Resartus*). OCC, 834. OC, 668. P, 9, 32

Thackeray, William Makepeace (English novelist, 1811-1863, author of *Vanity Fair* and numerous other works). OC, 689, 752. OCC, 936. I, 46

Than-Qui or Tortuga-Genio (Chinese monster). OCC, 660

Thangbrand (character in the *Njals Saga*). OCC, 888

Theodoro (Theodorus of Cyrene, Greek atheist philosopher and mathematician). OC, 661. P, 120

Thetis (in Greek mythology, a Nereid, mother of Achilles). PB, 244

Thibaudet, Albert (French literary critic, 1874-1936, author of *Histoire de la littérature francaise de 1789 a nos jours* and numerous other works on modern French literature). PB, 165

Thierry, Augustin (French historian, 1795–1856, author of *L'Histoire de la conquete de l'Angleterre par les Normands*, *Récits des temps mérovingiens* and other works). OCC, 963

Thilo, Christfried Albert (German theologian, author of *Die theologisiriende rechts- und staatslehre*, 1861, and other works). OC, 576n.

Thomas, Edward J. (author of *The Life of Buddha as Legend and History*). OCC, 781

Thomas a Becket, Saint (English martyr, politician and archbishop of Canterbury, 1118–1170). OCC, 654

Thomas a Kempis (Thomas Hammerlein or Hammerken, German monk, c.1379–1471, traditional author of *De Imitatione Christi*). OC, 450. I, 9

Thor (Thunaer or Thunor or Donar, Norse god of thunder). OC, 369, 726, 858, 883, 1081. OCC, 702, 707, 900n., 927, 929–30, 943, 952. A, 17. CONJ, 44, 51. LA, 146. OP, 365, 424, 493. P, 36. PB, 198–202, 224

Thorbjorn (character in the *Grettirs Saga*). OCC, 934. PB, 191–92

Thoreau, Henry David (American essayist, naturalist and poet, 1817–1862, author of *Walden*, *Civil Disobedience* and other works). BO, 65. ILN, 21, 22–23, 27. P, 38

Thorfinn Karlsefni (Icelandic leader of an attempt to colonize America, fl. 1002–1015). OCC, 940

Thorgils (Turgesius, 9th century Viking conqueror of Ireland). PB, 190

Thorgilsson, Gunnar (Icelander, 1816–1879). OP, 531

Thorkel (one of Gudrun's husbands in the *Laxdoela Saga*). OCC, 949

Thorkelin (Danish scholar who copied the *Beowulf* manuscript

and published it in 1815). OCC, 871

Thormod or Thormoth (character in the *Fostbroethra Saga* who dies singing). OCC, 941, 948

Thorolf (character in the *Egils Saga*). OCC, 937

Thorolf Mostrarskegg. PB, 200

Thorstein el Rojo (ancestor of Ari Thorgilsson). OCC, 949

Thorsteinn Uxafotr (Thorstein Oxfoot, Icelander whose adventures are narrated in the *Heimskringla*). OCC, 931

Thorvald Snorrason (character in the *Sturlunga Saga*, enemy of Hrafn Sveinbjornsson). OCC, 964

Thoth (Egyptian god). OC, 805. See also Hermes Trismegisto

Thrale (general, character in Borges story). OC, 463

Thrale, Ulrica (character in Borges story). OC, 463–64

Thrym (giant in the *Elder Edda* who stole Thor's ax). OCC, 930

Thunaer or Thunor. See Thor

Ti-chiang (Chinese monster). OCC, 630

Tiberio Graco (Tiberius Simpronius Gracchus, Roman political leader, 2nd century B.C.). CONJ, 24

Tichborne, Lady (Roger Charles Tichborne's French mother, who recognized the Claimant). OC, 302–5

Tichborne, Roger Charles (heir to the Tichborne baronetcy, whose disappearance, and the subsequent reappearance of someone claiming to be him, led to the longest case in British legal history). OC, 302–5

Tierra (Greek earth god). OCC, 645

Tifón (Typhon, a dragon-like monster in Greek mythology). OCC, 645

Tigre. See Bengolea

Tigre Blanco (in the mythology of Assam and China, the

animal that presides over the west). OCC, 701

Tigre del Espejo (tiger that lives in mirrors, according to people in Yunnan). OCC, 580

Tigre del Quequén (nickname for the gaucho outlaw Felipe Pacheco). P, 64, 113

Tigres (mythical tigers of Annam, presiding over the four corners of the universe). OCC, 701

Tillyard, E. M. W. (British scholar, author of *The Elizabethan World Picture* and *The Miltonic Setting*). OC, 747n.

Timrod, Henry (American poet, 1828-1867). ILN, 23, 27, 36

Timur. See Tamerlán

Tink, Juan (knife-fighter in Buenos Aires). OC, 128n.

Tiresias (in Greek mythology and literature, blind soothsayer). OP, 455. P, 87. SN, 41

Tirso de Molina (pseud. of Gabriel Téllez, Spanish dramatist, 1584?-1648, author of *El burlador de Sevilla* and numerous other plays). OC, 228n. OCC, 157, 696

Tiscornia, Eleuterio (Argentine scholar, 1879-1945, editor of the *Martín Fierro*). OCC, 513

Titanes (Titans in Greek mythology, twelve primeval deities). OCC, 747

Títere, el (character in the sainete *La Paloma*). OC, 110

Ti-Yiang (Chinese monster). OC, 283

Tokman (character in Suárez Lynch novella). OCC, 160, 170-73

Tola (name on runic inscription). PB, 190

Toland, John (British deist philosopher, 1670-1722). OC, 766

Tolosa, Rufo (gaucho, character in Ascasubi's *Santos Vega*). I, 63

Tolstoi, Leo (Russian novelist and philosopher, 1828-1910,

author of *War and Peace, Anna Karenina* and many other works). OC, 681. PB, 146

Tomás de Aquino. See Aquino, Tomás de

Tommaseo, Niccolo (Italian poet and critic, 1802-1874, author of dictionaries, a novel and a commentary on Dante). NED, 114, 148

Tonelada, Nene (character in Bustos Domecq story). OCC, 400, 401

Tonnelat (French scholar, editor with Colleville of the *Nibelungenlied*). OCC, 915, 967n.

Torito (knife-fighter). P, 63

Tornillo Sin Fin. See Tabacman

Toro (knife-fighter). P, 63

Torquemada, Tomás de (Spanish Dominican priest and inquisitor, 1420-1498). TE, 96

Torraca, Francesco (Italian literary scholar, 1853-1938, author of *Dante e la cultura sveva, Le donne italiane nella poesia provenzale* and other works). NED, 99, 106, 150n., 156. PB, 183

Torre, Guillermo de (Spanish critic, poet and translator, 1900-1971, husband of Norah Borges, author of *Manifiesto vertical ultraísta, Hélices, Literaturas europeas de vanguardia* and other works). OC, 32. OCC, 503. I, 73, 98, 160. IA, 70

Torre Nilson, Leopoldo (Argentine film director, 1924-1978). HE, 66

Torres Amat, Félix (Spanish literary scholar). OC, 720

Torres Villaroel, Diego de (Spanish poet, 1693-1770, author of a famous auto-biography). OC, 235. I, 7-14, 48, 75, 88. P, 79. PB, 171

Tortuga (one of the four magical animals in China). OCC, 619, 632. CONJ, 23

Tortuga Negra (in Chinese
mythology, animal which
presides over the north).
OCC, 701

Tortugo.  See Zalduendo

Tortugo Viejo.  See Loiácomo

Toscanini, Arturo (Italian
conductor, 1867-1957).  OCC,
404

Tostado, Alonso (Spanish
theologian, bishop of Avila,
d. 1455, author of *Libro de
las quatro questiones, Opus
aureum* and other works).
OCC, 319

Tostig (earl of Northumbria,
d. 1066, mentioned in
*Heimskringla*).  OC, 755,
756.    OCC, 949, 961-62

Toulet, Paul-Jean (French poet,
journalist and novelist,
1867-1920, best known for
the polished verse of *Les
Contrerimes*).  OC, 404, 445.
OCC, 78

Tourneur, Cyril (English
dramatist and poet, 1575?-
1626, author of *The
Revenger's Tragedy, The
Atheist's Tragedy* and other
works).   OC, 412, 638

Tourneur, Zacharie (critic and
editor of Pascal, author of
*Une Vie avec Pascal*, 1943).
OC, 704n.

Toussaint L'Ouverture, Francois
Dominique.   See Louverture,
Toussaint

Toynbee, Arnold Joseph
(English historian, 1889-
1975, author of *A Study of
History*).    P, 134

Toyo (character in Zen
Buddhist fable).  OCC, 773

Trachtenberg, Joshua (author
of *Jewish Magic and
Superstition*, 1939).   OCC,
613

Tracy, Spencer (American film
actor, 1900-1967).   OC, 285,
286.     BC, 48, 68

Traill, Henry Duff (English
journalist and biographer,
1842-1900, author of works on
Salisbury, Sterne, Coleridge
and others).   OC, 644n.

Trajano (Marcus Ulpius
Trajanus, Roman emperor,
c.53-117).  OCC, 827.
NED, 141, 143.  P, 72.  PB,
178, 179

Trapani, Emilio (character in
Borges story).  OC, 1044-47

Traversi, Clementina
(character in Borges-Levinson
story).  HE, 62

Trebio Negro (Trebius Niger,
quoted on several points in
natural history by Pliny).
OCC, 686

Trejo, Nemesio (Argentine
playwright, writer
particularly of *sainetes*,
1867-1916).   OC, 157

Trelles, José.   See Alonso y
Trelles, José

Treviranus, Franz (character
in Borges story).   OC, 499-
504, 507

Trigg, Montague (character in
Dickens' *Martin Chuzzlewit*).
OCC, 835

Trinidad (the Trinity of
Christian doctrine).   OC,
281, 283, 1065.  OCC, 956.
BC, 72.  C, 39.  CONJ, 15,
83.  ILN, 20.  LA, 104, 105.
OP, 384.  PB, 168, 191.
SN, 26

Tristán (Tristram, prince of
Lyonesse and lover of Iseult,
of legend and literature).
OCC, 138

Trismegisto.   See Hermes
Trismegisto

Tritones (sea creatures
in Greek myth).  OCC, 696

Troan (Priam's daughter,
according to the Snorri
Sturluson).   OCC, 952

Troilo (Troilus, Trojan prince
in poems by Homer, Chaucer
and Shakespeare).   OCC, 815

Trollope, Anthony (English
novelist, 1815-1882, author
of *The Warden, Barchester
Towers* and other works).
OCC, 319

Trolls (in Scandinavian
folklore, dwarfish or
gigantic creature of caves
and hills).   OCC, 702, 926

Trompa or Trompifay (character in Suárez Lynch novella). OCC, 174, 176, 177

Tror (Priam's son according to Snorri Sturluson). OCC, 952

Tse Yang (painter of tigers in poem by David Jerusalem). OC, 579

Tsepha (Hebrew name for a poisonous reptile, rendered by the Vulgate as basilisk). OCC, 594

Ts'ui Pen (great-grandfather of Yu Tsun, character in Borges story). OC, 475–79

Tucídides (Thucydides, Greek historian, c.460–400, author of important history of the Peloponnesian war). OCC, 357, 963

Tuiston (Tyr, Germanic god). OCC, 899, 900n.

Tula (mentioned in runic inscription). OCC, 924

Tule (son of Genghis Khan). OC, 418n. NED, 142. PB, 179

Tundal (Tundalus, legendary Irish knight and visionary, d. 1149, subject of *Visio Tundali*). OCC, 669, 670, 907

Tunk-poj (divine hunter of Siberian myth). OCC, 583

Tupac Amaru (José Gabriel Condorcanqui, Peruvian Indian leader, 1742?–1781). OCC, 175

Turco, el (knife-fighter). IA, 119

Turgenev, Ivan Sergeyevich (Russian novelist, 1818–1883, author of *Fathers and Sons* and other works). OCC, 850. ILN, 38. P, 100

Turgot, Anne Robert Jacques (French economist, comptroller general of finances, 1727–1781). ILN, 14

Turner, Joseph Mallard Wilson (English painter, 1775–1851). OC, 1054, 1105. OCC, 836–37. A, 80. CONJ, 80. OP, 383, 472. PB, 146. VA, 49

Turner, Lana (American film actress, b. 1920). OC, 285. BC, 67

Twain, Mark (pseud. of Samuel Langhorne Clemens, American writer, 1835–1910, author of *The Adventures of Huckleberry Finn, Roughing It, Life on the Mississippi, The Innocents Abroad* and many other works). OC, 197, 271, 345, 724, 734, 736. BC, 41. ILN, 14, 26, 27–28, 29. P, 50, 53, 81, 143. PB, 121–24, 188, 226

Twirl (character in Borges story). LA, 40, 41, 47, 52, 53, 55, 57–63

Twist, Oliver (main character in Dickens novel). P, 76

Tyr (Tuiston, Germanic god). OCC, 900n.

Tzetzes, Juan or Johannes (Byzantine grammarian and polymath, 12th century A.D., author of *Chiliades*, letters, commentaries on Homer and numerous other works). OCC, 650

Tzinacán (Maya priest, character in Borges story). OC, 596–99

Ubalde (owner of piston factory in Bustos Domecq story). OCC, 364

Ubalde, Félix (character in Bustos Domecq story, nicknamed El Indio). OCC, 381–91

Ugolino della Gherardesca (character in Dante's *Inferno*). OC, 610, 921. NED, 105–11

Ulf Sigurdarson (character in Borges story). LA, 112–13

Ulfilas (Gothic bishop, translator of the Bible into Gothic, c.311–383, also known as Vulfilas, Wufila and Lobezno). OC, 931. OCC, 861, 863–65

Ulises or Odiseo (Ulysses or Odysseus, king of Ithaca, husband of Penelope and father of Telemachus, main character in the *Odyssey*, also in poems by Dante, Tennyson, etc.). OC, 168, 228n., 241, 250, 263, 539, 540, 543, 544, 829, 843, 869, 897, 906, 931, 936, 1108, 1113, 1118, 1128. OCC, 15, 50, 501, 696, 741. BO, 37. CONJ, 25, 35, 45, 47. ILN, 25. NED, 113-18. OP, 387, 395, 423, 443, 455, 516, 519, 526. P, 82, 87, 171. PB, 168, 225, 242. SN, 26-31, 70, 88

Ulrica or Ulrikke (character in Borges story). LA, 25-31, 180

Ulupi (son of king Naga in the *Mahabharata*). OCC, 671

Umar Khayyam. See Omar Khayyam

Unamuno, Miguel de (Spanish novelist, poet, philosopher and critic, 1864-1936, author of *Niebla, Vida de don Quijote y Sancho, El sentimiento trágico de la vida* and numerous other works). OC, 13, 202, 353, 389, 667. OCC, 500. BC, 59, 60. BO, 27, 38. C, 9. I, 100-108. IA, 57, 102, 130, 174, 180. P, 55, 166. PB, 147-51, 169, 175, 203, 245. TE, 78, 114

Unicornio (fabulous animal). OCC, 619, 703-4, 705-6. OP, 384. P, 109. VA, 37

Unicornio Chino. See K'i'lin

Unwin (mathematician, character in Borges story). OC, 600-6

Upland Trouts (fabulous creatures of North America). OCC, 631

Urbach, Matilde (mentioned in poem by Gaspar Camerarius). OC, 852

Urbas (character in Bustos Domecq story). OCC, 315, 317, 318

Urbina. OC, 878

Urbistondo (character in Bustos Domecq story). OCC, 413, 414, 418

Urganda (the Lady of the Lake in *Amadís de Gaula*). OP, 527

Urgoiti (of Merlo, character in Borges story). LA, 72

Uriarte, Maneco (character in Borges story). OC, 1039-43

Uriburu, José Félix (Argentine general, polician and president, 1868-1933). OCC, 493. P, 55

Urien, Carlos M. (Argentine critic and historian). P, 138

Urizen (character in Blake's *Prophetic Books*). OC, 694. OCC, 840

Urmann (character in Borges story). OC, 522

Urnos (tribe in Borges story). LA, 111-119

Uroboros (monster that devours its own tail). OCC, 707, 712n.

Urquhart, Thomas (Scottish writer, 1611-1660, author of *Trissotetras, Logopandecteision* and *Ekskubalauron*, and translator of Rabelais). OC, 411

Urquiza, Justo José de (Argentine general, politician and president, 1801-1870). OC, 106, 114, 162, 573, 1001, 1049, 1111. OCC, 430, 521, 526. OP, 385, 554. P, 18, 64, 97, 138. TE, 6, 34

Urstein, Elsa (friend of Emma Zunz in Borges story). OC, 564, 565

Uspak (character in the *Bandamanna Saga*). OCC, 939

Uspenski, Petr Deianovich (Russian mystic, 1878-1947, author of *Tertium Organum*). OC, 278, 279, 394, 647

Ustáriz (character in Bustos Domecq story). OCC, 403, 404, 406, 407, 409, 421

Utgarda-Loki. See Loki

Uther (character in Layomon's *Brut*). OCC, 897-98

Vacarezza, Alberto (Argentine playwright, author of numerous *sainetes*, 1886-1959). OC, 653, 655

Vagts, Alfred (German poet and writer, b. 1892, author of

*Ritt in die Not: Gedichte*, a
*History of Militarism* and
other works).    I, 150–51
Vaihinger, Hans    (German
philosopher, 1852–1933).
OCC, 582
Valdemar I    (Waldemar I, the
Great, Danish king, 1131–
1182).    OCC, 972
Valdemar II    (Waldemar II,
Danish king, 1170–1241).
OCC, 970
Valentino    (Valentinus, founder
of the Valentinians, a
Gnostic sect, fl. c.135–
c.160).    OC, 213, 215
Valera, Cipriano de    (Spanish
humanist, priest and
translator of the Bible,
1532?–1602).    OC, 720.
OCC, 596, 753.    LA, 170.
P, 15
Valera, Juan    (Spanish diplomat
and novelist, 1824–1905,
author of *Pepita Jiménez*).
OCC, 78
Valerio Máximo    (Valerius
Maximus, Roman author, c.49
B.C.–c.30 A.D., author of
*Factorum ac dictorum
memorabilium libri*).    OCC,
972
Valerio Sorano, Quinto
(Quintus Valerius Soranus,
a Latin linguistic and
antiquarian scholar often
quoted by Varro, fl. 82
B.C.).    OC, 517, 750
Valeroso–Veloz–Impetuoso–Macho
(Japanese god).    OCC, 675
Valéry, Paul    (French poet and
critic, 1871–1945, author of
*La Jeune Parque*, the
*Cimetiere marin*, *La Soirée
avec Monsieur Teste* and
other works).    OC, 204, 211,
229, 289, 360, 445, 447, 449,
639, 686–87, 703.    OCC, 56,
58, 59, 468, 855.    C, 9.
ILN, 9.    P, 8, 53, 152, 163–
66.    PB, 144, 165, 247
Vali    (character in the
*Bandamanna saga*).    OCC, 939
Valjean, Jean    (character in
Victor Hugo's *Les
Misérables*).    OC, 921

Valle, Adriano de    (Argentine
writer, an editor of the
journal *Prisma*).    PJ, 57
Valle, Enrique del    (Argentine
writer, co-author with
Villamayor of *El lenguaje
del bajo fondo*, 1915).    OC,
654n.    OCC, 156
Valle-Inclán, Ramon del
(Spanish poet, playwright
and novelist, 1866–1936, author
of the *Sonatas* tetralogy,
*Guerra carlista* trilogy,
*Tirano Banderas*, *La pipa
de kif*, *Luces de Bohemia*
and other works).    OCC, 461, 501.
IA, 125
Vallejo, Antonio    (Argentine
poet associated with the
magazine *Martín Fierro*).
OCC, 497
Valmiki    (author of the
*Ramayana*).    OC, 668
Valquirias    (Valkyries, in
Germanic mythology, warrior
maidens of Odin).    OCC, 702,
708, 810, 878
Van Dine, S. S.    (pseud. of the
critic Willard Huntington
Wright, used to sign his
stories about the detective
Philo Vance).    OCC, 513.
ILN, 57
Van Doren, Mark    (American
critic and writer, 1894–
1972).    OC, 250n.
Van Schof    (17th century
translator of Camoes).    PB,
241
Van Vogt, Alfred Elton
(Canadian science fiction
writer, b. 1912, author of
*The Book of Ptah*, *Slan* and
other works).    ILN, 59–60
Van Winkle, Rip    (character in
Washington Irving story "The
Legend of  Sleepy Hollow").
ILN, 16
Vanasco, Alberto    (Argentine
poet, novelist and short-
story writer, b. 1925).
OCC, 371
Vance, Philo    (detective in S.
S. Van Dine's crime fiction).
ILN, 57

Vandier, Jacques (French
Egyptologist, author of *La
Réligion egyptienne*, 1949).
OC, 750

Vanini, Lucilio (Italian
philosopher and freethinker,
c.1585-1619, author of *De
admirandis naturae*). OC,
278n., 393. OCC, 579

Vantini (an obvious
misprint). See Vanini

Varela, Florencio (Argentine
poet and political figure,
1807-1848). OC, 183, 1048.
OCC, 520. P, 135

Varela, Juan Cruz (Argentine
poet and journalist, 1794-
1839, author of numerous
romantic and patriotic
compositions). OC, 179

Varo (Publius Quinctilius Varus,
Roman military leader in the
Rhine valley whose army was
destroyed by Arminius). OC,
580

Varsovia, don (nickname).
OCC, 182. See Fingermann

Vasco, Juan Antonio
(Argentine poet and
journalist, b. 1924). OCC,
371

Vasco da Gama. See Gama,
Vasco da

Vasseur, Alvaro Armando
(Uruguayan writer, b. 1878,
author of *Cantos augurales,
Cantos del Nuevo Mundo,
Cantos del Otro Yo* and other
works). TE, 61

Vathek (character in Beckford's
novel *Vathek*, based on Harun
Benalmotasim Vatiq Bila, the
ninth Abbasid caliph). OC,
250, 729-32

Vavassour, Dolores or Dollie
(character in Bustos Domecq
story). OCC, 75, 80, 82

Vaz Ferreira, Maria Eugenia
(Uruguayan poet, 1875-1924,
author of *La isla de los
cánticos*). TE, 62

Vázquez, María Esther
(Argentine writer and
journalist, author of *Los
nombres de la muerte* and
countless interviews, and

co-author with Borges of
*Literaturas germánicas
medievales*). OC, 351, 809.
OCC, 807, 862. P, 167-69

Vázquez Siruela, Martín
(Spanish writer, contemporary
and follower of Gongora).
IA, 68

Veblen, Thorstein (American
economist and social critic,
1857-1929, author of *The
Theory of the Leisure Class,
The Instinct of Workmanship,
The Theory of Business
Enterprise* and other works).
OC, 272

Vedia, Agustín de (Uruguayan
journalist, writer and
politician, 1843-1910). OC,
489

Vedia, Joaquín de (Argentine
theater critic, 1877-1936).
IA, 170

Vedia y Mitre, Mariano
(Argentine writer, historian
and politician, mayor of
Buenos Aires, 1881-1958).
PB, 137

Vega, Angel C. (Spanish priest,
translator of the *Confessions
of St. Augustine*). OC, 367

Vega, Carlos (Argentine
musicologist and folklorist,
1898-1966). OC, 159

Vega, Santos. See Santos Vega

Vega Carpio, Félix Lope de
(Spanish playwright, poet and
novelist, 1562-1635, author
of *La Dorotea, Fuenteovejuna*
and thousands of other
works). OC, 448, 688.
BO, 20. I, 25, 36. IA, 68,
96, 131. P, 46, 78, 112.
PB, 232. SN, 60. TE, 68,
103

Velázquez, Diego Rodríguez de
Silva y (Spanish painter,
1599-1660). OC, 145. IA, 29

Venturi, Pompeo (Italian
scholar, author of *La comedia
di Dante Alighieri*, 1751, and
editor of Dante's works,
1757). NED, 141n. PB,
178n.

Venus (Roman goddess of love,
identified with the Greek

goddess Aphrodite). OC, 364. OCC, 110, 191, 688. PB, 243. TE, 127

Verdussen (Dutch architect, character in Bustos Domecq story, author of *Organum Architecturae Recentis*, 1949). OCC, 334-35

Verdussen (editor of 1699 edition of Quevedo). TE, 39

Vereker, Hugh (character in James's *The Figure in the Carpet*). OC, 691

Verlaine, Paul (French poet, 1844-1896, author of *Poemes saturniens*, *Sagesse*, *Les Poetes maudits*, *Art poétique* and other works). OC, 9, 79, 116, 211, 841, 849. OCC, 304, 464, 484, 856. A, 46. C, 77, 101. ILN, 30. LA, 16, 53. OP, 546. P, 7, 85. PB, 226, 232, 233. SN, 153

Verloc, Adolf (character in Conrad's *The Secret Agent*). BC, 51, 52

Verne, Jules (French novelist, 1828-1905, author of *Vingt mille lieues sous les mers*, *Le Tour du monde en quatre-vingts jours* and other works). OC, 697. OCC, 130, 435. A, 34. IA, 101. ILN, 58. PB, 214

Vernher (Priester Wernher, author of a *Marienleben* or life of the Virgin Mary, 1172, entitled *Drei Lieder von der Jungfrau*). OCC, 907

Verónica (woman who allegedly used her veil to wipe the face of Jesus as he was on the way to Calvary). OC, 800

Viborita (character in Borges-Bioy filmscript). OCC, 199, 201-11. BC, 78

Vicente (character in Borges-Bioy filmscript). OCC, 204, 205

Vico, Giambattista (Italian philosopher and historian, 1668-1744, author of *Principii d' una scienza nuova* and numerous other

works). OC, 395, 497, 542, 543. P, 134

Victoria (queen of Great Britain and Ireland, 1819-1901). OCC, 394, 405

Vicuña de De Kruif, Loló (character in Bustos Domecq and Suárez Lynch stories). OCC, 80, 81, 149, 162-64, 166, 168, 169, 175, 176, 394, 405

Vidal (old Buenos Aires family). P, 78

Vidor, King (American film director, 1894-1982, director of *The Crowd*, *Hallelujah*, *Street Scene*, *Billy the Kid* and many other works). OC, 224. A, 67. BC, 33, 46

Viejo del Mar (character in the *Arabian Nights*). OCC, 267

Vielé-Griffin, Francis (French symbolist poet, 1863-1937). OCC, 323

Viertel, Berthold (Austrian film director, 1885-1953, director of *The Passing of the Third Floor Back*). BC, 42

Vigfus (grandfather of protagonist in *Viga-Glums Saga*). OCC, 939

Vigfússon, Gúdbrandr (Icelandic scholar, outstanding expert on old Norse history and literature, 1828-1889, author of *Túnatál* and an *Icelandic-English Dictionary*, editor of numerous sagas and co-editor of the *Corpus Poeticum Boreale*). OCC, 926

Vighi Fernández, Francisco (character in Bustos Domecq story). OCC, 185, 187

Vigilantes (characters in Borges-Bioy filmscript). OCC, 204, 205, 208, 212

Vigny, Alfred Victor, comte de (French poet, novelist and dramatist, 1797-1863, author of *Poemes antiques et modernes* and other works). OC, 383

author of a miscellany,
1791). OCC, 600, 668

Warburton, William (English
bishop and author, 1698–1779,
editor and collaborator of
Pope). P, 70–72

Ward, Artemus (pseud. of
Charles Farrar Browne,
American humorist, 1834–
1867). ILN, 27

Ward, John (young Englishman,
character in Borges poem on
the Malvinas war). CONJ, 95

Warren, Robert Penn (American
novelist, poet and critic, b.
1905, author of *All the
King's Men, Night Rider,
World Enough and Time* and
other works). ILN, 50

Washington, George (U. S.
president, 1732–1799). OC,
412. ILN, 12, 15, 63

Wate (hero in the *Gudrun*).
OCC, 917

Waterhouse, Gilbert (author of
a *Short History of German
Literature*). OC, 279–80

Watson, Doctor (character in
Doyle's stories about
Sherlock Holmes). OC, 414.
BO, 73. CONJ, 49–50.
ILN, 56

Watts, Alan Wilson (writer on
Zen Buddhism, author of *The
Way of Zen*). OCC, 781

Watts, George Frederic
(English painter and
sculptor, 1817–1904, subject
of a book by Chesterton).
OC, 629, 662, 672

Weatherhead, Leslie (author
of *After Death*, 1942). OC,
280–82

Weaver, Raymond (author of
*Herman Melville, Mariner
and Mystic*, 1921). P, 117

Weber, Albrecht (German
Orientalist, 1825–1901,
author of *Indische Streifen*,
1850, and *Indische Skizzen*,
1857). PB, 196

Weber, Carl Maria Friedrich
Ernst von (German composer
and pianist, 1786–1826).
OC, 747

Webster, John (English
dramatist, 1580?–1634, author
of *The Duchess of Malfi* and
other works). ILN, 43

Webster de Tejedor, señora
(character in Bustos Domecq
story). OCC, 438, 444

Weekley, Frieda. See
Lawrence, Frieda

Weidemann (character in Borges
story). OC, 1032

Weidenau, Julia de (character
in Hladík's verse drama *Los
enemigos*). OC, 510, 512

Weil, Gustav (German
Orientalist, 1808–1889, author
of *Biblische Legenden
der Musulmänner* and
translator of the *Arabian
Nights* and the *Koran*). OC,
398, 408, 410, 411, 525.
ILN, 16. SN, 73

Weimar, duke of. See Karl
Augustus, grand-duke of Saxe-
Weimar

Weird Sisters (characters in
Shakespeare's *Macbeth*).
OCC, 674. P, 142, 144–45.
PB, 226

Weiss, Otto (editor of
Schopenhauer's *Welt als Wille
und Vorstellung*). OC, 648n.

Weland (legendary maker of
swords, subject of the
*Volundarkvitha* and other
Germanic poems, also known as
Welund, Volundr and Volund).
OCC, 794, 846, 889, 930

Welles, Orson (American actor
and film director, 1915–1985,
director of *Citizen Kane* and
many other works). BC, 64–
65

Wellington, Arthur Wellesley,
duke of (British soldier and
statesman, 1769–1852). A,
15

Wells, Herbert George (English
author and social thinker,
1866–1946, author of *The
Invisible Man, The First Men
in the Moon, The Time
Machine, The Island of Dr.
Moreau, The Country of the
Blind, The Shape of Things to
Come, The World of William*

*Clissold, Outline of History*
and numerous other works).
OC, 55, 101, 220, 275-76,
280, 629, 639-41, 697-99,
723-24, 1104.   OCC, 65, 625,
847, 850.   A, 34.   BC, 43-
45, 58.   CONJ, 44.   ILN,
33, 38, 58.   LA, 68, back
cover.   OP, 382.   P, 24,
27, 100, 152.   PB, 172, 196n.,
224.   SN, 137
Welund.   See Weland
Wentling, John Philip
(American forester, author of
*The Farm Woodlot: a handbook
of forestry for the farmer
and the student in agri-
culture*, 1914, here cited
as an expert on the Squonk
resident in St. Anthony Park,
Minnesota).   OCC, 698
Wentscher, Max (German
philosopher, b. 1862, author
of *Fechner und Lotze*, 1924,
and other works).   OC, 257n.
Werfel, Franz (Austrian writer,
born in Prague, 1890-1945,
author of *Der Weltfreund,
Juarez und Maximilian, Das
Lied von Bernadotte* and
numerous other works).   OCC,
311
West, Rebecca (English novelist
and critic, b. 1892, author
of *The Return of the
Stranger, The Strange
Necessity* and other works).
OC, 691.   P, 102
Whately, Richard (English
prelate and writer, 1787-
1863, author of *Historic
Doubts Relative to Napoleon
Bonaparte*).   OC, 236
Wheeler, Post (British
folklorist and writer, 1849-
1956, author of *The Sacred
Scriptures of Japan* and
collections of folk tales of
Hawaii, Albania, Ethiopia and
other places).   OCC, 675
Whistler, James McNeill
(American painter, etcher,
wit and eccentric, 1834-
1903).   OC, 179.   OCC, 837.
P, 142, 173

White, William (American
bishop and theologian, 1748-
1836).   P, 156
White Goddess (mythical
figure, subject of book by
Robert Graves).   OCC, 855
White Knight (character in
Carroll's *Through the Looking
Glass*).   P, 109, 111
White Queen (character in
Carroll's *Through the Looking
Glass*).   P, 109
White Rabbit (character in
Carroll's *Alice's Adventures
in Wonderland*).   P, 109
White Whale.   See Moby Dick
Whitehead, Alfred North
(English mathematician and
philosopher, 1861-1947,
author of *Science and the
Modern World, Religion in
the Making, Symbolism* and
other works).   OC, 645.   CONJ,
79.   OP, 557
Whitman, Walt (American poet,
1819-1892, author of *Leaves
of Grass*).   OC, 13, 51, 157,
177, 206-8, 224, 249-53, 389,
578, 641, 660, 686, 694, 727,
736, 756, 858, 874, 913, 937,
975, 976, 1010, 1081, 1086,
1099, 1104, 1131.   OCC,
466, 467, 471, 474, 498, 796,
831, 840, 851, 852, 877, 880.
BC, 32.   BO, 68, 77.   C,
42, 105.   CONJ, 13, 44.
I, 91, 125.   IA, 109.
ILN, 9, 16, 21, 24-25, 26,
27, 31, 38, 42, 43, 45, 46,
48.   LA, 18-19.   OP, 365,
371, 376, 382, 408, 420, 469.
P, 8, 38, 39, 63, 82, 87,
112, 120, 128, 129, 133, 166,
170-74.   PB, 160, 166, 167,
171, 236
Whittier, John Greenleaf
(American poet and reformer,
1807-1892, author of *Snow-
Bound* and other works).
ILN, 31
Wiclif, John.   See Wyclif, John
Wieger, Léon W. (Orientalist,
1856-1933, author of *Vies
chinoises du Bouddha*).   OC,
742

Wieland, Christopher Martin
(German poet and novelist,
1733-1813, author of
*Geschichte des Agathon,
Oberon* and other works).
OCC, 794.    BO, 34

Wilcken, Ulrich (German scholar
of Saxo Grammaticus, 1862-
1944).    OCC, 972

Wilckinson    (character in
Bustos Domecq story).    OCC,
427

Wilde, Eduardo (Argentine
writer and politician, 1844-
1913, author of *Aguas abajo,
Prometeo y Cía., Tiempo
perdido* and other works).
OCC, 463.    IA, 155-62, 177.
PB, 123, 167.    TE, 6, 95

Wilde, José Antonio (Argentine
memorialist, 1813-1885,
author of *Buenos Aires
desde setenta años atrás,*
1881).    IA, 120

Wilde, Oscar (Irish poet, playwright, essayist and wit,
1854-1900, author of *The
Importance of Being Earnest,
The Picture of Dorian Gray,
Salomé, The Ballad of Reading
Gaol, De Profundis* and
numerous other works).    OC,
157, 162, 407, 464, 641, 691-
93, 697, 743.    OCC, 78, 149,
496, 836, 845-46, 849, 977.
A, 15, 68-69.    ILN, 52.
P, 29, 64.    PB, 157, 213,
224.    SN, 152, 153.    TE,
132-35

Wilder, Thornton (American
novelist and playwright, b.
1897, author of *The Bridge
of San Luis Rey, The Skin
of Our Teeth* and other works).
ILN, 53-54

Wilhelm, Eugen (German
Orientalist, 1842-1923,
author of works on ancient
Assyria).    OC, 772.    OCC,
705

Wilhelm II, Kaiser (king of
Prussia and emperor of
Germany, 1859-1941).    OC,
302

Wilkins, John (English
mathematician, scientist

and bishop, 1614-1672, author
of *Essay towards a Real
Character and a Philosophical
Language, The Discovery of a
World in the Moon* and other
works).    OC, 444, 706-9.
IA, 171.    LA, 36, 54.    P,
25, 26

Wilkins, Peter (character in
Paltock's *Peter Wilkins*).
OCC, 710

William of Occam.    See Occam,
Guillermo de

William the Conqueror.    See
Guillermo I de Inglaterra

Williams, Tennessee (American
playwright, 1914-198?, author
of *Streetcar Named Desire* and
numerous other works).
ILN, 54-55

Willoughby-Meade, Gerald
(British writer, author of
*Chinese Ghouls and Goblins,*
1928, and other works).
OCC, 607

Wilson, Woodrow (U. S.
president, 1856-1924).    ILN,
64

Winkelried, Arnold (Swiss hero,
d. 1386).    CONJ, 97

Winternitz, Moriz (German
religious scholar, 1863-1937,
author of *Der Mahayana-
Buddhismus, Religion und
Moral* and other works).    OC,
742.    OCC, 727, 736.    PB,
196

Winthrop, Ezra (character in
Borges story).    LA, 137-47

Winthrop, John (governor of
the Massachusetts Bay Colony,
1588-1649).    ILN, 10

Witcomb (founder of a photo
studio of the same name in
Buenos Aires).    OCC, 159

Wodan or Woden.    See Odin

Wolf, Friedrich August (German
philologist and critic, 1759-
1824, author of *Prolegomena
ad Homerum* and *Darstellung
der Altertumswissenschaft*).
OC, 164

Wolfe, Humbert (British writer,
1885-1940, author of *Shylock
Reasons with Mr. Chesterton,*
1920).    OCC, 311

Yama (Brahman god of death).
OC, 740.   OCC, 602

Yámila (character in the
*Arabian Nights*).   OC, 358n.

Yao (mythical first Chinese
emperor, reigned 2357-2255).
OCC, 632

Yaqub Almansur.   See Yacub
Almansur

Yarmolinsky, Marcelo (character
in Borges story).   OC, 499,
500, 506

Yasodhara (Gautama Buddha's
wife, sometimes Jasodhara).
OCC, 721, 723.   SN, 83

Yeats, William Butler (Irish
poet, playwright and
essayist, 1865-1939, author
of *The Celtic Twilight, In
the Seven Woods, The Wild
Swans at Coole, The Winding
Stair, The King of the Great
Clock Tower, Per Amica
Silentia Lunae, Mythologies,
A Vision, Autobiographies* and
other works).   OC, 249, 378,
496, 496, 561, 666, 686,
718n., 820, 1128.   OCC,
468, 475, 616, 814, 832, 854-
55.   A, 15.   ILN, 60.
P, 45, 62, 125, 148.   PB,
224.   SN, 30

Yehudá Haleví.   See Haleví,
Jehudá

Ygg (Scandinavian god of
death).   OCC, 929

Yocasta (mythical Greek queen,
wife and mother of Oedipus).
OCC, 627

Yolao (Iolaus, Greek
mythological hero, companion
of Herakles).   OCC, 645

Yorick (a skull in
Shakespeare's *Hamlet* once
belonged to this court
jester).   OCC, 820.   CONJ,
35, 44.   PB, 226

Yoske Nigger (New York
gangster mentioned in Borges
story).   OC, 312

Young, Edward (English poet,
1683-1765, author of *The
Complaint, or Night Thoughts
on Life, Death and
Immortality*).   OC, 752

Young, Brigham (American
Mormon leader, 1801-1877).
OC, 317.   P, 82

Young (owner of a meat-
salting plant).   OCC, 311

Youwarkee (mythical creature,
half-woman, half-bird,
character in Paltock's *Peter
Wilkins* also mentioned by
Browning).   OCC, 710

Yrigoyen, Hipólito (Argentine
politician, populist leader
and president, 1852-1933,
sometimes misspelled
Irigoyen).   OC, 81, 187,
526.   OCC, 427.   I, 132.
P, 55.   TE, 8

Yu Tsun (character in Borges
story, also the name of a
character in the *Hung Lu
Meng* or *Dream of the Red
Chamber*).   OC, 472-80

Yu el Grande (Chinese emperor,
ruled 2205-2198, founder of
the Hsia or Hia dynasty).
OCC, 660

Yusuf (Druse character in
Bustos Domecq story).   OCC,
26, 27, 30

Zacconne, Ernesto (Italian
comic actor).   OCC, 330

Zaid (character in Borges
story).   OC, 602-5

Zal (character in Firdusi's
*Shah-nama*).   OCC, 695

Zalduendo (character in
Borges-Bioy filmscript).
OCC, 225, 226

Zalduendo, Wenceslao
(character in Bustos Domecq
story, also known as Don
Tortugo Viejo).   OCC, 135-42

Zaleski (character in mystery
story).   OCC, 18

Zallinger, P. (Jesuit, d. 1736,
author of *Cartas
edificantes*).   OCC, 580

Zamora (character in Bustos
Domecq story).   OCC, 439

Zangwill, Israel (English
author, 1864-1926, author of
*The Big Bow Mystery,
Children of the Ghetto* and
other works).   OC, 600.   BO,
75.   ILN, 56

# Index of Titles

Acopio de pullas y de gracejos
(Mir y Baralt, 1934). OCC,
450

Acorazado Potemkin, El
(Eisenstein film about the
revolt on the battleship
Potemkin, 1925). OC, 224.
BC, 32, 33

Acquainted with the Night
(Frost). ILN, 47

Across the River and Into the
Trees (Hemingway, 1950).
ILN, 38

Acuario (Bonavena). OCC, 309

Acusador de si mismo. See
For the Defense

Adam's Curse (Yeats poem in
*In the Seven Woods*, 1904).
P, 45

Adelantos del progreso, Los
(Bustos Domecq). OCC, 13

Adiós pampa mía (tango by
Pelay, Canaro and Mores,
1945). OCC, 400

Adiós, que me voy llorando
(tango). OCC, 399

Adonais (Shelley elegy for
Keats, 1821). OCC, 833

Adone (Marino poem on Venus
and Adonis, 1623). OC, 731,
744

Advancement of Learning, The
(Bacon philosophical
treatise, 1605). OC, 715

Adventures among Books (Lang
essays, 1905). OC, 215n.

Adversus annulares (Juan de
Panonia work refuting the
idea of circular time). OC,
554, 555

Adversus mathematicos (Sextus
Empiricus philosophical work,
a critique of various
philosophical systems). OC,
770

Aelteste Deutsche Dichtung.
See Alteste deutsche Dichtung

Aeneid. See Eneida

Affaire Lerouge, L' (Gaboriau
detective novel, 1868). P,
47

Affentheuerliche
Geschichtschrift (Fischart
translation of Rabelais,
1575). PB, 160

After Death (Weatherhead,
1942). OC, 280–82

After the Fall (Arthur Miller
play, 1964). ILN, 56

Agente secreto. See The Secret
Agent

Agua del tiempo (Silva Valdés
book of poems, 1921). I,
61, 99. TE, 89

Agua secreta (Runeberg poem).
OC, 516n.

Agudeza y arte de ingenio
(Gracián, 1648). OC, 203.
OCC, 956

Aguila Diaria. See Brooklyn
Daily Eagle

Aguja de navegar cultos. Con
la receta para hacer
'Soledades' en un día
(Quevedo polemical work
against Góngora, 1613). OC,
445

Aholibah (Swinburne poem in
*Poems and Ballads*, here
misspelled "Awolibah"). PB,
157

Air-Conditioned Nightmare, The
(Henry Miller travel book
about the United States,
1945). ILN, 45

Al Kitab. See Alcorán

Al faro. See To the Lighthouse

Aladino y la lámpara (story in
the *Arabian Nights*). SN,
72, 73

Alas (Lugones, section of *El
libro de los paisajes*).
OCC, 479

Albergo Empedocle (Forster
story in *The Life to Come*,
1972). OCC, 856

Alcándara (Argentine avant
garde work). OCC, 499

Alcorán (the sacred book of
Islam, revealed by God to the
Prophet Muhammad, also called
Corán, Quran, Al Kitab,
Koran). OC, 209, 270, 341,
343, 380, 508, 582, 584, 587,
594, 600, 614, 688, 715,
1083. OCC, 349, 559, 599,
733, 818. BO, 17, 23.
NED, 123. OP, 368. SN,
128

Aleluya. See Hallelujah

Black Boy (Wright autobio-
graphy, 1945). ILN, 51
Black Christ, The (Cullen book
of poems, 1929). ILN, 49
Black Riders, The (Crane book
of poems, 1895). ILN, 34
Black Spring (Henry Miller
novel, 1936). ILN, 44, 45
Blanca soledad, La (Lugones
poem in *El libro fiel*).
OCC, 477-78
Blasón (Darío poem in *Prosas
profanas*, 1896). OCC, 466
Blast of the Book, The
(Chesterton story in *The
Scandal of Father Brown*).
PB, 141
Blessed Damozel, The (Rossetti
poem, 1850). OCC, 843.
NED, 161n.
Blicamcepero. OCC, 338
Blind Lover (Shand poem in
*Ferment*). P, 149
Blue Angel, The (Sternberg
film with Marlene Dietrich
and Emil Jannings, 1930).
OCC, 66
Bobalicón de las islas
inesperadas. See John
Bull's Other Island
Bocetos biográficos del doctor
Ramón S. Castillo (official
biography of Argentine presi-
dent, 1942-43). OCC, 145
Bocetos californianos. See The
Luck of Roaring Camp
Bodas del cielo y del infierno.
See The Marriage of Heaven
and Hell
Boina (Loomis book, 1916).
OCC, 321, 322
Bombay Gazette, The
(newspaper). OC, 414
Bombay Quarterly Review, The
(magazine). OC, 414
Bompiani encyclopedia. See
Diccionaire biographique des
auteurs de tous les temps et
de tous les pays
Bonheur, Le (L'Herbier film,
1934). BC, 36
Bonnie Scotland (Laurel and
Hardy film, 1935). BC, 47
Book of Martyrs (popular name
for Foxe's *Acts and Monuments
of these latter perilous

*times touching matters of
the Church*, Latin edition,
1559, English version, 1563).
C, 90. OP, 426
Book of Ptah, The (Van Vogt
science fiction work, 1948).
ILN, 59
Book of Roses, The (Parkman
work on gardening, 1866).
ILN, 16
Book of Tea, The (Okakura
Kakuzo, 1906). OCC, 780
Book of the Duchess, The
(Chaucer elegy on the duchess
of Lancaster, 1369). OCC,
815
Book of the Thousand Nights
and a Night. See Mil y una
noches
Bosque petrificado. See The
Petrified Forest
Bouddhisme (David-Neel, 1936).
OCC, 780
Bouquet de estrellas perfumadas
(Santiago Ginzberg collection
of poems). OCC, 338
Bouvard et Pécuchet (Flaubert
novel, 1881). OC, 259-62
Brahma (Emerson poem). OC,
251. OCC, 735. ILN, 22
Brazilian Mystic, A
(Cunninghame Graham book on
Antonio Conselheiro and the
Canudos uprising, 1925).
OCC, 839
Breta Sogur (sagas about
Wales, based on Geoffrey of
Monmouth's chronicle). OCC,
936
Breve examen del idioma
analítico de John Wilkins
(Ferri work, no doubt based
on Borges essay "El idioma
analítico de John Wilkins").
LA, 36
Breve historia de la literatura
inglesa. See Short History
of English Literature
Breviloquium (St. Bonaventura
theological work, 13th
century). OC, 775
Bric-a-Brac (Nierenstein Souza
anthology, published
posthumously by a group of
his friends, 1942). OCC,
311

Bridge of San Luis Rey, The
(Wilder novel, 1927).     ILN,
53
Bridge-Builders, The   (Kipling
poem, 1893).   OC, 659
Brief History of Moscovia, A
(Milton, published
posthumously in 1682).   SN,
154
Brisas de Fray Bentos   (Nieren-
stein Souza).   OCC, 313
Broadway Melody, The   (Beaumont
film, 1929).   OC, 223.   BC,
28
Bronce de Arezzo   (Greek
statue).   OCC, 685
Brooklyn Eagle   (newspaper,
1841–1955, where Whitman
worked from 1846 to 1848).
OC, 252.   ILN, 24
Brunanburh   (Old English ballad
included in the   Anglo-Saxon
Chronicle   for the year 937).
OC, 377, 906.   OCC, 885–86,
895.   OP, 466
Brunanburh   (Tennyson
translation).   OCC, 885–86
Brut   (Layomon's history of
Britain).   OCC, 897–98
Buda: Su vida, su obra, su
comunidad   (Oldenberg, 1946).
OCC, 781
Buddha and his Path to Self-
Enlightenment   (Fussell,
1955).   OCC, 780
Buddha's Law Among the Birds,
The   (Conze, 1955).   OCC,
780
Buddhacarita   (epic poem about
the Buddha attributed to
Asvaghosha).   OC, 742.
OCC, 727
Buddhism   (Humphreys, 1951).
OCC, 780
Buddhism, Its Essence and
Development   (Conze, 1951).
OCC, 780
Buddhismus nach alteren Pali-
Werken, Der   (Hardy).   OC,
741
Budismo nihilista   (Fatone,
1962).   OCC, 780
Buenos Aires desde su fundación
hasta nuestros días   (Manuel
Bilbao book, 1903).   OC, 82

Buenos Aires en tinta china
(Rossi book of drawings,
1951).   P, 127–28
Buey, El   (Silva Valdés poem in
Poemas nativos).   I, 62
Bundahishn   (Pahlawi religious
work of the 9th century, the
title of which means "The
Ground-giving," a manual of
religious knowledge).   OCC,
586
Busca de Averroes, La   (Borges
story, 1947).   OP, 508
Busca de Tai An, La   (supposed
film based on Bustos Domecq
story "La prolongada busca
de Tai An").   OCC, 254
Buscón, Historia de la vida del
(Quevedo picaresque novel,
written 1603–1608, published
in 1626).   OC, 662, 734.
I, 40.   P, 122
Cábala   (Kabbalah, Jewish
mystic interpretations of the
Scriptures, comprising the
Sefer Yetsirah and the
Zohar).   OC, 211, 627, 885,
997.   OCC, 322, 475.
OCC, 741, 762–63, 825, 880,
925.   BO, 16, 18, 48.
CONJ, 79.   I, 88.   ILN, 20.
P, 34, 121, 152, 161.   SN,
11, 125–39.   VA, 23
Cabala, The   (Wilder novel,
1925).   ILN, 53
Caballo, El   (Ipuche poem).
I, 60
Caballos de Abdera, Los
(Lugones story in   Las fuerzas
extrañas).   OCC, 495, 501
Caballos de la conquista.   See
The Horses of the Conquest
Cabaña del Tio Tom, La.   See
Uncle Tom's Cabin
Cabeza de Ramírez, La   (Lugones
poem in   Romances del Río
Seco).   OCC, 482
Caburé, El   (Cayol and de Bassi
sainete   with tangos, 1910).
IA, 137.   TE, 22, 29
Cadáver en fuga.   See The Case
of the Runaway Corpse
Caesar and Cleopatra   (Shaw
play, 1901).   OC, 713.
OCC, 848.   BO, 13
Caja de carpintero.   OCC, 322

sonnet in *Correo del otro mundo*). I, 10–11

Description of a City Shower (Swift poem, 1709). P, 127

Description of the Morning (Swift poem, 1709). P, 127

Descubrimiento de Europa por los chinos. See Espion chinois

Descubrimiento de un Mundo en la Luna. See The Discovery of a World in the Moon

Desert Gold (Grey novel, 1913). ILN, 61

Desesperé, Le (Bloy autobiographical novel, 1886). P, 34n.

Deshumanización del arte, La (Ortega y Gasset essay, 1925). P, 22

Desobediencia civil. See Civil Disobedience

Destiempo (magazine edited by Borges and Bioy Casares in 1936). OCC, 317

Destrucción de filósofos (Ghazali treatise, *Tahafut-ul-falasifa* or *The Incoherence of the Philosophers*). OC, 582

Destrucción de la destrucción (Averroes treatise, *Tahafut-ul-Tahafut* or *Incoherence of the Incoherence*). OC, 582, 583, 587

Destructive Element, The (Spender essay, 1935). OC, 640n. P, 102

Detrás del mostrador (Carriego poem in *Las misas herejes*). OC, 125

Deutsche Heldensage, Die (Jiriczek, 1902). OCC, 915. PB, 200

Deutsches Requiem (Borges story, 1946). OC, 629

Devil is a Woman, The (Sternberg film, 1935). BC, 39

Dhammapada (collection of the sayings of the Buddha). OCC, 745

Día de bronca (Carriego lunfardo poem). OC, 118

Día de lluvia, Un (Anglada essay). OCC, 50

Dial, The (literary organ of the American Transcendentalist movement, 1840–1844). ILN, 41, 42

Dialogo anglosajón. See Solomon and Saturn

Diálogo de los oradores. See Dialogus de Oratoribus

Diálogos (Plato dialogues: see also individual titles). PB, 196n.

Diálogos con Goethe. See Gesprache mit Goethe

Diálogos patrióticos (Hidalgo poem). OCC, 517

Dialogues between Hylas and Philonous (Berkeley philosophical dialogue, 1713). OC, 253n., 767

Dialogues Concerning Natural Religion (Hume). OC, 253n., 394, 708, 760. OCC, 151

Dialogus de Oratoribus (Tacitus). OC, 393. OCC, 588

Diario de noticias (newspaper). OCC, 30

Diario de un nazi (series of Soviet films on World War II). OC, 284. BC, 73

Diarios (Boswell's London and European diaries). OCC, 829

Días ociosos en la Patagonia. See Idle Days in Patagonia

Diccionaire biographique des auteurs de tous les temps et de tous les pays (Laffont-Bompiani, 1957–58). OCC, 321

Diccionaire de l'Académie francaise (the French Academy's dictionary, first published in 1694). OCC, 828

Diccionario (Villamayor). OCC, 156

Diccionario argentino (Tobías Garzón, 1910). OCC, 156

Diccionario argentino (Granada, 1910). OCC, 156

Diccionario de argentinismos, neologismos y barbarismos (Segovia, 1911). OCC, 156. IA, 180

Egoist, The (British magazine, 1914-1919). ILN, 42

Egyptian Cross Mystery, The (Queen novel). ILN, 57

Eheu! (Darío poem in *El canto errante*, 1907). OCC, 467

Einfuhrung in die Gottliche Komodie (Spoerri study of Dante, 1946). NED, 148

Eirikssaga Rautha (saga of Eric the Red). OCC, 940. PB, 190

Ejercicios (Jarnés book of essays, 1927). IA, 86

Ejército de la Ilíada (Lugones lecture, 1915). OCC, 489

Elder Edda. See Edda Mayor

Eleati, Gli (Albertelli, 1939). OC, 636

Elegía para un pueblo que perdió sus orillas (Molinari poem). IA, 133

Elegía a la muerte de su padre. See Coplas a la muerte de su padre

Elegías (Propertius elegies). OC, 664. P, 124

Elegido, El (Huergo story). OCC, 365

Elegie (Samain poem). OCC, 472

Elegies (Donne poems). OC, 700n.

Elemente der Kabbalah, Die (Bischoff, 1913). TE, 67

Elemento cornígero (Sbarbi). PB, 230

Elementos (Euclid treatise on geometry and theory of numbers). SN, 52

Elements of Drawing (Ruskin, 1863). OCC, 837

Elements of Perspective (Ruskin). OCC, 837

Elmer Gantry (Lewis novel, 1927). ILN, 35

Elogio de Ameghino (Lugones book on the Argentine paleontologist, 1915). OCC, 486-87

Elogio de la locura. See Encomium Moriae

Emanuel Swedenborg (Borges poem). P, 162

Emblemas morales (Covarrubias, 1610). I, 33

Emile (Rousseau book on education, 1762). OCC, 304

Emma Zunz (Borges story, 1948). OC, 629

Emoción aldeana (Lugones poem in *Los crepúsculos del jardín*). OCC, 473

Empire des Steppes, Attila, Genghis-Khan, Tamerlan, L' (Grousset, 1939). OC, 153

Emporio celestial de conocimientos benévolos (Chinese encyclopedia). OC, 708

Empresas (Covarrubias). See Emblemas morales

Empresas (Saavedra Fajardo). See Idea de un príncipe político christiano

En Belén (Gomensoro sonnet). OCC, 434

En Noche-Buena (Querol poem). OCC, 338

En camino! (Gomensoro ode). OCC, 434

En color exótico (Lugones poem in *Los crepúsculos del jardín*). OCC, 472

En el abismo (Almafuerte). IA, 41-42. P, 12-13

En el barrio (Carriego poem in *Las misas herejes*). OC, 125, 126, 127, 138, 142

En el principio fue el coche pullman (Anglada travel book, 1923). OCC, 48n.

En las siete selvas. See In the Seven Woods

En silencio (Carriego poem in *Las misas herejes*). OC, 142

Enciclopedia (Montaner y Simón). See Diccionario enciclopédico hispano-americano

Enciclopedia Sudamericana (encyclopedia published in Santiago, Chile, in 2074, of which we only have the article on Borges). OC, 1143

Enciclopedia de los Hermanos de la Pureza. OC, 688, 715

Encomium Moriae (Erasmus satire in praise of folly, 1509). P, 29. PB, 139

Fate of Homo Sapiens, The
(Wells, 1939).   OC, 724
Father Brown Stories
(Chesterton's five volumes of
detective stories about
Father Brown, *The Innocence
of Father Brown, The
Incredulity of Father Brown,
The Secret of Father Brown,
The Wisdom of Father Brown*
and *The Scandal of Father
Brown*).   OC, 694.   PB,
140–42.   SN, 74
Father and Son   (Edmund
Gosse biography of his
father, Philip Gosse, and
autobiography, 1907).   OC,
650
Faust   (Goethe drama, 1808
and 1832).   OC, 773.   OCC,
818.   PB, 229.   SN, 125.
TE, 12, 152.   VA, 15
Faust   (Gounod opera, 1859).
P, 29
Fausto   (Campo gauchesque poem,
1866).   OC, 139, 141, 186–
87, 192, 194, 232, 268, 953.
OCC, 520, 531, 537.   BC,
57.   I, 6, 55, 57, 82.
P, 28–31, 92, 94, 97, 113,
114–15.   TE, 11–17, 24, 152
Fe del cristiano   (Mather work
written in Spanish).   ILN,
10
Fear and Trembling.   See Frygt
og Baeven
Fears and Scruples   (Browning
poem in *Pacchiarotto*, 1876).
OC, 711
Fearsome Creatures of the
Lumberwoods   (Cox, 1910).
OCC, 698
Fechner und Lotze   (Wentscher
study of the two
philosophers, 1924).   OC,
257n.
Fedón.   See Phaedo
Fedora   (Sardou drama, 1882,
originally starring Sarah
Bernhardt).   OCC, 377
Fedro.   See Phaedrus
Felicia   (Saborido tango, c.
1910).   OC, 159
Fénix, The   (Old English poem).
See The Phoenix

Fénix y su historia natural, El
(Pellicer poem, 1630).   OCC,
588
Ferment   (Shand book of poems,
1950).   P, 148–50
Ferrocarril, El.   OC, 489
Fervor de Buenos Aires
(Borges's first book, poems,
1923).   OC, 13, 55, 759.
OCC, 499.   I, 5, 99.   P,
128.   PB, 172
Feu, Le   (Barbusse novel about
the First World War, 1916).
PB, 186
Feudo de los Gomensoro, El
(Nierenstein Souza, 1919).
OCC, 311
Ficciones   (Borges book of
stories, 1944).   PB, 171–73
Fierrazo, El   (tango).   OC, 160
Figure in the Carpet, The
(James story, 1896).   OC,
691.   ILN, 39
Figurín   (Lugones poem in
*Romancero*).   OCC, 481
Fihrist   (*The Index*, composed
by ad-Nadim in Baghdad in
988, a treatise on the
various languages and
literatures of Islam, with
sections also on foreign
religions and alchemy).   OC,
406
Fija, La   (periodical).   OCC, 21
Filipica   (the *Philippica* of
Theopompus, a world history
centering on Philip of
Macedon).   OC, 462n.
Film and Theatre   (Nicoll
study, 1935).   BC, 46–48
Films   (two Borges film
reviews, included in
*Discusión*).   OC, 177
Filosofia de la redención.
See Philosophie der Erlosung
Filosofícula   (Lugones book of
short prose and poems, 1924).
OCC, 495–96
Fin, El   (Borges story on a
final encounter of Fierro and
the Moreno, 1960).   OC, 483
Financier, The   (Dreiser novel,
1912).   ILN, 34
Finest Story in the World, The
(Kipling story about
reincarnation).   OC, 220

Fuente, La.   See The Fountain
Fuerza de la sangre, La
   (Cervantes exemplary novel).
   P, 44
Fuerzas extrañas, Las   (Lugones
   collection of short stories,
   1906).   OC, 1144.   OCC,
   495, 496, 500.   P, 24, 51
Fuga, La   (Saslavsky film,
   1937).   BC, 54–55
Fulminación del libro, La.
   See The Blast of the Book
Full of Life, Now   (Whitman
   poem).   OC, 252
Fundación mítica de Buenos
   Aires   (Borges poem, called
   originally "La fundación
   mitológica de Buenos Aires,"
   in Cuaderno San Martín).
   OC, 79.   PB, 125–26
Funes el memorioso   (Borges
   story about man with infinite
   memory, 1942).   OC, 483.   PB,
   167–68
Furioso.   See Orlando Furioso
Future of Painting, The   (W. H.
   Wright, 1923).   ILN, 57
G. F. Watts   (Chesterton study
   of painter, 1904).   OC, 662,
   709, 764.   P, 122
Galatea, La   (Cervantes
   pastoral novel, 1585).   OC,
   448, 668
Galileo Gelileo: Pensieri,
   motti e sentenze   (Favaro,
   1949).   OC, 716n.
Game with Shifting Mirrors, A
   (subtitle of Mir Bahadur
   Ali's The Conversation with
   the Man Called Al'Mu'tasim).
   OC, 414
Gangs of New York, The   (Asbury
   study, 1927).   OC, 311, 345
Ganzúa para Finneganns Wake.
   See A Skeleton Key to
   Finnegans Wake
Garden, The   (Sackville-West,
   1946).   OCC, 853
Garuda-Purana   (Hindu
   traditional book, the 17th
   Purana).   OCC, 634
Gate of the Hundred Sorrows,
   The   (Kipling story).   OC,
   1021
Gaucho, El   (Coni, 1945).
   OCC, 514

Gaucho, El   (book with preface
   by Borges, text by J. L.
   Lanuza and photographs by
   Burri, 1968).   P, 62–65
Gaucho, El   (Regules poem).
   OC, 1039
Gaucho Martín Fierro, El
   (first part of Hernandez's
   Martín Fierro, 1872,
   sometimes called the "Ida").
   OC, 195.   OCC, 515, 522,
   541, 565.   BC, 59.   P,
   89, 92, 94
Gaya ciencia   (Lugones poem
   in Romancero).   OCC, 480
Geheimwissenschaft im Umriss
   (Rudolf Steiner, 1920).
   OCC, 693
Genealogy of Fascism, The
   (Russell).   OC, 725
General Died at Dawn, The
   (Milestone film, 1936).   BC,
   52
General History of Labyrinths,
   A   (Haslam).   OC, 432
General Quiroga va en coche al
   muere, El   (Borges poem in
   Luna de enfrente).   OC, 55
General William Booth Enters
   into Heaven and Other Poems
   (Lindsay, 1913).   ILN, 48
Genese de l'idée de temps, La
   (Guyau, 1890).   OC, 278
Génesis   (first book of Bible).
   OC, 211, 638, 643, 651, 715,
   737, 1092.   OCC, 134, 655,
   661, 742, 743, 841, 888, 952.
   BC, 58.   BO, 69, 91.   I,
   149.   OP, 436, 497.   P, 26
Genesis   (Germanic poem).   OCC,
   903, 904
Génie du Christianisme, Le
   (Chateaubriand work of
   Christian apologetics, 1802).
   OC, 652
Genius, The   (Dreiser novel,
   1915).   ILN, 34
Geometría.   See Elements
Geórgicas   (Virgil poems on
   agriculture).   OC, 388, 512,
   541.   OCC, 304, 305, 321,
   601, 853.   BO, 21.   OP,
   462.   SN, 19, 59
Germanen der Volkerwanderung,
   Die   (Capelle, 1939).   OC,
   155

Germania (*De origine et situ Germanorum*, Tacitus monograph on the territory and the tribes east of the Rhine and north of the Danube). OC, 280. OCC, 787, 827, 861, 867, 899–900, 926. LA, 11. P, 73. PB, 224

Gerontion (Eliot poem). OCC, 679

Gerusalemme Liberata (Tasso poem, published without his consent in 1580, later revised under the title *Gerusalemme Conquistata*, published in 1593). OC, 264, 265n., 383, 744. P, 140. PB, 242

Geschichte der indische Literatur (Winternitz, 1905). OCC, 736

Geschichte der indischen Philosophie (Frauwallner, 1953). OCC, 753

Geschichte vom Gode Snorri (Niedner translation of *Eyrbyggja Saga*, 1920). OC, 381

Gesprache mit Goethe (Eckermann memoir, 1836–1848). OCC, 829. P, 38

Gesta Danorum (Saxo Grammaticus 13th century history of the Danes, sometimes called *Historia Danica*). OC, 756. OCC, 931, 958, 972–73, 975. OP, 496. P, 138. PB, 199

Gesta Dei per Francos (collection of Latin chronicles and historical documents on the Crusades, published in 1611). OC, 937. P, 140

Giant (Ferber novel, 1950). ILN, 33

Gift of the Magi, The (O. Henry story). ILN, 33

Gil Blas de Santillane (Lesage picaresque romance, 1715–1735). OCC, 41. SN, 71

Gilgamesh (Sumerian epic). OCC, 652. A, 80

Gimnasia para el adulto de clase media (Argentine film). OCC, 174

Gimnasio de la "Revista Nueva," El (Reyes anecdote in *Reloj de sol*). IA, 128

Gitanilla, La (Cervantes exemplary novel). P, 46

Gitanjali (Tagore prose poems, 1913). PB, 160

Glass Key, The (Hammett detective novel, 1931). ILN, 58

Glass Managerie, The (Williams play, 1945). ILN, 55

Gloglocioro (Planes). OCC, 322

Gloria de don Ramiro, La (Larreta historical novel, 1908). OC, 220

Glosario espiritual. See La vida inquieta

Glossarium ad scriptores mediae et infimae Latinitatis (Du Cange, 1678). OC, 523

Go Down, Moses (spiritual). OC, 296

Goa and the Blue Mountains; or, Six Months on Sick Leave (Burton, 1851). OC, 401

Gobierno gaucho (Campo poem in *Poesías*, 1870). OCC, 521

God of His Fathers (Jack London). ILN, 29

God of the Gongs, The (Chesterton story in *The Wisdom of Father Brown*). PB, 141

God of the Labyrinth, The (Quain mystery novel, 1933). OC, 461–62

God's Little Acre (Caldwell novel, 1933). ILN, 50

Goethe; or, The Man of Letters (Emerson essay in *Representative Men*). BO, 57

Gog und Magog, eine Chronik (Buber novel, 1949). OC, 751

Gold Bug, The (Poe story). BO, 76. ILN, 56. SN, 131

Gold Rush, The (Chaplin film, 1925). OC, 223. BC, 28

Golden Apples of the Sun (Bradbury novel, 1953). ILN, 60

Golden Bough, The (Frazer comparative study of

religion, 1890–1915). OC, 230. OCC, 569

Golden Era, The (newspaper and literary journal in San Francisco, 1852–1893). ILN, 28

Golden Legend, The. See Legenda Aurea

Golden Whales of California (Lindsay collection of poems, 1920). ILN, 48

Golem, Der (Meyrink novel, 1938). OC, 1066. OCC, 638. SN, 137–39

Golem, El (Borges poem, 1958). OC, 857. PB, 245, 246–47

Gongu-Hrolfs Saga (one of the *Fornaldar Sogur*). OCC, 971

Good Morning, America (Sandburg book of poems, 1928). ILN, 47

Gorboduc (one of the earliest of English tragedies, by Norton and Sackville, first performed in 1561). OC, 803

Gossip on Romance, A (Stevenson essay on narrative fiction, 1880). P, 22, 67, 74. SN, 13

Gotamo Buddha (Ladner, 1948). OCC, 780

Gotzendammerung (Nietzsche essay, 1888). NED, 93

Grace Abounding to the Chief of Sinners (Bunyan homiletic narrative, 1666). OC, 238

Gradus ad Parnassum (manual on Latin versification, many editions of which exist). OC, 371, 486, 487

Gráfico, El (newspaper). OCC, 74

Gramática de la Real Academia Española (official grammar of the Castilian tongue, first published in 1771). OC, 706. OCC, 595n. IA, 172, 173, 179. TE, 37–42

Gran Hotel Victoria (Latasa tango, 1906). TE, 29

Gran señora es la toronja (ballad formerly attributed to Zúñiga). OCC, 447

Gran sueño del siglo. OCC, 392

Grand Larousse encyclopédique (French encyclopedia

published between 1960 and 1964). LA, 48

Grande Argentina, La (Lugones political work, 1930). OCC, 493n.

Grandes más que Elefantes y que Abades (Góngora sonnet). I, 11

Grapes of Wrath, The (Steinbeck novel, 1939). ILN, 49

Grass Harp, The (Capote novel, 1951). ILN, 51

Great Gatsby, The (Fitzgerald novel, 1926). ILN, 41

Great God Brown, The (O'Neill play, 1925). ILN, 53

Great Good Place, The (James story). OCC, 850. ILN, 39

Greek Coffin Mystery, The (Ellery Queen mystery). ILN, 57

Green Hills of Africa, The (Hemingway book on big-game hunting, 1935). ILN, 37

Green Mansions (Hudson romance of the South American forest, 1904). OCC, 839

Green Pastures (Keighley film, 1936). BC, 57–58

Greguerías (Gómez de la Serna witty epigrams, 1911–1955). I, 93

Gremialismo (Baralt work in 6 vols., 1947–1954). OCC, 327

Grettis Saga (Icelandic saga about the deeds of Grettir the Strong). OC, 368, 381, 874. OCC, 934, 936, 938, 941. PB, 191–92

Grial (Grail legend). BC, 78. OP, 527

Griechische Denker: eine Geschichte der antiken Philosophie (Gomperz, 1896–1909). OC, 713

Grímnismál (didactic poem in the *Elder Edda*, in which Odin appears as the vagrant Grimnir or "the Masked One"). OCC, 929, 965n.

Guapo, El (Carriego poem in *Las misas herejes*). OC, 125, 127–29, 142. P, 40, 42, 64

Gudrun. See Kudrun

Guerra del Peloponese
(Thucydides history of the
war between Athens and
Sparta). OCC, 963

Guerra gaucha, La (Lugones
historical work, 1905).
OCC, 461, 496-97

Guerra judía. See Bellum
Judaicum

Guerreros en Helgeland. See
Haermendene pa Helgeland

Guía Lourenzo. OCC, 127

Guide to the New World: A
Handbook of Constructive
World Revolution (Wells).
OC, 723-24

Guide to Socialism. See The
Intelligent Woman's Guide to
Socialism and Communism

Guillaume Tell (Rossini opera,
1829). OCC, 330

Guitarra, La (Carriego poem in
Las misas herejes). OC, 127

Gulliver's Travels into Several
Remote Nations of the World
(Swift satirical work, 1726).
OC, 117, 261, 273, 422, 490,
660, 752, 1022. A, 72.
LA, 125. P, 119, 137.
VA, 45

Gulshan i Raz (The Mystical
Rose Garden of Mahmúd
Shabistarí, c.1320). OC,
594

Gunnlaugssaga Ormstungra
(Icelandic saga about the
rivalry of Gunnlaug and Hrafn
for the love of Helga).
OCC, 936-37

Guzmán de Alfarache (Alemán
picaresque novel, 1599 and
1602). OC, 203. I, 40, 140

Gylfaginning (the Beguiling of
Gylfi, part of Snorri
Sturluson's Prose Edda, which
includes stories about the
beginning and end of the
world). OCC, 952, 953-54

Ha caído una estrella (Silva
Valdés poem). TE, 89

Hablemos con mas propiedad!
(Bustos Domecq, 1932). OCC,
13

Hacedor de estrellas. See
Star Maker

Hacia una arquitectura sin
concesiones (Quincey, 1937).
OCC, 333

Haermendene pa Helgeland
(Ibsen play on the theme of
the Laxdoela Saga). OCC,
939

Hágase hizo (Tulio Herrera
novel, 1965). OCC, 344, 345

Hai ku (Japanese genre of
short poem). OCC, 775-76.
A, 91. OP, 462-63

Hail and Farewell (Moore
autobiography, consisting of
Ave, 1911, Salve, 1912, and
Vale, 1913). A, 15

Hakons Saga (Sturla Thordarson
saga about king Hakon of
Norway, who had instigated
the murder of Sturla's uncle,
Snorri Sturluson). OCC, 964

Hálfs Saga (Icelandic saga
about the legendary king
Hálf). OCC, 965

Hallelujah (Vidor film, 1929).
OC, 224, 295. BC, 33

Hamlet (Coleridge essay in
Notes and Lectures upon
Shakespeare). OCC, 561

Hamlet (Shakespeare tragedy,
1603). OC, 150, 202, 270,
383, 413, 446, 579, 617, 668,
669, 675, 700, 703, 755,
1066. OCC, 310, 553, 819-
20, 927-73. BO, 24.
CONJ, 33, 35, 44. NED,
110-11. OP, 496. P, 142,
144, 146. PB, 149, 154,
169, 226. SN, 17

Handy Guide for Beggars, A
(Lindsay prose work, 1916).
ILN, 48

Harlot's House, The (Wilde
poem). OC, 691. OCC,
846. A, 69. PB, 157

Harp Song of the Dane Women
(Kipling poem). OCC, 812,
846

Harvard Advocate (magazine).
ILN, 42

Has vuelto (Carriego poem,
published posthumously).
OC, 137, 138, 142

Háttalykill. OCC, 957

Háttatal (a list of verse
forms by Snorri Sturluson,

son Hadubrand). OCC, 901–2,
918
Himalayan (Kipling poem).
SN, 120
Himno Nacional Uruguayo. LA,
181
Himno a la luna (Lugones poem
in *Lunario sentimental*).
OCC, 474, 498
Himno de las torres (Lugones
prose piece in *Las montañas
de oro*). OCC, 470, 471, 474
Himnos para millonarios
(Anglada book of poems,
1934). OCC, 48, 49, 50
Himnos rojos (unfinished early
Borges work, also called "Los
ritmos rojos"). LA, 16
Hind in Richmond Park, A
(Hudson, 1922). OCC, 839
Hindustan Review (journal
published in Allahabad,
founded in 1903). OC, 414
Hipocresía de la hormiga
(Unamuno poem). PB, 149
Histoire de la littérature
francaise de 1789 a nos jours
(Thibaudet, 1936). PB, 165
Histoire de la philosophie
(Emile Bréhier). OCC, 581
Histoire de la philosophie
médievale (Wulf). NED,
117n.
Histoire Générale des Voyages
(Abbé Prevost miscellany in
many volumes, 1671, with a
sequel, *Nouvelle histoire
générale des Voyages*).
OC, 734
Histoires désobligéantes (Bloy
stories). OC, 711
Histoires tragiques
(Belleforest compilation of
tragic stories from Bandello
and other sources, 1559 and
later editions). OCC, 973
Historia (Herodotus history).
OCC, 667. SN, 54
Historia adversum paganos
(Orosius universal history,
c.417). OCC, 799
Historia animalium (Gesner,
1551–1558). OCC, 622
Historia biográfica de la
filosofía. See Biographical
History of Philosophy

Historia científica del
cinematógrafo (Anglada).
OCC, 67
Historia crítica de la
literatura uruguaya (Roxlo
work in 7 vols.). OC, 188.
P, 96
Historia Danica. See Gesta
Danorum
Historia de Inglaterra
(Macaulay). See History of
England
Historia de Inglaterra
(Milton). See The History
of Britain
Historia de Moscovia. See A
Brief History of Moscovia
Historia de San Martín y de la
emancipación sudamericana
(Mitre, 1887–90). PB, 131–
32
Historia de Sarmiento (Lugones
essay, 1911). OCC, 485,
486, 496. P, 131
Historia de cincuenta años de
desgobierno (Avellanos work,
published posthumously in
1939). OC, 1062
Historia de historias (one of
Torres Villaroel's *Sueños
morales*). I, 13
Historia de la dominación de
los árabes en España (Conde
work in 3 vols., 1820–1821).
OC, 231
Historia de la eternidad
(Borges book of essays,
1936). OC, 277n.
Historia de la filosofía
(Deussen). See Allgemeine
Geschichte der Philosophie,
mit besonderer Berucksich-
tigung der Religionen
Historia de la guerra europea.
See History of the World War,
1914–1918
Historia de la literatura
argentina (Rojas work in 8
vols., 1917–22). OC, 267,
268. OCC, 540, 559, 565.
P, 91, 92. PB, 152
Historia de la literatura china
(Giles). See History of
Chinese Literature
Historia de la literatura
uruguaya (Roxlo). See

Historia crítica de la
literatura uruguaya
Historia de la poesía hispano-
americana (Menéndez y
Pelayo, 1911). IA, 103
Historia de la revolución
francesa. See The French
Revolution, A History
Historia de la secta de los
Hasidim (Yarmolinsky study).
OC, 500, 501, 506
Historia de las filosofías y
religiones (Gregorovius,
perhaps a reference to his
*Geschichte der Stadt Rom im
Mittelalter*, 13 vols., 1859–
1872). OCC, 321
Historia de las ideas estéticas
en España (Menéndez y
Pelayo, 8 vols., 1882–1891).
IA, 72
Historia de las naciones
septentrionales (Olaus
Magnus work, 1555). OCC,
711
Historia de los Godos
(Jourdanes). See De rebus
Geticis
Historia de los heterodoxos
españoles (Menéndez y
Pelayo, 1880–1882). OC, 701
Historia de los jalifas
(Baladhuri's *Futuh ul-Buldan*,
a history of the early
expansion of Islam under the
Caliphate). OC, 324
Historia de los primeros reyes
de Noruega. See History of
the Early Kings of Norway
Historia de los reyes de
Noruega. See Heimskringla
Historia de mi muerte (Lugones
poem in *El libro fiel*).
OCC, 477, 478, 479
Historia del arrabal (Gálvez
novel, 1922). TE, 23
Historia del doctor Wassell.
See The Story of Doctor
Wassell
Historia del guerrero y la
cautiva (Borges story,
1949). OC, 629
Historia del Paraguay, Río de
la Plata y Tucumán
(Guevara). OCC, 485

Historia del Shorthorn en la
Argentina. OC, 1069
Historia Ecclesiastica Gentis
Anglorum (Bede's history of
the English people from the
Roman invasion to 731). OC,
643. OCC, 881–82, 883–85,
888, 897. NED, 125–34
Historia Natural de las
Serpientes y Dragones. See
Serpentum et draconum
historiae libri duo
Historia naturalis. See
Naturalis historia
Historia panorámica del
periodismo nacional
(Montenegro). OCC, 360
Historia philosophiae graecae
et romanae ex fontium locis
contexta (Ritter and
Preller, 1838). OC, 389
Historia Regum Britanniae
(Geoffrey of Monmouth
history of Britain, c.1150).
OCC, 936
Historia universal (Cantu).
See Storia universale
Historia universal (Orosio).
See Historia adversum paganos
Historia verdadera or Historia
verídica (Lucian satirical
work, the so-called "True
History"). OC, 627. P, 25
Historias trágicas. See Novelle
Historic Doubts Relative to
Napoleon Bonaparte
(Whately). OC, 236
History (Emerson essay, 1841).
OC, 679
History of Britain, The
(Milton, 1670). SN, 154, 156
History of Chinese Literature
(Giles, 1901). OC, 772
History of England from the
Accession of James II
(Macaulay, 1849–1861). OCC,
836
History of English Literature
(Lang, 1912). OCC, 857.
P, 117
History of English Literature
(Legouis and Cazamian, 1924).
OCC, 857
History of English Literature
(Saintsbury). See Short
History of English Literature

Inglinga Saga. See Ynglinga
  Saga
Inicial (literary magazine in
  Buenos Aires, 1923–1926).
  OCC, 497. TE, 154
Inmortal, El (Borges story,
  originally called "Los
  inmortales," 1947). OC,
  629. PB, 173
Inmortalidad de el Alma, con
  que se prueba la Providencia
  de Dios para consuelo, y
  aliento de los Cathólicos, y
  vergonzosa confusión de los
  Hereges (Quevedo). See
  Providencia de Dios
Innocents at Home, The (Twain,
  1870). PB, 122
Inquiry into Meaning and Truth,
  An (Russell work on meaning
  and empirical data, 1940).
  OC, 394
Inquisiciones (Borges book of
  essays, 1925). I, 5. TE,
  112
Inscripción de la Statua
  Augusta del Carlos Quinto
  en Aranjuez (Quevedo poem).
  IA, 62
Inscripción en cualquier
  sepulcro (Borges poem).
  OC, 759
Inscripciones (Haedo book of
  poems, 1923). OC, 849
Instrucción del estanciero
  (Hernández book on cattle
  ranching, 1881). OCC, 526,
  527
Instrucción secundaria, La
  (Amancio Alcorta, 1916).
  OCC, 137
Intelligent Woman's Guide to
  Socialism and Communism, The
  (Shaw, 1928). OC, 763
Intermezzo (Lugones series of
  poems in El libro de los
  paisajes). OCC, 480
Intimas (section of Carriego's
  posthumous poems). OC, 140
Introduction to Mathematical
  Philosophy (Russell book,
  1919). OC, 246, 256n., 277,
  392
Introduction a la vie dévote
  (St. Francis of Sales). OC,
  446n.

Introduction to Old Norse
  (Gordon, 1957). OCC, 974
Intruder in the Dust (Faulkner
  novel, 1948). ILN, 36
Intrusa, La (Borges story in
  El informe de Brodie). PB,
  245, 246
Invasión, La (Borges-Bioy
  script for film directed by
  Hugo Santiago, 1968–69).
  BC, 83
Invención de Morel, La (Bioy
  Casares novel, 1940). P,
  22–24
Invendable, L' (Bloy story).
  OC, 721
Invisible Man, The (Chesterton
  story in The Innocence of
  Father Brown). OCC, 189.
  BO, 78–79
Invisible Man, The (Wells
  novel, 1897). OC, 220n.,
  697, 698. OCC, 847. BC,
  43. P, 152
Ion (early Plato dialogue).
  OC, 263
Irish Poetry (Kuno Meyer,
  1911). OCC, 971n.
Isaías (book of Isaiah in the
  Bible). OC, 402n., 517,
  639. OCC, 125. TE, 64
Isla del Doctor Moreau. See
  Island of Doctor Moreau
Isla del tesoro. See Treasure
  Island
Isla oscura. See The Dark
  Island
Island of Doctor Moreau, The
  (Wells novel about
  vivisectionist). OC, 276,
  698, 699. OCC, 847. BC,
  43. P, 24
Islands Kultur zur Wikingszeit
  (Niedner, 1913). OC, 381
Islendigabók (Book of the
  Icelanders or Libellus
  Islandorum, Ari Thorgilsson's
  history of Iceland including
  a digression on the discovery
  and settlement of Greenland).
  OCC, 935, 936, 949
Ismaelillo (Martí poems for
  his son, 1882). OCC, 464
Itinerario de Carlos Anglada:
  trayectoria de un lírico
  (Formento). OCC, 48, 53

498, 499, 501, 658, 831.
I, 75. LA, 54. P, 60,
79. PB, 164, 166, 231
Lusíadas, Os (Camoes epic poem
about the history of Portugal
and the exploits of Vasco da
Gama, 1572). OC, 249, 832.
P, 8. PB, 234-45
Lusiads, The (Burton
translation). PB, 241
Luxe (magazine). OC, 444
Luz de provincia (Mastronardi
poem). OC, 163. PB, 166
Lyrical Ballads (Wordsworth-
Coleridge collection of
poems, 1798). OCC, 831.
P, 8
Lyrical Ballads (Wordsworth
preface to the second
edition, 1800). PB, 188
Lyrisches Intermezzo (Heine
collection of lyric poems,
1823, originally published
between two tragedies). PB,
159
Mabinogion (collection of
Welsh tales, compiled in the
14th and 15th centuries).
OC, 383, 1067. OCC, 931
Macbeth (Shakespeare tragedy,
c.1606). OC, 180, 270, 497,
498, 755, 773, 803, 1093.
OCC, 674, 819, 970. BC,
39. C, 49. OP, 437, 454.
P, 8, 138, 142-47, 172.
SN, 14, 129
Madame Bovary (Flaubert novel,
1857). OC, 259, 262, 265
Madrugar temprano (Tulio
Herrera book of poems, 1961).
OCC, 344, 345
Magnus Saga (Sturla Thor-
darsson's saga about king
Magnus of Norway). OCC, 964
Mahabharata (Hindu epic poem,
c.500 B.C.). OCC, 671, 736,
743, 751
Mahomet and His Successors
(Irving biography, 1849-
1850). ILN, 16
Main Street (Lewis novel,
1920). ILN, 35. P, 27
Majjhima Nikaya (the second
of four *Nikayas* in the
Buddhist scriptures). OC,
740

Major Barbara (Shaw play,
1907). OCC, 848
Major Trends in Jewish
Mysticism (Scholem, 1941).
OC, 886. OCC, 616
Maldon, Battle of (Old
English poem about a battle
between the Northmen and the
English in 991). OC, 755-
56, 1022. OCC, 811
Maldonado, El (tango). IA,
119
Malevo, El (Lugones poem in
*Romances del Río Seco*).
OCC, 483
Malón, El (poem).
OCC, 435
Malón, El (monthly bulletin,
organ of the Asociación
Aborigenista Argentina,
edited by Marcelo Frogman).
OCC, 153, 157, 184
Maltese Falcon, The (Hammett
novel, 1930). ILN, 57
Mamboretá (Carriego poem in
*La canción del barrio*).
OC, 135, 142
Man of the Crowd, The (Poe
story, 1840). OP, 438.
PB, 140
Man Versus the State (Spencer
essay on political
philosophy, 1884). OC, 719
Man Who Died Twice, The
(Robinson narrative poem,
1924). ILN, 46
Man Who Knew Too Much, and
Other Stories, The
(Chesterton stories, 1922).
OC, 694. PB, 140
Man Who Was Thursday, a Night-
mare, The (Chesterton novel,
1908). OC, 231, 629, 695,
731. OCC, 851. NED, 95-96.
P, 59. PB, 141, 181. SN, 74
Man and Superman (Shaw play,
1903). OC, 134, 236n., 281,
704n., 727, 748. OCC, 848.
BO, 51. P, 157
Man in the Cafe (Shand poem in
*Ferment*). P, 150
Man of Aran (Flaherty film,
1934). BC, 46, 47
Man that Corrupted Hadleyburg,
The (Twain novel, 1900).
OC, 724

Man who Sold the Moon
(Heinlein science fiction
novel, 1950). ILN, 59
Man with Two Beards, The
(Chesterton story in *The
Secret of Father Brown*).
PB, 141
Manalive (Chesterton, 1912).
OC, 261
Manequí de Mimbre. OC, 412
Manhood of Humanity, The
(Korzybski, 1921). OC, 198
Manifestación antiliberal, La
(Unamuno poem). PB, 149
Manisero, El (rumba). OC, 295
Manner of Men (Kipling
poem). SN, 119-20
Mansiones verdes. See Green
Mansions
Mantiq al-Tayr. See El
coloquio de los pájaros
Manual del gigante. See Libro
de la precisión y la revisión
Manual of Indian Buddhism
(Kern, 1896). OCC, 671, 780
Manuel raisonné (Moulonguet
cookbook, 1929). OCC, 325
Manuscript Found in a Bottle
(Poe story, 1833). OC, 731.
NED, 96. PB, 181
Manuscrito hallado en un libro
de Joseph Conrad (Borges
poem added to revised
editions of *Luna de
enfrente*). OC, 55
Many Inventions (Kipling book
of stories, 1893). OC,
220n.
Mapamundi (Lugones series of
poems in *El libro de los
paisajes*). OCC, 479
Máquina del Tiempo, La. See
The Time Machine
Maravillas de la creación
(al-Qazwini's *Atháru'l-Bilád*,
a treatise on geography).
OCC, 600, 695, 711-12
Maravillas del mundo y del
hombre, Las (one of the
"libros serios" Aquiles Molinari sees in Abenjaldún's
house). OCC, 25
Marble Faun, The (Hawthorne
romance, 1860). OC, 681,
682-83. ILN, 18

Marcha (Uruguayan weekly,
published from the forties
until 1974). OCC, 313
Marco Bruto, La vida de
(Quevedo historical work,
1631-1644). OC, 662. I,
43. P, 45, 121
Marcos (*Gospel of Mark* in the
New Testament). OC, 1070-
72. OCC, 864
Mardi (Melville novel, 1849).
P, 117
Maríu Saga (*Saga of the Virgin
Mary*, c.1200). OCC, 936
Marienleben (Wernher's life of
the Virgin Mary, 1172,
entitled *Drei Lieder von
der Jungfrau*). OCC, 907
Marienlyrik (Marian poetry, a
common element of medieval
religious poetry in Germany
and elsewhere). OCC, 907
Mark Twain's America (De Voto
biography, 1932). OC, 345.
P, 81. PB, 122, 123
Markheim (Stevenson novella,
1887). OCC, 845
Mármoles, Los (Fernández Irala
book of poems). LA, 35, 37,
38, 53
Marne, El (Arolas tango).
OC, 162
Marriage of Heaven and Hell
(Blake prose work, 1790).
OCC, 840. P, 13n., 160
Marruecos. See Morocco
Martian Chronicles (Bradbury
science fiction novel, 1950).
ILN, 60. P, 25-27
Martin Chuzzlewit, The Life and
Adventures of (Dickens
novel, 1843-44). OCC, 835
Martín Fierro (Hernández gauchesque poem, published in
two parts, *El gaucho Martín
Fierro*, 1872, and *La vuelta
de Martín Fierro*, 1879).
OC, 114, 115, 125, 131, 132,
134, 153, 162, 163, 165, 166,
167, 179, 181, 182, 185, 187,
188, 193-97, 223, 267, 268,
269, 519-21, 525, 563-65,
572, 629, 656, 658, 734, 797,
953, 1040. OCC, 18, 155,
482, 485, 513-565. BC, 29,
58. BO, 20-21, 24. I,

Miltonic Setting, The
(Tillyard). OC, 747n.
Mind (C. L. Dodgson work on
logic, 4 vols., 1894–95).
OC, 257
Mind of Man, A Textbook of
Psychology, The (Spiller,
1902). OC, 276, 647, 760.
BO, 30. I, 22. IA, 17.
SN, 35. TE, 53
Minuciosa relación. See
Lalitavistara
Miracle Plays (medieval dramas
based on sacred history or
the legends of the saints).
OCC, 817
Miriam (Capote story). ILN,
51
Mirror for Magistrates, A
(collection of tragic stories
in verse, planned by George
Ferrers and William Baldwin,
1559). PB, 142
Mirror of the Magistrate, The
(Chesterton story in The
Secret of Father Brown).
PB, 142
Misas herejes, Las (Carriego
book of poems, 1908). OC,
121–29, 142, 160. P, 41,
42
Miscelánea china (Wang Tai-hai
work, 1791). OCC, 600
Miscellaneous Papers (Carlyle
posthumous collection,
c.1900). OC, 726
Misérables, Les (Hugo novel,
1862). OC, 921
Mishnah (collection of Jewish
law). OC, 589, 763
Misionero, El (Almafuerte
poem). IA, 36, 37. P,
13, 40
Mister Higginbotham's
Catastrophe (Hawthorne short
story in Twice-Told Tales,
1837). OC, 684
Misterio del cuarto amarillo.
See Le Mystere de la chambre
jaune
Misterios. See Miracle Plays
Místico brasileño, Un. See A
Brazilian Mystic
Místicos y magos del Tibet.
See Mystiques et magiciens
du Thibet

Mitologia Nordica (Lun study,
1945). OCC, 920
Mitridates Eupator (Emerson
poem). PB, 172
Moby Dick, or The Whale
(Melville novel, 1851). OC,
229, 591, 660, 731, 1128.
OCC, 200, 712, 892. BC,
78. ILN, 26, 27. NED,
96, 118. P, 116, 117, 119.
PB, 181. SN, 30–31
Moderate Murderer, The
(Chesterton story in Four
Faultless Felons). PB, 141
Modern Electrics (magazine
published in New York, 1909–
1914). ILN, 58
Modern Painters (Ruskin
essays, 1843–1860). OCC,
836–37. NED, 86
Modern Painting (W. H. Wright,
1915). ILN, 57
Mogreb-el-Acksa (Cunninghame
Grahame travel book, 1898).
OCC, 839
Mohkam (ibn Sida). OC, 583
Mon ami Pierrot (song "Au
clair de la lune"). OCC, 40
Monadologie (Leibniz paper of
1714, published
posthumously). OC, 705.
NED, 139n.
Monarquía eclesiástica o his-
toria universal del mundo
(Pineda, 1576). I, 33
Monkey. See Viaje al Oeste
Monsieur Lecoq (Gaboriau
detective novel, 1869).
OCC, 15. P, 47
Montaigne; or, The Sceptic
(Emerson essay in
Representative Men). BO, 57
Montañas del oro, Las (Lugones
book of poems, 1897). OCC,
470, 471, 500
Monument to Saint Augustine:
Essays on Some Aspects of
His Thought (anthology of
essays published by Sheed and
Ward, 1930). OC, 367
Moonstone, The (Collins
detective novel, 1868).
OCC, 835. BO, 78. P,
47–48
Moralities (medieval dramatic
pieces in verse, in which

Nexus (Henry Miller novel, 1960, part of the *Rosy Crucifixion*). ILN, 45

Nibelungenlied (Middle High German heroic epic poem on Siegfried, written in Austria c.1200-1210). OC, 383, 592. OCC, 470, 844, 910-15, 917, 918, 920-21, 923, 975. LA, 30. P, 171

Nido del águila. See The Eagle's Nest

Nigger of the "Narcissus" (Conrad novel, 1898). OCC, 849. ILN, 26

Night Rider (Warren novel, 1938). ILN, 50

Night Thoughts ("The Complaint, or Night Thoughts on Life, Death, and Immortality," Young poem, 1742-45). OC, 752

Night and Day (Woolf novel, 1919). OCC, 853

Night in Bombay (Bromfield novel, 1940). ILN, 49

Nightmare (Fussele painting). SN, 42

Nightmare (Whelan film, 1942). BC, 70

Nikayas (four collections of the Buddha's sayings, which together form the *Sutta Pitaka* or *Basket of Discourses*, a division of Buddhist canonical books). OC, 740. OCC, 724, 777

Nirvana crepuscular (Herrera y Reissig poem in *Los parques abandonados*, 1909). OCC, 338

Njáls Saga (famous Icelandic family saga, story of the burning of the lawyer Njal and his family by his enemies, late 13th century). OC, 369, 381. OCC, 888, 932-33, 939-40, 941, 932-33, 939-40. PB, 200

Noche de garufa (Saldías tango, 1913). OCC, 259. TE, 29

Noche de los dones, La (Borges story in *El libro de arena*). LA, 180

Noche que en el Sur lo velaron, La (Borges poem in *Cuaderno San Martín*). OC, 79

Noche y día. See Night and Day

Noctes Atticae (Aulus Gellius miscellany, published c.180). OC, 277. P, 25-26

Nocturnos (Bustos Domecq). OCC, 13

Nocturnos (Silva poems). OCC, 464-65

Nombres de la muerte (Vázquez, 1964). P, 167-69

Nor-noroeste (Bonavena novel in 6 vols., the last published posthumously in 1939). OCC, 306, 307, 310

Nordische Mythologie im gemenverstandlichen Darstellung (Herrmann study, 1903). PB, 198

North of Boston (Frost book of poems, 1914). ILN, 46

Nosotros (Argentine literary magazine, 1907-1934). OC, 105, 113. OCC, 320, 338, 471n. TE, 154

Nothing Dies (Dunne treatise on time, 1940). OC, 646

Noticias. See Diario de Noticias

Nouveau Larousse (revised version of Larousse encyclopedia, 1897-1904). PB, 230

Nouveaux essais sur l'entendement humain (Leibniz essays, published posthumously in 1765). OC, 647

Nouvelle Revue Francaise (French literary magazine, 1908-1943, 1953-  ). OC, 445. I, 21

Novalis (Carlyle essay in *Critical and Miscellaneous Essays*). OC, 766

Novelas ejemplares (Cervantes short novels, 1613). OC, 448. P, 43-46

Novelle (Bandello collection of tragic stories, c.1550). P, 46

Now Voyager, The (Rapper film, 1942). BC, 69-70

Oso (Loomis work, 1911, later
called *Opus 1*). OCC, 320,
322

Otello (Verdi opera, 1887).
OC, 574

Othello (Shakespeare play,
1604). OC, 447, 803.
OCC, 820-21. P, 144.
PB, 162

Other Voices, Other Rooms
(Capote novel, 1948). ILN,
51

Otoño, muchachos, El (Carriego
poem, published post-
humously). OC, 135-36

Otra muerte, La (Borges story
in *El Aleph*). OC, 629

Otra vuelta de tuerca. See
Turn of the Screw

Otras inquisiciones (Borges
book of essays, 1952). OC,
52

Otro, El (Borges story in *El
libro de arena*). LA, 179,
180

Otro, el mismo, El (Borges
book of poems, 1964). OC,
857

Otro poema de los dones
book of sonnets, 1912).
OCC, 48, 50

Otro Whitman, El (Borges essay
in *Discusión*). OC, 177

Ottar (travel account in Old
English prose). OCC, 798-99

Our Knowledge of the External
World (Russell treatise on
epistemology, 1914). OC,
246

Our Theatres in the Nineties
(Shaw memoir, 1931). OC,
277

Our Town (Wilder play, 1938).
ILN, 53-54

Out of the Unknown (Van Vogt-
Hull science fiction, 1948).
ILN, 60

Outcasts of Poker Flat, The
(Harte story, 1869). ILN,
29. P, 83

Outline of History, The (Wells
work of universal history,
1920). OC, 697n.

Outsider, The (Wright novel,
1952). ILN, 51

Overland Monthly, The
(California magazine, 1868-
75, 1883-1935). ILN, 29.
P, 83

Oxford Companion to English
Literature (Harvey, first
published in 1932). OCC,
857

Pablo y Virginia. See Paul
et Virginie

Padrenuestro (Lord's Prayer).
OCC, 828, 893. P, 149

Página para recordar al coronel
Isidoro Suárez (Borges poem,
1954). PB, 245

Páginas de historia y de
autobiografía (anthology of
Gibbon's writings, edited by
Borges, 1961). P, 68-74

Páginas olvidadas (Evaristo
Carriego, the poet's grandfather, 1895). OC, 113

Pago (Silva Valdés poem in
*Poemas nativos*). TE, 90

Pagodas seniles, Las (Anglada
(Borges poem in *El otro, el
mismo*). OC, 857

Pain, Sex and Time: a New
Hypothesis of Evolution
(Heard essay, 1939). OC,
277-79

País de los ciegos. See The
Country of the Blind

Paisano Aguilar, El (Amorim
novel, 1934). PB, 134

Pájaros británicos (Hudson:
perhaps *Birds in a Village*,
1893). OCC, 839

Pájaros en Londres. See Birds
in London

Palabra del Buda, La
(Dragonetti, 1971). OCC,
780

Palabras a Pegaso (Anglada
manifesto, 1917). OCC, 48n.

Palais Nomades (Gustave Kahn,
1887). OC, 691. PB, 141

Pall Mall Gazette (literary
periodical founded in 1865
by Frederick Greenwood).
OC, 692

Palmeirim de Inglaterra
(Portuguese chivalric romance
by Francisco de Moraes,
written c.1544, published
in 1567, translated into

Pesadilla. See Nightmare
Peter Wilkins, The Life and
   Adventures of (Paltock
   romance, 1751). OCC, 710
Petit Larousse (short French
   dictionary and encyclopedia,
   first issued in 1924). OC,
   122
Petit Vaudois. OCC, 331
Petrified Forest (Mayo film,
   1936). BC, 41-42
Phaedo (Plato dialogue on
   Socrates's last conversations
   and death). BO, 29. OP,
   472
Phaedrus (Plato dialogue).
   OC, 215n., 713
Pharsalia (Lucan's Bellum
   Civile, a history of the
   Roman civil conflicts between
   Caesar and Pompey). OC,
   667. OCC, 573, 593, 594,
   669. NED, 103. P, 36,
   174. PB, 185
Philologus Hebraeo-Graecus
   generalis (Leusden
   dictionary, 1670). OC, 502
Philosophie au moyen age, La
   (Gilson, 1922). OC, 775
Philosophie de Platon, La
   (Fouillée study, 1869). OC,
   367
Philosophie der Bibel (Deussen,
   part of his Allgemeine
   Geschichte der Philosophie).
   P, 70
Philosophie der Erlosung
   (Mainlander work on the will
   to annihilation, 2 vols.,
   1876-1886). OC, 702
Philosophie der Griechen
   (Deussen, part of his
   Allgemeine Geschichte der
   Philosophie). OC, 367, 392
Philosophie des Mittelalters
   (Deussen, part of his
   Allgemeine Geschichte der
   Philosophie). OC, 367
Philosophy of Composition, The
   (Poe essay on "The Raven,"
   1846). OC, 1143. BO, 70.
   IA, 16-17. ILN, 18-20.
   OP, 419. P, 137, 167, 168
Philosophy of Style (Spencer
   essay, 1852). PB, 171

Phoenix, The (Old English poem
   in the Exeter Book). OCC,
   892
Photodramatist, The (film
   magazine, published in Los
   Angeles). BC, 46
Physiologus Graecus (Greek
   bestiary, some fifty fabulous
   anecdotes of natural
   history). OCC, 703-4, 711,
   713, 891
Pickwick Papers (The
   Posthumous Papers of the
   Pickwick Club, Dickens
   humorous sketches, 1836-37).
   OC, 733. OCC, 835
Picture of Dorian Gray, The
   (Wilde novel, 1891). OC,
   407, 691. OCC, 846, 977.
   A, 68
Piedra lunar. See The
   Moonstone
Piedras de Venecia. See The
   Stones of Venice
Piedras liminares (Lugones
   patriotic essays, 1910).
   OCC, 485
Pierre Menard, autor del
   "Quijote" (Borges story,
   1939). OC, 429
Pierrot negro, El (Lugones
   pantomime in the Lunario
   sentimental). OCC, 475
Piers Plowman, The Vision
   Concerning (Langland poem,
   c. 1360-1399). OC, 380.
   OCC, 813
Pilgrim's Progress from this
   World to that which is to
   come, The (Bunyan allegory,
   1678 and 1684). OC, 671,
   696. BC, 41. ILN, 44
Pilgrim, The (Chaplin film,
   1923). BC, 55
Pinta brava (Canaro tango-
   milonga, 1912). IA, 137
Pintores modernos. See Modern
   Painters
Pintura moderna. See Modern
   Painting
Pipa de Kif, La (Valle-Inclán
   poems, 1919). OCC, 461, 501
Pis-cuna (Formento book, 1929,
   an imitation of Anglada's Veo
   y meo). OCC, 49

Rainbow, The (Lawrence novel, 1915). OCC, 852

Ralph 124 C 4 (Gernsback science fiction novel, 1950). ILN, 58

Ramayana (Hindu sacred book). OC, 668. OCC, 634

Rana viajera, La (Camba humorous articles, 1920). OCC, 428

Rancho, El (Silva Valdés poem). I, 62, 63

Rats in the Wall (Lovecraft story). ILN, 59

Raven, The (Poe poem, 1845). BO, 69–70. ILN, 18–19

Razón, La (Buenos Aires afternoon newspaper). OCC, 25

Razón, La (Uruguayan newspaper). LA, 157

Rebusco de aragonesismos en algunos folletos de J. Cejador y Frauca (Bonfanti). OCC, 75

Rebusco en torno a las composiciones que por lo común se atribuyen a Maese Pedro Zúñiga, apodado asimismo el Molinero (Puga y Calsanz). OCC, 447, 451

Recado para don Martiniano Leguizamón (Clodomiro Ruiz's first book). OCC, 429

Recherche de l'absolu, La (Balzac philosophical novel, 1834). OCC, 311

Recuerdo de Año Nuevo, Un (Reyes essay in Reloj de sol). IA, 128

Recuerdos de provincia (Sarmiento autobiography, 1850). P, 129–33

Recuillement (Baudelaire sonnet, 1861). NED, 136n.

Red Badge of Courage, The (Crane novel, 1895). ILN, 33–34

Red Harvest (Hammett novel, 1929). ILN, 57

Red Planet (Heinlein science fiction, 1949). ILN, 59

Red Pony, The (Steinbeck short novel, 1937). ILN, 49

Reden an die deutsche Nation (Fichte nationalist treatise, 1808). OC, 725

Refalosa, La (Ascasubi poem in Paulino Lucero). OC, 185. OCC, 392, 536. P, 21, 82

Reflexiones (Marcus Aurelius autobiography, English title Meditations). OC, 395, 396

Reforma educacional, La (Lugones book on Argentine school reform, 1903). OCC, 488

Regalo, El (Lugones poem in Romances del Río Seco). OCC, 482

Reim in seiner Entwicklung und Fortbildung, Der (Mehring treatise on rhyme, 1891). P, 78

Reina Cristina. See Queen Christina

Relatos de lo grotesco. See Tales of the Grotesque and Arabesque

Religio medici (Browne religious work, 1642). OC, 393, 650, 704, 716, 1101. OCC, 823, 948. I, 33. OP, 381

Religión cristiana en la providencia divina. See Vera Christiana Religio

Religion des Buddha, Die (Koeppen, 1857). OC, 742

Religion egyptienne, La (Vandier study, 1944). OC, 750

Religion innehalb der Grenzen der blossen Vernunft (Kant's Religion within the Boundaries of Pure Reason, 1793). OC, 702n.

Religious Speeches (Shaw, 1965). OCC, 770

Reliques of Ancient English Poetry (Percy anthology of ballads and other poems, 1765). P, 148

Reloj de sol (Reyes book of short essays, 1926, the fifth series of Simpatías y diferencias). OC, 692n. IA, 124–31

Reposorio (Lugones, section of Las montañas de oro). OCC, 470

Representative Men (Emerson essays on Plato, Swedenborg,

Roughing It (Twain memoir of
life in California, 1872).
PB, 122
Rubaiyat of Omar Khayyam
(FitzGerald translation,
1859).   OC, 403, 689, 690,
993.   OCC, 842.   I, 128,
129.   P, 47.   PB, 122,
231
Ruedas del azar.   See The
Wheels of Chance
Ruin, The (Old English poem in
the *Exeter Book*).   OCC, 811,
877-78
Ruinas circulares, Las (Borges
story, 1940).   OC, 429, 464,
857
Ruiz, el cantor de las colonias
(Savastano doctoral disserta-
tion, 1971).   OCC, 432n.
Runes on Weland's Sword, The
(Kipling poem).   OCC, 846
Ruodlieb (Latin poem about the
fabulous adventures of a
young man named Ruodlieb,
written c.1030-1050 by a monk
of Tegernsee).   OCC, 906
Sabotage (Hitchcock film,
1937).   BC, 51-53
Sabueso de los Baskerville.
See Hound of the Baskervilles
Sacred Books of the East (vast
collection edited by Max
Muller, published by Oxford
in the late 19th century).
OC, 277.   PB, 195
Sacred Fount, The (James novel,
1901).   OC, 351.   P, 101
Sacred Scriptures of the
Japanese (Wheeler, 1952).
OCC, 675
Saemundar Edda.   See Elder Edda
Saga del Padre Brown.   See The
Father Brown Stories
Saga Library, The (Morris and
Magnusson collection, 1892).
OCC, 844
Saga of Billy the Kid (Burns
biography, 1925).   OC, 345
Sagas (Icelandic prose
narratives).   OCC, 563, 862,
887, 932-42, 963, 975.   BO,
59.   LA, 139, 142.   PB,
191n., 199n.
Sagrada Escritura.   See Biblia

Sagrada cripta de Pombo, La
(Gómez de la Serna
miscellany).   I, 124-26
Sailing to Byzantium (Yeats
poems in *The Tower*, 1928).
OC, 378, 718n.
Saint Joan (Shaw play, 1924).
TE, 99-102
St. Simeon Stylites (Tennyson
poem).   P, 165.   PB, 156
Saison en enfer, Une (Rimbaud
work, mixture of poetry and
prose, 1873).   OCC, 475
Salad of Colonel Cray, The
(Chesterton story in *The
Wisdom of Father Brown*).
PB, 141
Salammbo (Flaubert novel about
ancient Carthage, 1862).
OC, 55, 265, 412, 448.   P,
141.   PB, 186.   VA, 15
Salmo pluvial (Lugones poem in
*El libro de los paisajes*).
OCC, 479
Salmos or Psalmos (Biblical
psalms).   OC, 301, 395, 915,
976.   OCC, 680, 801, 824,
907.   I, 69.   OP, 365.
PB, 171.   TE, 78
Salmos del combate (Lugones
poem in *Las montañas de oro*).
OCC, 470
Salomé (Wilde play, written in
French, 1893).   TE, 134
Salomón y Saturno.   See
Solomon and Saturn
Salud no, ignorancia (Unamuno
sonnet).   PB, 149
Salut au monde (Whitman poem,
1856).   OC, 253.   ILN, 25
Salutación a Enbeita (Lugones
poem in *Poemas solariegos*).
OCC, 482
Samson Agonistes (Milton
dramatic poem, 1671).   OC,
701, 745n.   OCC, 588.
CONJ, 47.   PB, 161.   SN,
155, 156
Samuel (two books in Bible,
sometimes called *Reyes*).
NED, 144.   PB, 180
Sanctuary (Faulkner novel,
1931).   ILN, 36
Sanhedrin (book of the
*Talmud*).   OCC, 637

Sur, El (Borges story, 1953).
OC, 483. PB, 246

Suspiro, El (Herrera y Reissig
poem in *Los parques
abandonados*, 1909). TE, 55

Svarfdoela Saga (Icelandic
saga of ghosts and
*berserker*). OCC, 940

Sverris Saga (Karl Jónsson's
saga in which he tells of the
life of his friend Sverrir,
c.1200). OCC, 958

Swedenborg; or, The Mystic
(Emerson essay in
*Representative Men*). BO,
46, 57

Sweet Bird of Youth, The
(Williams play, 1959). ILN,
55

Swinburne as Poet (Eliot
essay, 1920). PB, 156

Switch on the Night (Bradbury
science fiction, 1955).
ILN, 60

Sylvie and Bruno (Lewis
Carroll narrative, 1889 and
1893). OCC, 838. P, 110.
SN, 70

Symbolic Logic (Dodgson,
1892). P, 108

Symphony in Yellow (Wilde
poem, 1889). OC, 691

System of Logic (Mill
treatise, 1843). OC, 245,
388, 650

Taba, La (Silva Valdés poem in
*Poemas nativos*). TE, 89

Tabaré (Zorrilla de San
Martín epic poem, 1888).
OC, 1069. TE, 60

Tablada, La (tango by Francisco
Canaro). OC, 159, 165

Tablas de Sangre (Rivera
Indarte book on Rosas, 1843).
LA, 11

Tahafut-ul-falasifa. See
Destrucción de filósofos

Tahafut-ul-Tahafut. See
Destrucción de la destrucción

T'ai P'ing Kuang Chi (Li Fang's
Chinese encyclopedia of
biography and other information, c.990). OCC, 629-30

Taita del arrabal (tango by
Luis Bayón Herrera). TE, 71

Tal vez (Loomis posthumous
work). OCC, 321, 322

Tale of a Tub, A (Swift
satirical work, 1696). P,
32-33

Tales of Old Japan (Mitford,
1871). OC, 345

Tales of the Grotesque and
the Arabesque (Poe, 1840).
OCC, 495. P, 27

Tales of the Hasidim. See Die
chassidischen Buchen

Talismán de la dicha (Lugones
story in *Filosofícula*).
OCC, 496

Talmud (body of Jewish laws).
OCC, 613, 616, 637, 661

Tamaño del espacio, El
(Lugones lecture on astronomy in 1921). OCC, 495

Tamburlaine (Marlowe play,
1590). OC, 803, 1140.
OP, 368, 416

Tango (Guiraldes poem in *El
cencerro de cristal*). IA,
117

Tango, El (Camino poem in
*Chaquiras*, 1926). IA, 115

Tanka (brief Japanese poems).
OCC, 775

Tantras (late Buddhist
writings). OCC, 752-53,
769

Tao Te King (Lao Tse religious
work, c.300 B.C.). OC, 439.
OCC, 114, 115, 117, 589, 634.
A, 80

Tapera, La (Regules poem in
*Versos criollos*). OC, 1039.
LA, 10

Tarde, La (Lugones poem in *Las
horas doradas*). OCC, 480

Tarde clara, La (Lugones poem
in *El libro de los paisajes*).
OCC, 479

Tarde con Ramón Bonavena, Una
(Bustos Domecq). OCC, 348n.

Tardes de topacio, Las
(Nierenstein Souza, 1908).
OCC, 311

Tatler, The (a 20th century
British periodical, not to be
confused with the one edited
by Steele from 1709-1711).
OC, 464. OCC, 334

Trabajos de Persiles y
Segismunda. See Persiles y
Segismunda
Trabajos y los días (Hesiod's
Works and Days, poem on the
virtues of work). OC, 619
Tradition and the Individual
Talent (Eliot essay). OC,
712n.
Tragedia de Louis Pasteur. See
Story of Louis Pasteur
Trahison des clercs, La (Benda
work on religion, 1927).
OC, 449
Traité des sensations
(Condillac philosophical
treatise, 1754). OCC, 581
Traspatio, El (Lugones poem in
Poemas solariegos). OCC,
482
Tratado (Nagarjuna treatise, a
fundamental work of Mahayana
Buddhism). OCC, 758-59
Tratado del amor conyugal
(Swedenborg, 1768, perhaps
his Treatise on the Nature of
the Influx). P, 159
Tratado del epíteto (Feijoo).
OCC, 336
Trau keinem Fuchs aut gruener
Heid und keinem Jud bei
seinem Eid (Nazi children's
book, 1936). PB, 155-56
Traum, Ein (Borges poem in La
moneda de hierro). OP, 470,
500, 508
Travels into Several Remote
Nations of the World. See
Gulliver's Travels
Traviata, La (Verdi opera,
1853). OCC, 327
Treasure Island (Stevenson
romance, 1883). OC, 101,
826. OCC, 845. PB, 172
Treatise of Human Nature (Hume
philosophical work, 1739-40).
OC, 760, 768
Tree of Knowledge, The (James
story). ILN, 39
Tree of Night, The (Capote
collection of stories, 1949).
ILN, 51
Treinta etimologías de Gaucho
(chapter in Costa Alvarez
book, El castellano en la
Argentina, 1928). OCC, 514

Treinta y tres orientales, Los
(Blanes painting). OCC, 528
Treintanueve escalones. See
The Thirty-Nine Steps
Tren expreso, El (Girondo poem
in Calcomanías). TE, 94
Tres besos, Los (Lugones fairy
tale play in Lunario
sentimental). OCC, 475
Tres comedias para puritanos.
See Three Plays for Puritans
Tres gauchos orientales
(Lussich poem, 1872). OC,
188. OCC, 522, 532n. P, 92
Tres kasidas, Las (Lugones
poem in Romancero). OCC,
481
Tres versiones de Judas
(Borges essay, 1944). OC,
483
Trésor (Latini encyclopedia in
eight books, c.1260). OCC,
573
Tribuna, La (Buenos Aires
newspaper published from
1853 to 1884 by the Varelas).
OC, 188. OCC, 522. I, 55
Trillo del Diavolo (Tartini
musical composition). OC,
642
Tripitaka (Pali religious
treatises). OCC, 766
Tristram (E. A. Robinson
dramatic narrative in blank
verse, 1927). ILN, 46
Tristan (Gottfried von
Strassburg poem in Middle
High German, c.1210, on the
legend of Tristan and
Isolde). OCC, 908
Tristeza del fauno, La
(Vilaseco poem, 1909). OCC,
347
Tristram Shandy, The Life and
Opinions of (Sterne novel,
1760-1767). I, 21
Triumph of Time, The (Swin-
burne poem). PB, 156, 157
Trobos de Paulino Lucero.
See Paulino Lucero
Troilus and Cressida
(Shakespeare play, c.1602).
PB, 162
Trois Mousquetaires, Les
(Dumas novel, 1844). NED,
121n. P, 41

# Index of Places

Africa (continent). OC, 66,
401-2, 411, 587, 697, 755,
1073.   OCC, 328, 573, 656,
679, 829, 848, 935, 938, 959.
A, 62.   ILN, 37.   P, 141.
PB, 191.   SN, 18, 63
Africa del Sur (Union of South
Africa).   OCC, 41, 46, 649.
ILN, 30.   PB, 241
Agraciada, La (town in
western Uruguay).   LA, 155
Agrigento (Agrigentum, ancient
port city in Sicily).   OC,
636, 661.   OCC, 690, 740.
C, 41.   P, 120.   SN, 88
Aguero (street in Buenos
Aires).   OC, 110.   OCC, 360
Ahura Mazdah.   See Ormuz
Aix-Les-Bains (town in France
on Lake Bourget, south of
Geneva).   OCC, 381
Ako (town in Japan west of
Osaka).   OC, 320, 321
Aksa (mosque in Jerusalem).
OP, 463
Al-Andalus.   See Andalucía
Alabama (state in United
States).   C, 33
Alahabad.   See Allahabad
Alamein, El (town in Egypt
west of Alexandria).   OC,
580
Alamo (building in San Antonio,
Texas, site of battle in
1836).   OC, 853, 901
Alamos, Los (ranch in Borges
story).   OC, 1068-72.   HE,
59, 70
Alaska (state in United
States).   ILN, 29, 57, 63
Albany (capital of state of
New York).   ILN, 28.   P,
81
Albert (town in northern
France near Amiens).   OC,
480
Albert Memorial (auditorium in
London).   P, 35
Alberuela (town in Spain).
OCC, 448, 451
Alcazarquivir (city in Morocco,
now Ksar el Kebir, where the
Portuguese king Sebastiao
died in battle in 1578).
OC, 831.   P, 165.   PB, 240

Alcana (market in Toledo where
Cervantes acquired the
manuscript of Cide Hamete
Benengeli).   C, 15
Alcázar de Fuego (underground
castle in Beckford's *Vathek*).
OC, 730, 731.   NED, 95.
PB, 181
Alejandría (Alexandria, port
city in Egypt).   OC, 213,
216, 285, 514, 533, 586, 713,
809, 1004.   OCC, 296, 579,
682, 711, 771, 828.   A, 11.
BC, 67.   BO, 13.   LA, 60.
OP, 513-14, 519.   P, 15.
SN, 61, 126
Alem, Leandro (street in Buenos
Aires, formerly the Paseo de
Julio).   OCC, 106, 282
Alemania (Germany).   OC, 279-
80, 302, 315, 371, 411, 412,
413, 472, 473,   558, 576,
577, 580, 581, 629, 668, 684,
695, 723, 725, 727-28, 754,
937, 991, 1116.   OCC, 463,
574, 613, 616, 624, 661, 708,
787, 826, 831, 832, 834, 835,
855, 865, 871, 874, 885, 887,
899-921, 923, 924, 930, 948,
952, 953, 958. 959, 974, 975.
A, 35, 46.   BC, 27, 55, 60,
65, 70.   BO, 20, 56, 58.
C, 23, 75.   I, 18, 146,
147.   IA, 159.   ILN, 15,
20, 23, 34, 38, 49.   LA, 14,
30, 179.   NED, 95.   OP,
392-93, 432.   P, 9, 32, 36,
37, 77, 100, 104, 105, 112,
140, 150, 159.   PB, 155-56,
158-60, 161, 173, 174, 189,
191, 229, 230, 232.   SN,
73, 117, 121, 128, 150, 159.
TE, 31
Alepo (Aleppo, city in northwestern Syria, now Halab).
OC, 1083.   OP, 367.   P, 145
Alfeo (Alpheus, largest river
in the Peloponnesus in
Greece).   OCC, 707
Alhama (town of southern
Spain, mentioned in the
*Romancero*).   IA, 56
Alhambra (Moorish palace and
fortress in Granada).   ILN,
15.   OP, 515

flows into the Somme at
Amiens). OC, 473

Andalucía or Al–Andalus
(region of southern Spain).
OC, 336, 337, 421, 583,654,
933. CONJ, 81. TE, 76

Andes (highest mountains in
South America, sometimes
called the Cordillera). OC,
24. OCC, 381. OP, 384,
536. P, 138. PB, 130

Andes, calle de los (street in
Buenos Aires). OP, 536

Andes, Universidad de los
(university in Bogotá). LA,
27

Angaco (site of a battle in
1841 between Mariano Acha
and Aldao). PB, 132, 152

Angeln (region of northern
Germany on the Danish
border). OCC, 787

Aniquilación (place in
allegorical poem by Farid
ud-din Attar). OCC, 695.
NED, 142. PB, 179

Annam (state in eastern
India). OC, 306. OCC,
701

Antártida (Antarctica). OC,
229. OCC, 318, 710. SN, 114

Antártidas, Islas (islands off
of the Antarctic Peninsula,
claimed by Argentina). OCC,
578

Antelo (place in Argentine
countryside). OP, 439

Antillas (Antilles). OC, 295.
OCC, 573

Antioquía (ancient Antioch in
Asia Minor, now Antakia).
OC, 213

Apulia (area in southern
Italy). CONJ, 37

Aqueronte (river in Hades).
OC, 790. OCC, 669. NED,
132, 139. PB, 177

Aquilea (city in Italy
destroyed by Attila in 452).
OC, 550, 554, 555

Aquitania (Aquitaine, ancient
province of France). OC,
253, 836. OCC, 919–20.
C, 31. PB, 189

Arabia (now Saudi Arabia).
OC, 401, 402, 587, 607.

OCC, 587, 590, 621, 653, 655,
729, 843, 852, 855, 892, 892,
948, 960. CONJ, 79. P,
34, 68, 73, 164n. PB, 190,
215. SN, 52, 65, 67, 72,
128

Arábigo, Golfo (Red Sea).
OC, 535

Aragón (region of northern
Spain, formerly a separate
kingdom). OCC, 87

Araoz (street in Buenos Aires).
OC, 590

Arapey (town in Uruguay north
of Salto). PB, 117

Arbela (town in Mesopotamia
near Nineveh, now called
Arbil, where Alexander the
Great fought a battle). A,
53. SN, 58

Arbol de la Ciencia (Tree of
Knowledge in Garden of Eden,
sometimes called the "Arbol
del Bien y del Mal"). OCC,
695, 879

Arbol de la Iluminación (Tree
of Enlightenment of Buddhist
legend, sometimes called
"Arbol del Conocimiento").
OCC, 723, 744

Arbol del Bien y del Mal. See
Arbol de la Ciencia

Arbol del Conocimiento. See
Arbol de la Iluminación

Arbol del Zobar. See Zobar

Archivo General de la Nación
(Argentine national archives,
in Buenos Aires). OC, 1049

Areco. See San Antonio de Areco

Arena, Mar de (one of the
marvels in the legend of
Prester John). OCC, 690

Arenales (street in Buenos
Aires). OC, 128. SN, 44.
TE, 44

Arenranguá (river in Uruguay
near which Dorrego was
defeated by Artigas). PB,
132

Arequipa (city in southern
Peru). OC, 1048

Arequito (town in Argentina,
in the province of Santa Fe).
P, 138

Arezzo (city and province in
Italy). OCC, 685

Atlántida (Atlantis). OCC,
682
Atlas (mountain in north
Africa). OC, 534
Atsuta (city in northern Japan
near Sapporo). OCC, 675
Austerlitz (town in
Czechoslovakia, known in
Czech as Slavkov, site of an
important battlefield in 1805
between Napoleon and the
Austrian-Russian alliance).
OC, 1113. OP, 387
Austin (capital of Texas).
OC, 9, 1138. OCC, 975.
C, 77. ILN, 33. LA, 67,
137. OP, 445. PB, 246
Australia. OC, 230, 301, 304,
750. OCC, 527, 852, 856.
VA, 36
Austria. OCC, 708, 907, 910,
911, 916. BO, 56. I,
147. SN, 39
Austria (street in Buenos
Aires). OC, 110
Austria-Hungría (Hapsburg
empire from 1867 to 1918,
also called the "Imperios
Centrales"). A, 46. BC,
36. P, 103
Avellaneda (industrial suburb
of Buenos Aires). OC,
128n., 133. OCC, 42, 51,
52, 56, 76, 78, 149, 160,
165, 320, 399
Avenida de Mayo (street in
Buenos Aires). OCC 349,
406. IA, 105
Aventino (one of the seven
hills of Rome). OC, 555
Averno (lake in Italy, an
entrance to hell in Roman
mythology and literature).
OC, 909, 925. NED, 95.
P, 71, 162. PB, 181
Avignon (city in Provence in
southern France). OCC, 646
Awomori (place in Japan).
OCC, 651
Axa (river whose delta marks
one of the borders of Uqbar).
OC, 432
Axum (city and former capital
of Ethiopia). OC, 411
Ayacucho (city in Peru, site
of decisive battle of wars

of independence in 1824,
formerly called Huamanga).
OC, 162, 191, 797, 1048.
OCC, 530
Ayacucho (street in Buenos
Aires). OCC, 424
Ayacucho (town in the province
of Buenos Aires). P, 93.
PB, 231
Azagouc (imaginary city in the
*Nibelungenlied*). OCC, 915
Azov (sea of Azov in the
Soviet Union). LA, 117
Azul (city in the province of
Buenos Aires). OCC, 240,
530
Babel (Tower of Babel in the
Bible). OC, 601, 875. I,
137. OP, 552
Babia. OCC, 405
Babilonia (ancient Babylon).
OC, 317, 456-60, 490, 607,
639, 692n., 702. OCC, 613,
642, 652, 822, 908. A, 52.
SN, 58
Bactria (ancient Greek kingdom
in central Asia, the capital
of which is now the city of
Balkh in Afghanistan). OC,
758n. OCC, 639, 746.
PB, 195. SN, 59, 64
Bagdad (Baghdad, capital of
Iraq). OC, 582. SN, 60, 73
Bagé (town in Rio Grande do
Sul, Brazil). OC, 564
Bahia (state in northeastern
Brazil). OCC, 51
Bahía Blanca (port city in
southern part of the province
of Buenos Aires). LA, 128.
VA, 48
Bajo (avenue along edge of
port in Buenos Aires). OC,
124n., 805-6, 1029. IA,
112, 117, 121, 168
Bajo Rhin (lower part of Rhine
valley). OCC, 900n.
Baker Street (street in London,
famous as the residence of
Sherlock Holmes). CONJ, 49
Balcarce (street in Buenos
Aires). OC, 128. OCC, 140.
SN, 44
Baleares (Balearic Isles in
Spain, Mallorca, Menorca and
Ibiza). OCC, 37

584, 625, 824, 1139.   OCC,
299.   A, 47.   CONJ, 23.
OP, 415
Bengala, Golfo de   (Bay of
Bengal).   BC, 54
Beocia   (Boeotia, region of
ancient Greece).   OCC, 15
Berazategui   (town between
Buenos Aires and La Plata).
OCC, 86, 134, 392, 397.
HE, 61, 70
Berenice   (ancient seaport on
Red Sea in Egypt).   OC, 533,
554
Bergen   (city in Norway).
OCC, 653
Berisso   (port town near La
Plata and Ensenada).   ILN,
52
Berlin   (city in Germany).
OC, 473, 480.   OCC, 193,
974.   NED, 115.   P, 77,
103.   PB, 174
Bermejo   (street in Buenos
Aires).   OC, 90.   OP, 536
Bermudas   (Bermuda).   ILN, 9
Berna   (Berne, city in
Switzerland).   A, 35.
CONJ, 38, 67
Bernardo de Irigoyen.   See
Irigoyen, Bernardo de
Beruti   (street in Buenos
Aires).   OC, 110
Bhuj   (city in India near
Bombay, sacred to the snake-
god Bhujanga).   OC, 593
Biarmaland   (old Norse name for
the Urals).   PB, 191
Bienaventuradas, Islas
(Fortunate Isles of Greco-
Roman mythology, sometimes
identified with the Canary
Islands or Madeira).   OCC,
843.   SN, 29
Biblioteca Episcopal   (in
Alicante).   OCC, 450
Biblioteca Nacional   (Argentine
national library in Buenos
Aires, on México street).
OC, 779, 809–10, 1009, 1049,
1107.   OCC, 357, 423, 459.
A, 54.   BO, 59.   LA, 36,
175.   SN, 145–47
Biblioteca de Alejandría
(ancient library at
Alexandria).   OCC, 682.

BO, 13.   LA, 60.   OP,
513–14
Biblioteca del Vaticano
(Vatican library).   OCC, 903
Bikanir   (city in Rajasthan,
India).   OC, 416, 542, 543.
LA, 170
Birmania   (Burma).   OCC, 309
Bizancio.   See Constantinopla
Bjarg   (town in northwestern
Iceland).   OCC, 934.   PB,
191
Blaaland   (old Norse name for
Ethiopia).   PB, 191.   VA,
28
Blanco Encalada   (street in
Buenos Aires).   OC, 134n.
Boca   (Italian neighborhood in
Buenos Aires).   OC, 81,
125n., 159, 164.   OCC, 548.
IA, 113
Bodleiana   (Bodleian Library,
Oxford).   LA, 111
Boedo   (street in Buenos
Aires).   OC, 142, 150, 160,
591.   OCC, 136, 354
Bogotá   (capital of Colombia).
LA, 27
Bohemia   (region in central
Europe, now in Czecho-
slovakia).   OC, 542, 578.
C, 17.   PB, 218.   SN, 73
Bolívar   (street in Buenos
Aires).   OC, 1009, 1034.
OP, 455
Bolivia   (country).   OCC, 41,
43, 331.   IA, 155.   LA,
44.   P, 17
Bollini   (street in Buenos
Aires).   OC, 149.   A, 26
Bombay   (city in India).   OC,
414, 416, 542.   OCC, 586,
846.   I, 46.   LA, 170
Borgarfjord   (fjord in eastern
Iceland).   OC, 755
Borgoña   (Burgundy or Bourgogne,
region of France).   OCC,
919.   PB, 199
Borneo   (large island in south-
west Pacific).   OCC, 600,
672.   OP, 544
Bosch   (hospital in Buenos
Aires).   OC, 594
Bósforo   (Bosphorus, strait in
Istanbul dividing Europe and
Asia).   A, 18

Bosque del Sur.   OCC, 185
Boston   (capital of the state
of Massachusetts).   OC, 684,
1053.   OCC, 974.   BO, 65,
70.   ILN, 10, 12, 13, 16,
18, 21, 49.   LA, 9, 138.
PB, 231.   SN, 156
Boulogne Sur Mer   (Argentine
town, suburb of Buenos Aires,
named for city in France
where San Martín died).
OCC, 353
Bourgogne.   See Borgoña
Bowery, The   (street and
neighborhood in New York).
OC, 315, 317
Bragado   (city in province of
Buenos Aires, sometimes
Bragao).   OC, 1070.   OCC,
240.   BC, 57   TE, 13
Brasil   (Brazil).   OC, 179,
303, 401-2, 433, 434, 491,
495, 545, 561, 563, 564, 627,
874, 1056, 1073.   OCC, 41,
46, 153, 171, 192, 309, 328,
516, 518, 526, 839.   A, 86.
BC, 69.   LA, 42, 50, 52,
55, 123, 127.   OP, 403,
477, 483.   P, 17, 92, 127,
135.   PB, 234, 244, 245.
VA, 43, 47
Brasil   (street in Buenos
Aires).   OC, 526
Bremen   (city in West Germany).
OCC, 32, 155.   C, 23.   LA,
111.   PB, 200
Breslau   (Wroclaw, city in
Poland).   OC, 411, 578, 593.
OP, 542
Bretaña   (Brittany, region of
France).   OC, 839, 878,
1067.   OCC, 592, 741, 787,
809, 814, 843, 868, 908n.,
920.   C, 73.   OP, 460.
PB, 238.   SN, 24
Bretland   (old Norse name for
Wales).   OCC, 959
Brighton   (city in southern
England).   OC, 414, 620
Brindisi   (city in southern
Italy).   OCC, 37
Bristol   (city in western
England).   OC, 602
Britania   (Britannia, Roman
name for British Isles).
OC, 552.   OCC, 867, 936

Británicas, Islas   (British
Isles).   OCC, 942.   P, 62.
PB, 174, 218
British Museum   (in London).
OCC, 707, 903.   LA, 54, 173
Broackway   (solecism for
Broadway in Bustos Domecq
story).   OCC, 398
Broadway   (street in New York
City).   ILN, 53
Brobdingnag   (imaginary land of
giants in the second book of
*Gulliver's Travels*).   OC,
422
Bronx   (northern borough of New
York City).   OCC, 427
Brook Farm   (Utopian community
in Massachusetts, 1841-1847).
OC, 684.   ILN, 18
Brooklyn   (borough of New York
City).   OC, 312, 1086.
ILN, 24, 44, 45, 58.   OP,
371
Bruges   (city in Belgium).
OCC, 323
Brunanburh   (site of battle in
937 between Aethelstan and
the Northmen).   OC, 377,
906.   OCC, 870, 885-86, 895,
937.   OP, 448, 466
Bruselas   (Brussels, capital of
Belgium).   OC, 630, 708.
C, 19.   IA, 155
Bucarelli   (street in Buenos
Aires).   OCC, 31
Buen Orden, cine.   See Select
Buen Orden
Buen Orden   (street in Buenos
Aires).   OC, 1050.   IA,
162
Buenos Aires   (capital city of
Argentina).   OC, 13, 17, 22,
32, 38, 55, 57, 63, 79, 81,
86, 90, 91, 101, 103, 105,
109, 112, 114, 128, 133,
134n., 139, 142, 158, 159,
164, 165, 177, 179, 186, 188,
268, 269, 270-71, 289, 421,
431, 483, 487, 514, 525, 526,
545, 546, 559, 561, 589, 612,
630, 635, 653, 654, 707, 727,
735, 793, 808, 857, 860, 862,
863, 922, 931, 933, 946, 947,
975, 982, 995, 1009-10, 1017,
1027, 1029, 1042, 1046, 1048,
1050, 1053, 1054, 1056, 1062,

1063, 1066, 1068, 1069, 1070,
1071, 1075, 1126, 1136, 1143,
1144, 1145.   OCC, 15, 16,
19, 21, 29, 43, 46, 47, 71,
80, 87, 102, 107, 114, 118,
149, 161, 171, 348, 376, 377,
382, 384, 399, 405, 413, 421,
422, 428, 459, 463, 466, 468,
471, 513, 514, 515, 520, 525,
526, 527, 558, 565, 612, 522,
528, 780, 781, 788, 807, 862,
948, 977.   A, 26, 38, 54,
57-58, 64, 76, 77, 84.   BC,
52-53, 54, 69, 79.   BO, 10,
22, 28.   C, 9, 12, 25, 35,
37, 45, 51, 77.   CONJ, 34,
95.   HE, 59, 65.   I, 26,
28, 79-83, 89, 96, 132, 138.
IA, 8, 18, 66, 103, 112, 132,
136, 147-51, 151-54, 155.
ILN, 8, 52.   LA, 14, 33,
36, 38, 39, 42, 43, 50, 51,
55, 56, 68, 69, 74, 125, 182.
OP, 366, 374, 412, 420, 470,
503, 511, 534, 536, 537, 543,
546, 547, 558.   P, 7, 9,
11, 17, 18, 22, 23, 25, 28-
29, 32, 34, 40-42, 49, 52,
54, 55, 58, 60, 61, 62, 64,
66, 68, 75-76, 77, 84, 86,
89, 91, 92, 96, 97, 112, 113,
127-28, 133, 135, 136, 142,
148, 151, 163, 167, 170,
PB, 125-37, 152, 158, 172,
174, 213, 230, 246, 247.
SN, 44, 90, 107, 148.   TE,
6, 7, 9, 16, 22, 78, 85, 105,
137, 141, 143-45.   VA, 45
Buenos Aires   (Argentine
province).   OC, 132, 150,
152, 558, 608, 735, 1025-28.
OCC, 304, 519, 525, 526, 527,
530, 552, 838.   BC, 57, 59.
C, 105.   P, 15, 31, 51, 89,
92.   PB, 122, 124.   TE, 84
Buenos Aires   (street in
Montevideo).   LA, 151
Buenos Aires, Universidad de.
OC, 805.   BO, 22.   CONJ,
95.   P, 68.   SN, 107, 149
Bulaq   (neighborhood in Cairo,
sometimes Bulak).   OC, 404,
411, 542-543
Bulgaria   (country).   OCC,
863.   PB, 218

Burdeos   (Bordeaux, city in
France).   OCC, 324.   PB,
190
Burlington   (city in New
Jersey).   ILN, 14
Burwash   (Kipling's home in
Sussex).   OCC, 847
Burzaco   (town south of Buenos
Aires near Almirante Brown
and Temperley).   OCC, 135,
137, 138, 139, 309, 369, 404.
HE, 51, 52, 57, 64, 70
Caballito   (street and
neighborhood in Buenos
Aires).   OCC, 341
Cabello   (street in Buenos
Aires).   IA, 153
Cabildo   (18th century Spanish
building on the Plaza de Mayo
in Buenos Aires).   PB, 129.
TE, 21
Cabo de Hornos   (Cape Horn).
OCC, 358.   P, 90
Cabrera   (street in Buenos
Aires).   OC, 863, 1035, 1070
Cachueta   (Turkish baths).
OCC, 173
Cádiz   (port city in southern
Spain).   OCC, 822.   P, 44
Caen   (city in Normandy,
France).   OC, 262
Café Procope.   OCC, 323
Café Tortoni   (old cafe and
restaurant near the Plaza de
Mayo in Buenos Aires).   OCC,
349, 350
Café del Globo (in Montevideo).
LA, 151
Cagancha   (site of battle in
Uruguay in 1839 between the
Uruguayan forces of Rivera
and the army of Juan Manuel
de Rosas).   OC, 184, 573,
968
Cahors   (city in south central
France).   OCC, 920
Cairo   (capital of Egypt).
OC, 338, 398, 400, 402, 582,
627.   A, 54.   SN, 61, 65,
70.   TE, 65
Cairo   (city in Illinois).
OC, 298
Calcuta   (Calcutta, city in
India).   OC, 407, 414, 416,
418

Caldea (lower region of
Mesopotamia). C, 53. OP,
374, 463, 523, 552, 555
Caledonia, La (ranch in Borges
story "El Congreso"). LA,
48-52, 57, 61
Cali (city in Colombia).
OCC, 336
California (state in United
States). OC, 250, 317, 318,
1136. OCC, 845. A, 32.
BC, 36, 62. HE, 52. ILN,
27, 29, 30, 44, 46, 49, 50,
53, 54, 57. OP, 478. P,
17, 81-83. PB, 246
California, La. OCC, 195
California, University of
(here, university campus in
Berkeley, California). ILN,
29
Callao (street in Buenos
Aires). I, 5. TE, 22
Calle 68 (street in La Plata).
OCC, 428
Calvo, Carlos (street in
Buenos Aires). SN, 11
Cámara de los Comunes (House
of Commons in British
Parliament). P, 72
Camargo (street in Buenos
Aires). IA, 88
Cambridge (city in England,
site of Cambridge
University). OC, 264, 718.
OCC, 826, 841, 842, 906, 931,
954n., 974, 975. P, 69.
PB, 201. SN, 154
Cambridge (city in
Massachusetts, site of
Harvard University). OC,
980-81. ILN, 44. LA, 9,
11, 16. PB, 246
Camden (city in New Jersey
where Whitman lived). OC,
913. ILN, 24
Camden (city in Ohio). ILN,
34
Camino de las Tropas (former
name of Avenida Sáenz, street
in Buenos Aires). OC,
1028. LA, 69
Campaldino (site of battle
between Florence and Arezzo
in 1289 in which Dante took
part). OCC, 902

Campania (region of southern
Italy). OC, 228n. OCC,
696
Campos Eliseos (Elysian Fields
of classical mythology).
NED, 100. P, 71. PB,
184. SN, 40-41
Canadá (country). OC, 1053,
1056. OCC, 399. A, 11-
12. ILN, 16, 24, 36, 59.
LA, 127. NED, 118
Cañada de Gómez (town in
province of Santa Fe near
Rosario). OCC, 526
Cancha Rayada (site of battle
in Chile in 1818 in which San
Martín was defeated by the
Spanish forces). OC, 1048
Candelaria (street in Buenos
Aires). IA, 132
Canelones (city in Uruguay
near Montevideo). OC, 734
Cangallo (city in Peru near
Ayacucho). OCC, 85
Cannebiere. OC, 446
Canning (street in Buenos
Aires). OC, 82, 108
Canterbury (cathedral city in
southern England). OC, 587.
OCC, 816, 817, 964. NED,
105
Canton (city in China). OC,
585. OCC, 580
Canudos (settlement in state
of Bahia in northeastern
Brazil where António Maciel
the "Conselheiro" lived with
his followers). OC, 516n.
Cañuelas (town in province of
Buenos Aires). OCC, 134,
240, 418, 419
Caos (chaos, the unformed
universe in Greek mythology).
OCC, 609
Capilla Sixtina (Sixtine
Chapel in Vatican). OCC, 69
Capilla Verde (the Green
Chapel in *Sir Gawain and the
Green Knight*). OCC, 814
Capital. See Buenos Aires
Capitolio (hill in Rome where
the temple of Jupiter was
located). OCC, 826. P, 70
Capurro, Hotel (hotel in
Montevideo). OCC, 312

Caraguatá (river in Uruguay).
OC, 491

Carcasona (Carcassonne, walled
city in southern France).
OC, 711

Cardiff (city in southern
Wales). OC, 602

Cardoso. See Lagunas del
Cardoso

Caribdis (Charybdis, whirlpool
in a narrow channel of the
sea, an obstacle in the
*Odyssey*). OC, 250. OCC,
299

Caribe (Caribbean Sea). OC,
306, 1062, 1065

Carmen de las Flores. OCC,
239, 240

Carouge (town in Switzerland
near Geneva). LA, 19

Cárpatos (Carpathian mountains
in central Europe). P, 103

Carrasco (street in Buenos
Aires). OCC, 70, 286

Carretas, Plaza de las. OCC,
222

Carrión (river in Old Castile
in Spain, next to which the
Cid fought a battle). P, 80

Cartagena (city in south-
eastern Spain). OCC, 595n.

Cartagena (city on Caribbean
coast of Colombia). OC,
1056, 1062

Cartago (ancient Carthage,
near Tunis). OC, 55, 235,
236, 265n., 383n., 552, 674,
812, 875, 880, 894, 983,
1063, 1091. OCC, 358, 683,
684, 962. A, 20. BO, 37.
C, 17, 43, 45. CONJ, 37-
38, 39, 43, 93. OP, 435,
522. PB, 121. SN, 119.
TE, 102

Casa Colorada (in Lomas in
Buenos Aires). LA, 67-77

Casa Rosada (Argentine
government house on the
Plaza de Mayo). P, 59. PB,
129. TE, 144

Casa del Arte. OCC, 48, 58,
62

Casa del Catequista. OCC, 86,
127

Casa del Oculista. OCC, 155

Caseros (town near Buenos
Aires, site of decisive
battle in 1853 in which Rosas
was defeated). OC, 100,
106, 623, 792, 994. OP,
491. P, 18, 93. TE, 34

Caseros (street in Buenos
Aires). OCC, 140

Casilda (town in the province
of Buenos Aires). LA, 42

Castellammare (place of origin
of Sangiácomo family, perhaps
Castellammare del Golfo in
Sicily). OCC, 64

Caspio, Mar (Caspian Sea in
Soviet Union). OC, 625

Castilla (Castile, region in
central and northern Spain).
OC, 654, 667, 823. OCC,
851. BO, 40. I, 8. IA,
18. OP, 527. PB, 128,
151, 240, 244. TE, 95, 144

Cataluña (Catalonia, region in
eastern Spain). OC, 654.
SN, 128

Catamarca (province in northern
Argentina). OCC, 38, 39,
46. LA, 92

Catamarca (street in Buenos
Aires). OCC, 114

Catedral (the cathedral in
Geneva). A, 56

Caucaso (the Caucasus, region
north of Turkey). OC, 688

Caulacau or Kaulakau (Gnostic
heaven of heavens). OC,
214, 750n.

Cavdor (Cawdor, area in
Scotland of which Macbeth was
thane). P, 145

Celeste Imperio. See China

Cementerio del Norte (in
Buenos Aires). OCC, 527

Cementerio del Oeste (in
Buenos Aires). OCC, 329

Centenario, Parque (park in
Buenos Aires). OC, 786

Centro (center of Buenos
Aires). P, 128

Centroamérica (street in
Buenos Aires, now called
Pueyrredón). OC, 107-8.
IA, 152

Cepeda (place in the province
of Buenos Aires, site of

battle in 1859 between
Urquiza and Mitre). OC, 86,
185, 186, 1048.   OCC, 520,
526.     OP, 471.     P, 28
Cercano Oriente   (Middle East).
ILN, 35, 37
Cerrito   (hill by harbor in
Montevideo).   OC, 295, 935,
965, 967.     OCC, 112, 114,
115, 129.   LA, 155.   TE,
33
Cerro Alto.   OC, 1048, 1049,
1051, 1052
Cerro Bermejo.   OC, 1048
Cerro Largo   (town in Uruguay).
OC, 629, 1058
Cerro Presidente.   OCC, 130
Cerros Blancos   (Uruguayan
battlefield).   LA, 152
Cerviño   (street in Buenos
Aires).   OC, 130
Ceuta   (Spanish city on the
coast of Morocco).   OC, 336.
SN, 29
Ceylán   (Ceylon or Sri Lanka).
LA, 70.   PB, 242
Chacabuco   (town in the
province of Buenos Aires).
OC, 792, 1048, 1070.     OCC,
50, 559.     PB, 129, 130
Chacabuco   (park in Buenos
Aires).   OCC, 316
Chacabuco   (street in Buenos
Aires).   OC, 128
Chacarita   (cementery in Buenos
Aires).   OC, 79, 90–91, 109,
160, 626, 1037.   OCC, 24,
346, 439
Chaco   (semi–arid region in
Bolivia, Paraguay and
Argentina).   OC, 789.
OCC, 357
Chacra de Pueyrredón   (home of
Juan Martín de Pueyrredón,
the hero of Argentine
independence, where José
Hernández was born).   OCC,
525
Chalons   (town in France).
OC, 161, 217
Charcas   (province in Bolivia).
CONJ, 70
Charcas   (street in Buenos
Aires).   OC, 119, 796.   A,
57.   SN, 40

Charles   (river in Boston).
OC, 980.     LA, 9, 179
Charleston   (city in North
Carolina).   ILN, 23
Charlone   (street in Buenos
Aires).   OCC, 30
Charlottenburg   (city in
Germany).   BC, 46
Charlottesville   (city in
Virginia where the University
of Virginia is located).
ILN, 57
Chartres   (cathedral city near
Paris).   C, 19
Chascomús   (city in province of
Buenos Aires).   OCC, 240.
TE, 32
Chavango   (street in Buenos
Aires).   OC, 111
Checoeslovaquia   (Czechoslo-
vakia).   OC, 723
Cheshire   (county in west
central England).   OCC, 635
Chicago   (city in Illinois).
OCC, 13.   ILN, 30, 35, 45,
47, 48, 51.     P, 130
Chihuahua   (city and state in
northern Mexico).   OC, 318
Chile   (country).   OC, 179,
301, 302, 522, 1029.     OCC,
515.     P, 131, 133, 134,
137, 138.     PB, 130, 213.
SN, 67
Chile   (street in Buenos
Aires).   OC, 128, 132n.,
146, 148, 159, 590, 1063.
A, 40.   CONJ, 83.     LA,
56.   OP, 455.   SN, 44
Chilecito   (street in Buenos
Aires).   OC, 284.   BC, 73
Chilkoot   (pass in Alaska near
Haines).   ILN, 29
China   (country, sometimes
Tsin, Imperio Central,
Celeste Imperio, Sin).   OC,
153, 283, 306–310, 413,
418n., 558, 583–85, 593, 633–
35, 679, 769, 999–1000.
OCC, 105, 118, 589, 607, 619–
20, 629–30, 632, 633, 658,
660, 672, 678, 695, 701, 705–
6, 713–14, 727, 731, 751,
761, 766–68, 772, 832, 848,
911, 948.     A, 41, 48, 58,
80.   BC, 70, 72.   C, 105.

Confitería del Aguila.   LA,
89
Confitería del Gas.   OCC,
173.   LA, 39, 43
Confitería del Molino   (cafe
in Buenos Aires).   OCC, 382,
387, 390, 391
Congo   (country).   OCC, 761
Congo Suizo   (solecism for
Belgian Congo).   LA, 127.
VA, 47
Congreso   (congress building
in Buenos Aires).   OCC, 329,
423.   BC, 54
Congreso del Mundo   (secret
world congress in Borges
story).   LA, 35–63, 180
Congreso del Uruguay
(Uruguayan congress).   LA,
43
Connaught   (county in western
Ireland).   OC, 492
Connecticut   (state in United
States).   ILN, 11, 51
Constantinopla   (Constantinople
or Istanbul, capital of
Turkey, sometimes Estambul,
Miklagard, Bizancio).   OC,
368–69, 397, 552, 755, 1133.
OCC, 690, 827, 863, 865, 938,
941, 943, 959.   A, 18.
LA, 117.   OP, 410.   P,
73.   PB, 191
Constanza   (Konstanz or
Constance, city in Germany
near Swiss border).   OCC,
905
Constitución   (train station in
Buenos Aires and the
surrounding neighborhood).
OC, 526, 527, 591, 617, 874,
1129.   OCC, 136, 137, 382,
414, 415, 428.   IA, 115,
120, 135.   NED, 96.   PB,
181–82
Contarf   (site of battle in
medieval Ireland).   LA, 101
Copacabana   (neighborhood in
Rio de Janeiro).   OCC, 286
Copenhague   (Copenhagen,
capital of Denmark).   OCC,
871, 925
Córcega   (Corsica, French
island in the Mediterranean).
OCC, 254, 829
Cordillera.   See Andes

Córdoba   (city in Argentina,
capital of the province of
Córdoba).   OC, 181, 833,
933, 1121.   OCC, 513, 565.
C, 51.   OP, 401.   P, 135.
TE, 87
Córdoba   (city in southern
Spain).   OC, 582, 583, 586,
587, 933, 937.   C, 51.
IA, 68, 123.   OP, 463.
SN, 64.   TE, 32, 129
Córdoba   (Argentine province).
OC, 132n.   OCC, 350, 520,
612.   LA, 14.
Córdoba   (street in Buenos
Aires).   OC, 525, 1124, 1129.
C, 59.   OP, 405.   P, 87
Corinto   (Corinth, city in
Greece).   OC, 658.   OCC,
605, 656.   PB, 194, 195
Cork   (city in Ireland).   OCC,
669
Cornwall   (region of western
England).   OC, 600, 604
Coronel Díaz   (street in Buenos
Aires).   OC, 108, 128, 1044.
IA, 152
Coronel Pringles.   See Pringles
Corrales   (old Buenos Aires
neighborhood, derived from
the former stockyards at
Caseros and Rioja, now a
street name).   OC, 86, 95,
128, 166, 329, 888, 1029,
1034.   IA, 115, 119, 120,
152
Correo Central   (main post
office in Buenos Aires).
OCC, 423, 425
Corrientes   (Argentine
province).   OC, 1054
Corrientes   (street in Buenos
Aires).   OC, 123, 133, 419,
433.   OCC, 312, 360, 366,
423.   IA, 105
Cortada   (street in Buenos
Aires, perhaps Cortada de
Rauch).   OC, 119
Cosmos   (the universe).   PJ, 61
Cosquín   (resort town in
the mountains of Córdoba
province).   OCC, 413
Costa Brava   (Buenos Aires
neighborhood).   OC, 955,
1026

Costa Rica (street in Buenos
Aires). OCC, 78, 140

Costanera (avenue along the
River Plate in Buenos Aires).
OC, 134n.

Craigenputtock (Carlyle's
home). P, 37

Craigie (street in Cambridge,
Massachusetts). OC, 980

Crefeld (Krefeld, city in
Germany near Dusseldorf).
ILN, 29. P, 81

Creta (large Greek island of
Crete). OC, 569-70, 604.
OCC, 54, 345, 664, 699. A,
37, 60. CONJ, 24. SN,
43

Croacia (Croatia, region of
Yugoslavia). PB, 218

Crocodile (bar in Geneva).
LA, 19

Cuareim (island in southern
Brazil). OC, 546

Cuba (country). ILN, 30, 34

Cuchilla Negra (range of hills
in Uruguay). OC, 441.
LA, 48

Cuchilla de Haedo (range of
hills in northern Uruguay).
OC, 968

Cuernavaca (city in state of
Morelos, Mexico). OC, 830

Cuerno de Oro (Golden Horn
in Istanbul). A, 18

Cuyo (region and former
province in Argentina,
currently the provinces of
Mendoza, San Juan and San
Luis). OC, 1143

Dahomé (former name of the
republic of Benin). OC, 402

Dakar (capital of Senegal).
OC, 66

Damasco (Damascus, capital of
Syria). OC, 517, 586

Danubio (Danube river in
Europe). OC, 383, 550, 557,
576. OCC, 823, 863, 899,
914, 969. C, 17. SN, 111

Dardanelos (the Dardanelles or
Hellespont, strait between
the Balkan peninsula and
Anatolia). OCC, 831

Dardania (Roman province north
of Macedonia, now part of
Yugoslavia). OC, 552

Darjeeling (city in west
Bengal in India). OCC, 761

Darragueira (town in the
province of La Pampa near
Bahía Blanca). OCC, 415

Dársena Sur (part of port of
Buenos Aires). OC, 1009.
OCC, 314

Dartmoor (plateau in Devonshire, England). OCC, 15

Deán Funes (street in Buenos
Aires). OCC, 107, 108, 111,
115-18

Delaware (state in United
States). ILN, 49

Delhi (capital of India).
OC, 614

Delicias, Las (hotel in
Adrogué). VA, 13

Delos (Greek island). BO, 29

Delta (Paraná delta west of
Buenos Aires). OCC, 45

Dent du Chat (mountain in the
Alps). OCC, 381

Denver (capital of state of
Colorado). OCC, 323

Depford (probably Deptford,
borough of London). P, 144

Devonshire (region in western
England). OCC, 832

Deyá (town in Mallorca). A,
51-53

Diagonal 74 (street in La
Plata). OCC, 428

Dijon (city in France). ILN,
44

Dinamarca (Denmark). OC, 675,
711, 1025. OCC, 653, 787,
790, 792, 809, 811, 813, 867,
868, 870, 871, 873, 875, 876,
885, 917, 920, 937, 938, 949,
952, 958, 959, 967, 970-73.
CONJ, 50. LA, 44. OP,
453, 459, 466, 472, 496, 553.
P, 142. PB, 198, 240.
SN, 17, 150, 157

Dnieper (river in Soviet
Union). OCC, 960

Doce de Fierro (in Buenos
Aires). IA, 152

Dodona (ancient sanctuary of
Zeus in Epirus, famous for
its oracle). OC, 242n.

Dolores (town in province of
Buenos Aires). OCC, 240.
C, 57. P, 128

Erzerum (city in eastern
Turkey). OC, 432
Erzgebirge (German name for
various mountain ranges rich
in minerals, in Tuscany,
Czecoslovakia and Germany).
P, 103
Escandinavia (Scandinavia).
OCC, 653, 674, 699n., 707,
708, 747, 787, 789, 813, 843,
861, 869, 886, 887, 896, 901,
918, 923–73, 975. A, 18.
BO, 59. LA, 143, 146, 169.
NED, 118, 126. OP, 469,
495. P, 145, 153. PB,
189–93, 220. SN, 150, 151
Escocia (Scotland or
Caledonia). OC, 773, 1074.
OCC, 592, 598, 616, 641, 703,
809, 819, 826, 827, 830, 831,
839, 845, 879, 885, 949, 959,
964. BC, 47. BO, 69.
IA, 108. ILN, 26. LA,
60, 70, 173. NED, 95. P,
35, 38, 81, 143, 145, 146.
PB, 232. SN, 71. VA, 28
Esepo (supposed Homeric name
for the Nile river, though
Homer calls the Nile the
Aegyptos; there is a Mysian
river called Aesepus in
Hesiod). OC, 240, 535
Esja, Hotel (hotel in
Rekjavik). A, 59
Esmeralda (street in Buenos
Aires). OC, 419. OCC,
76. A, 58. P, 29
Esmirna (Smyrna, city in
Turkey, now Izmir). OC, 533
España (Spain). OC, 163,
271, 280, 582, 587, 658, 667,
688, 723, 794, 799, 876, 878,
931, 1081, 1138. OCC, 358,
517, 559, 560, 817, 822, 831,
924, 956, 959. A, 85.
BC, 36. BO, 20, 96. C,
51. I, 15, 18, 39, 45, 82,
96. IA, 68, 97, 167, 174,
179. ILN, 9, 15, 16, 32,
35, 37, 38, 47, 64. OP,
365, 385, 445, 483, 516.
P, 7, 28, 44, 46, 53, 75, 78,
86, 112, 126, 127, 132, 135,
138, 143, 147, 156, 164, 165.
PB, 117, 122, 128, 130, 131,
142, 147, 148, 150, 152, 166,

175, 176, 191, 192, 198, 218,
229, 230, 232, 233, 238, 244,
245. SN, 62, 102, 109,
116, 118, 128, 156. TE,
76, 80, 96, 125
Espora, Avenida (street in
Buenos Aires). HE, 60
Estadio de River (soccer
stadium in Buenos Aires).
OCC, 360
Estado. See Argentina
Estado Occidental (imaginary
South American country in
Borges story). OC, 1062,
1063
Estado Oriental. See Uruguay
Estados del Plata (the
countries of the River Plate
region). PB, 213
Estados Unidos (United States
of America). OC, 208, 234,
678, 684. OCC, 377, 399,
427, 631, 834, 835, 837, 848,
850, 855, 933. BC, 27, 42,
54, 55, 62. BO, 58, 65,
79. ILN, 8–67. LA, 20,
71, 125, 181. PB, 121–24,
167, 229. OP, 382
Estambul. See Constantinopla
Estephano. OCC, 335
Estigia (Styx, mythical river
in hell). OC, 203. OCC,
282, 437
Estocolmo (Stockholm, capital
of Sweden). OC, 517. BO,
45, 46. P, 154. PB, 246
Estrasburgo (Strasbourg,
capital of Alsace in France).
OCC, 908
Estrella, La (bar and house of
prostitution in Borges
story). LA, 91
Eter (the ether in Ptolemaic
cosmology). OCC, 609
Etiopía (Ethiopia or
Abyssinia). OCC, 602, 608,
621, 663, 684. VA, 28
Etna (volcano in Sicily).
OC, 661. P, 121. SN,
111
Etruria (ancient region of
Italy, home of the
Etruscans). PB, 190
Etzelnburg (Attila's capital).
OCC, 914
Eucópolis. OCC, 863

Civil War). OC, 1113. C, 33. OP, 387, 540

Ghizeh (city in Egypt near Cairo, site of Pyramids). C, 31

Gibraltar. OCC, 959. PB, 191, 198

Ginebra (Geneva, city in Switzerland). OC, 9, 213, 423, 819, 880. OCC, 303, 326. A, 38, 56, 64, 74. BO, 96. C, 25, 51, 77. CONJ, 14, 33, 97. ILN, 10. LA, 10, 11, 16. OP, 454, 506. P, 53, 100. PB, 246

Giribone (street in Buenos Aires). OCC, 154

Glasgow (city in Scotland). OC, 1078. OCC, 829. ILN, 29. P, 81

Glew (town in the province of Buenos Aires). LA, 69, 73

Globe Theatre (theatre in London of which Shakespeare was a part owner). P, 144

Gloria. See Paraíso

Gnitaheidr (place where the dragon Fafnir lives in the *Fáfnismál*). OC, 592

Goa (city in India on the Malabar coast, formerly a Portuguese colony). OC, 1118. OP, 395, 463. PB, 238

Godoy Cruz (street in Buenos Aires). OC, 108. OCC, 404, 410

Golconda (town near Hyderabad in southern India). PJ, 57

Gólgota (mountain near Jerusalem, also called Calvary). OC, 20, 1070. OCC, 378, 879. C, 17. P, 14

Gómez, Valentín (street in Buenos Aires). OC, 148. OCC, 95

Gorchs. OCC, 91

Gorriti (street in Buenos Aires). OCC, 320

Gouveia, Hotel y Fonda de (hotel in Bustos Domecq story). OCC, 126

Gran Aldea (nickname for Buenos Aires). P, 96

Gran Bretaña (Great Britain). OC, 724. OCC, 703, 830, 853. ILN, 16. P, 148

Gran Pizzería Los Hinchas (pizzeria in Bustos Domecq story). OCC, 22

Granada (city in southern Spain). OC, 107n. OCC, 560. BC, 59. ILN, 15. OP, 515. PB, 136. SN, 64

Grecia (Greece). OC, 242, 283. OCC, 559, 604, 609, 616, 621, 627, 656, 664, 692, 694, 707, 740, 741, 747, 764, 831, 833, 843, 855, 863, 876, 925, 935, 938, 943, 952, 956, 959, 960, 970. A, 23, 25–26, 29, 37, 44, 80. BC, 28, 69, 72. C, 41. CONJ, 16. ILN, 34, 44, 52, 53. LA, 81. NED, 114, 135. OP, 367, 374, 393, 457. P, 70, 162, 173. PB, 190, 195, 196, 219, 230. SN, 14, 27, 41, 57, 58, 62, 103, 120, 125, 131, 139, 152, 153. VA, 40

Greensboro (city in North Carolina). ILN, 33

Groenlandia or Gronland (Greenland). OCC, 923, 924, 925, 940, 941. IA, 130. NED, 118. PB, 190

Guadalete (river in southern Spain, near which a battle was fought in 711 between the Moors and the Visigoths). OC, 413

Guadalquivir (river in southern Spain). OC, 582, 586, 587

Guadalupe (church in Palermo in Buenos Aires). OC, 1049

Guadalupe (lake in Buenos Aires area). OC, 329

Gualeguay (river and city in the province of Entre Ríos). OC, 564, 571

Gualeguaychú (city in the province of Entre Ríos). OC, 571, 573. OCC, 427, 429

Guatemala (street in Buenos Aires). OC, 81

Guayana francesa (French Guyana). P, 17

Holanda. See Países Bajos
Hollywood (part of Los Angeles
  where film industry is
  centered). OC, 162, 223,
  224, 230, 284, 285, 313, 356,
  399, 589, 658. BC, 29, 32,
  33, 36, 38, 67, 69, 72, 73.
  ILN, 55. PB, 161
Holmgard (old Norse name for
  Novgorod). OCC, 938. PB,
  190
Honduras (country). ILN, 33,
  52
Honduras (street in Buenos
  Aires). OC, 103, 117, 119,
  157. TE, 25
Hong Kong (British possession
  in China). ILN, 53
Horeb (mountain in Bible).
  OC, 402n. IA, 38
Hormiga Negra (street name in
  Bustos Domecq story). OCC,
  444
Hornstrandir (place mentioned
  in the Grettirs Saga). OCC,
  934. PB, 191
Hotel, L'. See Alsace, Hotel d'
Hoy (one of Orkney isles).
  OCC, 916
Hradcany (palace in Prague).
  OC, 510
Huincó. OCC, 176
Huisne (French river). OCC,
  681
Humahuaca (street in Buenos
  Aires). OCC, 88, 360
Humberto I (street in Buenos
  Aires). OCC, 21, 32
Humboldt (street in Buenos
  Aires). IA, 88
Hungría (Hungary). OC, 522,
  579, 1119. C, 41. OP,
  396-97
Iberia (the Iberian peninsula,
  Spain and Portugal). OCC,
  959. PB, 219
Idaho (state in United States).
  ILN, 41
Ilión. See Troya
Illescas (town in Spain near
  Toledo). OC, 572
Illinois (state in United
  States). OC, 298. ILN,
  37, 47, 48, 60. P, 26
Imola (city in Italy). NED,
  106

Imperio Británico (British
  empire). OC, 694. OCC,
  846. OP, 370. PB, 158,
  159, 228
Imperio Central. See China
Imperio Lusitano (Portuguese
  empire). PB, 244
Imperio Romano (Roman empire).
  OCC, 686, 787. NED, 140.
  PB, 178
Imperios Centrales. See
  Austria-Hungría
Indapur (town east of Bombay).
  OC, 416
India (country). OC, 200,
  271, 354, 415, 511, 613, 630,
  646, 741. OCC, 599, 608,
  623, 671, 705, 729, 730, 732,
  733, 742, 744, 745, 757, 760,
  761, 765, 766, 770, 836, 846,
  848, 853, 917, 943. A, 80.
  ILN, 12, 20. LA, 174.
  NED, 118. PB, 196, 244.
  SN, 58, 59, 61, 64, 67, 78,
  81, 86, 90, 93, 120. VA,
  29
India Muerta (site of battle
  in Uruguay in 1845 in which
  Rosas's forces under Urquiza
  defeated Fructuoso Rivera).
  OC, 573
Indiana (state in United
  States). OC, 1136. ILN,
  34. OP, 413
Indias (here, the West
  Indies). OCC, 157. CONJ,
  81. OP, 460. SN, 62.
  TE, 142
Indias Orientales (the East
  Indies). OC, 671. ILN, 17
Indo (Indus river). NED,
  140. PB, 195, 244
Indoamérica (term which refers
  to the Latin American
  countries with large Indian
  populations). OCC, 357, 367
Indochina. OCC, 772
Indostán (region in northern
  India). OC, 413, 416, 483,
  583, 612, 739, 740, 741, 742,
  743, 794, 837. OCC, 589,
  671, 684, 692, 701, 727, 728,
  729, 733, 742, 765, 766, 927.
  BO, 95. LA, 44, 171.
  NED, 142. P, 141. PB,
  178, 195, 196, 201

51.    LA, 112, 113, 138, 139, 142, 143, 147.    OP, 409–10, 470, 493, 494, 529–30, 531.    P, 113.    PB, 190–93, 219.    SN, 10, 152. VA, 15, 28
Israel (country).    OC, 384, 522, 523, 640, 643, 715, 717, 737, 915, 996, 997, 1021. OCC, 876, 882, 889.    CONJ, 17, 33, 63.    ILN, 9, 28. NED, 143.    P, 80.    PB, 155–56, 179.    SN, 63, 64, 101, 128, 139.    TE, 96
Itaca (Ithaca, island in Adriatic ruled by Odysseus). OC, 843.    OP, 455, 484, 526
Italia (Italy).    OC, 105, 235, 268, 446, 557, 636, 754, 836, 858, 991.    OCC, 64, 81, 533, 559, 562, 626, 641, 814, 816, 822, 824, 831, 833, 841, 842, 852, 864, 874, 885, 898, 909, 933, 935, 959. A, 46, 64.    BC, 53, 54. BO, 20, 56.    HE, 63.    I, 22, 31.    IA, 112.    ILN, 18, 37, 38, 41, 42, 61. LA, 55, 73.    NED, 102, 140. OP, 495.    P, 37, 44, 46, 70, 112, 124, 127, 163. PB, 128, 142, 177, 226, 228, 229, 230, 232, 238.    SN, 9, 12, 117, 128, 156
Italia, Plaza (plaza in Palermo section of Buenos Aires, next to zoo and botanical garden).    OC, 108
Itálica (Roman town in Spain, near Seville).    I, 102.    IA, 48, 97, 107.    P, 165
Ituzaingó (town in the province of Corrientes, Argentina, site of a battle in 1827 in which Argentine and Uruguayan forces defeated the Brazilians).    OC, 185, 194, 487, 797, 816, 1048. OCC, 559
Izumo (town in Japan).    A, 89–91
Jaén (city and province in southern Spain).    OC, 336
Jaipur (city in India south of Delhi).    OCC, 745

Jamaica (country). OC, 306. OCC, 218
Jamestown (first English settlement in Virginia). ILN, 63
Japón (Japan).    OC, 157, 375n.    OCC, 651, 675, 766, 772–76, 855.    A, 35, 38, 83–84, 90.    C, 101–2. CONJ, 67.    ILN, 61.    OP, 416, 520.    SN, 64, 77, 79, 80, 86, 93
Japonés, Parque (amusement park in Buenos Aires).    OCC, 426
Jaramí (sugar mill).    OCC, 38
Jardín Botanico (botanical garden in Palermo neighborhood in Buenos Aires).    OC, 108
Jardín Zoológico (old zoo in Palermo in Buenos Aires). OC, 108, 783.    OCC, 320, 403, 409, 412, 414, 425. SN, 143
Jardín Zoológico (zoo in Aberdeen).    VA, 27
Jarrow (city in northwestern England by Newcastle-upon-Tyne).    OCC, 883.    NED, 125
Java (island in Indonesia). OC, 589
Jena (university city in Germany, site of battle in 1806 between Napoleon and the Prussian army).    OCC, 975
Jerusalén (Jerusalem, city in Israel).    OC, 411, 418, 551. OCC, 588, 599, 709, 956, 959. BO, 48.    P, 140.    PB, 173, 198.    SN, 30
Jockey Club (elite club in Buenos Aires).    OCC, 18, 160
Johns Hopkins University (in Baltimore).    ILN, 30
Jomsburg (Wolin, ancient town in Pomerania, Germany). OCC, 971
Joplin (town in Missouri). ILN, 48
Jorasán (Khorasan, province of Iran).    OC, 101, 324, 326, 402n., 432, 594.    PB, 172
Jordán (river in Israel and Jordan).    OC, 296.    OCC, 430, 431, 596, 956, 964

Laguna de Gómez (lake in province of Buenos Aires). OC, 1070

Lagunas de Cardoso (lake in province of Buenos Aires). OC, 562

Lahore (city in Pakistan). OC, 733, 1021. VA, 28, 38

Lancaster (county town of Lancashire, England). OCC, 815

Langres (town in eastern France). OC, 363

Lanús (industrial suburb of Buenos Aires). OC, 564, 566. HE, 56

Laprida (street in Buenos Aires). OC, 441, 863. OCC, 323. A, 77. SN, 44

Larga (former name of two streets in Buenos Aires). OC, 1050

Larkland (Norse name for some part of North American coast). OCC, 940

Las Heras (avenue in Buenos Aires). OC, 110, 111, 129, 130, 148, 1035. OCC, 51, 426. IA, 166. SN, 11

Latmos (mountain in Turkey, now called Besparmak Dagi). OP, 524

Laureles, Los (quinta). OC, 486, 1039. OCC, 235, 239

Lausanne (city in Switzerland). OCC, 331, 826. P, 69, 72

Lauterbrunnen (town in Switzerland). A, 85

Lavalle (street in Buenos Aires). OC, 113. A, 56. BC, 54. P, 29

Lavalle, Plaza (square in Buenos Aires, by Teatro Colón). P, 138

Laxardalr (Laxaldalur, name of three different valleys in Iceland). OCC, 939

Leandro Alem. See Alem

Lebtit (Andalusian city mentioned in the *Arabian Nights*). OC, 336

Lehmann (lake mentioned in Bustos Domecq story, perhaps Lake Leman in Switzerland). OCC, 331

Leiden (Leyden, city in the Netherlands). OC, 922. I, 31. LA, 81

Leipzig (city in Germany). OC, 356, 411, 542. OCC, 963, 975. LA, 111

León (city and region of Spain). OCC, 595. IA, 95

León de Armenia (store in Bustos Domecq story). OCC, 277, 288

Lepanto (Naupactus in Greece, site of naval battle in 1571 between Spaniards and Turks in which Cervantes lost his left hand). OC, 448, 1096. OCC, 851. OP, 441, 528

Lerna (swamp where the Hydra lives). OC, 363. OCC, 645

Leteo (river Lethe in hell). OC, 812, 918. BO, 34. C, 66. IA, 77. NED, 90

Leubucó (Ranquel Indian capital in the Argentine pampas visited by Mansilla). OCC, 126

Levante (the Levant or Orient). PB, 240

Leyden. See Leiden

Lhasa (capital of Tibet). OC, 698

Liang (one of several places of this name in Malaysia, Indonesia and China). OC, 248

Líbano (Lebanon). OCC, 26, 32. A, 26

Libertad (street in Buenos Aires). OC, 132n. TE, 22

Libia (Libya). OCC, 593

Lichfield (town in Staffordshire, England). OCC, 828. LA, 68

Licia (Lycia, ancient name for mountainous region of Turkey). OCC, 685

Lilliput (land discovered by Lemuel Gulliver). OC, 422, 490

Lima (capital of Peru). OP, 459

Lima (street in Buenos Aires). LA, 63

Limbo (part of hell reserved for unbaptized good people). NED, 99. PB, 183. SN, 22

Machua (bazaar in Calcutta).
OC, 416

Macon (town in Georgia).
ILN, 30

Madagascar (island off east
Africa). OCC, 589, 639

Maddaloni (town in the
Campania, Italy). OCC, 70

Madison (capital city of
Wisconsin). ILN, 53

Madras (city in southern
India). OC, 416

Madrid (capital of Spain).
OC, 653, 654, 655. OCC,
780. A, 75. I, 8, 10,
96. P, 53. PB, 149.
TE, 95. VA, 16

Magadha (ancient kingdom in
India, part of Bihar south of
the Ganges). OCC, 725

Magdeburg (city in Saxony,
Germany). OP, 550

Magnolias, Las (Benito Larrea's
*quinta* in Bustos Domecq
story). OCC, 375, 376, 380

Magreb (Arabic name for the
west). SN, 72, 73

Maiden (town in Massachusetts).
ILN, 57

Maine (state in United States).
ILN, 17, 23, 46

Maipo (plain near Santiago,
Chile, site of a battle
between San Martín and the
Spanish forces in 1818, often
spelled Maipú). OC, 162,
1048. PB, 129, 130, 131

Maipú (street in Buenos Aires).
OC, 134. OCC, 76, 116,
117, 120. A, 57. CONJ,
70. VA, 13, 14

Malabia (street in Buenos
Aires). OC, 119

Malagnou (street in Geneva).
LA, 10

Malaver (street in Olivos,
suburb of Buenos Aires).
OCC, 268

Malaya (country, now Malaysia).
OC, 231. OCC, 701, 940.
A, 62. BO, 66. SN, 67

Maldon (place in Essex, England
where battle of Maldon was
fought in 991). OC, 755,
1022. OCC, 811, 886–87.
LA, 139, 143. PB, 245

Maldonado (small river which
crosses the city of Buenos
Aires, now covered over).
OC, 82, 105, 109, 110, 130,
329, 331, 332, 366, 765, 963,
1029, 1034. OCC, 405.
IA, 149. LA, 62. PB, 128.
TE, 139

Mallorca (one of the Balearic
isles to the east of Spain).
A, 51, 70. I, 89. PB,
246

Malmo (city in southern
Sweden). OC, 518, 565

Malvinas (Malvinas islands, in
dispute between Britain and
Argentina). CONJ, 91–92, 95

Mamaroneck (town in New York).
ILN, 14

Manantiales (battlefield in
Uruguay). OC, 1058

Manantiales (ranch in Bustos
Domecq story). OCC, 141

Mancha, La (region in south
central Spain). OC, 239,
667. BO, 67. IA, 12,
13, 18. P, 44. PB, 207,
209, 211. SN, 129

Manchester (industrial city in
England). BO, 58

Manhattan (central part of New
York City). OC, 252, 937.
C, 31, 42, 102. OP, 511.
P, 172

Mansilla (street in Buenos
Aires). OCC, 323, 439, 445

Mantua (city in Italy). NED,
88

Mar del Plata (city on the
Atlantic coast of the
province of Buenos Aires).
OC, 471. HE, 52

Marconi, Hotel (hotel in the
Once neighborhood). OCC,
336

Marchenoir (town in France
near Orléans). OC, 576

Marienburg (town in West
Prussia, now Malbork in
Poland). OC, 576

Marion (town in Virginia).
ILN, 35

Markland (Old Norse name for
Newfoundland). PB, 191

Marquesas (islands in the
south Pacific). ILN, 26

Marrakesh (city in Morocco).
OC, 587. OCC, 388

Marruecos (Morocco). OC,
223, 583. BC, 29

Marte (the planet Mars). OC,
275, 697. OCC, 727.
NED, 90, 140. P, 26–27.
PB, 178

Martínez (suburb in northern
Buenos Aires) OCC, 569

Maryland (state in United
States). ILN, 57

Maschwitz. OCC, 433, 434, 437

Massoler (town in north
central Uruguay where a
battle took place in 1904,
resulting in the defeat and
death of Aparicio Saravia).
OC, 571–75

Massachusetts (state in United
States). ILN, 9, 10, 26,
31, 38, 44, 57, 63. PB,
121, 231

Matanzas (river and town in
province of Buenos Aires).
TE, 26

Matheu (street in Buenos
Aires). OCC, 328

Matriz, Plaza (main square in
Montevideo). LA, 158

Mayflower (ship which brought
Pilgrims to Massachusetts in
1620). ILN, 9, 10, 63

Mayo, Avenida de (street in
Buenos Aires, running from
the Casa Rosada and Plaza de
Mayo to the Congreso). IA,
105. TE, 22

Mayo, Plaza de (main square in
Buenos Aires, surrounded by
the Casa Rosada, the Cabildo,
the Central Bank, the
Cathedral and several
ministry buildings). OC,
130, 1009. OCC, 347, 402,
526. P, 95, 97. PB, 129.
TE, 46

Mazandaran (province of Iran).
OCC, 586

Meca (Mecca, holy city of
Islam, in Saudi Arabia).
OC, 402. OCC, 599. NED,
142. PB, 178, 241. TE, 32

Medellín (city in Colombia).
OCC, 336

Medina (city in Saudi Arabia).
OC, 401. PB, 241

Mediterráneo (Mediterranean
Sea). OCC, 844. ILN, 45.
PB, 240

Méjico. See México

Melo (town in northeastern
Uruguay). OC, 608

Melton Mowbray (town in
Leicestershire, England).
OC, 463

Memphis (city in Tennessee).
OC, 440, 442. ILN, 51

Mercado Común (Common Market
or European Economic
Community). LA, 127. VA,
47

Mercado de Abasto. See Abasto

Mercado de Frutas (fruit
market in Buenos Aires).
OCC, 222

Merced (church in Buenos
Aires). OC, 134

Mercedes (city in Uruguay).
OCC, 311. A, 73. LA,
152

Mercia (one of the kingdoms
of Anglo-Saxon England). OC,
839. OCC, 895

Mercurio (the planet Mercury).
NED, 90

Merlo (Buenos Aires suburb
in the province of Buenos
Aires). OC, 1037. OCC,
86, 191. HE, 61. LA, 72

Mermaid (ship in Borges story
about the Tichborne Claimant,
really called the Bella).
OC, 302

Merseburgo (Merseburg, town
near Leipzig, Germany).
OCC, 918

Meru (mountain in Buddhist
legend). OCC, 722, 737,
738, 743. SN, 81

Merv (an oasis and town in
Soviet Central Asia, old
capital of Khorasan). OC,
324

Metauro (river in Umbria, site
of battle between Romans and
Carthaginians in 207 B.C.).
OC, 1090, 1113. OP, 387,
435

México (country, often spelled
Méjico). OC, 150, 316, 317,

Monterrey (city in northern
Mexico). OCC, 385
Montes de Oca (street in
Buenos Aires). OC, 148.
OCC, 417
Montevideo (capital of
Uruguay). OC, 63, 124n.,
152, 179, 181, 183–85, 486,
545, 546, 547, 571, 762, 853,
935, 936, 994, 1048, 1068,
1086. OCC, 515, 516, 517,
520. A, 35. BO, 40. C,
77. I, 133. IA, 111,
113. LA, 56, 63, 151, 153,
158, 181. OP, 371, 478, 491.
P, 17, 18, 92, 128, 133.
PB, 130, 133, 213, 230, 246.
TE, 33, 137, 148
Montevideo (street in Buenos
Aires). OCC, 82, 107, 118,
129
Montfaucon (name of several
towns in France). OC, 315
Montiel (region of La Mancha,
Spain). OC, 799, 971
Montmartre (section of
northern Paris). OC, 271
Montpellier (city in southern
France). OC, 445. I, 31
Moreno (town mentioned in song
in Borges-Bioy filmscript).
OCC, 240
Moreno (street in Buenos
Aires). OC, 1032. OCC, 118
Morgue, Rue (Paris street in
famous Poe story). OCC, 18.
BO, 74
Morón (Buenos Aires suburb in
province of Buenos Aires).
OC, 150, 181, 1025, 1027,
1036, 1037, 1044, 1127.
OCC, 222, 240, 358, 517.
P, 50, 60
Mosa (Meuse river in Belgium
and France). SN, 111
Moscú or Moscovia (Moscow,
capital of Soviet Union).
OC, 284. BC, 73. P, 86.
SN, 154
Mozambique (country). PB, 243
Muchas Musas, santuario de las
(eclectic modern building in
Potsdam, by the architect
Otto Julius Manntoifel, in
Bustos Domecq story). OCC,
334

Muerto, Mar (Dead Sea). BC,
57
Mulhouse (town in Alsace in
France). OCC, 363
Munchen. See Munich
Mundo Animal (a wild animal
park Borges visited). A, 48
Munich (city in southern
Germany). OCC, 683, 780,
903. ILN, 57
Munro (Buenos Aires suburb).
OCC, 404, 421
Munster (province in southern
Ireland). OC, 492. LA,
101
Muralla de Adriano (Hadrian's
Wall in northern England).
OCC, 809
Murano (town in Italy near
Venice). OCC, 52
Murcia (province of
southeastern Spain). OCC,
599
Musée Grevin. OCC, 16
Museo Británico. See British
Museum
Museo Histórico Nacional
(historical museum in Buenos
Aires, in Parque Lezama).
OC, 1051
Museo de Bellas Artes (art
museum in Buenos Aires, near
the Recoleta). OCC, 350
Museo de La Plata (natural
history museum in city of La
Plata). OCC, 431
Mysore (state of southern
India). OC, 593
Ñaembé (battlefield where the
forces of López Jordán were
defeated in 1871). OCC,
526. P, 92
Naglfar (death ship in
Scandinavian mythology).
OCC, 927
Nalanda (town in Bihar, India).
OCC, 757
Namur (fortified town in
Belgium). OC, 576
Ñancay (river in the province
of Entre Ríos). OC, 571,
574
Napa (city and county in
California). A, 32
Nápoles (Naples, Italy). OC,
228n. OCC, 37, 696. SN, 111

Nara (town in Japan near Osaka). A, 84. C, 51. CONJ, 11

Nashville (city in Tennessee). OC, 442

Natchez (city in Mississippi). OC, 299, 300

Ñato, Quinta del (nickname for cemetery, ñato being a flat-nosed person, here a skull). OC, 964. OCC, 87, 948

Navarro (town in province of Buenos Aires). OC, 958. OCC, 240, 358

Nazaré (Nazareth, city in Israel). PJ, 71

Nebraska (state in the United States). OC, 230

Necochea (town on the Atlantic coast of the province of Buenos Aires). OCC, 351, 352, 353

Negra, La (ranch in Bustos Domecq story). OCC, 397

Negro, Mar (Black Sea). OCC, 924. A, 18. LA, 117. PB, 190, 218

Nepal (country). OCC, 623, 721, 724, 772, 777. SN, 77, 79

Neptunia. OCC, 74

Neptuno (the planet Neptune). OCC, 584

Nettesheim (town in Germany). OC, 256, 261, 541. C, 41. I, 88

Neuquén (city, river and province in southern Argentina). I, 25

Nevada (state in United States). OC, 317

New Amsterdam (former name for New York City). ILN, 63

New England (sometimes Nueva Inglaterra). OC, 311, 980, 982, 983. BO, 65. ILN, 10, 20, 27, 31, 38, 42, 46, 47, 49, 53. LA, 179–80. OP, 485. P, 100, 118, 147, 170

New Hampshire (state in United States). OC, 685

New Jersey (state in United States). ILN, 14, 33

New York City. See Nueva York

New York (state in United States). P, 81, 170

New York University (university in New York City). OCC, 427

Newark (city in New Jersey). ILN, 33

Niágara (falls near Buffalo, New York). A, 85

Nicaragua (street in Buenos Aires). OC, 82

Nicea (ancient city of Asia Minor, now Isnik in Turkey). OC, 737. PB, 168

Nicodemia (probably typographical error for Nicomedia, ancient bishopric, now Izmit in Turkey). OCC, 863

Niflheim (the land of the dead in the *Nibelungenlied*). OCC, 913

Nighthawk (restaurant in New York City). LA, 144

Nihon (place in Japan, perhaps Nihommatsu or Nihongi). C, 101–2

Nijni-Novgorod (city in Russia). OC, 146. IA, 32

Nilo (Nile river). OC, 402, 543, 837, 885. OCC, 431, 602, 707. PB, 197

Nimes (city in southern France). OC, 444, 445, 447, 450n. OCC, 55

Niños Expósitos (orphanage in Buenos Aires). P, 17

Nishapur (province of Iran, in northern Khorasan, and the capital city of province). OC, 326, 418n., 493, 688, 690. NED, 140, 141. OP, 465, 519. PB, 177, 178, 231

Nithur (Nittur, city in Mysore state, India). OC, 593

Nitria (ancient monastery in the Wadi Natron in Egypt). OC, 553

Nord, Hotel du (hotel in Borges story "La muerte y la brújula"). OC, 499, 503

Norman (university city in Oklahoma). OP, 388

Normandía (Normandy, France). OC, 689, 1087. OCC, 813,

Occidente    (Occident, the
   West).   OC, 794, 809, 832,
   837, 1067.   OCC, 107, 621–
   22, 728, 743, 745, 769, 787,
   826, 856.   A, 18, 23, 38.
   C, 9, 25, 96.   NED, 140.
   OP, 445, 498.   P, 67, 72,
   101, 133, 140.   PB, 177,
   222, 223.   SN, 57–59, 62–
   63, 67, 70, 96, 125.   VA,
   20, 28
Ocho Nubes    (Japanese mountain).
   OCC, 675
Odeón    (theater in Buenos
   Aires).   PB, 134
Odesa    (Odessa, city in
   southern Russia).   OC, 224.
   BC, 32
Oeste    (western United States).
   ILN, 8, 15, 24, 27–30, 33,
   35, 48, 60–61.   OP, 429
Oeste, cementerio del
   (cemetery in Buenos Aires).
   OC, 1051
Ohio    (state in United States).
   ILN, 34, 49, 61
Ohio    (Ohio river).   OC, 296
Ojo de Agua    (place in the
   southern part of province of
   Santiago del Estero where
   Facundo Quiroga is warned
   of ambush).   OC, 1122.
   OP, 401
Oklahoma    (state in United
   States).   LA, 123.   OP,
   388.   P, 104.   VA, 43
Oliden    (street in Buenos
   Aires).   OCC, 256, 288
Olimar    (river in eastern
   Uruguay).   OC, 489
Olimpia    (Olympia, ancient
   religious center in Greece).
   OCC, 604
Olimpo    (Olympus, mountain in
   Greece, fabled home of the
   gods).   OP, 455
Olisipo    (ancient name for
   Lisbon).   OCC, 601
Olivos    (northern suburb of
   Buenos Aires).   OCC, 266,
   269, 271, 275, 438
Ombú    (street in Buenos Aires).
   OCC, 442.   IA, 115
Once    (neighborhood in Buenos
   Aires surrounding the Once
   railroad station).   OC, 86,

152, 610, 790, 1010, 1017,
   1050, 1070.   OCC, 86, 88,
   107, 109, 116, 133, 191, 211,
   212, 336, 341.   A, 57.   C,
   37.   IA, 115, 120.   LA,
   51.   P, 55, 60
Once, Cine    (movie theatre in
   Buenos Aires).   OCC, 116
Once de Abasto.   OCC, 360
Once de Setiembre    (street in
   Buenos Aires).   OC, 128,
   620.   IA, 135
Orbis Tertius    (imaginary
   planet in Borges story).
   OC, 434
Orcadas    (Orkney Islands).
   OCC, 916, 964.   LA, 170,
   173, 174
Oregon    (state in United
   States).   OC, 179, 318.
   P, 90, 135
Orense    (province in north-
   western Spain).   OC, 654
Oriente    (the Orient, the East).
   OC, 249, 384, 587, 627, 809,
   813, 831, 832, 837, 850, 853,
   1067, 1084, 1086.   OCC,
   108, 110, 118, 609, 723, 756,
   767, 769, 777, 827, 833, 856,
   868, 875, 907, 924, 959, 960.
   A, 20, 23, 38, 84.   BO, 16,
   17.   C, 9, 15, 25, 89, 91.
   ILN, 22, 23.   NED, 85, 136,
   140.   OP, 368, 369, 370,
   416, 435, 462–63, 517, 521.
   P, 68, 101, 140.   PB, 177,
   190, 191, 195, 237.   SN,
   15–16, 57–70, 118.   TE, 99.
   VA, 20, 28
Orinoco    (river in Venezuela).
   OC, 295
Ormuz    (Hormuz or Hormoz,
   island and strait in Iran).
   OCC, 586
Oroño    (street in Buenos
   Aires).   OCC, 375
Osa Mayor    (Ursa Major, the
   constellation).   OCC, 828
Oslo    (capital city of Norway).
   LA, 28
Otford    (town in Kent,
   England).   OCC, 895
Otsego    (lake in New York
   state).   ILN, 14
Ottawa    (capital city of
   Canada).   OC, 1053

and park). OC, 107, 110,
111. OCC, 21, 22, 35, 45,
51, 53, 57, 62, 70, 72, 78,
84, 85, 105, 140, 149, 179.
IA, 152
Pennsylvania or Pensilvania
(state in United States).
OCC, 698. ILN, 40, 41, 5C
61
Pennsylvania, University of
(university in Philadelphia).
ILN, 41, 50
Pentreath (in Borges story, a
port in Cornwall; there is a
town of this name in Wales,
but the only association of
the name with Cornwall is
with Dolly Pentreath of
Mousehole, the last speaker
of the Cornish language, who
died in 1777). OC, 601, 604
Pequod (the name of Captain
Ahab's ship in *Moby Dick*,
taken from the Pequot tribe
native to Connecticut). OP,
485
Perelandra (a fabulous land in
the fiction of C. S. Lewis).
OCC, 576
Pergamino (town in the
province of Buenos Aires).
OC, 561, 562, 1042. OCC,
240
Pergamo (perhaps Pergamon or
Bergama, ancient Greek city
in Asia Minor famous for the
Altar of Zeus now in Berlin,
called "Satan's throne" in
Revelation 2:13). OC, 552
Perla, La (café in Buenos
Aires, in Bustos Domecq
stories). OCC, 97, 116
Persépolis (ancient city in
Persia, near Shiraz). OC,
1083. OCC, 586. CONJ, 23.
OP, 367, 541. PB, 172
Persia (now Iran). OC, 25,
338, 406, 476, 589, 688, 836.
OCC, 586n., 613, 735, 764,
853, 855, 876, 880, 882, 902.
A, 51. BO, 66. ILN, 20,
39. OP, 370, 379, 394,
425, 432, 464, 465, 469, 514,
538. PB, 194, 229. SN,
57, 58, 59, 61, 64, 65, 66,
67, 70, 72, 103, 117, 118

Perú (country). OC, 24, 295,
561, 562, 762, 862, 1052,
1066. OCC, 70, 76, 79,
822. C, 95–96. ILN, 16.
LA, 11, 44. OP, 480. P,
132. SN, 156
Perú (street in Buenos Aires).
OC, 119, 1009
Pharos (island in Alexandria
where great lighthouse was
located). OC, 591
Philadelphia. See Filadelfia
Piamonte (Piedmont, area in
northwestern Italy). OCC,
320
Pichincha (mountain near
Quito, Ecuador, site of
battle in 1822 in which Sucre
defeated the Spanish forces).
PB, 132
Piedad (church in Buenos
Aires). OC, 131, 1010
Piedad (street in Buenos
Aires). OC, 1050. OCC,
211. A, 84. LA, 89
Piedras (street in Buenos
Aires). A, 40. CONJ, 87.
OP, 403
Pigall. See Royal Pigall
Pigué (town in southern part
of province of Buenos Aires).
IA, 13
Pilar (church in Buenos
Aires). OC, 128n., 591.
PB, 132, 152
Pilar (town in province of
Buenos Aires near Luján).
OC, 1055. OCC, 52, 54, 55,
60, 64, 77
Pirámides (Great Pyramids of
Giza in Egypt). OCC, 709.
A, 82. C, 31. I, 35
Pireo (Piraeus, port by
Athens). OCC, 924. PB,
190
Pirineos (Pyrenees, mountains
on border between France and
Spain). P, 34
Pisa (city in Italy). OC,
921. NED, 105
Pittsburgh (city in western
Pennsylvania). OC, 444
Pizzería Jardín Zoológico (in
Bustos Domecq story). OCC,
412

Plácido, Golfo (one of the geographical landmarks of the imaginary Estado Occidental). OC, 1062

Plata, La (avenue in Buenos Aires). SN, 11

Plata, La (capital city of the province of Buenos Aires, founded in 1882). OC, 1129. OCC, 131, 133, 140, 427, 428, 514, 526. P, 128. VA, 17

Plata, Mercado del (market in Buenos Aires). OC, 797

Plata, Río de la (River Plate, wide estuary at the mouth of the Paraná and Uruguay rivers). OC, 168, 181, 653. OCC, 311, 521, 839. I, 57. LA, 155. P, 18, 64, 113, 136. PB, 213

Plata, Río de la (River Plate region). A, 74. P, 133

Platte (river in Nebraska). OC, 250

Plymouth (early settlement in Massachusetts). ILN, 63

Po (river in Italy). OCC, 823

Podolsk (city in Soviet Union near Moscow). OC, 499

Poitiers (city in France). OC, 441

Polo Norte (North Pole). OC, 711

Polo Sur (South Pole). OC, 697. SN, 15

Polonia (Poland). OC, 496. OCC, 920. I, 147. ILN, 33

Pombo (bar in Madrid, favorite meeting place of avant garde writers). I, 15, 17, 124, 126

Pomerania (coastal territory of Prussia, now in Poland). OCC, 794, 889, 971

Popayán (city in southern Colombia). LA, 28

Popolare (favorite restaurant of some Bustos Domecq characters). OCC, 410, 412, 413, 416, 417, 420, 423, 425

Port Said (port city in Egypt, at northern entrance to Suez Canal). P, 151

Portland (city in Maine). ILN, 23

Portones (in Buenos Aires). OC, 1050. TE, 30

Portugal (country). OC, 831, 832, 933. OCC, 790, 831, 917. A, 86. CONJ, 43. I, 7, 8. ILN, 35. OP, 463. P, 78, 112. PB, 218, 236, 237, 238, 240, 241, 243–45. SN, 103

Posadas (capital of the Argentine province of Misiones). P, 52

Potsdam (city in Germany near Berlin). OCC, 334

Pozos, Combate de los (street in Buenos Aires). OCC, 342, 347, 391

Praga (Prague, capital city of Czechoslovakia). OC, 508, 522, 885, 887, 1066. OCC, 638, 903. P, 103. PB, 176n.

Pretilla (some place in the neighborhood of Zaragoza). OCC, 447

Primera Junta (street in Buenos Aires). OC, 129

Primera Luz (bar in Buenos Aires). OC, 111

Primrose Hill (London neighborhood). OC, 304

Princeton (university town in New Jersey). ILN, 11, 40, 52, 53

Pringles, Coronel (town in the province of Río Negro, Argentina). OC, 1126

Provence or Provenza (region of southern France). OCC, 933. ILN, 23, 42, 43

Providence (capital city of Rhode Island). ILN, 58

Prusia (area of northern Germany and Poland). OC, 698. OCC, 358. A, 77. BC, 70. ILN, 14, 29. P, 81

Puán (town in southern part of the province of Buenos Aires). OCC, 126

Puente Alsina (bridge over the Riachuelo in Buenos Aires, subject of a tango). OC, 86, 110, 134n., 163, 164. P, 127

Puerto Mariscalito. OCC, 128

Puerto Rico (Caribbean island, a U. S. colony since 1898). ILN, 47

Puerto Ruiz (near Gualeguay). OC, 169

Pueyrredón (street in Buenos Aires). OC, 128. OCC, 95. SN, 11

Pujato (town in the province of Santa Fe where Bustos Domecq was born in 1893). OCC, 13, 34, 84, 104, 121, 133, 142, 147, 195, 402, 421 402, 421, 437, 444

Punjab (region of northwestern India). OC, 616. VA, 28

Punta del Este (resort city in Uruguay). LA, 36

Purgatorio (Purgatory). BO, 60. NED, 88, 89, 90, 92, 114, 145, 155, 158. PB, 169. SN, 15, 20, 22, 29, 30, 63

Pyramid Forty (hill in Wisconsin or Minnesota where the Gillygaloo nests). OCC, 631

Qaphqa (sacred letrine in Babylon). OC, 458

Quartier Latin. See Barrio Latino

Quebracho (town in Uruguay, site of battle in 1886 in uprising against the government of general Santos). OC, 488

Queensland (state in northeastern Australia). OC, 620

Quema de basura (former garbage dump in southern Buenos Aires). OC, 91. IA, 169

Quequén (coastal town in southeastern part of province of Buenos Aires). OCC, 47, 61, 195. P, 64, 113

Querétaro (city and state in central Mexico). OC, 625

Quiaca, La (Argentine town on Bolivian border in province of Jujuy). OCC, 36

Quilino (town near Deán Funes in province of Cordoba). OCC, 612

Quilmes (industrial suburb of Buenos Aires). OC, 617. OCC, 240, 396, 838. P, 136

Quintana (street in Buenos Aires). OC, 988, 1009. OCC, 410

Quito (capital city of Ecuador). P, 173

Ragusa, Hotel (hotel in Bustos Domecq story). OCC, 181

Raij (island mentioned in Lane translation of *Arabian Nights*, perhaps Borneo). OCC, 672

Rambla de Madera (the boardwalk in Necochea). OCC, 353

Ramos Mejía (town in western Buenos Aires). OC, 1068, 1070

Rapallo (town near Genoa, Italy). ILN, 41, 42

Ratisbona. See Regensburg

Ravena (Ravenna, city in Italy near Venice). OC, 557, 558, 560, 807. OCC, 257, 260, 683, 909–10. SN, 26

Recoleta (cemetery in Buenos Aires, as well as the surrounding neighborhood). OC, 18, 79, 91–92, 762, 785, 1009, 1017. OCC, 184, 226. IA, 119, 120, 165. LA, 62. TE, 21

Reconquista (street in Buenos Aires). TE, 22

Red Cedar (river in Michigan). OP, 503

Red River (river in Louisiana). OC, 299

Regensburg (city in Bavaria in Germany, ancient Ratisbona). OCC, 669, 908

Reikiavik (Reykjavik, capital city of Iceland). A, 59

Reino Unido (United Kingdom of Great Britain and Northern Ireland). OC, 305

Repatriación de los Restos (highway in Bustos Domecq story). OCC, 444

República Dominicana (Dominican Republic). P, 85

Requeté, El (grill in Suárez Lynch novella). OCC, 174

Resistencia (city on the
Paraná River in Argentina,
capital of the province of
the Chaco). OCC, 429

Retiro (train station in
Buenos Aires and the
surrounding neighborhood).
OC, 159, 163n., 965, 969,
1017, 1042. OCC, 24, 36,
173, 179, 285.   A, 11.
IA, 119, 136.   OP, 437.
P, 17

Retiro, el (ranch).  OC, 1093

Rhin or Rin (Rhine River).
OC, 217.  OCC, 340, 787,
809, 867, 899, 912, 914, 919,
966, 968, 969.   C, 75.
CONJ, 73.   OP, 432.  SN,
111

Rhode Island (state in United
States). ILN, 58

Riachuelo (small river which
flows into the River Plate at
Buenos Aires).  OC, 81,
125n., 1045.   OCC, 243,
251, 252, 287, 399.   BC,
54.  IA, 113, 134.   LA,
62.  PB, 128

Ribera. OCC, 138

Richmond Park (park in London).
OCC, 839

Rifeos (mountains where the
hippogriff comes from).
OCC, 647

Rimini (town in Italy).  NED,
100.  PB, 183

Rin.  See Rhin

Rincón de San Gregorio.  See
San Gregorio

Rincón Viejo (ranch belonging
to Adolfo Bioy Casares).
OCC, 296

Río Bamba (Riobamba, city in
Ecuador).  PB, 132

Rio Grande do Sul (state in
southern Brazil).  OC, 433,
491, 545, 546, 564

Río Negro (province and river
in Argentina).  OC, 488,
571, 872

Río Santiago (port town near
La Plata in the province of
Buenos Aires).  P, 54

Río Tercero (town in Argentina
near Córdoba).  OCC, 36

Rio de Janeiro (former capital
of Brazil). OC, 302.  IA, 156

Río de Piedras (one of the
marvels of the realm of
Prester John).  OCC, 690

Río de la Plata.  See Plata,
Río de la

Riobamba (street in Buenos
Aires).  OCC, 424

Rioja, La (Argentine province).
OCC, 82, 527

Rivadavia (street in Buenos
Aires).  OC, 526.   OCC,
111, 140, 269.  P, 92

Rivadavia, centotafio de (tomb
and monument to Rivadavia in
the Plaza Miserere, by the
Once train station in Buenos
Aires).  OCC, 53

Rivadavia, Hospital (hospital
in Buenos Aires).  OC, 107,
110.  A, 26

River (football team and
stadium in Buenos Aires).
OCC, 411

Rivera (city in Uruguay on the
Brazilian border, adjoining
Sant'Anna do Livramento).
OC, 629

Rivera (street in Buenos
Aires, now called Córdoba).
OC, 82, 148, 1124.   OP, 405

Riviera (Mediterranean coast
of France and Italy).  OCC,
111, 261

Rivington (neighborhood in New
York City, site of a gang
battle involving Monk
Eastman).  OC, 314

Roanoke (the Lost Colony
founded by Sir Walter Raleigh
in North Carolina).  ILN, 63

Ródano (Rhone river).  OC,
880.   OCC, 646.  A, 56, 73.
CONJ, 33, 73.   LA, 11, 180.
OP, 511, 550

Rodas (island of Rhodes in the
Aegean).  OC, 149, 226.
OCC, 585

Rodona (place mentioned in the
Orlando Furioso).  OCC, 647

Rodríguez Peña (street in
Buenos Aires).  OC, 779

Rojas (town in the province of
Buenos Aires near Pergamino).
OC, 562

Rojo, Mar (Red Sea). OC, 533, 542, 603, 1076. OCC, 621, 810

Roma (Rome, capital of Italy, here sometimes "la Ciudad de los Césares," "Romeburg" and so on). OC, 216, 263, 506, 515, 518, 534, 536, 542, 552, 557, 671, 683, 684, 702, 728, 742, 750, 800, 805, 812, 839, 858, 863, 875, 894, 931, 1086, 1131. OCC, 279, 334, 358, 621, 622, 650, 656, 657, 682, 686, 692, 711, 809, 825, 826-27, 836, 861, 867, 876, 887, 898, 899, 906, 909, 920, 925, 928, 964. A, 9. BO, 59. C, 17, 45, 53, 77. CONJ, 16, 37, 38, 39, 44, 70. I, 20. ILN, 53. NED, 99, 102, 143, 149. OP, 370, 408, 425, 462, 495, 541. P, 62, 68-74, 86, 100, 162, 165. PB, 179, 183, 189, 190, 218, 224, 232. SN, 41, 62, 150, 151. VA, 15, 36

Romeburg (Anglo-Saxon name for Rome). See Roma

Roncesvalles (village in northern Spain, site of battle in 778 in which Charlemagne was defeated and Roland lost his life). OC, 836

Ronda (town in southern Spain). C, 13

Rosa Argentina, La (Argentine merchant ship on which Ascasubi worked in 1819). P, 17

Rosario (second city of Argentina, in province of Santa Fe). OCC, 13, 63, 64, 81, 127, 347, 376, 377. P, 128

Roscommon (county in Ireland). OC, 461

Rosedal or Rosaleda (rose garden in Palermo Park, Buenos Aires). OC, 134n. TE, 105

Rosetti (street in Buenos Aires). OCC, 24, 29

Rouen (city in France, ancient capital of Normandy, called Rudhaborg by the Vikings). PB, 198

Royal (hotel or restaurant). HE, 55

Royal Keller (restaurant in Buenos Aires much frequented by the modernist writers). OC, 115. OCC, 321

Royal Pigall (famous tango bar in the 1920's, on Corrientes). OCC, 405

Rubicón (small stream of ancient Italy, crossed by Julius Caesar in 49 B. C. in defiance of the Senate). OCC, 331

Ruderverein. OCC, 74

Rudhaborg. See Rouen

Rugby (town in Warwickshire, England). OCC, 837

Runnerstadt. OCC, 910

Rusaddir (town in Morocco, also called Melilla). OC, 555

Rusia (Russia or Soviet Union). OC, 146, 577, 754, 1083, 1086. OCC, 41, 42, 45, 559, 685, 848, 923, 938, 959, 960, 968. BC, 32, 38. I, 147. IA, 32. ILN, 10, 34, 63. LA, 10, 14, 15. OP, 367, 370. P, 22, 37. PB, 190, 228. PJ, 60, 67, 71

Russell (street in Buenos Aires). OC, 1045

Ruthwell (town in Scotland). OCC, 879

Ruzafa (town in Syria). OC, 587

Ryoan-Ji (Japanese garden). OCC, 776

Saavedra (Buenos Aires street and neighborhood). OC, 131, 149. OCC, 51, 101, 103. IA, 165. TE, 9, 21, 142, 144

Sahara (desert in northern Africa). A, 82. SN, 52

St. Anthony Park (town in Minnesota). OCC, 698

Saint Germain (church and surrounding neighborhood in Paris). OCC, 18. BO, 73

St. Louis (city in Missouri). ILN, 42

St. Paul (capital city of Minnesota). ILN, 40

San Nicolás (town in the
province of Buenos Aires).
OC, 116.  OCC, 240.  P,
31, 64.  PB, 153
San Pablo (Sao Paulo, largest
city in Brazil and capital of
state of Sao Paulo).  OP,
390
San Pedrito (street in Buenos
Aires).  OCC, 154
San Pedro (city on the Paraná
river between Buenos Aires
and Rosario).  OCC 240
San Remo (national park in
Argentina which Shirley
Temple visited in the company
of Hortensia Montenegro).
OCC, 160
San Salvador (church in Buenos
Aires).  OC, 1045
San Telmo (old neighborhood in
Buenos Aires).  OC, 1038.
SN, 146
San Vicente (suburb in
southern Buenos Aires).
OCC, 136, 240
Sanam (fortress in Khorasan
where Al-Moqanna held out
against the caliph Mahdi).
OC, 328
Sant'Anna do Livramento
(Brazilian town on the
Uruguayan border where Jose
Hernández wrote part of the
*Martín Fierro*).  OC, 441.
OCC, 526.  P, 92
Santa Fe (Argentine province).
OC, 113, 132n., 558.  OCC,
13, 69, 552, 977.  LA, 38,
48.  PB, 154
Santa Fe (street in Buenos
Aires).  OC, 128n.  OCC,
140.  P, 87
Santa Irene (ranch).  OC, 573.
OP, 471
Santiago (capital of Chile).
OC, 301, 1143.  P, 131
Santiago de Compostela (city
in Galicia in Spain,
pilgrimage center).  OC,
338.  OCC, 964
Santiago de la Vega (town in
Jamaica, now St. James).
OC, 306
Santiago del Estero (oldest
city in Argentine, capital of

province of same name).  OC,
1121.  OP, 401.  P, 128
Santiago del Estero (street in
Buenos Aires).  OCC, 132.
LA, 35
Santos (port near Sao Paulo,
Brazil).  OC, 627
Sao Paulo.  See San Pablo
Sarandí (street in Buenos
Aires).  OCC, 397.  P, 53
Sarandí (street in Montevideo).
LA, 158
Saratoga Springs (resort in
upstate New York).  ILN, 33
Sarmiento (street in Buenos
Aires).  OC, 593, 786.
OCC, 442
Sarón (Sharon, plain in
central Israel).  OC, 383
Saskatchewan (province in
western Canada, here spelled
Saskatchawara).  ILN, 59
Satsuma (province of Japan).
OC, 321, 323
Saturno (the planet Saturn).
NED, 90
Saucourt (town in France, site
of battle in 881).  OCC, 906
Sauk Center (town in
Minnesota).  ILN, 35
Saxland.  See Seaxland and
Sajonia
Scannapieco (pharmacy in
downtown Buenos Aires).
OCC, 180
Schleswig-Holstein (region of
West Germany on Danish
border).  OCC, 868
Seaxland (old Norse name for
Saxony).  OCC, 868, 959.
PB, 191
Sebastopol (Russian city on
the Black Sea, sometimes
called Sevastopol).  OC,
146.  IA, 32
Select Buen Orden (movie
theater in Buenos Aires).
OCC, 173, 185
Sena (Seine river in France).
OCC, 823
Sendai (city in Japan, north
of Tokyo, on Sendai Bay).
OC, 323
Senlis (town in northern
France).  ILN, 49

Serbia (region of southern Yugoslavia). OCC, 911

Serkland (old Norse name meaning Land of Saracens, perhaps Spain or Algeria or Asia Minor). OCC, 959. LA, 117. PB, 191

Serrano (street in Palermo neighborhood in Buenos Aires where Borges lived as a child). OC, 81, 86, 108, 796, 1045. SN, 46. TE, 27

Serre (river in northern France). OC, 472

Sésamo (cave in the *Arabian Nights*). OP, 517

Severn (river in Wales and England). OCC, 897

Sevilla (Seville, city in Spain). OCC, 639. I, 76, 96. P, 106. PB, 190. SN, 29. TE, 75

Shang-Tu (Chengdu, capital of Szechwan province, China). OC, 644

Shanghai (city in China). OCC, 113

Shiraz (city in Iran). OC, 325, 593

Si-Kiang (Sui Jiang, river in China which empties into the sea at Macau). OC, 309

Siberia. OCC, 583. A, 47

Sicilia (Sicily, large island in south Italy). OCC, 626, 690, 959, 960. ILN, 51. SN, 111

Sidón (ancient Phoenician port city, now in Lebanon). OC, 362, 383n., 1105. OP, 383

Sierra Chica (location of a prison in Buenos Aires). OCC, 352

Sils-Maria (town in south-eastern Switzerland). OC, 250

Silvaplana (town in south-eastern Switzerland near Sils-Maria). OC, 253, 388

Sin. See China

Sin Kalan. See Canton

Sin Nombre (alleged street name). OCC, 352

Sinai (peninsula in Egypt). OCC, 752. TE, 33

Sind (river in India). OC, 593

Sing Sing (prison in Ossining, New York). OC, 315

Sión (Zion, Biblical name for part of Jerusalem). NED, 89

Siria (Syria). OC, 715. NED, 142. PB, 178

Sirkar (Persian word for Mogul supreme authority in India). OC, 415

Socorro (church in Buenos Aires). OC, 91, 128n.

Sodoma (one of the "cities of the plain" in the Bible). OC, 400. OCC, 655

Sol (sun). NED, 90

Soler (street in Buenos Aires). OC, 625, 863. SN, 46

Solingen (town in Germany near Dusseldorf). OC, 785

Solís (street in Buenos Aires). OC, 125n. OCC, 343

Sorbona (Sorbonne, University of Paris). ILN, 42

Soterraño (Bustos Domecq reference to the Buenos Aires subway system, usually called "subterráneo" or "subte"). OCC, 73

Southampton (city in southern England). PB, 131

Spalding (town in Lincolnshire, England). OCC, 895

Spokane (city in Washington state). ILN, 48

Springfield (capital city of Illinois). ILN, 48

Sravasti (city in India). OCC, 736

Staffordshire (midland county in England). OC, 473

Stamford Bridge (site of important battle in 1066 between West Saxons and Norwegian invaders). OC, 542, 543. OCC, 896. P, 143

Stanford (university in Palo Alto, California). ILN, 49

Staubbach (waterfall in Switzerland). A, 85

Stormen (place mentioned in the *Gudrun*). OCC, 917

Stratford-on-Avon (town in England, home of Shakespeare).

Greek mythology).  OCC, 504,
740
Tashilhunpo  (monastery in
Tibet).  OC, 417
Tasmania  (island south of
Australia).  OCC, 335.
LA, 56
Teatro Colón  (opera house in
Buenos Aires).  OC, 186.
OCC, 327.  P, 18.  PB, 137
Teatro Nacional  (in Buenos
Aires).  IA, 112.  PB, 130
Tebas  (Thebes, Greek city).
OC, 240, 551.  OCC, 627.
CONJ, 44.  OP, 455.  PB,
162
Tebas Hekatompylos  (Thebes,
city in Egypt).  OC, 533,
534, 543
Tehran  (capital of Iran).
OC, 324
Temperley  (Buenos Aires
suburb).  OCC, 88, 254, 256,
259, 269, 274, 283, 328.
HE, 54.  LA, 70
Temple, del  (street in Buenos
Aires).  OC, 125n., 145,
159, 994.  IA, 31
Templo de Zeus  (at Olympia).
OCC, 604
Termópilas  (Thermopylae, site
of battle between Greeks and
Persians).  OC, 798, 901
Terranova  (Markland or
Newfoundland).  PB, 191
Terre Haute  (city in Indiana).
ILN, 34
Tesalia  (Thessaly, a district
of northern Greece).  OC,
539.  OCC, 604, 605, 692
Tetuán  (Tetouan, city in
Morocco).  OC, 589
Texas  (state in United States).
OC, 318, 933, 937, 989, 1136,
1143.  OCC, 37, 358, 975.
C, 33.  ILN, 33, 63.  LA,
123, 137, 138, 140, 141.
LA, 28, 67.  OP, 413, 459.
P, 135, 172.  VA, 43
Thames  (street in Buenos
Aires).  OC, 964, 1030,
1044, 1045
Thingeyrar  (town in Iceland,
site of ancient monastery).
OCC, 958

Thorgate  (one of the gates in
the old walls around York,
England).  LA, 27, 28, 29
Thorney  (town near
Peterborough, England).
OCC, 895
Thrudheim  (old Norse name
for Thrace).  OCC, 953
Thule.  See Islandia
Tiber  (river in Rome).  OC,
459
Tibet  (country, now part of
China).  OCC, 615, 724, 727,
761–65
Tientsin  (Tianjin, city in
China).  OC, 476
Tierra  (the planet earth).
OCC, 579, 585, 660.  C, 67.
CONJ, 34.  NED, 89.  P,
25.  SN, 52
Tierra Adentro  (term for
the interior of the pampas
region).  OC, 558, 559.
LA, 92.  PB, 231
Tierra Santa or Tierras Santas
(the Holy Land).  ILN, 28.
PB, 198.  See also Israel
Tierra del Fuego  (poor
neighborhood of Buenos Aires
at the turn of the century).
OC, 111, 128, 166.  A, 26.
IA, 120.  TE, 25
Tigre  (town on the Paraná
delta near Buenos Aires).
A, 62, 80
Tilsit  (former German name for
city of Sovetsk in the Soviet
Union).  OC, 577, 579n.
Ting-Kvei  (perhaps Ting Kau,
in Hong Kong).  OC, 309
Tiro  (Tyre, ancient Phoenician
city, now in Lebanon).  OC,
215, 362.  CONJ, 38.  SN,
119
Tirol  (province of south-
western Austria).  OCC, 909,
916.  P, 103
Tlon  (imaginary planet in the
literature of Uqbar).  OC,
432, 434–441
Toboso, el  (town in Spain,
noted for the palace of the
lady Dulcinea).  OC, 799
Tokio  (cafe and bar frequented
by characters in Suárez Lynch
novella).  OCC, 157

forces of Urquiza defeated
those of Mitre in 1874).
OP, 549.   P, 28
Verona (city in northern
Italy). OC, 419. OCC,
909-10
Versailles (palace near Paris).
OC, 727.   OCC, 165.   PB,
158
Vértigo (place mentioned in
poem by Farid ud-din Attar).
OCC, 695. NED, 142. PB,
179
Vértiz, Plaza Virrey (square
in Buenos Aires).   OC, 149
Vesali (Vaishali, district in
India on the Ganges). OCC,
726
Vesubio (Vesuvius, volcano
near Naples). OCC, 37.
SN, 111
Vía Media (the Middle Way in
Buddhist doctrine). OCC,
725, 749-50, 758
Vía Pestífera. OCC, 334
Viamonte (street in Buenos
Aires). CONJ, 95
Vicente López. See López,
Vicente
Victoria (street in Buenos
Aires).   OC, 857.   P, 127
Victoria, plaza de la (plaza
in Buenos Aires). OC, 563,
791.   BC, 59
Vieille Ville (in Geneva).
A, 39
Viejo Mundo (Old World).
ILN, 44
Viena (Vienna, capital of
Austria). OCC, 165, 261.
P, 103
Vietnam (country). A, 26
Vilcapugio (site in Bolivia of
a battle between Belgrano and
the Spanish royalist forces
in 1813). OCC, 358
Villa Alvear. OC, 82.   TE,
22, 144
Villa Castellammare
(Sangiácomo residence in
Argentina). OCC, 67, 71,
76, 79, 81
Villa Crespo (Buenos Aires
neighborhood). OC, 134n.,
164.   OCC, 395

Villa Devoto (Buenos Aires
neighborhood). OCC, 73
Villa Domínico (town south of
Buenos Aires near
Avellaneda). OCC, 395, 397
Villa Gallinal (supposed
Buenos Aires neighborhood in
Bustos Domecq story). OCC,
415
Villa Luro (Buenos Aires
neighborhood). OC, 1022.
OCC, 395
Villa Malcolm.   TE, 139
Villa María (town in the
province of Córdoba). OCC,
97
Villa Mazzini. OCC, 23, 30, 32
Villa Ortúzar (Buenos Aires
neighborhood). OC, 71.
TE, 9
Villa Santa Rita (Buenos Aires
neighborhood). OC, 329
Villa Urquiza (Buenos Aires
neighborhood). OC, 149,
591.   TE, 9, 144, 145
Villas Miserias (shanty towns
around Buenos Aires). OCC,
363
Vinland (Norse name for
America). OCC, 923, 940,
959.   PB, 190
Virginia (state in United
States). OC, 250.   ILN,
18, 35, 50, 57, 63
Vístula (Wisla, river in
Poland).   LA, 112
Vizcaya (one of Basque
provinces in Spain). PB,
151
Wabash Avenue (street in
Chicago). BC, 54
Walden Pond (pond in Concord,
Massachusetts). ILN, 22
Wall Street (street in New
York City, center of
financial district). OC,
446.   OCC, 170
Wapping (neighborhood in
London). OC, 301, 302
Warnes (street in Buenos
Aires). OC, 566.   OCC,
182
Washington (capital of United
States). OCC, 698.   ILN,
31

## ABOUT THE COMPILER

DANIEL BALDERSTON is Assistant Professor of Spanish at Tulane University. He is the author of *El precursor velado: R. L. Stevenson en la obra de Borges* and has contributed articles to *Revista Iberoamericana, Folha de Sao Paulo, Travessia, Modern Language Notes*, and *Discurso Literario*.